DON'T TELL
ME TO WAIT

DON'T TELL ME TO WAIT

. . . .

How the Fight for Gay Rights Changed America
and Transformed Obama's Presidency

Kerry Eleveld

BASIC
BOOKS
A Member of the Perseus Books Group
NEW YORK

Published by Basic Books,
A Member of the Perseus Books Group

Books published by Basic Books are available at special discounts for bulk
purchases in the United States by corporations, institutions, and other
organizations. For more information, please contact the Special Markets
Department at the Perseus Books Group, 2300 Chestnut Street, Suite 200,
Philadelphia, PA 19103, or call (800) 810-4145, ext. 5000, or e-mail
special.markets@perseusbooks.com.

Designed by Linda Mark

Library of Congress Cataloging-in-Publication Data.
Eleveld, Kerry, author.
  Don't tell me to wait : how the fight for gay rights changed America and
transformed Obama's presidency / Kerry Eleveld.
    pages cm
  Includes bibliographical references and index.
    ISBN 978-0-465-07489-1 (hardback)—ISBN 978-0-465-07349-8 (e-book)
1. Gay rights—United States. 2. Same-sex marriage—United States. 3. Obama,
Barack—Political and social views. 4. Presidents—United States—Election—2012.
5. Gays—Political activity—United States—History—21st century.
6. Homosexuality—Political aspects—United States—History—21st century.
7. United States—Politics and government—2009– 8. United States—Social
policy—1993– I. Title.
  HQ76.8.U5E44 2015
  323.3'264--dc23
                                                                2015024502

10 9 8 7 6 5 4 3 2 1

To my father, for helping me envision what could be.
And to the activists who made it possible.

CONTENTS

INTRODUCTION

C HICAGO WAS ELECTRIC THAT NIGHT. AS RETURNS POURED
in on November 4, 2008, showing that Barack Obama would
become the country's first black president, not a cab could be
found. People from every corner of the city streamed into Grant Park
to get a glimpse of the man who had helped them find new hope in
America.

"It's been a long time coming," President-elect Obama told the rapt
crowd, "but tonight, because of what we did on this day, in this election,
at this defining moment, change has come to America."

Not for all. Across the nation a wildly different scene was beginning
to unfold in the streets of San Francisco. Gay Californians and their allies
who had spilled into the Castro to revel in Obama's victory were learning that a majority of their fellow citizens had likely voted to strip same-
sex couples of their marital rights. It wasn't a right that had come easily.

San Francisco mayor Gavin Newsom had jump-started the state's
marriage equality movement when he ordered city clerks to start issuing
marriage licenses to same-sex couples on February 12, 2004. It was the
first time in the history of the country that a mass of same-sex couples
had an opportunity to get marriage licenses. Within the first three days,
city officials had already performed nine hundred marriages. Expectant
couples—many of whom had been together decades—pitched tents

outside of City Hall in hopes of finally getting their turn to commit their lives to one another. Gift bouquets flooded in from across the country—ordered anonymously and delivered to happy couples that had just wed. Twenty-nine days and some four thousand marriages later, the California Supreme Court shut it down. By August, the high court had invalidated every single marriage that had been performed in what came to be known as the Winter of Love.[1]

The following year, the state legislature became the first in the nation to pass a marriage equality bill after a nearly two-year push by LGBT advocates that ultimately succeeded when Latino and African American leaders threw their strong support behind it. But this achievement was just as short-lived; the bill was swiftly vetoed by Governor Arnold Schwarzenegger, who asserted that the courts should decide the matter. In 2007, the California legislature delivered a repeat performance after another sustained push by LGBT activists and gay lawmakers, but Schwarzenegger stonewalled again. When the issue finally did reach the state's high court (which held a 6-to-1 majority of Republican appointees), it ruled 4 to 3 on May 15, 2008, that lesbians and gays did indeed have a constitutional right to marry.

But by the time the dust had settled from election night, the voters had reached a different conclusion by a margin of 52 to 48 percent. The number of states that performed legal same-sex marriages was summarily halved, leaving Massachusetts as the sole marriage equality state in the union. (A little over a week later, though, Connecticut would pick up where California left off as the state's first same-sex couples began to wed following a Connecticut Supreme Court decision in October affirming their right to marry.)

As I tapped out an election-night story in the wee hours of the morning from my Chicago hotel room, news from the West Coast drama peppered my inbox. I wasn't just any journalist that night; I was a journalist working for the LGBT news magazine *The Advocate*. This one was personal. And as I tried to reconcile Grant Park's euphoria with the Castro's heartbreak, I faced an uncomfortable truth: the culmination of one great movement was joyously settling into the soul of America just as another movement realized that the most fundamental piece of their humanity was still not welcome, even in a progressive stronghold like California.

Barack Obama had been central to both dramas.

THREE MONTHS EARLIER, Obama and his Republican rival, Senator John McCain, had agreed to appear at a two-hour forum with Evangelical Pastor Rick Warren at Saddleback Church in Orange County, California, a famously conservative enclave nestled against the southern coastline of a state that is arguably the most liberal in the union. The two presidential hopefuls were there for one reason: to woo the Christian vote. McCain's rap as a moderate Republican widely distrusted by social conservatives had left a rare opening for Obama. If he could present as a moderate but devout Christian, he might shave a point or two from an influential voting bloc that had risen to prominence in the '80s with the founding of the socially conservative advocacy groups the Moral Majority and later the Christian Coalition and had largely eluded Democrats ever since.

Obama talked the talk: confirming he was a Christian and telling Warren that he was "redeemed" through his faith in Jesus Christ. That set up the question everyone was waiting for. Warren glanced down at his notes, then back up, settled his gaze squarely on the Democratic nominee for president and said simply, "Define marriage."[2]

Obama did not hesitate. "I believe that marriage is the union between a man and a woman. Now, for me as a Christian . . . " he paused as the crowd's eruption drowned his words. "For me as a Christian," he continued, looking at Warren resolutely, "it's also a sacred union. Ya know, God's in the mix."[3]

Those thirty critical words became his most definitive and high-profile articulation on the matter that election. Warren, the celebrated author of *The Purpose Driven Life*, had served up the perfect platform, televised at a time when voter interest was revving up for the final few months of the '08 campaign. Obama had to have practiced his response to the marriage question. It was sure to come up in the Evangelical forum and he and his political advisers had clearly concluded that appearing to waver on the issue would make him vulnerable at the polls. The sentiment echoed across the nation, but in California it had a nuclear effect.

Californians that fall faced two historic decisions: The first was whether to elect the nation's first black president. The second was whether to prohibit same-sex marriages in the Golden State by passing a ballot measure known as Proposition 8.

The effort to pass "Prop 8" was launched in response to the California Supreme Court ruling earlier that year that same-sex couples had a constitutional right to marry. All told, Prop 8 became one of the nation's most expensive ballot battles in history, with both sides sinking a combined $80 million-plus into its fate. Though twenty-eight other states had passed ballot initiatives restricting same-sex marriages, California's measure stood apart because it actually took away rights that had already been granted by the state's high court, immediately calling into question the validity of some eighteen thousand marriages that had taken place in a five-month legal window.[4]

Obama's answer to Warren's inquiry ultimately provided the perfect weapon to anti-gay forces eager to overturn same-sex marriage. Golden State voters would overwhelmingly favor Obama over McCain, and Prop 8 supporters needed some of those Obama voters to defect on the question of marriage equality. They repurposed his pronouncement at Saddleback as the centerpiece of a robocall that targeted portions of the state. The narrator framed Obama's declaration by telling voters it was the candidate's definition of marriage "in his own words" and ending with, "Proposition 8 defines marriage as a union between a man and a woman. Vote 'yes' on 8 if you agree with that definition."

The campaign by Prop 8 supporters worked; Obama won California by twenty-four points on election night, but marriage equality lost by four. The battle over Prop 8 and Obama's complicity in its passage, however unwitting, marked the beginning of a complicated relationship between the LGBT community and President Obama. On the one hand, he believed himself to be a leader on issues of fairness and equality. On the other, he had willingly deployed an oft-repeated conservative trope about "traditional marriage" in pursuit of his ascension to the highest office in the land. To put it more bluntly, he had used bigotry as a stepping-stone to the presidency and, in so doing, had carelessly harmed LGBT Americans across the nation.

In 2008, it was one thing for politicians to support civil unions as an alternative to full marriage equality. All of Obama's serious rivals for the Democratic nomination had taken similar positions. In fact, most LGBT Americans accepted the notion that the country wasn't ready to elect a candidate who supported same-sex marriage. Obama's charge was that although he didn't support the freedom to marry, he did endorse providing the same legal rights and benefits to gay couples through civil unions that flowed to heterosexual couples through marriage. Those benefits—more than eleven hundred in total federally—included things as crucial as being eligible to visit one's partner in a hospital, to get health coverage through a spouse's employer, or to receive Social Security survivor benefits after a spouse has passed away. It was often a matter of life or death, financial solvency or hardship, and Obama made perfectly clear that these rights should be afforded to same-sex couples.

But for many LGBT Americans, civil unions would not suffice. Marriage was by no means the only gay issue that mattered and for some it wasn't even the most important, but it is still the institution by which society measures and values love. And to be gay is to be defined by whom you love, so being denied the opportunity to consecrate that love necessarily denigrates the very core of one's being. Some of the earliest efforts to petition the courts for the right to marry dated back to the '70s. But that was long before the country or the courts were ready to seriously consider such a right. By the '90s, however, that consideration began in earnest when several same-sex couples sued the state of Hawaii in 1991 for its refusal to issue them marriage licenses. In 1993, the State Supreme Court ruled that the government's failure to do so may have violated the state's prohibition on sex discrimination, launching the broader debate as we know it today about the constitutionality of banning same-sex marriage.

But what Obama had asserted at Saddleback was altogether more repugnant than a simple discrepancy over the semantics of marriage versus civil unions. To call marriage "a sacred union" that lesbians and gays were somehow intrinsically disqualified from because "God's in the mix" was to deem same-sex partnerships unholy and somehow unnatural. In one breath, Obama declared gays too spiritually corrupt for marriage and in the next breath he professed to advance their cause.

This was the type of duality on the topic of LGBT equality that would become a constant source of controversy throughout Obama's first term as president. Obama considered himself a man of conviction—someone who played "the long game" and transcended Washington politics to govern on his own terms. And yet the politics that he, his campaign, and eventually his administration employed appeared to be driven by precisely the same political homophobia that had consumed

Washington since the turn of the millennium. It was a politics of convenience, not urgency, and it was one in which Obama embraced doing things when it "made sense" rather than forcing the issue.

LGBT Americans were not alone in their dismay at the outset of Obama's presidency. Progressives more broadly saw the heart of their legislative agenda on the environment, reproductive freedom, immigration, and labor organizing largely sidelined during Obama's first two years in office—which would also be the height of his power. But queer activists, partly because of their profound heartache on election night while much of the nation celebrated, would become the first members of Obama's base to both vocalize their discontent and mobilize against his administration.

Letter writing and lobbying weren't enough for them. They sought to disrupt the tidy universe of Washington by repeatedly protesting the very same man for whom 70 percent of them had voted. This meant showing up to the president's speeches and explicitly shouting him down even as a crowd full of his supporters verbally and sometimes physically intimidated the protesters. It meant pulling financial support from the president and the Democratic Party—a particular leverage point since gay supporters had traditionally contributed heavily to Democratic coffers. And it meant purposely pushing a narrative of discontent in the national media that threatened to undermine President Obama's reelection.

All of these efforts, taken together, helped LGBT activists accomplish something no other specific progressive constituency did during Obama's first term: getting a signature piece of legislation across the finish line before Democrats lost control of the House of Representatives to Republicans in January of 2011. On December 18, 2010—just four days before the close of the 111th Congress—the Senate gave final approval to the Don't Ask, Don't Tell Repeal Act of 2010, ensuring the demise of the military's nearly twenty-year statutory ban on allowing lesbians and gays to serve openly. That monumental achievement set the stage for a political tipping point that would render LGBT issues and eventually even marriage equality a political winner after decades of defeat.

In 2008, Barack Obama had sacrificed gay marriage in his bid to become the first black president of the United States. It was a position that most Americans agree was born of political necessity. But in

2012, he defied conventional wisdom, endorsed same-sex marriage, and won reelection anyway. His declaration was a watershed moment in the struggle for LGBT equality, foretelling historic wins at the ballot box in 2012 and the Supreme Court in 2013 that opened the floodgates for same-sex marriage nationwide. By the time President Obama stood on the 2013 inaugural platform and likened the struggle of LGBT activists to those of the African-American and women's-rights activists who came before them, he looked like a man transformed—a leader whom history would finally remember as the faithful steward of a civil rights struggle for a new generation.

Two years later, the White House would be bathed in rainbow to celebrate the birth of same-sex marriage in America. In the Rose Garden, President Obama would tell the nation marriage equality was more than just the consequence of a Supreme Court decision. "It is a consequence of the countless small acts of courage of millions of people across decades who stood up, who came out, who talked to parents," he said.[5]

"What a vindication of the belief that ordinary people can do extraordinary things," he added. "They should be very proud. America should be very proud."

But what happened in those intervening years—between Obama's statement on Warren's stage and his unequivocal embrace of gay marriage by 2015—is a matter of some dispute. Was Obama's evolution born of principle or political expediency? Did he lead the nation or follow it? What personal and political forces moved the man who had accepted an invitation to Saddleback Church knowing full well he would be asked about gay marriage and then had spent nearly four years dodging the issue as president? And what did his 2012 pronouncement in favor of the freedom to marry mean for the trajectory of his presidency?

President Obama, for his part, believed that he was pushing the envelope on gay rights. And to some extent, he was. But his timeline was too slow and the wheels of Washington too glacial for those who felt they were living in a system of gay apartheid—where lesbian, gay, bisexual, transgender, and queer Americans lived under a different set of laws than everybody else.[6]

For the most part, these were LGBT activists who had rooted for Obama in 2008 only to find the man they had elected was an incrementalist to his core, not the revolutionary they had voted for. He was neither hero nor villain, neither angel nor demon. But whatever he was, he wasn't getting the job done in their eyes and therefore they had to leave him and his aides with no good option other than to do the right thing on a host of LGBT issues.

When President Obama finally came out for same-sex marriage in 2012, he was answering a relentless call to justice that had been bending his ear since the very moment he stepped into the Oval Office.

He wasn't ahead of the times or behind the times, but rather smack dab in the middle of the electorate. And while his pronouncement followed the opinion of half the nation, it still preceded the other half. His endorsement helped clear the way for many who were trailing the trend lines to come along. After all, there was no greater authority in the nation on prejudice than the first African American President of the United States.[7]

Ultimately, the issue of LGBT rights did as much for Obama's presidency as he did for it, and it will undoubtedly be one of his most consequential legacies, alongside that of health care reform and helping to turn the corner on the devastating economic recession. None of those three accomplishments came without a fight, but two began as the Holy Grail of the administration while the other forced its way onto the first-term agenda. And while the administration never found a way to turn health care reform or the slow-paced economic recovery into votes come election time, Obama's gains on gay rights scored him badly needed points with his progressive base and became a uniquely positive force at the polls. In fact, equal rights for LGBT Americans grew more popular with each successive year of Obama's presidency.

President Obama will indeed go down in history as the president who helped launch a new era of equality in America, but it was the LGBT activists themselves who gave that legacy life.

THE INAUGURAL INSULT • 1

ROBIN MCGEHEE WAS EXHAUSTED AFTER SPENDING AN EIGHT-hour day in October of 2008 canvassing for her candidate, Barack Obama, in Fresno, situated in the heart of California's central valley. Unlike the Golden State's two most prominent cities, Los Angeles and San Francisco, Fresno is smack dab in the middle of the state and its politics lean center-right. At the time, Fresno County had broken Republican in every presidential election since 1980, save one: 1992, when a dazzling young Bill Clinton charmed the moveable middle of this country straight into office.[1]

McGehee and her Obama "HOPE" signs were proving to be a hot commodity in the waning campaign days of 2008. The Democratic Party wasn't applying a full-court press in Fresno the way it was in more liberal parts of the state. Much of the canvassing there was left up to local organizers like McGehee, who would drive over three hours north to San Francisco to pick up signs from the Obama for America HQ in the city's SoMa district.[2]

But McGehee had her eye on another prize: defeating Proposition 8. As the mother of two young children who had married her lesbian partner in June of 2008 during the narrow window when it was legal, McGehee was also pilfering as many "No On 8" signs as possible for transport back to Fresno. The effort to thwart the anti-gay ballot measure was being headed up by an unusually large executive committee of more than a dozen LGBT advocates—including, most notably, leaders from Equality California, the Los Angeles Gay and Lesbian Center, and the National Center for Lesbian Rights—along with some paid political consultants. No On 8 was ultimately well funded, taking in a total of about $44 million from wealthy to small-dollar LGBT donors and allies. (Supporters of the ban raised about $40 million, with more than half of it coming from members of the Mormon Church.) The No On 8 campaign's San Francisco office was just up Market Street from the Democrats' HQ, about a block away from the heart of the Castro district. And much like the Democrats, No On 8 organizers were focusing their energy on more progressive strongholds to the north and south.[3]

After knocking on around one hundred doors that day, McGehee opened the door to her own home, went straight for a glass of water and some food, then checked her messages. There it was—the robocall she'd heard about. Barack Obama saying he considered marriage to be "a sacred union" between man and woman. "You know, God's in the mix."[4]

You've got to be kidding me, she thought. McGehee was working her butt off trying to get Obama elected and stop the ballot bashing in her state. On some days, she even enlisted the help of her five-year-old son, Sebastian, and two-year-old daughter, Jackson, who wore matching junior-sized "Team Obama Nation" T-shirts (yellow with a silkscreened white collar and blue tie on the front). Yet there was her candidate, in a moment she would rather forget, speaking out against her and her family—and with audience applause to boot.

The message sank in. McGehee stewed. But several minutes later, she shrugged it off. They were going to win both battles, she figured, the election and Prop 8. Obama was just doing what needed to be done to get elected. The country wasn't ready to accept marriage equality yet. She understood that. But once Obama was in office, his advocacy on behalf of lesbian, gay, bisexual, and transgender Americans would trump his anti-gay marriage rhetoric. She was certain of it.

MCGEHEE HAD FALLEN for Obama at the same time many other Americans had—during his 2004 Democratic National Convention speech when he was still just a candidate for US Senate. During his oft-quoted ode to red states and blue states, Obama had added what at the time was an unusual reference. "We coach Little League in the blue states, and, yes, we've got some gay friends in the red states," he explained, weaving the commonalities of our citizenry throughout a list of assumptions often used to divide conservatives and liberals.[5]

It may seem like a pittance today, that one word. *Gay*. It wasn't even a plea for rights and freedoms, only an acknowledgement of our existence. But just being seen from that stage, in that convention's keynote address, at that political moment, meant something.

LGBT Americans were under attack that year. Republicans had launched an all-out offensive on gay rights in the form of eleven proposed state constitutional amendments that would prohibit same-sex marriage. President George W. Bush's campaign chief Karl Rove famously hoped the "moral values" push would simultaneously draw more social conservatives to the polls and deliver the GOP a second term. Bush did win, of course, but not necessarily because of the marriage referenda—even though that's what many people assume. Many political scientists and pollsters concluded that the ballot measures did produce higher turnout, but they did so among both Republicans and Democrats (many of whom still opposed same-sex marriage). Ultimately, terrorism—and whom people trusted to handle it—had a more statistically significant impact on inflating Bush's numbers from 2000 to 2004. Even Rove himself later noted that Bush's share of the vote increased in 2004 by almost the exact same number of points on average in states with and without referenda.[6]

But on election night, the facts weren't overly scrutinized in the media scrum to instantaneously explain Bush's win. As often happens in politics, once the notion that the marriage measures had tanked John Kerry's presidential bid cleared the bar of conventional wisdom, it became lore in Washington. Bush's win in tandem with the eleven successful marriage amendments would be wielded as indisputable evidence that gay issues were losers for the next several election cycles.

But at the convention—before anyone knew the outcome of the marriage amendments sweep—Obama's single-word affirmation felt incredibly validating. For McGehee, a Gen Xer, Senator Obama was starting to look a lot like Bill Clinton had once looked to gay Baby Boomers. Fresh.

Clinton had defied his predecessors by openly courting gay voters. He had also accepted money—more than $2.5 million of it—that was bundled for him by gay and lesbian donors. It was the first presidential election in which gay Americans had really flexed their monetary muscle, and it was very much a sign of times to come. When it came time for Clinton to make his nomination acceptance speech at the 1992 Democratic convention, he also gave a nod to gay Americans.[7]

"We must say to every American: Look beyond the stereotypes that blind us," Clinton told the nation on July 16, 1992. "For too long politicians have told the most of us that are doing all right that what's really wrong with America is the rest of us. Them. Them, the minorities. Them, the liberals. Them, the poor. Them, the homeless. Them, the people with disabilities. Them, the gays . . . But this is America. There is no them. There is only us."[8]

It was an historic first for a nominee. Clinton had raised the profile of lesbian and gay Americans in his campaign and provided great hope to many in the LGBT community. Of course, those hopes were largely dashed by a presidency that yielded the legacy of the "don't ask, don't tell" (DADT) law banning gays from serving openly in the military and the Defense of Marriage Act (DOMA), which prevented the federal government from legally recognizing same-sex marriages. But in 1992, Clinton's candidacy felt like a political spring for gay America after a dark decade in which the federal government had largely denied its very existence even as gay men died of AIDS by the thousands.

In much the same way, 2008 felt like a rebirth for LGBT Americans after the deep freeze of the socially conservative Bush years. McGehee may have had her heart set on Barack Obama from the start, but he was by no means the only viable Democratic candidate for LGBT voters. In fact, Senator Hillary Clinton had been adored by gay men and lesbians alike for years—ever since she became the first First Lady to march in a Gay Pride Parade in New York City in 2000. And John Edwards, Kerry's 2004 running mate, had also made inroads with some prominent LGBT activists, especially those who opposed the Iraq War and liked his emphasis on antipoverty issues.

Gays had been treated like a piñata by Republicans and social conservatives with increasing intensity over the past decade. Between 1998 and 2006, a total of twenty-six states passed ballot measures prohibiting same-sex marriage. Politically, the question rarely seemed to be, "How will Democrats help aggressively advance the rights of LGBT people?"

It was usually, "Which Republicans will launch the most masterful attacks on gays and, in response, how will Democrats effectively telegraph empathy without risking any moderate votes?" But in the 2008 primary, with a field full of viable Democratic candidates fighting over progressive votes, that all changed.[9]

NO ONE COULD have anticipated just how far Hillary Clinton and Barack Obama would be pulled in a new direction on LGBT rights when they kicked off their seventeen-month nomination quest at the outset of 2007. The lengthy slugfest that ensued benefitted every progressive constituency as the candidates made promise after promise to woo voters along the way. But LGBT Americans—who far and away represent the smallest slice of the progressive pie—watched the two presidential hopefuls compete for their votes as never before.

In fact, the 2008 election was tailor-made for the LGBT community. First, every vote truly did count as Clinton tried desperately to edge her way back into the race after a disappointing showing in February—Obama won twenty-one states to Clinton's nine—that left her trailing by more than 150 delegates. But Clinton had a distinct edge over Obama with lesbian, gay, and bisexual voters. A Hunter College poll in November 2007 showed LGB voters favoring Clinton over Obama by a margin of 63 to 22 percent. Clinton needed to keep a lock on that lead.[10]

Second, even though Democrats in Washington had spent the past decade running away from gay issues, mainstream America had started to embrace lesbians and gays. Ellen DeGeneres had defied conventional wisdom in Hollywood and become a megastar even after coming out on the cover of *TIME* magazine in 1997. The TV sitcom *Will & Grace*, centered around a gay lawyer and his neurotic female roommate, had warmed the hearts of Americans for nearly a decade during its eight-season run from 1998 to 2006. Even certain sectors of government were advancing: the Supreme Court had overturned sodomy laws nationwide in 2003, Massachusetts was four years into marrying same-sex couples, and twenty state legislatures had enacted laws protecting gays in the workplace (though protections for transgender workers hadn't progressed as far). In other words, America was far ahead of Washington on accepting gays and that meant the Democratic candidates would have to step up their game in order to avoid seeming antiquated.

Third, and perhaps paramount in terms of the election, LGBT Americans had cultivated a vibrant blogging community. The Internet had proven to be a fantastic resource for populations that were smaller or underrepresented in mainstream media. Gay people had naturally sought out community through a medium that connected them and catered to them in ways that mainstream media never had. In the 2008 election, as candidates really began to leverage the power of the blogosphere, bloggers took on a major political role that was even more pronounced in the queer world. Sites like Pam's House Blend, run by the ever-pithy Pam Spaulding out of North Carolina, had a distinctly grassroots following, as did the Indiana-based blog, Bilerico Project, run by Bil Browning and Jerame Davis. There were news aggregators like Andy Towle's blog Towleroad in New York, which offered the best in gay from across the web. A number of blogs, like Jeremy Hooper's Good As You and Alvin McEwen's Holy Bullies and Headless Monsters, also specialized in tracking right-wing, virulently anti-LGBT activists. Joe My God, Queerty . . . the list goes on.

Then there was the influential inside-the-Beltway site, AMERICAblog, which covered both LGBT and mainstream news. The editor, John Aravosis, and his deputy editor, Joe Sudbay, were both forty-something gay men who had logged a combined thirty-six years in Washington by the time the 2008 Democratic primary rolled around. Aravosis, a first generation Greek American who spoke five languages, had worked on Capitol Hill for a handful of years as a foreign policy adviser in the late '80s and early '90s before taking a post at the World Bank and eventually landing a job as politics editor for About.com. When he founded AMERICAblog in 2004, it quickly gained notoriety as one of the top-rated political blogs, in part because it pulled no punches about Washington politics. In 2005, the left-leaning site MyDD ranked it No. 5 on its list of most-trafficked political blogs, while it registered at No. 9 in *PC Magazine*'s 2008 list of "20 Best Political Web Sites." Sudbay, who hailed from Maine, had written for the site since 2004, though he mainly made his living as a political consultant for liberal causes. Sudbay had cut his teeth in political advocacy working on gun safety issues for six-plus years at Handgun Control, Inc., from 1994–2000.[11]

The two men would play a key role on LGBT issues during both the election and the forthcoming Obama administration. The relationship they forged with the Obama campaign during the general election, along with the blog's profile in Washington, gave Aravosis and Sudbay unmatched access and leverage among the LGBT blogs at the outset of the administration. They had enough credibility with Washington insiders, along with enough reach into liberal America, to help shape the narrative about how President Obama was faring on a host of progressive concerns and, in particular, LGBT issues.

Their first major encounter with the Obama campaign put the blog on the radar of campaign staffers and foreshadowed a certain tension that would continue once many of those staffers eventually set foot in the White House. That prophetic introduction came in the fall of 2007, at a time when the polls still favored Hillary Clinton. Pundits were beginning to wonder aloud if young senator Obama was mounting a failed primary bid against a Washington powerhouse that was too big to fail. The Obama campaign decided to launch a gospel tour aimed at wooing black voters in the critical primary state of South Carolina, where Clinton was still giving Obama a run for his money with African American Democrats. In fact, a national CNN poll conducted in mid-October 2007 found that among registered black Democrats, Clinton led Obama by 24 points (57 percent to 33 percent).[12]

On October 19, the Obama campaign blasted out an e-mail announcing that the "40 Days of Faith & Family" tour would show voters "how Barack Obama's family values and faith have shaped his leadership and commitment to bringing all people together around his movement for fundamental change." The campaign's national religious director, Joshua DuBois, boasted, "This is another example of how Barack Obama is defying conventional wisdom about how politics is done."[13]

Their unity message had one fatal flaw. Among the entertainers the campaign had chosen to headline the tour was a man named Donnie McClurkin, a Grammy Award–winning gospel singer and minister who said he had struggled with same-sex attraction in the past. In 2004, a controversy had arisen over McClurkin's participation in the Republican National Convention due to his assertion that gays could be cured through religious intervention. The *Washington Post* had reported then that McClurkin had publicly vowed to fight "the curse of homosexuality."

And in 2002, McClurkin wrote on a Christian website, "I've been through this and have experienced God's power to change my lifestyle. I am delivered and I know God can deliver others, too."[14]

But initially, McClurkin's past statements had been missed in the mainstream media. Aravosis caught wind of McClurkin's history and pounced. On AMERICAblog, he noted that "sucking up to anti-gay bigots" and "giving them a stage" was certainly "defying conventional wisdom" about how to get a Democrat elected president. He posted the story on a Saturday morning, a day when most news stories die.[15]

But the story didn't disappear. That evening, an African American author and political commentator, Earl Ofari Hutchinson, advanced the story with a Huffington Post blog entry titled, "Obama Should Repudiate and Cancel His Gay Bash Tour, and Do It Now."[16]

Hutchinson charged that Obama had "ripped a page straight from the Bush campaign playbook" by trying to tap into anti-gay sentiment among "blacks in South Carolina, especially black evangelicals," many of whom, he said, openly and quietly "loathe gays." Hutchinson pointed to a Joint Center for Political and Economic Studies poll in 2004 that found blacks opposed gay marriage by a far larger margin than the overall population. The fall 2004 poll found that 46 percent of African Americans opposed any legal recognition of gay relationships while only a little over a third of the general population shared that view. Among black subgroups, fully 62 percent of Christian conservatives rejected any legal recognition for same-sex unions, as did 57 percent of those who lived in the South.[17]

"Desperate to snatch back some of the political ground with black voters that are slipping away from him and to Hillary," Hutchinson wrote, "Bush's black evangelical card seems like the perfect play."

The post caught people's attention. On Sunday, a number of gay bloggers weighed in. Pam Spaulding led with this simple headline: "Why Is Obama Touring with 'Ex-Gay' Homophobe Donnie McClurkin?" By Monday, it was a full-blown story, with mainstream outlets seeking comment from the candidate. The Associated Press reported that the Human Rights Campaign, the largest national LGBT group, had "urged" Obama to cut ties with the gospel singer.[18]

Any time the Human Rights Campaign, or HRC, weighed in, it was considered an important measure of where the LGBT community stood on certain issues. HRC, founded in 1980, was the most visible gay rights group in Washington. For many, its logo—a yellow equal sign set against a square blue backdrop—had become a simple statement of support for equality and could be found on bumper stickers across the nation. In 2007, its budget hovered around $40 million, making it the consummate eight-hundred-pound gorilla in the room whenever politicians took up LGBT issues.[19]

But HRC was also as mainstream as gays could get. It often failed to represent the wide-ranging views of the greater LGBT constituency, which is irrepressibly opinionated and notoriously diverse—including members of every race, religion, ethnicity, gender, and socioeconomic class. For years, the counterbalance to HRC had been the National Gay and Lesbian Task Force, which had closer to an $8 million budget. The Task Force was further left than HRC and often staked out positions that were at odds with its brawnier counterpart. In the fall of 2007, for instance, a controversy developed around whether the Democratic-led House of Representatives should try to pass a workplace nondiscrimination bill that simply protected gays, lesbians, and bisexuals against being fired (i.e., focused on sexual orientation only) or one that also covered transgender individuals (i.e., was gender identity inclusive). HRC eventually joined the bill's chief sponsor and Washington power broker, openly gay Representative Barney Frank, in supporting passage of the sexual-orientation-only version of the bill. They said it would be easier to pass and would also build momentum for a victorious vote on a transgender-inclusive bill in the next Congress (the GOP controlled the Senate in 2007 and any pro-gay measure would be dead on arrival in that chamber anyway). The Task Force helped lead a coalition of more than three hundred smaller organizations that adamantly opposed leaving transgender Americans behind. Despite those vehement objections, Democratic leadership did finally put the sexual-orientation-only bill to vote and it cleared the House, 235–184.[20]

But the controversy left a deep rift within LGBT advocacy circles and further solidified the perception that HRC was both supported and run by a richer and less marginalized segment of the greater LGBT community. HRC leaders exhibited a certain elitism, viewing themselves as the real political professionals. All the other advocates were just amateurs, toiling away in the margins. HRC had lobbyists and big extravagant galas, and its leaders relished being Washington "insiders," just like every other sizeable Beltway group. Yet in spite of HRC's supposed Washington prowess, its leadership turned out to be dead wrong about the benefits of passing the workplace protections bill in 2007. The transgender-inclusive bill did not gain momentum in the next Congress—the one that would count historic Democratic majorities in both the upper and lower chambers.

Yet for all HRC's political clout in 2007, they could not move Obama's campaign on the McClurkin question. Over HRC's objection, on Monday night, a campaign spokesman said they had no plans to drop McClurkin from the lineup. Instead, Obama issued a written statement in which he said he believed strongly that African Americans and the LGBT community must "stand together" in the fight for equal rights. "I strongly disagree with Reverend McClurkin's views and will continue to fight for these rights as President of the United States to ensure that America is a country that spreads tolerance instead of division," the statement said.[21]

If the campaign hoped that would be the end of it, it miscalculated. The controversy roared through the week. On Wednesday, two Obama advisers held a conference call to soothe the campaign's LGBT supporters. They stressed Obama's "unequivocal" support for gay rights and announced that an openly gay minister would be opening the concert tour with a prayer. But the campaign's attempt to smooth over the kerfuffle got bizarrely worse when people learned the gay minister they had chosen to open the black gospel tour was white. Supporters and critics alike were dumbfounded, but none more so than members of the LGBT African American community. Blogger Pam Spaulding, a black lesbian living in the South, called it "mind-boggling" that the campaign had selected a white pastor to address homophobia in the black religious community. "We're talking Politics 101," she wrote. "The last thing a crowd of black folks who have a problem with homosexuality needs is: 1) to be 'told' by the Obama campaign that a message about tolerance must be delivered from a white voice of faith, and 2) to have their beliefs confirmed that being gay is 'a white man's perversion.'"[22]

The campaign was in serious trouble. They had managed to pit one key Democratic constituency against another—sloppy at best, a fundamental miscalculation at worst—and then they totally bungled the cleanup. Worse still, they had yet to grant a single interview to any reporter from an LGBT outlet, vastly underestimating their influence. I had been chasing them for a cover story for *The Advocate* magazine for several months. In fact, we had been chasing all three leading candidates—Clinton, Edwards, and Obama—for a cover, but only Clinton had agreed. Her interview with my colleague Sean Kennedy hit the stands as our cover story in October. Nonetheless, I kept asking the Obama camp, relentlessly. Getting an interview with a sought-after politician is a little like being in a bad relationship—you just keep throwing yourself at them again and again until they eventually decide they need you.

Finally, in the midst of this media nightmare, the Obama campaign decided the candidate needed me. A spokesperson e-mailed me to offer a fifteen-minute phone interview that Friday morning. Though the campaign clearly wanted the interview published so they could say that Obama had addressed the debacle head on, they also hoped the story would finally fade into the Friday evening sunset.

I started with the most basic question: Was McClurkin vetted?

"Not vetted to the extent that people were aware of his attitudes with respect to gay and lesbians and LGBT issues," Obama explained, "at least not vetted as well as I would have liked to have seen." He was speaking very slowly and deliberately, with a good number of pauses. As an interviewer, it was painful. I found myself silently cursing his cautious cadence—fifteen minutes would disappear in no time.[23]

I told the senator that some black gay activists I had spoken with said the McClurkin choice gave them pause about the campaign, even if they generally trusted in Obama himself. "Do they really understand the nuances of these issues?" I said, recounting those conversations; "Are they really sitting down and talking with gay folks? Because it seems like this decision came purely through the lens of faith."

Obama countered by noting his willingness to take LGBT issues head on in front of a multitude of audiences, including people of faith. It was true. Obama had addressed homophobia in front of religious audiences several times. In 2006, for instance, Rick Warren had invited Obama to speak at Saddleback Church's Global Summit on AIDS on World AIDS Day.

"Like no other illness, AIDS tests our ability to put ourselves in someone else's shoes—to empathize with the plight of our fellow man," Obama had told the crowd of roughly two thousand people. While many people contract the disease through no fault of their own, he said, "it has too often been easy for some to point to the unfaithful husband or the promiscuous youth or the gay man and say 'This is your fault. You have sinned.' I don't think that's a satisfactory response. My faith reminds me that we all are sinners." [24]

Obama told me that breaking down barriers between religious individuals and LGBT Americans was the partial impetus for his emphasis on religious voters.

"Part of the reason that we have had a faith outreach in our campaigns is precisely because I don't think the LGBT community or the Democratic Party is served by being hermetically sealed from the faith community, even though we may disagree with them," he said. "We can try to pretend these issues don't exist and then be surprised when a gay marriage amendment pops up and is surprisingly successful in a state. I think the better strategy is to take it head on, and we've got to show up."

I acknowledged that his campaign had found itself in a difficult position. "But by keeping McClurkin on the tour," I said, "didn't you essentially choose your Christian constituency over your gay constituency? I mean . . ."

"No, I profoundly disagree with that," he responded, cutting me off. "This is not a situation where I have backed off my positions one iota. You're talking to somebody who talked about gay Americans in his convention speech in 2004, who talked about them in his announcement speech for the president of the United States, who talks about gay Americans almost constantly in his stump speeches."

The candidate seemed to feel misunderstood, or perhaps, underappreciated for his actions. But time was dwindling. The campaign spokesperson had already cut in to tell me the interview would soon be over.

"One thing that I do want to make sure is included in this article," Obama said, is that on issues from "don't ask, don't tell" to DOMA to the gay marriage amendment to adding gay people as a protected class to the Illinois human rights ordinance, "there has not been a stronger and more consistent advocate on LGBT issues than I have been."

"And it is interesting to me," he continued, "and obviously speaks to the greater outreach that we have to do, that that isn't a greater source of interest and pride on the part of the LGBT community."

I couldn't let that comment slide. I had been chasing his campaign for an interview for many months—as had many other LGBT reporters—precisely so that we could cover his record, whatever it might reflect.

"I will say that we put in more than a few requests to try to interview you so that we could do an article that did focus on those issues," I responded. Then, as any reporter would, I immediately slipped in one more question about whether he would sign an employment nondiscrimination bill that specifically included protections for transgender individuals.[25]

The spokesperson chimed in again, annoyed. "Kerry, he really has to get going now." That, of course, was her job. The interview had already run almost exactly fifteen minutes and every new question was a potential liability.

"Alright guys," Obama said, wrapping things up. "Kerry, we'll try to have more frequent conversations."

I thanked the senator for his time and we hung up.

After raging all week, the controversy seemed to quiet a bit over the weekend. The interview got good pickup in mainstream outlets like the *New York Times* and *Politico*, as well as making the rounds on the LGBT blogs. The fact that Obama had taken the time to speak with a gay outlet seemed to mitigate some of the damage. That is, until Sunday, the day of the tour's first performance. As many LGBT Americans had feared, McClurkin used the stage Obama had given him to launch into a full-blown anti-gay revival toward the end of the concert.

As the *New York Times* reported: "He approached the subject gingerly at first. Then, just when the concert had seemed to reach its pitch and about to end, Mr. McClurkin returned to it with a full-blown plea: 'Don't call me a bigot or anti-gay when I have suffered the same feelings,' he cried. 'God delivered me from homosexuality,' he added. He then told the audience to believe the Bible over the blogs: 'God is the only way.' The crowd sang and clapped along in full support."[26]

Meanwhile, the presence of the gay pastor, Reverend Andy Sidden, had been completely underwhelming. CNN characterized Sidden's opening prayer as "notably brief" and "anti-climactic," and delivered "when the arena was only about half full."[27]

The McClurkin story yielded two major takeaways, one for future denizens of the White House and another for members of the LGBT community. For the Obama campaign, it became a shining example of what the gay blogosphere could do—take what many mainstream reporters might have once considered a fringe story and land it on the front pages of the nation's biggest news outlets. McClurkin stole headlines from the Obama camp for a solid week at a time when Hillary Clinton had opened up a staggering twenty- to thirty-point lead over Obama in national polls. As the *New York Times* put it, "Tamping down that conflict between two important Democratic constituencies has been an unwelcome distraction for Mr. Obama as he tries to revitalize his campaign." Wisely, campaign staffers decided to reach out to the man who originally lit up the story. Aravosis ended up hearing from both Joe Rospars, the chief digital strategist, and Steve Hildebrand, the campaign's deputy director who was also openly gay. It was the beginning of an ongoing conversation that would extend straight into Obama's presidency.[28]

But for members of the LGBT community, the imbroglio was mystifying. Whether one was a friend or foe of the Obama campaign, no gay person could come up with a feel-good explanation for the campaign's disastrous handling of the situation. I was inclined to believe that their choice of McClurkin had been a mistake rather than an intentional strategy to exploit a rift between gays and the black religious community. Nonetheless, they demonstrated a willful ignorance of the sentiment in the queer community from beginning to end. Obama said he was surprised that gays weren't more interested in his record, yet he hadn't given them the opportunity to be. His record was decent, but he hadn't spent much time selling it. If he wanted to be judged by his actions—as he said he did in the interview—keeping McClurkin on the tour was not going to help his case. Instead, it seemed as if he had entirely turned his back on lesbian, gay, bisexual, and transgender Americans. Furthermore, if Obama wanted to bridge the divide between socially conservative Christians and LGBT people, the McClurkin incident had rendered him an unmitigated failure.

McClurkin represented what I came to see as one of Obama's greatest weaknesses on LGBT issues as well as other progressive issues—his inability to digest negative feedback. He viewed himself as a progressive, certainly on most social issues like LGBT rights. And he seemed to feel so secure with the fact that he was doing the right thing by gay people that he couldn't accept the suggestion that he may have done the wrong or hurtful thing. Politicians make trade-offs, for sure. His trade-off on gay rights was that he was advocating for legal equality and addressing homophobia even if he wasn't willing to declare his full support for same-sex marriage during the 2008 election. At the time, that may have been a totally fair bargain. His LGBT supporters certainly thought so. But the notion that something he and his campaign originated had advanced the very root of homophobia he claimed to be dismantling was anathema to him. Obama's ability to internalize criticism on issues in which he felt morally justified was lacking. And that blind spot would become more glaring to LGBT activists as the early years of his presidency unfolded.

OBAMA HAD A LOT to learn from the McClurkin incident and he would continue to face calls to reaffirm his commitment to gay rights. Voters wanted to know how he was different from Hillary Clinton on the issues, and the pressure quickly intensified. For reasons of her own, Clinton was becoming much more vocal about LGBT equality.

Though she had certainly beaten Obama to granting the first major LGBT interview, early in her campaign, Clinton, like the other candidates, wanted to say as little as possible on issues that might hurt her in the general election—and that included gay rights. But by the spring of 2008, as she worked to make up for the delegate deficit she suffered during the February primary contests, Clinton developed a whole new relationship with LGBT issues. They were her best friend. And she did what every candidate does who's behind in a campaign; she started granting interviews. Lots of them, to all kinds of media outlets.

So after granting one singular interview to *The Advocate* in 2007, she suddenly gave an unprecedented string of interviews to local gay papers, most notably in Ohio, Texas, and Pennsylvania—key states she needed to pick up in order to remain a contender for the nomination. In the three weeks following the February 5 Super Tuesday vote, she did interviews with the *Washington Blade* in Washington, DC, the *Gay People's Chronicle* and *Outlook Weekly* in Ohio, and the *Dallas Voice* in Texas. It worked. Hillary supporters were cheering all the access she was giving to LGBT press while Obama supporters struggled to justify his absence. Although his campaign made an ad buy for four full-page ads in the gay tabloids and Obama published an open letter on the blog Bilerico.com, he was looking insular. Hillary's full-court press left the perception that Obama didn't think he needed to woo LGBT voters any longer—his eyes had shifted toward the general election.[29]

It all came to a head on April 4, 2008, when the *Philadelphia Gay News* published its interview with Clinton under the headline: "Clinton Talks, Obama Balks." The Q&A with Senator Clinton ran on one-half of the front page opposite a blank space where Senator Obama's interview would have run had he granted one. The paper's publisher, Mark Segal, said he had tried to get an interview for over a month in advance of the publication but had consistently gotten the runaround from the campaign. The paper's weekly editorial charged, "With all due respect, Senator, you haven't spoken to the local LGBT press since 2004. Isn't it about time?"[30]

The Clinton campaign relished the moment. "We can't imagine why Sen. Obama hasn't granted many interviews with press in the LGBT community," campaign spokesman Jin Chon told the *Dallas Voice*. "Hillary Clinton has no qualms about being asked the tough questions."[31]

The pressure finally reached the Obama campaign. I had never stopped chasing them for a wide-ranging sit-down, and a day before the public flogging they took in Philly, they reached out to me. By April 7, 2008, I was sitting in a glass-encased conference room at the Obama campaign headquarters at 233 North Michigan Avenue. The space was abuzz with dozens of twenty-something staffers tapping away at their computers when Obama strolled into the office in dark sunglasses, a black suit, and white shirt, loose at the collar with no tie. He had just flown in from a fundraiser in San Francisco the night before and a couple of campaign aides trailed him, bringing him up to speed on the latest news.

When Obama finally arrived, he introduced himself and apologized for not wearing a tie, explaining that he had just gotten off a five-hour flight across the country.

"It doesn't bother me a bit," I said, noting that I had chosen to wear a vest rather than a suit, so we were both erring on the informal side. Why I was attempting to ease the conscience of the current Democratic frontrunner about his dress code, I will never know. But with that we started in.

Since Obama's lack of accessibility had been driving headlines, I asked, why the silence?

He pushed back. "I don't think it's fair to say 'silence' on gay issues. The gay press may feel like I'm not giving them enough love. But basically, all press feels that way at all times." He glossed over the fact that he had actually given multiple interviews to both African American and Spanish-language outlets and instead noted that he had been consistently speaking to general audiences about gay issues. "I talked about the need to get over the homophobia in the African American community," he said, referencing a speech he gave a few months earlier on the eve of Martin Luther King Jr. Day at Atlanta's Ebenezer Baptist Church, where Dr. King had served as pastor. "When I deliver my stump speeches, routinely I talk about the way that anti-gay sentiment is used to divide the country and distract us from issues that we need to be working on, and I include gay constituencies as people that should be treated with full honor and respect as part of the American family."[32]

I told him the "underlying fear" of the LGBT community was that we would be last on his priority list if he got elected. But Obama parried again, noting that his willingness to speak to general audiences was more "indicative" of his commitment to the issues rather than just checking off a "special interest" box. "It's easy to preach to the choir," he added. "What I think is harder is to speak to a broader audience about why these issues are important to all Americans."[33]

When I asked what he could "reasonably get done" in office, the first line out of his mouth was, "I reasonably can see 'don't ask, don't tell' eliminated." Obama then proceeded to tick through a list of other legislative priorities he would push for, but on the military's gay ban, he was resolute.

He also said he was "very interested" in making sure that federal benefits were available to same-sex couples who had civil unions.

"I assume you're talking about the Defense of Marriage Act," I clarified.

"Absolutely," he said. "I for a very long time have been interested in repeal of DOMA."

As I listened, I started thinking that his answer on "don't ask, don't tell" had been all too swift and easy. I decided to press him on one of the factors that had sunk President Bill Clinton's 1993 effort—opposition in the military.

"Back to 'don't ask, don't tell' real quick—you've said before you don't think that's a heavy lift. Of course, it would be if you had Joint Chiefs who were against repeal. Is that something you'll look at?"

"I would never make this a litmus test for the Joint Chiefs of Staff," he said, delivering a discernable piece of news that would later be picked up by mainstream outfits like the Associated Press. "Obviously, there are so many issues that a member of the Joint Chiefs has to deal with, and my paramount obligation is to get the best possible people to keep America safe."[34]

It was clearly an answer geared toward the general electorate and not one LGBT activists would be happy to hear. The Joint Chiefs' opposition to ending the ban on gay service members in 1993 became one of several insurmountable stumbling blocks to changing the policy. If Obama wasn't prioritizing support for repeal as one of his criteria for choosing the chairman of the Joint Chiefs of Staff, then repeal wasn't such a sure thing after all.

While getting him to "make news" on "don't ask, don't tell" was a mini coup for me, I wanted to push hard on his support for civil unions over marriage. Many activists lamented civil unions as a throwback to "separate but equal" institutions—a view I shared—but he had already been asked about that contradiction. I decided to frame my question using a narrative I had heard both Obama and his wife, Michelle, reference often as a classic civil rights dilemma—being warned that *now* isn't the right time.

"Both you and your wife speak eloquently about being told to wait your turn and how if you had done that, you might not have gone to law school or run for Senate or even president," I said. "To some extent, isn't that what you're asking same-sex couples to do by favoring civil unions over marriage—to wait their turn?"

"I don't ask them that," he retorted, shaking his head. "I don't think that the gay and lesbian community, the LGBT community, should take its cues from me or some political leader in terms of what they think is right for them. It's not my place to tell the LGBT community, 'Wait your turn.' I'm very mindful of Dr. King's 'Letter from Birmingham Jail,' where he says to the white clergy, 'Don't tell me to wait for my freedom.'"

The comparison I had drawn between his experience of facing down discrimination and what he was prescribing for the LGBT community showcased his thinking on the parallels between the two movements. Yet the contrast fell short of sparking a realization about the broader implications of what his stance meant—he was advocating for a position that put him on the wrong side of history. For as much hope as he had inspired, Obama was a politician first, and was still constrained by the limitations of what he thought was politically possible in the moment.

"My perspective is also shaped by the broader political and historical context in which I'm operating," he explained. "I'm the product of a mixed marriage that would have been illegal in twelve states when I was born. That doesn't mean that had I been an adviser to Dr. King back then, I would have told him to lead with repealing an antimiscegenation law, because it just might not have been the best strategy in terms of moving broader equality forward."

I decided to try again on marriage. "Is it fair for the LGBT community to ask for leadership? In 1963, President Kennedy made civil rights a moral issue for the country."

"But he didn't overturn antimiscegenation. Right?" Obama responded.

"True enough," I conceded.

Though Obama wasn't leading the way on marriage equality, he clearly felt satisfied with the leadership he was showing by chipping away at homophobia in the general public. Since he often talked about speaking to African American audiences, I tried to draw him out about his insights on homophobia in the black community, but he stopped me short of articulating the question.

"I don't think it's worse than in the white community," Obama responded. "I think that the difference has to do with the fact that the African American community is more churched and most African American churches are still fairly traditional in their interpretations of Scripture."

Did he have a different prescriptive, I wondered, for addressing homophobia in the black community?

"Well, I think what's important is to have some of that church leadership speak up and change its attitudes, because I think a lot of its members are taking cues from that leadership," he said.

Indeed. *They were taking their cues from people like Donnie McClurkin,* I thought.

"Do you have any regrets about the South Carolina tour?" I said. "People there are still sort of mystified that you gave Donnie McClurkin the chance to get up onstage and do this, and he did go on sort of an anti-gay rant there."

"I tell you what, my campaign is premised on trying to reach as many constituencies as possible and to go into as many places as possible, and sometimes that creates discomfort or turbulence," Obama acknowledged. "The flip side of it is, you never create the opportunity for people to have a conversation and to lift some of these issues up and to talk about them and to struggle with them, and our campaign is built around the idea that we should all be talking."

The senator—who had given far more interviews to hungry reporters at that point than I had conducted of cagey politicians—ran around my question. Had I been a better interviewer, I would have forced the issue with a follow-up question like, "So, no. You have no regrets." But his answer spoke for itself. Obama surely never indicated any misgivings about the fact that McClurkin had ultimately delivered what so many LGBT activists had feared.

The press aide interjected to say that Obama had to leave for another meeting. They had promised me twenty minutes and we had already run past the twenty-three-minute mark. Obama looked at me, "We good?" he asked. Yes, I said, shaking his hand one last time. He turned around and headed out the door. "Oh and by the way," he jested, never looking back, "I'm glad you saved some money on your dry cleaning. That's important." It was a final zing about my failure to wear a suit to the interview. Then he was gone. I took it in good humor, as I'm sure it was intended. But Senator Obama had most certainly gotten the last word before disappearing. So much for trying to set a future president at ease for his informal dress code.

THE INTERVIEW WAS generally received well by those who wanted to receive it well, and received poorly by those who did not. By then, an all-out war had broken out between the pro-Obama and pro-Hillary factions of the LGBT world. The fact that Obama had made time for a wide-ranging interview allowed his followers to save face. But changing anyone's mind at that point wasn't really the point. Like most voters, LGBT folks had decided they liked one candidate or the other for reasons ranging from their sensibilities to their stylistic approach to a sense that one candidate just *got* them. Once that decision was made, they filtered every new development through that lens.

Those who liked Clinton were obsessed with Obama's McClurkin meltdown and what that said about his inability to relate to the LGBT experience. Those who liked Obama generally focused on Bill Clinton's record and the fact that Hillary only wanted to repeal section three of DOMA—the section that prohibited the federal government from recognizing same-sex unions. She suggested leaving in place section two—the section that said states couldn't be required to recognize gay marriages from other states. Depending on which candidate you favored, you either thought Hillary's stance was strategically brilliant because it could attract more support from lawmakers by leaving states to decide their own fate; or you thought it was an act of political cowardice because she was compromising full equality for something that might be sellable on Capitol Hill.

But the longer the campaign drew out, the more complicated the questions got. By late April, supporters of Proposition 8 announced they had obtained 1.1 million signatures to put the anti-gay measure on the ballot in November, far surpassing the nearly seven hundred thousand necessary that year. They had presaged the California Supreme Court's May 15 decision legalizing same-sex marriage by several weeks. And on June 7, 2008, LGBT Democrats would unite behind a single candidate after Hillary Clinton conceded the race to Barack Obama.[35]

Now that he was assured the Democratic nomination, Obama faced the conundrum of how to address what was fast becoming the nation's highest-profile battle for the right of same-sex couples to marry. Arizona and Florida would also have anti-marriage equality measures on the ballot that year, but nowhere was the battle more pitched than in California, where thousands of same-sex couples would marry in advance of the November vote.

When the California high court ruling came down May 15, 2008, and the Golden State became only the second state in the union to grant same-sex couples the freedom to marry, gay activists were ecstatic. My inbox lit up with victory e-mails. Not only did the ruling find that same-sex couples had a constitutional right to marry, the broadly worded 4–3 decision also declared that any state law discriminating against lesbians and gays moving forward would be constitutionally suspect in the same way that laws discriminating against other minorities are. "An individual's sexual orientation—like a person's race or gender—does not constitute a legitimate basis upon which to deny or withhold rights," wrote Chief Justice Ronald George, who was appointed to the bench by Governor Ronald Reagan. Putting gays in a similar category to other protected minorities was a step beyond the rationale the US Supreme Court had used to overturn sodomy laws in 2003, and a particularly bold move from a 6-to-1 majority-Republican court that was viewed as moderate to conservative.[36]

The day of the ruling, Obama issued a statement saying that he had "always believed same-sex couples should enjoy equal rights under the law." As president, he said he would "fight for civil unions." But he added that he respected the court's ruling and continued to believe "that states should make their own decisions when it comes to the issue of marriage."[37]

The statement didn't please queer activists at all. With the nomination wrapped up, Obama was angling toward a general-election audience. There was no hint of congratulations to the same-sex couples who had waited so long and had jumped through so many hoops—political, legislative, and legal—before their marriage rights were acknowledged by the state. Instead, Obama had restated his support for civil unions, which by his rendering would be a separate-but-equal institution. He also pounded home the notion that marriage was a states' rights issue. Since he didn't support full marriage equality, he was using the right of states to self-determine as a way to avoid having to denounce the ruling.

Activists were disillusioned, even if the statement was classically political. Obama, a former constitutional law professor, seemed to be ignoring the long history of legal decisions that had overturned this kind of discrimination. The Supreme Court had found *separate* institutions were "inherently unequal" in its landmark 1954 *Brown v. Board of Education* decision making segregated schools unconstitutional. And while it was true that the federal government had essentially deferred to the states on the definition of marriage since the nation's founding, states' rights were also most closely associated with arguments made by those who wanted to perpetuate the racist practices of slavery in the nineteenth century and segregation in the twentieth century. Further, in *Loving v. Virginia*—the 1967 Supreme Court decision that struck down laws in sixteen states banning interracial marriage—the court held that a state's power to regulate marriages is indeed con-

stricted by the Equal Protection and Due Process Clauses of the Fourteenth Amendment. Put more simply, states get to decide who can get
married and who can't only insofar as they are not infringing upon an
individual's fundamental freedoms for no good reason.[38]

The pro-civil unions, pro-states' rights position was particularly hard
to swallow from a man who was the product of a mixed-race marriage
and who routinely noted that when he was born, his parent's union wasn't
valid in at least a dozen states. Paradoxically, the same personal history that
made Obama's marriage stance seem so outlandish also gave him a sort of
Teflon quality on the matter. How could one look at Barack Obama and
charge that he didn't understand the implications of his policy positions?
This was a line that I found myself constantly walking as a reporter. It was
one of the reasons that in my interview I chose not to ask him whether
his marriage stance amounted to hypocrisy. As a white woman, I couldn't
imagine looking him in the eye and suggesting that I knew more about
separate-but-equal institutions. Instead, I had attempted to use his own
words about "not waiting his turn" to impugn his stance.

But gay activists weren't the only ones sizing up the ruling and how
it might affect the elections. Just like President Bill Clinton had grappled
with what not signing DOMA might mean for his reelection bid in 1996
and Senator John Kerry had struggled to carve out a position that seemed
appropriately tolerant without being too aggressively pro-gay in 2004,
Obama was now faced with the same dilemma. Conventional wisdom
held that the 2003 Massachusetts court decision legalizing gay marriage
had caused a conservative backlash among voters that was a boon to
Republicans. There was perhaps good reason to think that California's
ruling would be similarly harmful. Democrats weren't interested in a
2004 repeat during the 2008 election, and Obama had acted accordingly.

On May 17, 2008, two days after the decision, the *New York Times*
editorial board hailed the "momentous" ruling and called for Obama and
McCain, the Republican Party nominee, to "support Mr. Schwarzenegger in opposing a constitutional amendment" in California. McCain,
who was fighting to gain credibility with the Christian right, did no such
thing. His campaign issued a statement saying he supported "the right"
of California voters to define marriage as "the union between a man and
a woman." After several weeks, the candidate went even further, saying
he also supported "the efforts" to do so.[39]

Obama's campaign, as mentioned, initially issued a statement reiterating his support for both the rights of same-sex couples and the right of states to decide. The official campaign statement, which was sent out broadly to all reporters, only included those two elements. But to certain LGBT advocates, the campaign included an extra line: "On the issue of constitutional amendments, Senator Obama has been on record for some time: He opposes all divisive and discriminatory constitutional amendments, state or federal. That includes the proposed amendments in California and Florida." For obvious reasons, most news reports missed that line about California's amendment and it went largely unnoticed, at least by mainstream outlets.[40]

But pressure continued to mount over the month of June—Gay Pride month—for the new standard-bearer of the Democratic Party to weigh in more definitively on California's ballot measure. Instead, Obama managed to work in his line, "marriage is between a man and a woman"— something he had been saying repeatedly—in an ABC interview on June 16. The next day, the LGBT blog Bilerico Project published a post titled, "Shut the Hell Up." "If I hear 'Marriage is between one man and one woman' one more time from Obama's mouth—or any Democrat's mouth—I'm going to scream," wrote blogger Sara Whitman. "How is this change? Leadership? Hope? Or do only straight people get to hope?"[41]

Later that month, the campaign finally took a higher profile stand on Proposition 8 and sent a letter to a gay Democratic club in San Francisco explicitly denouncing the measure. It was read aloud on June 29 at the Gay Pride brunch of the Alice B. Toklas LGBT Democratic Club.

"I am proud to join with and support the LGBT community in an effort to set our nation on a course that recognizes LGBT Americans with full equality under the law," said the statement, "that is why I oppose the divisive and discriminatory efforts to amend the California Constitution, and similar efforts to amend the US Constitution or those of other states."[42]

Importantly, it came from the candidate himself (i.e., was written in first person) rather than a spokesperson on his behalf. It still wasn't the first time Obama had used first person to say he opposed divisive and discriminatory marriage measures. As early as February 2008, he had used such language in response to a candidate questionnaire from the Houston GLBT Political Caucus. But since it was his first statement to specifically mention California's initiative, *The Advocate* headline read, "Obama Announces Opposition to California's Ballot Measure." The campaign didn't seem to like all the attention the letter was getting. A spokesperson wrote me to say that we had "overplayed" the statement. "This wasn't new today," he wrote, noting that Obama had used similar wording in the past.[43]

Clearly, Obama's advisers were skittish about seeming too pro-gay on marriage-related issues. They also had to contend with the McCain camp, which was drawing attention to the statement by saying Obama had flip-flopped on his marriage stance. They could be forgiven for their confusion; Obama's stance was hard to pin down—he thought the definition of marriage should be left up to the states but he opposed amendments that would prohibit same-sex marriages even though he also opposed those very same marriages in theory. The Obama campaign had hoped to signal LGBT support without making mainstream headlines, which is exactly why they resurrected an old statement and sent a letter to one LGBT club rather than issuing a campaign statement to a wider universe of reporters and supporters.[44]

But that type of visibility on the senator's marriage stance wouldn't emerge again until late August when Obama and McCain had their televised sit down with Rick Warren. The two had a history of meeting on common ground around their belief in God even if they were at odds on things like abortion and gay rights. When I had interviewed Obama the previous year, he talked glowingly of the courage it took for Warren to lend him his stage at Saddleback on World AIDS Day in 2006.

"He was under enormous heat because, among his constituency, my position on LGBT issues and my position on abortion is anathema," Obama said, recalling that antiabortion activists had urged Warren to rescind the invitation. "To his credit, he allowed me to speak, in his church, from his pulpit, to 2,000 Evangelicals. And I didn't trim my remarks, I specifically told them, 'I think you guys are wrong when it comes to issues like condom distribution.' And by the way, I got a standing ovation."[45]

So here Obama was again, on Warren's stage in Southern California, a little over two months away from the November election. And if there were two things he knew he would be asked about, they were gay marriage and abortion. They were two of the biggest issues for Warren's flock of Evangelicals. Marriage was so big, in fact, that Warren ultimately recorded a personal endorsement of Proposition 8 and posted the video to his website a week before the vote, as well as e-mailing a statement to some twenty thousand members of his church, urging them to "vote yes on Proposition 8—to preserve the biblical definition of marriage." Failing to quiz the presidential nominees on those two issues would have been a dereliction of duty. So there is no question that Obama had practiced his answer repeatedly about what marriage meant to him. And there's no question, either, that when Obama delivered the line, "Now, for me as a Christian . . . it is also a sacred union. God's in the mix," his chief strategists hailed it as a home run. As long as Obama wasn't too scary on social issues—especially same-sex marriage—he could appeal to more independents and moderates and maybe even a few conservatives who weren't thrilled with McCain.[46]

The crowd ate up Obama's answer. They applauded after he defined marriage as being between "a man and a woman." They applauded after he said God was "in the mix." They even applauded after he declined to support a federal constitutional amendment because marriage has always been "a matter of state law." And they applauded after he endorsed civil unions and closed with, "I think my faith is strong enough and my marriage is strong enough that I can afford those civil rights to others, even if I have a different perspective or different view."

The exchange had lasted less than two minutes yet the potentially hostile crowd had given him love four separate times. It went swimmingly compared to his answer on abortion and being pro-choice, in which he rambled on for about three-and-a-half minutes to deafening silence from the crowd.

Warren never asked Obama about Proposition 8 explicitly, but the presidential hopeful had passed the marriage test with flying colors. While it was nice that Obama made a plug for affording lesbian and gay couples certain civil rights, he did so, as usual, against the backdrop that he didn't support full marriage equality. While some viewed Obama's approach as a cautious push for an expansion of our rights, his framing held an insidious dark side. In essence, he was telling people they could deny us the deepest expression of our love through marriage and yet be fair by granting us certain legal rights like hospital visitation. There was something troubling about the notion of making people feel that their actions were righteous even when they were discriminatory.

PERHAPS LGBT AMERICANS should not have been that surprised. It was not the first time Obama had made different appeals to separate audiences on the way to winning an election. During his primary bid for the US Senate in 2004, Obama told LGBT voters that his support for civil unions had tactical underpinnings. But when he faced his Republican challenger in the general election, he framed his rejection of same-sex marriage in religious terms—or what conservative Christians considered to be moral terms.

In January 2004, Obama faced a handful of other progressive candidates who were all vying for LGBT votes, including one, Gery Chico, who supported full marriage equality. That month, Chicago journalist Tracy Baim, publisher of the LGBT newspaper *Windy City Times*, interviewed Obama. During the interview, Obama asked her to turn off the tape recorder at one point so they could speak candidly about marriage versus civil unions. Obama was trying to understand why LGBT people cared so much about the word and not just the rights. He reasoned that if civil unions could offer the same rights and benefits as marriage, wouldn't that be an acceptable alternative?[47]

The exchange seemed very academic to Baim—this was a professor in learning mode, not a candidate in spin mode. Baim tried to explain to him that civil unions would have lesser import no matter how many rights came with it. Marriage holds a symbolic value in this country that makes the institution itself so much greater than the sum of its 1,100-plus benefits.

"It's a tradition that has both a legal and religious sense," she told him, "there's no way to separate those two things anymore in this country. So as a tradition, if you're going to say you're fully supportive of LGBT rights, you can't stop short of the most important tradition that binds our families together."[48]

Some activists actually would have preferred to separate the religious ceremony from the civil institution, but that would also mean disentangling the two for all Americans. As Baim noted, changing that long-standing tradition was a virtual impossibility.

When she turned the recorder back on, Obama told Baim that he was most concerned about securing the rights for same-sex couples.

"I am not a supporter of gay marriage as it has been thrown about, primarily just as a strategic issue," he said. "I think that marriage, in the minds of a lot of voters, has a religious connotation. I know that's true in the African American community, for example. And if you asked people, 'should gay and lesbian people have the same rights to transfer property, and visit hospitals, and et cetera?' they would say, 'absolutely.' And then if you talk about, 'should they get married?' then suddenly . . . "[49]

Baim interjected, noting that over one thousand federal benefits come with marriage. Then she posited, "But you think, strategically, gay marriage isn't going to happen so you won't support it at this time?"[50]

"What I'm saying is that strategically, I think we can get civil unions passed," Obama said, referring to an Illinois bill that was working its way through the state legislature. "I think that to the extent that we can get the rights, I'm less concerned about the name."[51]

But that was during the primary. After Obama won, his religious turn on marriage came during the general election where he faced Republican Alan Keyes, a firebrand conservative commentator who made social issues like abortion and gay marriage a cornerstone of his campaign. Keyes—who told gay radio host Michelangelo Signorile that Vice President Dick Cheney's daughter Mary Cheney was a "selfish hedonist" because she was a lesbian—accused Obama of "deceiving the voters" on same-sex marriage.[52]

After several days of criticism from Keyes, who was also African American and very much competing for the state's black vote, Obama gave a radio interview asserting that his views on the matter were guided by his Christian faith.[53]

"I'm a Christian," Obama told the Chicago radio station WBBM-AM in September of 2004. "And so, although I try not to have my religious beliefs dominate or determine my political views on this issue, I do believe that tradition, and my religious beliefs say that marriage is something sanctified between a man and a woman."[54]

It was a general-election pronouncement that sparked an emergency meeting of Obama's LGBT supporters, who were shocked by the revelation. Baim chronicled that meeting extensively in multiple interviews she conducted for her 2010 book, *Obama and the Gays: A Political Marriage.*[55]

During the hastily arranged meeting, Obama sat in the middle of about twenty LGBT activists at his campaign headquarters. They voiced their concerns and asked, "What do your religious views have to do with your political views?" recalled LGBT advocate Michael Bauer. Another

Obama supporter, David Munar, remembered the candidate explaining that he wasn't supporting same-sex marriage, he was supporting equality for lesbians and gays in terms of rights and privileges. "He understood the cause for equality," Munar told Baim, "but also the political reality, that to push for marriage was not pragmatic, not feasible . . . that the cause for equality was more important than the symbolism of using the actual word, 'marriage.'"[56]

Few of the activists were entirely satisfied by Obama's explanation, but they also had nowhere else to go at that point. Keyes was an absolutely scary candidate, and many appreciated that Obama took the time to engage and hear them out.[57]

The strategy worked in 2004 and Obama retrod that road map in 2008—emphasizing the equal rights part of his marriage stance in the primary and then the religious aspect of his views in the general election. Only as a presidential candidate, the stakes were much higher. Obama had a national profile and the power of his declaration on Warren's stage had repercussions across the country. Ballot measures were on the line, tens of thousands of same-sex couples had already married by then and, perhaps most tragically, LGBT youth were told once again that their love was somehow unholy and unworthy of recognition. It was one thing for Obama to play the religion card during his 2004 Senate bid, but quite another to do it four years later in pursuit of the presidency.[58]

Of course, no one can definitively say that Obama's marriage pronouncement at Saddleback guaranteed the passage of Proposition 8, but it certainly didn't hurt. He had given marriage equality opponents a plethora of perfect sound bites that could be used in print, audio, or video—a messaging trifecta. They capitalized on it, using the audio for the robocall that reached Robin McGehee's home and the text from a *Hardball with Chris Matthews* appearance for a flier that was mailed out about five days before the vote. "I'm not in favor of gay marriage, but I'm in favor of a very strong civil union," Obama had told MSNBC's Chris Matthews in April. But in campaigns, the second half of a statement like that is left for dead. The flier, which included a large photo of Barack Obama grinning with his wife beaming at him in the background, featured huge block letters reading simply, "I'm not in favor of gay marriage." Below the quote, they added Obama's Saddleback remarks and then included an Obama for

America insignia that made the flier appear like an official campaign ad. The only words on the page bigger than Obama's quote were, "Vote YES on Prop 8." As soon as the flier emerged, the Obama campaign quickly issued a statement clarifying that Obama opposed the amendment, but the damage was done. Voters get the fliers, they get the robocalls, they see the ads. They don't get the clarifications.[59]

Marriage equality proponents, by contrast, declined to use verbiage from the letter Obama sent to the Alice B. Toklas Club. A consultant who was in charge of the No On 8 campaign later remarked, "That was a close call. Maybe we should have."[60]

But in some ways, the most important repercussion of Obama's performance on Warren's stage and the robocalls that followed was that queer activists like McGehee would never forget it. After Proposition 8 passed, the activists were like tinder. If Obama was going to avoid igniting them, he would have to deliver on his promises to the LGBT community. Any sign that he didn't plan to do so was sure to enflame those who already felt betrayed by the guy they had donated to and canvassed for and given their vote.

Yet in the fervor of election night, it was easy to forget some of that frustration. To cover it, I flew to Chicago and embedded myself with the city's LGBT community. A returns party was held at a local gay bar called Sidetrack. Between drinks, merriment, and people taking pictures alongside a life-sized Obama cutout, occasional ominous announcements crept in about California's Prop 8 vote. But *The Advocate*, which was based in Los Angeles, had plenty of people reporting on the ballot measure. I kept my focus on Chicago and headed to Grant Park around 9:30 p.m., after Ohio had been called for Obama.

When I arrived, the crowd of roughly 240,000 was alive with the smell of victory. At 11:00 p.m. Eastern/8:00 p.m. Pacific, the polls closed on the West Coast and news agencies finally announced what had become crystal clear over the past few hours—Barack Obama would be the next president of the United States. The crowd erupted.[61]

Barack and Michelle Obama walked out onto the blue-carpeted runway, each waving to the crowd with one hand while holding the hand of one of their daughters, Malia and Sasha, with the other. Against a backdrop of about a couple of dozen American flags lining the recesses of the stage, Obama took to the podium.

"Hello Chicago!" Obama called out, surveying the revelers. Buoyed by his achievement, he began, "If there is anyone out there who still doubts that America is a place where all things are possible, who still wonders if the dream of our founders is alive in our time, who still questions the power of our democracy, tonight is your answer."[62]

But as inspiring as witnessing that moment was, it couldn't insulate me from the dispiriting results in California.

The more I pondered how a little known African American politician from Illinois could be elected to the US Senate in 2004 and then clinch the highest office in the land just four years later, the more I bought into the idea that maybe change comes from the middle of the country. If you can get a relatively moderate state like Illinois to buy into something—such as the fledgling candidacy of an unknown upstart—then perhaps it was marketable to the rest of the country. Maybe the country simply wasn't ready for gay marriage, I thought. Maybe it was too soon for the movement to focus its energies there when we had yet to push a single major piece of pro-LGBT legislation through Congress.

"Even as California's marriage battle drags on," I wrote for *The Advocate* that night, "and New York and New Jersey are poised to advance their marital quests legislatively, I am reminded of how many states and how many people exist somewhere in between the passions of America's coasts. Ultimately, I don't think our movement should settle for anything less than full equality, and that includes marriage rights. But as a Midwesterner by birth who has lived six years in South Carolina, five in San Francisco, and now four in New York, I still find wisdom in the center—where a confluence of interests, customs, and differing points of view bleed into each other to yield a softer palette. Just as our country pushes forward to form a more perfect union, so should we. But let us not deify marriage to the exclusion of pursuits like employment nondiscrimination, hate crime protections, and basic partnership recognition."[63]

To some extent, covering Obama had made me wonder if pushing for civil unions over marriage might be a more pragmatic route to securing important rights and protections for same-sex couples in the short term. And to some extent, I was simply trying to make sense of a disorienting blow to the LGBT community.

But perhaps my thinking was a luxury born of location. In the days following the election, tempers flared in the streets of California as protests swept the state. On the first Sunday after the vote, LGBT advocates focused their energy on the very religious institutions they held most responsible for pushing Prop 8: about one thousand activists gathered in Lake Forest to protest outside of Rick Warren's Saddleback Church, and in Oakland, a protest of several hundred people at a prominent golden-spired Mormon Temple forced the California Highway Patrol to shut down two highway ramps nearby. About 2,500 protesters also assembled at the steps of the state's capitol in Sacramento.[64]

But maybe the biggest indication of how widespread the discontent was came from activists Amy Balliett in Seattle and Willow Witte in Cleveland. Deeply frustrated by the outcome, the two former college buddies built an interactive website called Join the Impact, where activists could post and publicize marriage equality rallies. The site went live on the Friday following the election, and by Sunday night, it was receiving more than fifty thousand hits an hour. After the site crashed several times due to the sheer volume of traffic, they got a bigger server and a little technical help. By the following week, they had received over a million views and organized hundreds of rallies that would take place on Saturday, November 15, in all fifty states, eight countries, and more than three hundred cities around the world. This was not business as usual. A sleeping giant had been poked one too many times. It was an extensive and undeniable rejection of the status quo. Denying gays basic human rights wasn't acceptable to a critical mass of people anymore. Even if they weren't the majority, they were paying attention, they were hungry to get involved, and they wanted their voices to be heard. It was just a matter of finding a way to parlay that energy into a sustainable force for change.[65]

BACK IN WASHINGTON, preparations began for the inaugural ceremony. By December, even LGBT activists seemed excited to put the Prop 8 drama on hold for a time and revel in Obama's moment. Then the news came: the Presidential Inaugural Committee had chosen none other than Rick Warren—who had personally championed Proposition 8—to give the invocation at the inauguration.

It was a baffling decision. Hadn't the committee vetted Warren? Weren't they aware of his very public pronouncement on Proposition 8?

His own video message, after all, posted just a couple weeks before the vote, had left nothing to the imagination. "Now let me just say this really clearly," Warren said on October 23, 2008, "We support Proposition 8, and if you believe what the Bible says about marriage, you need to support Proposition 8. I never support a candidate, but on moral issues, I come out very clear." Warren even referenced quizzing Obama and McCain on the matter at his candidate forum and cited their unanimous agreement with him that marriage remains between "one man and one woman."[66]

Perhaps Obama's new team simply believed that Warren had a legitimate policy disagreement with LGBT Americans on a matter that we considered a fundamental human right. This at least seemed to be the sentiment President-elect Obama conveyed at one preinaugural press conference where he was asked about the upheaval surrounding Warren's inclusion in the ceremony.

"I think that it is no secret that I am a fierce advocate for equality for gay and lesbian Americans," Obama asserted on December 18, 2008. But, he added, it was also important "for America to come together," despite our differences on some social issues. "During the course of the entire inaugural festivities, there are going to be a wide range of viewpoints that are presented. And that's how it should be because that's part of what America's about. That's part of the magic of this country is that we are diverse and noisy and opinionated," Obama told reporters, "And that's, hopefully, going to be a spirit that carries over into my administration."[67]

It was a stunning turn of events for LGBT activists. Warren, who had used his position of piety to vilify gay citizens and delegitimize their relationships, would be blessing the president-to-be and his leadership of the American people. This, we were told, was part of the magic of the country.

The day before that press conference, Richard Socarides, who had served as a special assistant advising President Bill Clinton on LGBT issues, got an inquiry from *New York Times* reporter Jeff Zeleny wondering if he would be willing to speak on the record about Warren. Zeleny was having trouble getting prominent Beltway gays to talk about the pick—few LGBT people wanted to get on the wrong side of an incoming Democratic administration after being relegated to the hinterlands of Republican rule for eight years. It literally does not pay to be an outcast in Washington. People trade on access, they sell the strength of their contacts and their ability to land a meeting with a big politico. Alienating yourself by publicly criticizing your party's president-elect before he even sets foot in the Oval Office is a risky business if you want to be part of Washington's "in" crowd.[68]

But Socarides, who was then working as an attorney in New York, agreed to talk. Though many LGBT advocates faulted him for Clinton's wanting gay rights record, his former title made him a perfect source for reporters. Clinton had originally appointed Socarides to a post at the Department of Labor in 1993, but in 1994 Clinton advisor Marsha Scott pulled him in for advice as she assembled the very first gay outreach office at the White House. He eventually took over the office in 1996 when Scott left to work on Clinton's reelection campaign.

Socarides worried that the Warren development was a particularly bad sign for where gay issues fell on the totem pole of priorities for the incoming administration. If others weren't willing to say anything, he was. He told Zeleny that Obama's team had made a "serious miscalculation" if they thought selecting Warren would just slide by or be otherwise excused or overlooked.[69]

"It's not like he's introducing Obama at some campaign rally in the South," Socarides said in the article, an obvious reference to McClurkin. "He's been given this very prominent, central role in the ceremony which is supposed to usher in a new civil rights era."[70]

Also quoted in the article was Reverend V. Gene Robinson, the nation's first openly gay Episcopal bishop, who had been a prominent early supporter of Obama during the contentious primary battle. After the Warren announcement, Robinson called his contacts in the campaign to express his disappointment. According to the piece, they had told him that "Obama was trying to reach out to conservatives and give everybody a seat at the table."[71]

"I'm all for Rick Warren being at the table," Bishop Robinson told the *New York Times*, "but we're not talking about a discussion, we're talking about putting someone up front and center at what will be the most watched inauguration in history, and asking his blessing on the nation. And the God that he's praying to is not the God that I know."[72]

The Human Rights Campaign also ended up weighing in on the dispute with an editorial in the *Washington Post* titled, "Obama's Inaugural Mistake," penned by HRC president Joe Solmonese. The fact that HRC was moved to act signaled just how bad Obama's transgression was. The last thing HRC's leadership wanted to do was put distance between themselves and the incoming administration, but remaining silent on the selection of Warren simply wasn't an option. If the movement's most conservative actor, HRC, was taking Obama to task in the *Post*, the grassroots was livid.

In response to the fallout, Obama's top lieutenants replicated the campaign's South Carolina strategy. They invited Robinson to give the invocation at the Lincoln Memorial kickoff event for inaugural week. The committee insisted that Robinson's inclusion had been in the works before the controversy erupted. But Robinson's slot would not get even close to the same visibility as that of his anti-gay counterpart, Warren, who would lead off the actual inauguration itself. In fact, much like Reverend Andy Sidden's opening prayer in South Carolina, which barely gained an audience and was soon forgotten, Robinson's prayer slipped through the cracks as well. HBO began televising the event at 2:30 p.m. on January 18, 2009, but since Robinson was scheduled to begin his prayer at 2:25 p.m., it was not televised nor was it included by any broadcast outlet that carried HBO's feed, such as NPR, which later devoted a follow-up segment to Robinson's exclusion.[73]

It is a provocative prayer, I thought, as I listened to him from the press corral to the left of the stage, completely unaware that the rest of the nation was tuned out. Robinson drew inspiration from a fourfold Franciscan blessing that invites "restless discomfort."

"Oh, God of our many understandings," he began, "we pray that you will bless us with tears; tears for a world in which over a billion people exist on less than $1 a day, where young women in many lands are beaten and raped for wanting an education, and thousands die daily from malnutrition, malaria, and AIDS.

"Bless this nation with anger," he continued, "anger at discrimination at home and abroad, against refugees and immigrants, women, people of color, gay, lesbian, bisexual, and transgender people."[74]

He also prayed for the new president-elect's safety and asked for patience and understanding "that our new president is a human being, not a messiah."

Those close to the stage could hear him just fine, but there did seem to be some glitch with the PA system. As the program commenced, the audio kinks seemed to fade. The thousands who filled the stretch between Lincoln's somber gaze across the reflecting pool to the Washington Monument were treated to soaring performances from the likes of Beyoncé, Bruce Springsteen, and U2. So when I started getting word about Robinson's omission from the televised programming, it was a jarring disconnect from an otherwise uplifting afternoon. At first, I thought it was simply a PA failure. But when I later realized his entire prayer had been cut from the broadcast as well, I thought, *There must be some mistake—how could this have happened?*

An HBO producer told the website AfterElton.com that the Presidential Inaugural Committee "made the decision to keep the invocation as part of the pre-show." HBO executive Jeff Cusson agreed, saying, "You'll have to talk to PIC about all of the scheduling decisions. We had a set broadcast time and went forth accordingly."[75]

The next day, committee spokesperson Josh Earnest issued a statement saying, "We had always intended and planned for Rt. Rev. Robinson's invocation to be included in the televised portion of yesterday's program. We regret the error in executing this plan."[76]

I, like many others, found myself struggling. I wasn't prone to conspiracy theories, but a pattern of willful negligence at the very least was developing. How many times could they screw up the gay thing, then apologize, then screw it up again? Warren and McClurkin were starting to look less like singular slipups than emblems of a deeper problem. Obama's team either wasn't LGBT-conversant enough to foresee these landmines before they triggered them or, worse yet, they weren't persuaded by the impending collateral damage to bother to course correct in advance. Regardless of which, it did not bode well for how gay, bisexual, and transgender concerns would be handled in the Obama White House.

LOSING THE RELIGION · 2

J ONATHAN LEWIS AND HIS POLITICAL ADVISER PAUL YANDURA
were at odds over whether the newly inaugurated Barack Obama
would address a conference of mega-moneyed progressive donors
they were attending at the glamorous Biltmore Hotel in Coral Gables,
Miami. It was early March, 2009, and Lewis, son of billionaire Peter
Lewis who built Progressive Insurance into an auto insurance giant, figured that Obama might make an appearance. Attendees had been told
that an Obama "official" would be coming. But these were the people
who had helped pave the way for Obama's 2008 victory, giving hundreds
of thousands and, in some cases, millions of dollars to elect Democrats.
Lewis hoped the new president might surprise them, which would be
an early indication of the tenor his administration would strike while in
office. But Yandura, who had once worked in the Clinton White House
and understood the political realities of such an appearance, was much
more skeptical about whether this president, for all his promises, would
be any different from his predecessors.[1]

The group of donors, known as the Democracy Alliance, was founded
in 2005 by Democratic strategist and former Clinton official Rob
Stein as the liberal answer to the conservative funding machine that
took down—or perhaps more appropriately, "swift-boated"—the 2004
Democratic nominee, John Kerry. Peter Lewis, hedge fund pioneer and
philanthropist George Soros, and Golden West Financial cofounders

Herb and Marion Sandler, were initial backers of the Democracy Alliance. Both Lewis and Soros had contributed heavily to the 2004 effort to oust President George W. Bush, with Lewis committing about $25 million and Soros around $50 million to left-leaning political groups. Members of Democracy Alliance—roughly 100–200 donors in 2009—were required to give at least $200,000 a year to liberal groups hand-picked by the organization, plus a $30,000 annual maintenance fee. The Alliance was initially intended to be a clearinghouse of information for progressive donors looking for advice about which left-leaning groups to funnel their money to. Democracy Alliance, then, was an effort to help progressive donors with cash on hand be smarter and more collaborative about their giving.[2]

Yandura had been the younger Lewis's adviser since 2004, when Jonathan first got interested in political giving, in part, because his father started talking about lavishing large sums on the 2004 cycle. Jonathan had been burned once before in politics, and he contracted Yandura to help make sure his father wouldn't make a similar mistake. Around the turn of the millennium, Jonathan had donated $1 million to the Human Rights Campaign when its leaders were raising money to establish a permanent home for the organization. They would eventually accomplish that goal in style, purchasing and handsomely renovating an impressive eight-story building on the corner of Rhode Island and 17th Street, right in the thick of DC's own gayborhood, Dupont Circle, and just a ten-minute walk north of the White House. The doors opened in 2003 on October 11—National Coming Out Day—complete with a row of panels in the entryway bearing the names of the couple hundred donors who had given generously to the cause. But Jonathan and his family had a separate dedication for their outsized contribution. Just past the front desk and across from the elevators leading to the main offices, a brushed silver plaque inscribed with black lettering read: "This lobby was made possible by a generous gift from Helen and Joseph Lewis, Peter B. Lewis, Jonathan D. Lewis & Roberto Posada." That plaque eventually became a focal point for Lewis's anger—physical evidence of money down the drain and a reason to look elsewhere for agents of change on gay rights. Lewis's frustration with HRC would ultimately lead him to invest in a type of activism that represented the antithesis of HRC's approach.[3]

But originally, at the very moment that HRC had been looking for big donors, Lewis and his Colombian-born partner of a decade-plus were struggling with the legal discrimination many same-sex couples faced. They were searching for a way for Posada to either get a visa or establish permanent residency so they could live together at Lewis's home in Miami. He couldn't simply get a green card by marrying Lewis the way hetero couples could. After years of hiring lawyers in New York, Washington, and Miami to no avail, Lewis decided to invest in some political advocacy on the issue. HRC approached him at the perfect moment. He was most taken with the idea of helping the group establish a tangible symbol of the LGBT community in the heart of Washington and a place that gay youth could call home. And since the organization was fighting for LGBT interests, Lewis also hoped it might play a role in helping him and his partner and other same-sex couples resolve their immigration issues.

Lewis's hopes were quickly dashed. After handing over the money, he started watching HRC like a hawk and quickly became disenchanted. As a businessman, he didn't think the group was very effective at securing rights. Though HRC had a high profile and a fancy building, they had never managed to pass a single piece of legislation through Congress. Worse yet, they seemed more interested in being accepted by the Washington establishment than challenging it. Lewis later came to view that investment as one of the worst in his life.[4]

So when his father began talking about dropping millions on politics in 2004, Lewis wanted to do what he could to help insulate him from disaster. Not that his father necessarily needed his help, but a protective instinct still kicked in. That's when he enlisted Yandura, who was one-half of the DC-based consulting firm Scott+Yandura. Yandura, with his dark beard, might have passed for a lumberjack if he were wearing a plaid shirt and carrying a pickax. He knew Washington politics and LGBT circles as intimately as almost anyone in the Beltway and was the classic insider-turned-out. Through working at the White House and then for the Democratic National Committee in the '90s, Yandura got an unfettered view into what happens behind closed doors regardless of what the insiders might be saying publicly. He would use that knowledge during the first years of Obama's presidency to harness the energy from Prop 8 and turn it into a force for change in Washington. So understanding Yandura's point of view as the consummate Washington insider who eventually chose exile is essential to understanding why many LGBT activists adopted such an aggressive posture toward the White House, in particular.

Lewis, on the other hand, would provide the resources to turn Yandura's ideas into action. He was not your typical donor; he didn't like going to prestigious political dinners or positioning himself for appointments to largely ceremonial positions like ambassadorships. In fact, Lewis had an inherent distrust of politics and politicians alike. His first political memory centered around sitting at the dinner table and being told by his parents that they were both on the second installment of President Richard Nixon's infamous "enemies list," which was made public in 1973. His parents had landed on the dark side of Nixon's moon for being major contributors to Democratic presidential nominee George McGovern. Lewis, an impressionable young teen at the time, found the news unsettling. He was terrified that such a list existed and perhaps wary of becoming too involved or recognizable in a world where this kind of blacklisting was a reality. Whatever the reason, Lewis gravitated toward remaining an outsider. Fitting in didn't come naturally to him. He was gay, Jewish, wealthy, and, although one would never guess it by his fit physique and square jaw line offset by a pair of stylish thick-rimmed glasses, Lewis had struggled with his weight as a young man. As a donor, he was more interested in seeing the tangible gains of his giving than in reaping the political benefits.[5]

If Lewis more or less inherited a political legacy, Yandura's initiation into politics—and Washington politics, more specifically—was more fortuitous. It came through a strange twist of fate in 1994 when he was in his mid-twenties. He had landed a spot volunteering at the White House and was attending an orientation in an auditorium full of a couple hundred of his compatriots at the Eisenhower Executive Office Building, an imposing edifice situated right next to the West Wing that houses most of the White House staffers. A Secret Service officer was in the midst of scaring the interns silly about all the awful things that could happen to them if they stole so much as a paper clip when a petite woman wandered in and whispered in his ear. The agent got flummoxed, blushed a bit, and then inquired whether this had to happen at that very moment. She assured him it did, at which point he turned to the group of aspiring interns and asked, "Is anyone in the room gay?" Yandura froze. His eyes nervously darted around the room. The agent surveyed the cohort for several seconds . . . no takers. The LGBT community was still reeling from having lost scores of gay men to AIDS in the 1980s and early 1990s. Most gay Washington operatives were still closeted at work. In fact, until President Clinton changed the policy in 1995, lesbians and gays were still prohibited from getting high-level security clearances. It simply was not a safe time for gay people to proclaim their sexuality, especially in Washington, DC.[6]

After a few beats of panicked paralysis, Yandura slowly rose from his chair, which was not-so-conveniently located in the middle of a row. Everyone turned to stare at him as he displaced a line of his seated peers en route to the aisle. He was waved to the front of the room and promptly led out by the woman, whose name, he later learned, was Wendy Heistad. "We are going to have so much fun!" she chirped at Yandura, who was still terrified and entirely unclear about where and how this diversion would end. He trailed behind Heistad as she navigated her way through the building to the office of Marsha Scott, for whom she was an assistant. She introduced the two strangers. It was the start of a lifelong friendship for Yandura and Scott, who later became business partners. Scott was a high school friend of Bill Clinton's and one of his most trusted Arkansas confidants. She worked in political affairs and had been given the task of forming the very first White House Office of Gay and Lesbian Outreach in order to help Clinton repair his relationship with gays following his botched effort to lift the ban on gay service members.

Clinton had basically tripped over the issue only a week after being elected, as he was leaving a Little Rock Veteran's Day event in November of 1992. A CNN producer shouting questions in the rope line asked the president-elect whether he planned to keep his campaign promise to let gay service members serve openly. Clinton could have ignored the question—a tried-and-true tactic for politicians—but instead he responded. "We need everybody in America who has a contribution to make and is willing to obey the law and work hard and obey the rules," he said. "That is the way I feel."[7]

That answer essentially became his first public policy pronouncement as an incoming president and the nascent administration wasn't even remotely prepared for the forces that statement would unleash against it. Along with the fact that the military has historically been one of the most powerful lobbies on Capitol Hill, Democratic Senator Sam Nunn of Georgia—whom many believed felt snubbed after Clinton passed him over as head of both the Department of State and the Department of Defense—became a one-man wrecking ball on the matter. He quickly began telling reporters he opposed lifting the ban and that the president couldn't simply make a unilateral decision. Nunn, who chaired the Senate Armed Services Committee (making him an essential player in any change in military policy) was publicly shaming President Clinton before he even got out of the starting gate. "Nunn Emerges as Power Player as White House Tries to Lift Gay Ban," proclaimed an Associated Press headline on January 30, 1993, even as the freshly inaugurated commander in chief was still struggling to formulate his new policy. The young president, it seemed, was an amateur being schooled in the ways of Washington by a veteran Senator from his own party. White House aides were desperate to change the conversation and wipe the insinuation from the front pages of the nation's newspapers. In July of 1993, they settled on "don't ask, don't tell" as a compromise that would ostensibly allow lesbians and gays to serve as long as they kept quiet about their sexual orientation. While the new policy managed to quell a revolt by the military's top brass, it infuriated gay groups.[8]

The new gay outreach office was an effort to extend an olive branch. Scott, who was straight, informed Yandura that his mission was to help her shape the office. Then she promptly marched him out of the building, across the parking lot and into the West Wing where President Clinton was working in a private study next to the Oval Office. When they entered the room, Clinton looked up from his desk with his reading glasses on and Scott explained that Yandura would be helping her with the new endeavor. Clinton stood up to greet Yandura and clutched the hand of the befuddled twenty-six-year-old, who was speechless. He was donning his first and only suit that day and had somehow gone from managing fight-or-flight impulses to meeting the leader of the free world in the span of about twenty minutes. Yandura barely managed a reply, and then it was over. It all might have seemed like a dream had he not gone on to work in the White House for two more years before working for Clinton's 1996 reelect as the first gay and lesbian outreach director and later raising money for the Democratic National Committee.[9]

As an internal fixture at the White House, Yandura experienced first-hand how the administration approached the LGBT constituency. The idea was to seem accessible, especially to relatively friendly and financially powerful groups like HRC, but not actually yield much ground. (After all, the Human Rights Campaign had contributed $3 million to Clinton's 1992 campaign.) When more subversive forces—like AIDS activists, who routinely held headline-grabbing arrestable actions—protested the White House, Clinton officials exhibited no fissures externally even if they felt panicked internally. The main point was to keep the politics of the LGBT community in check. The administration had lost control of the narrative on the gay ban almost immediately. Now aides needed to keep gays close, pleasing them when it was deemed possible and managing them when it was not. The gay and lesbian outreach office was a positive step to be sure—it opened up a channel of communication that had never existed before and was a profound improvement on previous presidents' refusal to even acknowledge gay Americans, let alone their concerns. But it was by no means a guarantee that the LGBT community would be consulted on major policy decisions.[10]

After working as a Democratic insider for about a decade, Yandura eventually made nearly as flashy an exit from the inner circle as he had an entrance. In 2005, he started pressing Howard Dean and the DNC to advocate more publicly against a new round of marriage referenda that would be on state ballots across the nation in 2006. When he finally decided his pleas were falling on deaf ears, he sent an e-mail to a small group of major donors and their advisors criticizing Democrats for their lack of action.[11]

"For many months, a number of us have made appeals to Howard Dean and party officials to care about and defend the dignity of gay and lesbian families and friends, in the same way they defend the dignity of other key constituencies," Yandura wrote on April 20, 2006, noting that Republicans had announced their intent to use gay marriage as a wedge issue again in the midterms that year. "Neither the DNC, nor any of the national committees (DCCC, DSCC), have a strategy to combat this hatred (unless you count avoidance as a strategy)," Yandura continued. "Why are gays and lesbians continually left to fight these battles alone? Where are our allies? All progressives need to be asking how much has the DNC budgeted to counter the anti-gay ballot initiatives in the states. We also need to know why the DNC and our Democratic leaders continue to allow the Republicans to use our families and friends as pawns to win elections."[12]

Yandura, who had been viewed by many as a Democratic Party loyalist up to that point, ended the letter by advising the LGBT donors not to give any more money to Democrats until the DNC could provide answers to the questions he had posed. Yandura knew how much pain he could inflict on the party with this kind of move; he had raised money for the Democrats during two separate presidential elections and knew what a cash cow gay donors had become for the party. In fact, in 2000, the DNC had specifically created the Gay and Lesbian Leadership Council (GLLC) in order to track how much money LGBT donors contributed to the DNC's arsenal. Yandura served as the council's first director and, by his estimates in a sworn affidavit, the GLLC helped raise upwards of $5 million for the DNC in its inaugural year. But the DNC's openly gay treasurer, Andrew Tobias, put that number closer to $10 million to $18 million (the sum total of individual donations from gays and those taken in through LGBT-organized fundraisers that included both gays and straight allies).[13]

Yandura's appeal went public shortly after he wrote it when portions of the letter were published by the left-leaning blog MyDD and then were later covered by *Washington Blade* reporter Lou Chibbaro Jr. The assault helped fuel a certain distrust of the DNC and came on the heels of news that Democratic Party Chair Howard Dean had eliminated the DNC's gay outreach desk, which was separate from the fundraising post Yandura once held.

The DNC wasn't pleased, and the fallout from the release of Yandura's letter quickly became personal. At the time, Yandura's partner, Donald Hitchcock, was the director of the GLLC. But not for long. The DNC had originally recruited Hitchcock in June of 2005, after the position had been open for months. But a little over a week after Yandura's letter became public, Hitchcock was fired.

DNC spokesperson Karen Finney explained the move to the *Washington Blade:* "It was decided we needed a change. We decided to hire a proven leader."[14]

Yandura countered, "This is retaliation, plain and simple."[15]

The fact that Howard Dean had started to make a heavy push in 2006 to woo Evangelical voters didn't help the optics. Early in 2005, Dean had eliminated the LGBT outreach desk, which included two nonfundraising posts the community had fought hard to establish in order to foster communication between the Democratic Party and the gay constituency. DNC officials said Dean had simply eliminated all the constituency desks in an effort to "streamline" the system. Yet he and his chief of staff, Leah Daughtry, quietly began building the DNC's Faith in Action initiative to boost religious outreach in 2005. In October 2007, a *New York Times* profile of Daughtry noted that she had hired the organization's first religious outreach director and the team "now counts seven staff members." The Democrats, it seemed, were courting the very constituency that was targeting gays. Worse yet, they appeared to be prioritizing religious voters despite the fact that Evangelicals weren't a key Democratic constituency and didn't contribute heavy sums to Democratic coffers. The lessons from Bush's 2004 win, fueled by the perception that the anti-gay marriage amendments had boosted his vote share, appeared to have taken hold in the party. But if their goal was to peel off Evangelical votes, the Democrats had an image problem. They were too closely associated with gay rights, and that was an absolute nonstarter with so-called "Values Voters."[16]

As is turned out, Democrats were not wholly unsuccessful in their religious outreach in 2006. White Evangelicals and born-again Christians accounted for nearly 25 percent of all voters nationwide in 2004 and 2006, which is what consistently made them such a coveted voting bloc. But while they favored President Bush over Senator Kerry by a margin of 78 to 21 percent in 2004, two years later they only chose Republican candidates over Democrats 70 to 28 percent—an eight-point slip during a midterm election that delivered control of both chambers of Congress to Democrats. Midterms aren't exactly comparable to presidential elections. Still, in some ways, the strategy appeared to be making an inroad even if it was causing consternation among the base.[17]

Hitchcock, Yandura's partner, eventually filed a discrimination and defamation suit, *Hitchcock v. DNC Services Corp. et al.*, in April of 2007. Though the DNC originally said the case had "no merit," a judge disagreed and allowed the lawsuit to move forward. DNC Chair Howard Dean and other top officials were forced to testify in the case in the spring of 2008, and some embarrassing internal e-mails in which DNC staffers disparaged the gay press started to surface. The DNC then offered Hitchcock $100,000 to settle the case. He declined in August 2008, just before the big Democratic convention in Denver. Finally, in January of 2009, they settled the case out of court for an undisclosed amount.[18]

Though the settlement prevented a slew of internal DNC documents from being released, a couple of years' worth of seditious headlines and bad press for the DNC had begun to foment discontent among the LGBT ranks. With the exception of when Dean was finally deposed, the mainstream media barely batted an eye. But LGBT blogs and weekly newspapers found the Hitchcock-DNC showdown tantalizing. Any gay person who was paying close attention to constituency politics started to wonder whether the Democrats were really on our side, despite what they said.

As Andrew Belonsky, the editor of the popular gay blog Queerty, wrote in January of 2008: "Gay voters, myself included, are torn: do we support the party that offers us at least nominal inclusion, or do we strike off and find a more independent-minded politico? More astute voters will realize, however, that we don't have much of a choice."[19]

THROUGH THE ENTIRE DNC ordeal, Jonathan Lewis stuck with Yandura as his political adviser (as did Yandura's business partner, Marsha Scott, with whom he continued to co-own a consulting business). Lewis had been turned off from gay politics by his HRC experience and, more than anything, was completely stunned by how uniquely unsuccessful the LGBT movement had been at the federal level. There was not a single piece of major pro-equality legislation to be shown for all the work, all the money, all the fundraisers. Lewis was more drawn to investing in the nation's youth. They were the only group of people that consistently inspired him and gave him hope that the nation could change for the better.

So between 2004 and 2008, Yandura helped Lewis and his family direct almost $13 million toward increasing youth participation in politics through enterprises like the Youth Voter Alliance (a 2004 youth voter field operation in five battleground states), Wake Up Everybody (a 2004 hip-hop album aimed at young voters and produced in collaboration with America Coming Together), and Youth Voter PAC (which solely supported candidates who took youth seriously or were young themselves).[20]

The youth investment was a savvy move, though not one that most political donors had come around to yet. Lewis and Yandura were driven by two things: research suggesting that any young person who voted for a particular party in three consecutive cycles would likely identify with that party for life; and the fact that, at 80 million strong, Millennials would eventually rival the Baby Boomers in numbers. Yet when Yandura and Lewis started the venture in early 2004, political operatives were generally in the habit of ignoring the youth vote. For two presidential election cycles in 1996 and 2000, for instance, the turnout rate for voters aged 18 to 24 was close to 36 percent (by contrast, the 65 and older crowd turned out at nearly 70 percent both years). Given young people's political antipathy, most wondered why they should waste their time and resources on them. Of course, that notion was upended in the decade to come. In 2004, youth participation spiked to 47 percent, and by 2008 it topped out at nearly 49 percent. Though it slid back to 41 percent in 2012, the youth vote came to be seen as a critical part of the progressive voting coalition that Democrats needed to win elections, and Millennials were, as of 2013, widely viewed as the voting juggernaut of the future.[21]

Though there's no way of knowing how much Lewis's giving contributed to a turnaround in the trend, the investment was indicative of his style. First, his instincts were good, even if his overall impact was hard to substantiate. Second, he relished in committing resources to something that went against the prevailing wisdom of the day.

Heading into the 2008 elections, Lewis and Yandura were careful about throwing their support behind any one Democratic candidate too quickly. Lewis leaned toward Hillary but maxed out at $2,300 to both candidates during the primary. Obama seemed like a solid fallback position to him. He had met Obama only once. In Aspen in the summer of 2006, a friend called Lewis and asked whether he could make time to meet with a young senator from Illinois who was considering a presidential run. Lewis invited several of his family members over and they sat around chatting for an hour or two with Senator Obama on a gorgeous

Colorado summer day. Obama, who was still a relative outsider at the time, came across as sharp and impressive. But it wasn't a particularly revelatory meeting. It was the first time Lewis had inserted himself into the political process at that level and that early in an election, but he wasn't sold just yet.[22]

As Obama's candidacy gained momentum, however, Lewis started to look back on the afternoon with greater fondness. In his view, he'd had the opportunity to meet Obama at a more grassroots level—before he was a household name. And like so many other progressives, Lewis felt the wave of optimism that swept the nation with Obama's election, a yearning for a change from business as usual in Washington.

So by the time Lewis reached the Democracy Alliance meeting at the Biltmore Hotel in March of 2009—with a newly elected progressive president safely in office and full Democratic control of Congress—he was ready for something big. He was confident, too, that the Democracy Alliance could have a hand in aiding the new administration's success. This was exactly the type of gathering, he figured, at which a newly elected president might make an appearance.

Yandura was more muted in his enthusiasm about the change Obama's election would bring. *Proof's in the pudding*, he thought, and there wasn't any pudding yet. He was also much less optimistic about Obama's attendance at the meeting. Having seen this dog and pony show before, he tried to tamp down Lewis's expectations.[23]

"I don't think Obama's gonna show," Yandura told him.

But Lewis remained undeterred. "I wouldn't be so sure about that."

Yandura scanned the premises as they walked through the lavish lobby—barrel-vaulted ceilings, Corinthian-style columns, marble floors. Nice. But none of the telltale signs that a president was coming. No stanchions for the ropes that hold people back as a president enters and exits. No Secret Service in sight. And attendees hadn't been required to send their names, social security numbers, and birthdates in advance for background checks.

But when they entered the meeting room, a shade of doubt arose in Yandura's mind. The room was set up theatre-style with a couple hundred chairs facing the front and a row down the middle. But the windows had been thoroughly covered over with blackout curtains, blocking out the sunlight and gorgeous views of a sprawling, palm-tree-studded pool, while casting an eerie hue over the entire room. Yandura recognized the curtains as one of the number one rules of a presidential advance team—never allow a direct line of vision to the commander in chief from outside the room. *Maybe I was wrong*, he thought.[24]

But when it came time for the big moment, the new White House deputy chief of staff, Jim Messina, entered the room unceremoniously through a side door and took the stage. Lewis felt the elation and excitement drain from his body instantly. *This is who they sent?* he thought. Lewis found Messina to be distinctly unimpressive and even condescending. He started talking in distant "We's"—*We're going to need some time* and *We can't get to everything right away* and *We have an awful lot of constituencies to deal with*. In some ways, it felt as if the donors were being scolded. It was only two months into the administration and Obama's top lieutenants were already laying the groundwork for disappointment. Instead of feeling connected to the administration, Lewis felt alienated. If Obama had inspired a sense of hope that drew millions from these donors, Messina had effectively deflated that enthusiasm in the course of a few minutes, at least for Lewis. Messina wasn't sent to have an exchange with these high-powered progressive donors or enlist their help, he was sent to set expectations low—very low. For Lewis, the message was essentially, "Hey, thanks for the election, we'll get back to ya."[25]

At that moment, Lewis completely recalibrated his expectations of what the Democracy Alliance was capable of achieving and whether it could cooperate with the Obama administration. He knew the progressive movement was in trouble. He knew the LGBT movement was in trouble. He exchanged knowing glances with some other like-minded donors seated nearby. Then he leaned over to Yandura and said, "We've got to do something." What that something was, neither had any idea.

PERHAPS LEWIS HAD held out hope for the new president because he believed that the Democracy Alliance could actually play a strategic role in the administration—helping to fund polling or studies related to certain policy prescriptions. But the fact was, he was just now experiencing the completely dispiriting sensation that a number of other LGBT activists had felt ever since Obama picked Rick Warren to bless his leadership of the nation.

Nonetheless, LGBT advocates in Washington persisted with relatively high hopes for the first one hundred days. In some ways, it was just a relief to have a Democrat back at the helm again. At least the White House doors were finally open again to progressive groups.

The Gay & Lesbian Victory Fund, a Washington-based group that mainly focuses on getting more LGBT Americans into elected office, had amassed and vetted some 1,400 resumes of qualified LGBT candidates for various administrative posts. The binder of applicants, which was handed over to the Obama transition team, was supposed to put the LGBT community's best and brightest right at the fingertips of the incoming administration's decision makers. The effort was hailed as a model for other constituencies and the hope was that President Obama would finally appoint history's first openly gay cabinet member. But it didn't take long for the administration to dash that dream. By mid-December 2008, it was clear that our last, best hope for a cabinet-level appointee, John Berry, had been passed over in favor of Senator Ken Salazar for secretary of the interior. Berry ultimately became the highest-ranking LGBT official administration-wide when Obama chose him to lead the Office of Personnel Management, which serves as the human resources department for the federal government's approximately two million civilian employees. It was a big job and a very important one to gay rights since the federal government still had a long way to go to ensure workplace equity for its LGBT employees. But it didn't hold the same prestige or visibility that a cabinet post would have.[26]

The highest-ranking gay official at the White House became Brian Bond, a veteran of LGBT advocacy circles in Washington. Bond had once served as executive director of the Gay & Lesbian Victory Fund. The Obama campaign had plucked him from his post heading up the DNC's Gay and Lesbian Leadership Council (GLLC), where he replaced Donald Hitchcock, Yandura's partner. In that sense, Bond was a trusted Democratic company man—more prone to steadying the boat than rocking it. After serving as the Obama campaign's national constituency director, a role in which he fostered communication between the campaign and key Democratic constituency groups, Bond was chosen to serve as deputy director of the White House Office of Public Engagement, which meant he became the de facto White House liaison to the LGBT community.[27]

Although Bond had been given a position at the White House, he was still kept at arm's length from the commander in chief, at least initially. He was never designated an "assistant" to the president, a title that helps separate the wheat from the chaff in the building. Generally speaking, the highest-ranking White House officials carry the titles of assistant to the president, deputy assistant, and special assistant (in order of descending rank). But anyone who has an "assistant" title generally has a higher level of access at the White House and is more likely to be part of the president's "inner circle." In the Clinton White House, Marsha Scott, who was straight but was also officially named the first White House liaison for gay and lesbian issues in 1995, was part of that circle; she served as a deputy assistant to the president. Richard Socarides, who succeeded Scott, was a special assistant. Bond may not have had that kind of access to Obama, but perhaps more importantly, no LGBT official did. President Obama, unlike his Democratic predecessor, didn't have anyone who officially represented the LGBT constituency serving as a core part of his inner circle of White House advisers—at least insofar as titles were concerned.

The way LGBT advocates responded to these kinds of slights during the first hundred days of Obama's presidency became a point of departure between those who were counseling patience and those who were stoking urgency. While not everyone in Washington was of like mind, certainly people inside the Beltway were more likely to be giving Obama the benefit of the doubt than grassroots activists were. The administration had not produced any major breakthroughs; John Berry's appointment to head the Office of Personnel Management (OPM) came the closest. OPM, formerly known as the US Civil Service Commission, was once responsible for scrubbing gays from the federal government. Now the agency would claim a gay man as its leader. But that didn't mean much in practical terms to activists outside of Washington, even if insiders were cheering it. In fact, it seemed that what Washington LGBT groups were hailing as promising advancements were little more than baby steps built upon President Clinton's efforts nearly two decades earlier.[28]

To be sure, Obama was already well on pace to surpass Clinton in the number of openly LGBT people he appointed to serve in his administration. Clinton had appointed 150 openly gay people, including the first out lesbian and gay man ever confirmed by the Senate—Roberta Achtenberg and Bruce Lehman, respectively. Obama, meanwhile, appointed at least 37 openly gay and transgender officials in his first one hundred days alone. But many of Obama's appointments came from the Clinton administration, which had truly made groundbreaking advancements on gay inclusion in federal government. John Berry's career in government, for instance, was boosted significantly when President Clinton appointed him as assistant secretary for policy, management, and budget at the Department of the Interior in 1997.[29]

Meanwhile, on the big-ticket items, the administration wasn't showing much promise. Initially, activists were focused on four key pieces of pro-LGBT legislation. First on the agenda was a hate crimes bill, which was first proposed in 1997 by President Bill Clinton and introduced by Senator Edward "Ted" Kennedy. It was subsequently renamed the Matthew Shepard and James Byrd Jr. Hate Crimes Prevention Act after a gay Wyoming college student who was brutally beaten and killed because of his sexuality and a Texas man who was dragged to his death behind a car because he was black. Among other things, the legislation sought to expand the federal hate crimes law enacted in 1968 to include sexual orientation, gender, gender identity, and disability. Second was the Employment Nondiscrimination Act (aka ENDA), which would have made it illegal to discriminate against gay and transgender workers simply because of their sexual orientation or gender identity. Though 90 percent of Americans already believed that type of discrimination ran afoul of federal law, it was actually perfectly legal in most states to tell someone they were being fired because they were lesbian, gay, or transgender. The third piece of legislation was repeal of the military's "don't ask, don't tell" policy. And the fourth: repealing the Defense of Marriage Act, a bill that became known as the Respect for Marriage Act. These were the major milestones LGBT activists were pulling for, whether they were achieved legislatively or, alternatively, through the courts. From a legislative standpoint, LGBT advocates and many congressional lawmakers had an informal agreement that they would go in that order—hate crimes, ENDA, DADT repeal, and DOMA repeal— conceivably from easiest to hardest.[30]

Short of passing legislation, advocates were also looking for the president to take executive action that could help equalize treatment for

LGBT Americans, particularly in the workplace. One initiative included adding nondiscrimination protections for federally employed transgender workers. Another action would require that contractors employed by the federal government had policies to protect LGBT workers from bias.

By 2009, workplace protections already existed within the federal government for lesbian and gay employees. But it had been a long, slow process. In 1953, President Dwight D. Eisenhower had signed Executive Order 10450, which included "sexual perversion" among a list of attributes that were deemed a security risk and therefore grounds for dismissal in the federal government. Within the first year of the order's existence, at least 618 civil servants either resigned or were terminated due to the sex perversion clause. The policy also had the unintended effect of giving rise to one of the gay rights movement's pioneering activists when it triggered the dismissal of Frank Kameny, a Harvard PhD, from the US Army Map Service in 1957 for being a "sexual pervert." Kameny sued the federal government, appealing his case all the way to the Supreme Court, which ultimately declined to hear it in 1961. That same year, Kameny cofounded the Mattachine Society of Washington, an early gay advocacy group with several chapters in other metropolitan areas. But Kameny and his cohort adopted far more aggressive tactics than their peers. Inspired by the direct-action tactics of the civil rights movement, they organized the first gay protests of the White House and other government agencies in 1965.[31]

The signs that Kameny and his colleagues carried, reading "First Class Citizenship for Homosexuals" and "Fair Employment Applies to Homosexuals too," were as relevant when Barack Obama entered office as they had been in the '60s. To be sure, the federal government had gone some way toward addressing Kameny's demands, but it continued to deny gay "security clearances." In 1975, the US Civil Service Commission announced that homosexuality would no longer be a basis for excluding gays from government employment. In 1998, President Bill Clinton finally signed an executive order expressly prohibiting discrimination on the basis of sexual orientation within the federal government. Advocates hoped that President Obama would sign a similar executive order to expand that definition to include transgender employees. The next goal was to bring fair employment practices, which was within reach for government employees, to the rest of the country.[32]

But one hundred days into the administration, there were no signs of life for either major executive action or LGBT legislation. "Don't ask, don't tell" had received the most attention in the White House briefing room, in part because the mainstream press corps remembered it as one of Obama's most prominent campaign promises. Now, White House press secretary Robert Gibbs seemed to be backing away from it. On a number of occasions in the first several months, Gibbs had begun to push forward a precept that would become the White House mantra on the gay ban for the bulk of two years—repeal must be achieved through a "durable, legislative solution." A California-based think tank called The Palm Center, which was dedicated to the study of sexual minorities in the military, produced a report showing that President Obama could temporarily halt discharges of lesbian and gay soldiers through an executive order even as the legislative process ran its course. But the White House was officially rejecting that notion out of hand, placing the full burden of ending discharges on Congress rather than on the executive. Congress tends to move at a glacial pace, so there was little chance that repeal would happen quickly, considerably delaying the time frame in which the White House would have to deal with the other LGBT issues on the agenda.[33]

Worse yet, Gibbs wasn't the only one signaling a stall on repeal. Even more blunt pronouncements were coming from the president's pick for secretary of defense, Robert Gates. A holdover from the Bush administration, Gates held a considerable amount of cachet in Washington as he attempted to perform cleanup on the bungled wars in Afghanistan and Iraq. If he was showing resistance to repeal, it was unlikely that Congress would take up the matter on their own.

Gates was asked about the repeal timetable on Fox News on March 29, 2009. "That dialogue," he said, "has really not progressed very far at this point in this administration. I think the president and I feel like we've got a lot on our plates right now and let's push that one down the road a little bit."[34]

While Gates's answer would not please LGBT advocates, at least it was straightforward. He had said everything Gibbs couldn't say. Gates wasn't constrained by the same politics as the White House and, if anything, he had a distinct interest in lowering expectations on how quickly repeal would progress. He was a perfect civilian steward for the military:

a process man who liked things to be done according to code. Gates was not interested in adhering to timelines that merely advanced a political end—regardless of whether it was driven by a Republican or a Democrat. If "don't ask, don't tell" was going to end on his watch—as President Obama had pledged—Gates was going to shepherd the change through slowly and in orderly fashion. In his first major discussion with the president about repeal on April 13, Gates warned against executive action. He told Obama he would "appoint a task force to study the impact of changing the policy and how best to implement such a change."[35]

The smoke signals coming from multiple corners of the administration were causing consternation for the organizations that were specifically dedicated to achieving repeal: Servicemembers Legal Defense Network (SLDN) and Servicemembers United in Washington, and The Palm Center on the West Coast. They expected a repeal in Obama's first term, and it was beginning to dawn on them that it might not happen, especially if it wasn't achieved in the first two years. At that point, none of the organizations really had a playbook for what to do if the administration wasn't proceeding apace on certain issues in their eyes. So the repeal advocacy groups essentially started writing that playbook on the fly—each in their own way. On April 28, 2009, Aubrey Sarvis, executive director of SLDN, took out a full-page ad in the Capitol Hill publication *Roll Call* titled "President Obama: Keep Your Word," urging the president to include repeal in the Department of Defense budget he would soon be submitting to Congress. Sarvis followed up a month later with a blog entry he penned on Huffington Post, which began: "President Obama is a brave man. He doesn't hesitate to take great political risks." Sarvis praised the president's leadership and noted that Obama's approval rating in the most recent *ABC News/Washington Post* poll was at 69 percent. "Not since Ronald Reagan's first 100 days has a president done so well." Given his considerable political capital, Sarvis argued, "Now is the time to lead."[36]

SLDN's message, while one of accountability, was still fairly complimentary of Obama. But it wasn't nearly as glowing as what the multi-issue LGBT groups like HRC and the National Gay and Lesbian Task Force were pushing out. In a piece I wrote for *The Advocate* on the one-hundred-day mark, April 29, HRC president Joe Solmonese toed the party line, reminding people that the White House had a lot of other priorities to contend with. It was a very similar message to the one White House aide Jim Messina had peddled at the Democracy Alliance gathering.

Knowing full well that not everyone in the LGBT community was pleased with the progress, I pressed Solmonese about the relative lack of major accomplishments. "I've been impressed," he responded. "Given all that this president and this administration has encountered coming in—the most daunting economic crisis in a generation, the war in Iraq and heightening situation in Afghanistan and the Middle East, and, quite frankly, all they have had to undo from the Bush administration—I'm optimistic and inspired by the first 100 days."[37]

Rea Carey, executive director of the National Gay and Lesbian Task Force, pushed a similar message, focusing on how inclusive the administration had been since Obama took office. "I've been doing Washington advocacy work since 1989, and this particular administration feels not only more inviting or receptive of the community but, quite frankly, more proactive," Carey observed.[38]

The big groups, perhaps predictably, were proving to be more focused on what might be called *access advocacy*, where access is primary and advocacy is secondary. Of chief importance to access advocacy is having a seat at the table. If you aren't at the table, the thinking goes, you have no clout—either within the administration or inside Washington. There's certainly a case to be made that having access is important—it gives one the chance to educate administration officials on certain issues and express concerns behind closed doors, preferably before policy decisions are made. But access is a double-edged sword. Administration officials can also use the threat of cutting you out to coerce you into giving up or compromising your priorities.

And herein lies the conundrum: if you prize access for access's sake—if you air your grievances privately but refrain from being publicly critical no matter what—what is that access actually worth? Keeping quiet may boost your public image and your fundraising operation because people perceive you as powerful based on your relationship with the White House. But if you are never willing to sound the alarm bells when things are going south, those ancillary benefits come at the expense of the core issues for which you are advocating. And even more importantly, they come at the expense of the constituency you serve.

Sarvis, unlike Carey and Solmonese, was trying to be constructively critical while also lauding the president. Like the other LGBT leaders, Sarvis had been included in early White House meetings related to LGBT issues. But at the end of one hundred days, he took his concerns public, compromising the number one rule of access advocacy: loyalty. Each issue and each administration has a different threshold for how much betrayal will be tolerated. Where the line is, you usually don't know until you've crossed it. Sarvis was testing that line and, eventually, that would have consequences.

One person who knew a lot about the dance the groups were engaged in with the White House was a man who had been on the other side of that two-step in the '90s: Richard Socarides. Socarides felt like he was watching a replay of the Clinton administration's second-term handling of LGBT issues. Clinton White House officials were so gun-shy after "don't ask, don't tell" blew up in their faces that it became nearly impossible to make progress on gay-related policies in the second term. Socarides remembered trying to line up President Clinton for a speech at the Human Rights Campaign in 1997. Clinton ultimately agreed, but Socarides recalled it being almost as hard as trying to get the president to make his first visit to China. Now he feared the Obama administration had learned the first-term lesson of the Clinton administration too well—steer clear of gay issues at all costs.[39]

Socarides was right to be concerned. Sixteen years later, Obama's White House was full of Clinton retreads, many of whom still harbored some form of PTSD (post-traumatic stress disorder) on the issue. Chief among them was Rahm Emanuel, Obama's first chief of staff and the driving force behind execution of the White House agenda and congressional strategy during the administration's first couple years. In 1993, Emanuel had a front row seat to Bill Clinton's stumbles on allowing gays to serve in the military and reforming health care. Many political observers believed Clinton's early missteps on the gay ban crippled his ability to tackle bigger issues such as health care reform. In fact, Emanuel initially counseled President Obama against pushing health reform in the early months of the administration. But Obama was resolute, and Emanuel took his boss's decision to heart. This time around, it seemed, Emanuel was determined to sidestep one impediment on the way to finally making good on the other. Obama was staking his presidency on health care reform. Emanuel was likely loathe to watch a second president sacrifice an achievement that had eluded presidents past for nearly a century over an issue that would surely hurt the Democrats in the midterms. At best, overturning the policy would amount to a Pyrrhic victory, even if a morally sound one.[40]

"Don't ask, don't tell" was not only a gay issue, it was also distinctly progressive. Rahm was a chief purveyor of the notion that Democrats couldn't win at the polls on progressive issues, certainly not the social ones. Gay rights, immigration, gun control, a woman's right to choose were all losers. As leader of the Democratic Congressional Campaign Committee in 2006, Emanuel actively recruited moderate-to-conservative Democrats to run in more traditionally red districts and hopefully capitalize on the unpopularity of President George W. Bush. It worked; House Democrats won thirty new seats that year, giving them majority control of the House for the first time in twelve years. But it set conservative Democrats—known as the "Blue Dog" coalition—on course to have a major impact on the Democratic caucus in the next several years to come. By the 111th Congress (2009–2010), House Blue Dogs reached the pinnacle of their influence, controlling 52 seats of the Democrats' 256 seats overall. In order to reach the 218 votes necessary to pass legislation, Democrats would need at least a dozen Blue Dog votes on any bill that couldn't attract Republicans. So if Obama hoped to gain their support for health care reform, he would need to go easy on them when it came to anything that might be viewed as a "hard vote"—and that included progressive legislation like "don't ask, don't tell."[41]

Socarides believed that the political moment was ripe to advance repeal. Polling supported it, Obama still had the political capital to spare, and he had promised to do it repeatedly during his campaign. But after seeing no positive signs in that direction in the first one hundred days, it dawned on Socarides: *Oh my God*, he thought, *they're not going to touch gay issues for months if not years. It was just too painful last time around.* Socarides felt compelled to draw attention to the path he was afraid the administration was heading down.[42]

He set out to write an op-ed that he doubted anyone would take—getting op-eds published in major newspapers is actually quite a feat given all the competition for the space. You have to be a verifiable expert, your subject has to be top of mind, and your point must be perfectly crisp. As he suspected, the *New York Times* rejected it, so Socarides moved on to the *Washington Post*. They responded right away—they wanted it. The *Post* ran the piece in the May 2, 2009, print edition under the headline, "Where's our 'Fierce Advocate'?" A copy editor at the *Post* had come up with the title, and Socarides thought it was perfect.

"In December, while trying to quiet the furor over his invitation of Rick Warren to take part in his inauguration, Barack Obama reminded us that he had been a 'consistent' and 'fierce advocate of equality for gay and lesbian Americans,'" Socarides wrote. "But at the end of its first 100 days, his administration has been neither."[43]

Socarides argued that delaying on gay issues was "bad strategy." "President Obama will never have more political capital than he has now, and there will never be a better political environment to capitalize on. People are distracted by the economy and war, and they are unlikely to get stirred up by the right-wing rhetoric that has doomed efforts in the past," he wrote.

It was an impassioned piece, but Socarides didn't get much positive feedback from Washington advocates. They dismissed his assessment as grousing from a Clintonite who, in their eyes, hadn't produced many positive gains when he was at the White House anyway. Nonetheless, the piece unleashed an outpouring of conversation on LGBT listservs and blogs. It had struck a chord. And perhaps more importantly, the placement in the *Post* alerted the hungry Beltway media that Obama might have a problem in his progressive ranks. Gays were getting restless.

It didn't take long for a response to come from the administration. The following week, the White House invited a few LGBT groups to a strategy session led by deputy chief of staff Jim Messina, who reported directly to Emanuel and had been given the LGBT portfolio of issues. Group leaders emerged from the meeting issuing public assurances that the administration was on the move. Of course, they could offer no details.

"They have a vision. They have a plan." HRC's Joe Solmonese told Sheryl Gay Stolberg of the *New York Times* on May 6, 2009. But that was all.[44]

It was easy for the advocates to claim—as Solmonese did to me in a follow-up interview—that not only were they not at liberty to share the plan but doing so could jeopardize the administration's course of action.

Longtime LGBT activist David Mixner, who had not attended the meeting, appeared in the same article in the *Times* offering a counterbalance to the enthusiastic Washington establishment. "How much longer do we give [Obama] the benefit of the doubt?" he asked.[45]

Mixner was an irreplaceable voice in the gay rights movement. He had a long and unimpeachable record of activism, having cut his teeth in politics as a civil rights activist and eventual antiwar activist who helped organize two major national protests against Vietnam in the late '60s. While Socarides was still considered a Clinton guy, Mixner had originally backed John Edwards for the Democratic nomination because of his advocacy for ending the Iraq War. When Edwards dropped out in January 2008, a group of his LGBT supporters debated whether to throw their support behind Clinton or Obama. Mixner favored Obama for two reasons. One was his opposition to US involvement in Iraq, which Obama had laid out in a speech as early as 2002 when he was still a state senator. But another was Mixner's sense that more than anybody, someone whose ascendancy had been made possible by the civil rights movement of the '60s would understand the civil rights movement of the next generation. Some in the group shied away from referring to LGBT equality as a civil rights issue—African Americans were sometimes resistant to the comparison and generally found the idea of comparing the two movements offensive. But Mixner was convinced that until we really defined ourselves as a civil rights movement—beyond partisan identity, beyond political identity, and certainly not as a political interest group—we would not be successful. So he and another big Edwards supporter, Eric Stern, convinced a cadre of a couple dozen prominent LGBT advocates to put their weight behind Obama en masse.[46]

But by April 2009, Mixner was faced with the prospect that his candidate-turned-president wasn't honoring his promises to the gay community. Mixner may have wept on Obama's inauguration day, but his commitment wasn't to the man, it was to an ideal. It was all-too-familiar territory for the sixty-two-year-old New Jersey native. Mixner had helped Bill Clinton, an old friend from their antiwar days, in his 1992 presidential bid by raising over $3 million from gay donors. He then worked on Clinton's transition team after his triumph.[47]

But when Clinton stumbled on the gay ban controversy early in his presidency, Mixner's close relationship with the White House soured. A couple of weeks after Clinton's July 1993 announcement of the "don't ask, don't tell" compromise—which would purportedly remove the all-out ban on gay military service but fell far short of Clinton's pledge to allow gays to serve openly—Mixner and about thirty other high-profile gay rights activists were arrested protesting in front of the White House. Mixner's loud and public criticism of Clinton's betrayal of the community drew ire from the White House. Political director Rahm Emanuel told the *Wall Street Journal* that Mixner had "unjustly criticized" the president and was now "persona non grata" at the White House. Mixner, who made his living as a Democratic political consultant at the time, had four major clients and he lost all of them within twenty-four hours. He couldn't work for nearly four years. But he had gone into the protest with his eyes open and understood the risks. Few people know what it's like to be faced with the prospect of losing your livelihood in order to stand on principle. Mixner did, and for that he was considered a hero in the LGBT activist world.[48]

This time around, he had a lot less to lose. He wasn't an insider (though he still had some friends who were), he lived in New York, and he wasn't about to be screwed over again by letting another Democratic president use gay rights as a stepping-stone to the presidency and then renege on his promises. On May 20, 2009, in the wake of Messina's mysterious strategy session with LGBT group leaders, Mixner took to his blog. "As this Administration sits in offices plotting timeline charts on what rights they feel comfortable granting us this year, clearly it is time for us to gin up our efforts and stop waiting for them to hand us our God given entitlements. Enough. I really can't stomach any more being told 'not now'. As nice as it would be, no one is going to give us our freedom; we are going to have to continue to fight like hell for it," he wrote.[49]

It was a call to arms, and Mixner was one of the few gay leaders not associated with a major organization who had the gravitas and reach to do it. He called on the leaders of LGBT groups to organize a march on Washington in the fall. But well aware of how unlikely that prospect was given their cozy relationship with the White House, he added, "and if they don't, I appeal to our young to come together and provide the leadership."[50]

The answer to Mixner's call was already in the making out in California. For Robin McGehee, the loss on Proposition 8 had taken a deeply personal turn when the principal of her son's Catholic elementary school, St. Helen's School, called her four days after the election and asked her to step down as president of the Parent Teacher Association due to her involvement with the No On 8 campaign. Her son Sebastian had thrived at the school, but once administrators barred her from volunteering there, she decided to enroll him elsewhere.[51]

This battle was no longer about Prop 8, it was about silencing those who disagreed with the measure. She decided she would not be silenced anymore. She would fight until they won. She hatched the idea of "Meet in the Middle 4 Equality," a marriage equality rally that finally came to fruition in Fresno on May 30, 2009, ten days after Mixner's plea.

Marchers gathered in Selma, California, early that Saturday morning to march a 14.5-mile stretch to the steps of Fresno City Hall. The idea was that in order to potentially flip the outcome of a future ballot initiative, gay marriage supporters would have to make inroads with conservative people in the middle of the state rather than simply focusing on the more urban coastlines. As a critical mass of marchers started to form slightly before 8:00 a.m., McGehee took to a bullhorn that slain gay rights hero Harvey Milk had used in the '70s. Milk, the subject of a 2008 Academy Award–winning film of the same name, gained nationwide attention after running a high-profile campaign to become the first openly gay elected official in California. He won a seat on the San Francisco Board of Supervisors in 1977 but was assassinated just a year later. A disgruntled colleague who had resigned his supervisor post shot both Milk and San Francisco Mayor George Moscone at City Hall on November 27, 1978.[52]

Milk was famous for many things, including a phrase he uttered often, "You gotta give 'em hope!" But that morning, McGehee drew on Milk's constant insistence that people come out of the closet and let their fellow Americans get to know them.

"You have got to reach into those communities that struggle to understand us," she told hundreds of people prepping for the march, reported the *San Francisco Chronicle*.[53]

By the time they reached Fresno, several thousand people had joined the cause, carrying signs that read "'I DO' Support the Freedom to Marry" and "Separate is NOT Equal."

The speakers ranged from celebrities like Oscar-winner Charlize Theron to seasoned activists like Cleve Jones, who had been a friend of Harvey Milk, to Lieutenant Dan Choi, a new activist who had recently come out publicly on *The Rachel Maddow Show* and would soon take up the banner of repealing "don't ask, don't tell" in the months to come.

When it came time for McGehee to speak, she addressed the crowd as a mother first.

"I am just a mom who really loves her kids," she said, tears filling her eyes. "And I am tired of having to drive all across this state to convince other people that it should be OK for me to ride my bike with my kids, to play in the park with my kids, and do everything else another parent wants to do."[54]

But as the speech progressed, McGehee began to leverage the political moment. Acknowledging all the reporters present, McGehee directed her comments at the man she had believed in since 2004, the man she had canvassed for, and the man whose triumph she had celebrated even as her heart broke on election night.

"If you can get a message to Barack Obama and Michelle Obama, I have something I'd like to say," she told the crowd, her emotions rising again. "Although I heard him say on election night that our community was part of his plan, my answer to that is: show me you have the courage, show me you have the courage to produce change."

"I believed in you," she charged, flanked by her partner and two children, "and now I'm asking you to prove it."

A BRIEF INTERVENTION · 3

WHILE THE OBAMA ADMINISTRATION WAS STALLING ON LGBT legislation, another gay issue was brewing that they would be forced to face. Throughout the country, states and courts were beginning to legally recognize same-sex couples, regardless of what the president had to say on the matter. When the Iowa Supreme Court issued a decision legalizing gay marriage on April 3, 2009, Iowa became the third (and only Midwestern) state in the nation to extend marriage rights to same-sex couples.[1]

It was also the first such advancement since Obama had taken office. So it provided the perfect opportunity for me to leverage my new role as the Washington correspondent for *The Advocate* and prod the administration on an achievement they might otherwise have wanted to ignore. It was a Friday, and I requested a statement from the White House press office at about 2:00 p.m. The ruling had been posted at around 9:00 a.m., and the court's website had immediately begun crashing from the crush of traffic. Activists were ecstatic and had been hailing the win all day even as right-wing organizations issued a stream of dire predictions about where the country was heading. Then, at a little after 8:00 p.m., the White House response came—a perhaps unsurprisingly lackluster regurgitation of campaign talking points.[2]

The President respects the decision of the Iowa Supreme Court, and continues to believe that states should make their own decisions when it comes to the issue of marriage. Although President Obama supports civil unions rather than same-sex marriage, he believes that committed gay and lesbian couples should receive equal rights under the law.[3]

As soon as I posted the statement, activists became outraged, Friday night be damned. We were still licking our wounds from California and picking up a state in the heartland was a huge victory. Yet all Obama could do to mark the moment was state that he "respects the decision" and reiterate his preference for civil unions. The first statement the White House sent me even had a typo in it—they left out the words "equal rights" and simply said that gay couples "should receive *protection* under the law." I had posted it without commentary, but the bloggers immediately skewered the weak language.

"So, let's see," wrote Pam Spaulding, "it should be left to the states so that as gay couples travel across state lines, they are married, not married, civil unioned, domestic partnered . . . yeah that sounds like equal protection under the law. *Oh wait—the press release didn't use the word EQUAL, did it?*"[4]

I got back in touch with my press contact, Shin Inouye, and asked whether they meant "equal protection." For legal reasons, they likely did not want to use the phrase "equal protection"—it would imply that Fourteenth Amendment constitutional protections should be applied to same-sex couples. Inouye sent me a corrected version using Obama's preferred phrasing, "equal rights," a little after 9:00 p.m.[5]

That historic Friday ruling was succeeded by another milestone the following Tuesday: Vermont lawmakers overrode a veto from Governor Jim Douglas to become the first state in the union to extend marriage rights through legislation rather than a judicial ruling. The White House declined to issue another statement even though I, and likely others, requested one. Fair enough. The president's position hadn't changed, and they weren't prepared to put out something more celebratory. So why invite a second black eye from disgruntled activists? Plus, this dance was all new. It was a new White House. I was on a new beat and approaching it quite aggressively. Marriage equality was still a relatively new phenomenon. In retrospect, I think they were trying to figure out where the boundaries were for what did and didn't require a response. And maybe more importantly, what the right formula was for keeping the LGBT constituency pacified. Clearly, putting out a statement had not done that.[6]

At that early juncture, the administration had been taking clear and decisive steps on a good number of mainstream issues: they had enacted a $787 billion stimulus bill, the largest in history; they had committed seventeen thousand more troops to Afghanistan; and they had canned the CEO of General Motors and orchestrated a government takeover of the ailing company. None of these things was without controversy, but they were bold, forceful decisions, whether one agreed with the policy or not. Yet on gay relationships, the White House was suffering from a complete lack of inspiration.[7]

That evening, I penned a piece with the headline, "The White House Office of Missed Opportunity." I was trying to channel the anger that had surfaced after I posted the Iowa response. It was so tone-deaf. Some people e-mailed me personally to express their displeasure, while a number of others registered their dissatisfaction on an LGBT listserv to which I was subscribed. Many people still weren't ready to go public with their anger—they so badly wanted Obama to be the president they had hoped for. But the Iowa response and subsequent silence on Vermont had thrown them.

"Sometimes, the culture pushes forward even when politicians aren't ready for it," I wrote on April 7, 2009. "Last week, the middle of the country gave mainstream cred to supporting marriage equality. This week, Vermont made equal protection a legislative ideal as much as a judicial one. If President Obama and his top generals are too busy to take on LGBT issues, then the time is right for someone with the vision and rank to find a contemporary groove on our issues. . . . And if that person existed already, the statement issued last Friday would not have struck such a discordant note with the vibe of the day."[8]

One month later, Maine followed Vermont's lead, passing legislation legalizing same-sex marriage that Governor John Baldacci signed into law only minutes later on May 6, 2009.[9]

The number of gay marriage states, now totaling five, had more than doubled since Obama took office, and with every new development, the media was becoming more attuned to the issue. In the past, LGBT rights had often been viewed as a fringe social issue by mainstream reporters. It was more a question of politics suited to the campaign trail then it was a matter of governance, at least at the federal level. But now, as the marriage equality states ticked up, the media began to smell trouble for the president. The culture was beginning to surpass Obama—the guy who had positioned himself as ahead of the times on gay rights. Although I had been the one to ask the White House for a comment on Iowa, it was a mainstream reporter, Jake Tapper, then with ABC, who asked press secretary Robert Gibbs whether the president had a reaction to the development in Maine.[10]

Gibbs tried to put the issue to bed immediately. "No, I think the President's position on same-sex marriages has been talked about and discussed." No news here, he was saying. Move along.

Tapper wasn't persuaded. "He opposes same-sex marriage," he stated.

"He supports civil unions," Gibbs corrected, offering the other side of the same coin.

But the following week, Tapper still wasn't satisfied.

"The President opposes same-sex marriage, but he supports giving same-sex couples the same rights as married people," he said on May 12, 2009. "What's your response to critics of his policy who say this is exactly separate but equal?"[11]

Gibbs noted the president had been asked the question on "multiple occasions" during the campaign. "I can pull you something on that," he said, reiterating the president's strong support for civil unions.

Gibbs was right. The separate-but-equal question had been asked. I had witnessed one instance at an LGBT debate in Los Angeles sponsored by HRC and Logo TV in 2007. But Tapper's delivery was far more blunt and the press corps in the briefing room a much less friendly audience than the room full of Democrats in Los Angeles had been.[12]

After attending White House press briefings for the better part of two months, I was gathering up the nerve to level my first question at Gibbs. Obama had campaigned on repealing the Defense of Marriage Act, which expressly prevented the federal government from recognizing the new wave of gay marriages soon to be performed in Iowa, Vermont, and Maine (along with those already happening in Connecticut and Massachusetts). The predicament provided an ideal opening for a question about the administration's progress on overturning DOMA. It was newsworthy and an issue that presumably the White House had an interest in addressing based on recent developments; it mattered greatly to my readership; and it was something no other reporter had thought to ask. While "don't ask, don't tell" had already received a good bit of attention and most mainstream reporters had a handle on that issue, many didn't fully grasp DOMA or its implications yet. In fact, I wondered if even half the reporters in the White House briefings could recite the meaning of the acronym.

My chance came on May 18, 2009, a day when the briefing room held only a smattering of reporters. Usually, Gibbs consistently called on every reporter in the first two rows first. Those seats were assigned to the big outlets: wire services like the Associated Press, print publications like the *New York Times* and *Washington Post*, and broadcast outfits from the three major networks to cable news sources like CNN, Fox, and MSNBC. That left only a few precious minutes for him to answer questions from the rest of us. There was never enough time, and Gibbs could pick and choose based on whom he did or didn't want to take a question from. But at the time, I was still an unknown quantity to him. I was one of the squatters who took whatever seat might be available if there was one at all. As Gibbs worked his way down my row that day and it dawned on me that the moment had finally come, my heart started thumping. *Good Lord, what am I doing here? Do I really have the chops for this?* When he called on me, I nearly fumbled the question.

"The president supported the Defense of Marriage Act—the repeal of that—during the election," I said, correcting myself. "Now that same-sex couples can marry legally in five different states, what is the President doing to make sure those marriages can be recognized at the federal level, and what's the timeline for something like that?"[13]

My fledgling jitters were met with equal dismay from Gibbs, who had not yet perfected answers for LGBT-related issues outside of same-sex marriage and "don't ask, don't tell." While Obama's position on marriage and DOMA had been thoroughly probed during the campaign, as president, his stance on marriage was still largely symbolic since he had no conceivable path to legalizing it. But DOMA was a statute and therefore it was an issue of governance. The concept that the president would now be held accountable for finding a remedy to the harms DOMA was inflicting on same-sex couples was new to Gibbs. Over time, Gibbs would grow completely comfortable with LGBT questions, even when he had no good answers for them. But he had yet to perfect the nonanswer nonchalance he would eventually effect.

"I will . . . I have to go check on that, I . . . I honestly don't know the answer to that," Gibbs replied, stammering out an answer in three seconds flat before calling on the next reporter.[14]

Brief as it was, that twenty-second video clip became a mini YouTube sensation among activists hungry to see the administration get to work on LGBT rights. "Gibbs Punts on DOMA," screamed the headline from Pam Spaulding at Pam's House Blend. Meanwhile, John Aravosis of AMERICAblog announced: "Gibbs Questioned on Timeline for DOMA Repeal," followed simply by a text-link to the video that read, "He didn't have an answer."[15]

It was the beginning of a symbiotic relationship between the bloggers and me. I would ask probing questions in a generally neutral tone, and the bloggers would broadcast those exchanges to the queer community in the most unrelenting terms. Since Gibbs rarely gave substantive answers on anything, the trick for me was to ask a question that rendered even the lack of a response newsworthy. As Aravosis pointed out, "he didn't have an answer," and that in and of itself meant something.

I was certainly not the first reporter from an LGBT outlet to be granted White House press credentials—that distinction belongs to the *Washington Blade*'s Lou Chibbaro Jr., and Lisa Keen, both of whom began covering the White House during the AIDS crisis in the '80s. But I was the first to participate in the White House briefings on a weekly basis. My presence served several purposes. First, I was a constant reminder of a constituency that had almost always been forgotten after the votes were counted. Every election cycle, Democrats would swoop in like dashing suitors and make entreaties to the gays for money and votes, then summarily drop them afterward. But every time I raised my hand to ask a question, Gibbs faced the dilemma of whether to address an LGBT concern on that particular day.[16]

Second, after I earned my stripes in the briefing room and developed a rapport with some of the other correspondents, my questions helped mainstream reporters gauge what was important to the LGBT community and what progress was being made on our top issues.

But third and critically, Gibbs's responses to my questions provided a constant reminder to LGBT activists that the White House appeared to be doing little to nothing on things like "don't ask, don't tell" repeal and overturning DOMA. Whereas President Obama had talked about LGBT equality issues regularly on the campaign trail, Gibbs mostly shrank from my questions, especially as they became less theoretical and more specific. It was a little like Chinese water torture. The drip, drip, drip amounted to something intolerable over time, and the LGBT community was now getting a slow-but-steady trickle of intel straight from the White House press briefings.

EVEN AS ADDITIONAL STATES were legalizing gay marriage, a number of new legal cases were being filed on behalf of same-sex couples who couldn't legally marry or whose legal marriages were not being recognized by the federal government. One of those cases, *Gill v. Office of Personnel Management* (aka *Gill*), sought to effectively overturn DOMA. Another, *Perry v. Schwarzenegger* (aka *Perry*), was a constitutional challenge to Proposition 8 that many hoped would reach the Supreme Court and secure same-sex marriage rights nationwide. These two cases would have important legal implications in the battle to achieve equal treatment for same-sex spouses. But equally as significant, they would help dramatically shift the political landscape on which the struggle to pass pro-LGBT legislation was being waged.

In fact, while incredible progress was made toward achieving equality during Obama's presidency, the legal effort to secure full marriage rights and the political effort to advance LGBT legislation would move along separate tracks. But in the eyes of the American public, the legal and political continually intermingled, helping to produce the combustible moment that would unfold over just a handful of years.

Gill was filed on March 3, 2009, under the stewardship of Mary Bonauto, civil rights project director of the LGBT legal group Gay & Lesbian Advocates & Defenders (GLAD). The case sought to overturn section three of DOMA—the portion that prevented the federal government from recognizing same-sex couples' state-sanctioned marriages. *Gill v. Office of Personnel Management* challenged the denial of federal benefits and protections to Massachusetts couples that were legally married. It was a crafty approach targeting the most insidious and questionable piece of the law rather than going after the whole thing outright.[17]

The federal government's refusal to recognize same-sex marriages denied those couples marital benefits that flowed from some 1,100 provisions of federal law. Gay spouses, for instance, were taxed like strangers on a deceased partner's estate rather than being able to use the many tax advantages afforded to heterosexual spouses. Gays also could not receive their spouse's Social Security survivor benefits, which sometimes meant that surviving spouses could no longer afford things like the home the couple had once lived in together. Same-sex spouses of federal employees were also blocked from receiving health benefits under their partner's plan. And US citizens were prevented from sponsoring their foreign-born spouses for residency, which forced many couples to either live in separate countries or relocate to a country that would recognize their marriage. The list goes on and on.

DOMA was truly a cancer that managed to infect every area of the federal government's interaction with wedded couples, from taxation to immigration to health care and more.

Although DOMA was introduced and enacted in an incredibly swift four months in 1996, its sweeping consequences would not be fully brought into relief until 2004, when same-sex couples first began to marry. Discrimination, once codified into law, seeps through the many halls of government. Bad law begets bad policy, which begets more bad policy and sometimes more bad law. Its tentacles stretch into nearly every agent of the government and the process of untangling that stranglehold is a complicated and messy business.[18]

What made section three of DOMA so egregious and legally vulnerable was the fact that the federal government had a long-standing practice based on settled constitutional doctrine of deferring to state definitions of marriage. A 1975 US Supreme Court decision had called regulation of domestic relations "a virtually exclusive province of the States." Therefore, if the state said you were legally married, it should have been proof enough for the federal government. But DOMA was a complete departure from that practice, and the unprecedented change in public policy would require government lawyers to prove that the shift served some governmental interest beyond prejudice. As Supreme Court Justice Sandra Day O'Connor had emphasized in her concurring opinion in *Lawrence v. Texas*—the landmark 2003 ruling that overturned state laws criminalizing sodomy—"Moral disapproval of a group cannot be a legitimate governmental interest under the Equal Protection Clause."[19]

Gill was not the only pending legal challenge to DOMA, but it was the first case that law scholars considered legally sound, and as such had the LGBT community abuzz. GLAD and Bonauto had amassed a particularly strong track record of pro-LGBT lawsuits in the Northeast, including winning the history-changing case, *Goodrich v. Department of Public Health*, which in 2004 made Massachusetts the very first state in the nation where same-sex couples could legally wed.[20]

The other case, *Perry*, was brought by a pair of attorneys who formed a powerful political odd-couple—conservative stalwart Ted Olson and David Boies, one of the foremost liberal lawyers in the country. The two had famously rivaled each other in *Bush v. Gore*, the legal battle in 2000 that ultimately ended the agony of Florida's "hanging chad" recount and delivered the presidency to George W. Bush. Olson had been recruited for the suit by Hollywood director Rob Reiner, a prominent Democratic activist who thought a conservative like Olson, who had won forty-four of the fifty-five Supreme Court cases he had argued, would be best positioned to make the case to the court's conservative justices. Olson suggested bringing on David Boies so that liberals wouldn't distrust the effort.[21]

Perry would eventually make it to the US Supreme Court in 2013, as Olson and Boies and the group that hired them, the American Foundation for Equal Rights (AFER), had hoped. Though it took much longer than they intended. But in 2009, with state cases and legislative votes succeeding, the wisdom of launching a federal legal push for constitutional marriage rights was hotly debated. The overwhelming consensus among LGBT legal experts was that it was far too soon to put a marriage equality case in front of the conservative-leaning Roberts court—especially a broad case seeking nationwide impact that was designed for Supreme Court review within six months. A Supreme Court loss, many feared, would set the movement back decades. At the time, LGBT advocates had lost every marriage battle at the ballot box with one exception: in 2006, Arizona voters had rejected a sweeping measure to ban same-sex marriage and both gay and straight domestic partnerships.

But two years later, those same voters promptly reversed course by passing a more narrowly worded constitutional amendment prohibiting just same-sex marriage, making voters' anti-gay intentions crystal clear. That one-for-thirty-one record was unlikely to convince the Supreme Court that the nation was indeed ready for same-sex marriage.[22]

But legal considerations aside, the challenge to Prop 8, the brainchild of Reiner and AFER cofounder Chad Griffin, then a California-based Democratic consultant, was an enormous political boost to the marriage movement. To rally support for the case, Olson and Boies embarked on a nationwide talking tour. The idea of interviewing the duo that faced off in *Bush v. Gore* was like catnip to reporters. They had star power and they appeared on TV, radio, in numerous print articles, and at forums and fundraisers across the country. Strategically, having a conservative hero like Ted Olson making the case to the country that same-sex couples are indeed guaranteed the right to marry by the US Constitution was worth its weight in gold. In fact, on May 27, 2009, Jake Tapper of ABC used Olson's support for marriage equality as a jumping-off point in the briefing room.

"Today in California, Ted Olson, former solicitor general for President Bush, and David Boies are introducing a lawsuit against the state of California, saying that by denying same-sex couples the right to marry, the ability to marry, they are violating the equal protection rights under the US Constitution for same-sex couples," Tapper noted. "Olson, a very conservative lawyer, [is] saying that is a violation of the Constitution." Tapper reiterated President Obama's preference for civil unions over same-sex marriage and concluded, "Why is [his position] not a violation of the Equal Protection Clause?"[23]

Gibbs responded the way he often did when he didn't want to answer a question. "Jake, let me have somebody take a look at the pleading that they're going to make," he said.

"Forget the specific argument," Tapper continued, "I'm just talking about their general argument . . . by not allowing same-sex couples to marry, it is a violation of equal protection."

It was a no-win for Gibbs. He didn't want to say that President Obama believed relegating gays to civil unions was a violation of the Equal Protection Clause—that would suggest Obama believed in the constitutional right of gays to marry. But he also didn't want to say that denying same-sex couples the right to marry was constitutional—that would spark an LGBT rebellion.

"Well," Gibbs offered, "the president's position, we're all aware of. I hesitate to be general about the legal underpinnings of an argument based on some portion of the Constitution."[24]

President Obama, for his part, was trying to have it both ways. He wanted to show his support for a very vocal and financially prolific swath of his base, but he was wary of forcing the issue nationwide. In some ways it was a very legalistic approach to public policy—applying a scalpel to dissect it a piece at a time rather than articulating a sweeping vision that would overhaul the entire system. While Ted Olson was talking about the constitutional right of same-sex couples to marry, President Obama and his team were preparing to issue a presidential directive in June that would provide *some* benefits to federal employees with same-sex partners—as long as those benefits were not blocked by DOMA or some other federal statute. The Office of Personnel Management and the State Department spent months identifying which benefits could be granted to same-sex partners but, ultimately, the administration determined that health insurance and retirement plans could not be among them. (That decision came despite the fact that two federal judges in California had concluded exactly the opposite in two separate rulings a few months earlier; the judges ordered the federal government to extend health benefits to the same-sex partners of two federal workers, and the government ignored the orders.) The administration's conclusion meant that most federal employees were only eligible for benefits such as taking sick leave to care for their partner or their partners' children (which they would be prevented from doing if they weren't legally related) and adding their partner to long-term care coverage. It was like the Swiss cheese of benefits—substantive yet riddled with holes since it didn't include things like health care and pension.[25]

At the State Department, however, the order had more powerful implications due to the demanding nature of working abroad. The State Department had the authority to change the regulations included within the Foreign Affairs Manual, and Secretary of State Hillary Clinton charged her team with researching such changes almost immediately after taking the helm at the agency. Her instructions to Patrick Kennedy, the undersecretary for management and a thirty-eight-year veteran of the agency, and Jim Thessin, the deputy legal adviser, were, "Let us do everything that I in my powers can do to resolve this."[26]

Before Clinton took charge of the State Department, same-sex partners of foreign service officers (FSOs) stationed overseas were ineligible for a number of benefits available to their heterosexual counterparts: use of medical facilities at US posts, help in processing travel documents like passports, evacuation in emergency situations, being counted in their partner's family size for housing allocations, and receiving language and security training. For gay FSOs who were moving their families abroad, these types of limitations posed very real hurdles. The department's LGBT advocacy group, GLIFAA, had been calling for these reforms for several years, so lesbian, gay, and transgender employees at the State Department were particularly heartened by the news that they would finally be enacted.[27]

But these advances were so deep in the weeds that they were difficult for mainstream Americans to absorb. Instead of viewing Obama's directive as a sizable step forward, for example, the White House press corps was hard-pressed to understand how something that didn't include the two most meaningful benefits—health care and retirement—was worth much. They also knew that many LGBT Americans wanted something more than half-measures from the Obama administration. At the press briefing, Jennifer Loven, then of the Associated Press, asked Robert Gibbs to "talk about why people should see this as more than kind of an empty gesture or just a symbolic move on [Obama's] part?"[28]

Gibbs responded that the president saw it as a matter of "fairness."

"But wouldn't it also be fair to extend benefits such as the right to have health insurance—a health insurance plan or pension plan?" wondered Loven.

"Well, that requires not an executive order or presidential memorandum but a change in the law," Gibbs answered, referring to DOMA.

Loven's was the first of a number of questions that June day about the legal implications of DOMA, the president's timeline for overturning it, and widespread political unrest among the president's LGBT supporters. Reporters in the White House press corps were certainly familiar with marriage-related issues, and they all knew that Obama had embraced civil unions over marriage as a candidate—that was straightforward enough. But really grasping the intricacies of the president's contradictory positions on federal DOMA, state marriage equality, and anti-gay ballot initiatives would require a fair amount of catch-up for mainstream reporters. Reporters like Loven and Tapper were already zeroing in on President Obama's increasingly tortured and convoluted positions on marriage and relationship recognition. Not coincidentally, journalists' questions about these issues would gradually get more precise, more bold, and more dogged over the course of the next several years until their inquiries became altogether unbearable. LGBT activists and bloggers were no longer the only ones hounding Obama on gay rights.[29]

On June 3, 2009, New Hampshire became the sixth state to legalize same-sex marriage, thereby tripling the number of marriage equality states since Obama took office. That evening, NBC's Brian Williams tried a different approach to the marriage question in a prerecorded prime time interview, "Inside the Obama White House."

"Do gay and lesbian couples who wish to marry in this country have a friend in the White House?" he asked President Obama, as they sat in the stately Cabinet Room, the American flag and the official flag of the president situated behind Obama.[30]

"I think gays and lesbians have a friend in the White House," Obama responded, "because I've consistently committed myself to civil unions, making sure that they have the ability to visit each other in hospitals, that they are able to access benefits, that they have a whole host of legal rights that they currently do not have."[31]

To average Americans, it may have sounded perfectly reasonable. To mainstream journalists, it was just more of the same predictable talking points. But to activists, it was added salt in the wound. Blogger David Badash at The New Civil Rights Movement penned a disgruntled post with the headline: "Obama: Gays, Not Gay Marriage, Have a Friend in the White House."[32]

DESPITE THE CONSTANT drumbeat of questions from journalists, administration officials didn't seem to understand that they had a festering and potentially volatile problem on their hands until the Justice Department filed its first brief defending DOMA on June 11, 2009, in a case called *Smelt v. United States.*[33]

In the months leading up to the filing, AMERICAblog editors Aravosis and Sudbay, both of whom had law degrees though neither was a practicing attorney, had been tracking the legal challenges to DOMA. In the first few months of the administration, they had reached out to campaign staffers who were now at the White House in the hopes of having a collaborative relationship with the administration. Aravosis had dreamt of having an occupant in the White House who was a friend of the LGBT community. He figured that he and Sudbay finally had enough experience in the movement to offer some practical advice from time to time on strategic decisions affecting LGBT issues. But the administration had already gotten off to a decidedly rocky start on that front. No one could have foreseen how quickly the relationship between Obama and the LGBT community would start to sour. And Aravosis, much like Jonathan Lewis, was perhaps overly optimistic about how open the administration would be to outside input.[34]

By spring, Sudbay's "early warning system" (as Aravosis called it) was being set off. He had his eye on the progression of *Gill v. Office of Personnel Management* and he kept reminding Aravosis that the Department of Justice would soon have to file a brief in it. That meant the administration would have to decide whether to continue defending a law that President Obama had explicitly called "abhorrent" as a candidate for US Senate in 2004 and discriminatory as a presidential candidate in 2008.[35]

During his primary showdown with Hillary Clinton, Obama had published an open letter to the LGBT community in which he took a swipe at Clinton's recommendation to only repeal section three of DOMA and keep intact section two, the portion that protected states from having to recognize marriages performed in other states. "While some say we should repeal only part of the law," Obama wrote, "I believe we should get rid of that statute altogether. Federal law should not discriminate in any way against gay and lesbian couples, which is precisely what DOMA does."[36]

Given Obama's firm stance on DOMA during his candidacy, Sudbay knew activists wouldn't take kindly to the administration defending the statute against legal challenges. He also realized something that had as yet failed to dawn on the White House or even most of Washington's political establishment—the anger over Prop 8 had entirely changed the political landscape. LGBT activists, he reasoned, were unlikely to turn a blind eye to politically motivated decisions on LGBT concerns that might have once seemed necessary if unfortunate. In an effort to head off what seemed an inevitable clash, Aravosis reached out to Brian Bond, the LGBT liaison, to schedule a meeting. On March 19, 2009, three months before the filing, he headed over to the Eisenhower Executive Office Building next to the White House to meet with Bond, Shin Inouye, the White House director of specialty media, and Christina Reynolds, the White House director of media affairs and special assistant to the president. They met at the staff cafeteria, which reminded Aravosis of his elementary school lunch program, complete with little trays and an apron-clad employee behind a glass plate plopping food on your plate.

The four sat at a table for about an hour and Aravosis tried to relay to them how much discontent was simmering in the community. They had endured Rick Warren and watched the White House waffle on "don't ask, don't tell" and marriage, and now with the DOMA cases on the horizon, Aravosis explained, it was a recipe for disaster. The meeting was pleasant enough overall, but Aravosis walked away feeling like they had no idea how badly things were going with LGBT activists and how much worse relations could possibly get. At that point, Obama was still radiating that rock star glow that had illumined his path to the White House. Spectators across the country were still giddily waving at the presidential motorcade as it passed by. Media outlets were reporting that the Obamas had revived "the era of the cocktail party" with their regular Wednesday night soirees at the White House; who would make the guest list and what would be served was highly sought after information. In short, President Obama and his coterie were still the essence of chic, and it must have been difficult for his team to imagine that any progressive group was as disgruntled as Aravosis was suggesting. Not to mention the fact that the administration was getting a completely different message from most of Washington's LGBT advocacy groups, which seemed more intent on tamping down the expectations of LGBT activists than they were on holding the administration's feet to the fire.[37]

A few months later, Sudbay would encounter a similar reaction not from White House staff, but from Washington LGBT advocates. In early June, just days before the Justice Department filed its first DOMA brief, Sudbay was invited to the Human Rights Campaign headquarters for a meeting about hate crimes legislation. It was a room full of the usual suspects in Washington's gay advocacy circles. The president and vice president of HRC, Joe Solmonese and David Smith, plus the legislative director, Allison Herwitt, and an HRC media consultant, Mary Breslauer; two prominent lobbyists in town that HRC kept on retainer: Steve Elmendorf of Elmendorf Strategies and Robert Raben of The Raben Group; Hilary Rosen, a former recording industry lobbyist and long-time HRC Foundation board member who was working at the PR firm the Brunswick Group at the time; and Winnie Stachelberg, who in 2006 had joined the powerful progressive think tank the Center for American Progress after spending eleven years at HRC. In this group, Sudbay, who worked as a consultant in addition to his blogging, was mostly an outsider. He had done some consulting for HRC in the past but no more. In this instance, he was specifically invited to the meeting to provide an alternative perspective to the insular group.

The Human Rights Campaign was having a hard time getting hate crimes legislation passed. Since it was June and Pride month, the White House was hungry for an LGBT victory it could tout to buffer itself against an increasingly impatient activist undercurrent. In May, President Obama had made a point of holding an Oval Office meeting (complete with photo op) with Judy Shepard, the mother of hate crime victim Matthew Shepard and a tireless advocate for the legislation. The bill, which had been passed by both chambers in 2007 only to perish under a veto-threat from President George W. Bush—had sailed through the liberal-leaning House in April 2009 with 249–175 votes. But the measure was in trouble in the Senate, where the foremost champion of LGBT equality at the time, Senator Ted Kennedy, was in failing health. No one in the entire chamber held as much gravitas or power as Kennedy. Without the help of its key ally, HRC was having trouble finding Senate floor time and a legislative vehicle for the bill. (In the Senate, smaller measures are routinely passed as attachments to larger bills.)[38]

Hate crimes was the bill everyone had taken for granted given its passage in previous sessions. In December of 2008, David Smith, who had been with HRC more than a dozen years, had described the bill to me as "low-hanging fruit" because it was "so ripe and so ready to go." That same month, HRC had included signing "hate crimes legislation into law within 6 months" as part of its "Blueprint for Positive Change" for the new president. They blasted the blueprint to their entire membership list of about 750,000 people and urged President-elect Obama to commit to the five-point plan in order to "turn the corner" on the Rick Warren fiasco. Enacting hate crimes legislation shouldn't have been a problem; after all, the Senate Democrats now had 59 votes, eight more than when the bill had passed in 2007.[39]

Yet six months into the Obama administration, HRC was now hosting a meeting of some of the most senior people in the movement—the ones who were not only the likeliest to know how to get things done on the Hill but many of whom were also paid to do so—to find a way to advance a bill that everyone had considered a gimme. Hate crimes would eventually be passed as an attachment to the Department of Defense's budget bill, but not until several months later on October 22, 2009. Both the White House and HRC would feel as if they didn't get enough credit for finally pushing the bill through. It was the first major piece of pro-LGBT civil rights legislation ever passed by Congress and also the first time the phrase "lesbian, gay, bisexual, and transgender" was entered into the US code. But what the two entities failed to understand was that many activists had long considered hate crimes a foregone conclusion, a remnant of the '90s that, while important, should have been a done deal years earlier. LGBT Americans now wanted more from the government than the assurance that, if they got beaten to a pulp or killed, the crime might exact higher penalties and the federal government could assist in the investigation.[40]

That sentiment wasn't lost on Sudbay as he sat at HRC on that summer day in June. More than anything, he was worried by the tenor of the meeting. As a blogger who was privy to a continual feedback loop from reader comments on his posts, he could sense the unrest among activists. Solmonese suggested that all the agitation would just fade once hate crimes legislation passed, but Sudbay didn't think that was true at all. The community *expected* hate crimes to pass, he said, and had moved on to DOMA and "don't ask, don't tell." As the brainstorming session drew to a close, Sudbay raised the alarm bells about the impending DOMA briefs.[41]

"The administration is going to have to decide by end of the month if they're defending DOMA, and if they do, there's going to be a serious problem," he said.[42]

Others in the room disagreed. The Obama administration had no choice but to defend the statute, they argued.

Sudbay remained firm. "They don't have to defend DOMA, and if they do, that big fundraiser at the end of the month is going to be a huge problem," he warned, referring to the LGBT Pride fundraiser the DNC holds in Washington every year. That was the last strategy session Sudbay was ever invited to at HRC.

Several days later, on June 12, 2009, Sudbay and Aravosis broke the news of just what exactly was contained in the first Justice Department brief filed in defense of DOMA. It was not good.

"We just got the brief from reader Lavi Soloway," wrote Aravosis. "It's pretty despicable, and gratuitously homophobic. It reads as if it were written by one of George Bush's top political appointees. I cannot state strongly enough how damaging this brief is to us. Obama didn't just argue a technicality about the case, he argued that DOMA is reasonable. That DOMA is constitutional. That DOMA wasn't motivated by any anti-gay animus. He argued why our Supreme Court victories in *Romer* and *Lawrence* shouldn't be interpreted to give us rights in any other area (which hurts us in countless other cases and battles). He argued that DOMA doesn't discriminate against us because it also discriminates about [sic] straight unmarried couples (ignoring the fact that they can get married and we can't)."[43]

The brief used case law involving underage brides (sixteen years of age) and incestuous marriages (an uncle to a niece) to build a rationale for why states might resist recognizing same-sex marriages performed in other states. If as a matter of public policy, the states had refused to recognize such marriages—even if they were performed legally in another jurisdiction—then surely, according to the brief, they should have the same authority to reject same-sex marriages. The implied equivalency was revolting to LGBT Americans, even if legal observers considered it a legitimate defense of the law.[44]

Aravosis and Sudbay vehemently denounced the brief in the strongest possible terms, setting the tone for how it would be received. The AP had posted a more basic report on the filing the night before but the news wasn't on anyone's radar until AMERICAblog put it there. Their post went up at around 9:45 a.m. on a Friday morning and was picked up immediately by bloggers at outlets like *Politico, The Atlantic,* and the Huffington Post. By the afternoon, nearly every LGBT organization, including HRC, had joined the outcry. "The Administration apparently determined that it had a duty to defend DOMA in the courts," read a statement from Joe Solmonese that hit my inbox at 2:09 p.m. "The President has just as strong a duty to put his principles into action, and end discrimination against LGBT people and our families." HRC had little choice—it was nearly impossible to defend the brief or even dismiss it given the way it was written. It was not only culturally insensitive, it advanced legal arguments that were particularly harmful to any future DOMA challenge that might reach the Supreme Court, such as the notion that the statute was consistent with the constitutional principles of due process and equal protection.[45]

The White House went into full damage control, dispatching people to defend the administration's course of action. The strong reaction to the *Smelt* brief had totally blindsided people in the West Wing, despite the fact that LGBT activists and legal advocates alike had tried to focus the administration's attention on the matter. In fact, before GLAD even filed *Gill* in March, Mary Bonauto had met with Melody Barnes, director of the White House Domestic Policy Council, to warn her that a lawsuit was coming. DOMA, as an issue, should have been on their radar, but that was all water under the bridge now.[46]

Most people who took the administration's side advanced the concept that the Justice Department *must* defend laws duly enacted by Congress. Robert Raben, a gay man and former Justice Department official under Clinton told the *Washington Blade*, "The statute sucks. It's disgusting. We've opposed it from day one. We'll continue to oppose it, but the Department of Justice is doing what the Department of Justice does, which is defend the statute."[47]

As I scrambled to make sense of it, the White House press office offered me legal heavyweights like Harvard constitutional law professor Laurence Tribe and former Clinton Assistant Attorney General and Solicitor General Walter Dellinger. Tribe, who fully wanted to see DOMA overturned, gave a strategic reason for gay rights activists to be thankful the Justice Department had defended it. *Smelt* was a weak case, he explained, unlikely to yield a positive outcome if it were to make it to the Supreme Court.

"Even though I personally believe that DOMA is unconstitutional, I think that this particular lawsuit is very vulnerable; it's not anywhere near as strong as the [*Gill* case] that was brought in the federal district court in Massachusetts," he told me. "A strategic Justice Department interested in a litigation strategy that has some realistic chance of success certainly would not have taken this case as the one in which the constitutional vulnerabilities of DOMA should be explored."[48]

Though Tribe, Raben, and others provided reasons for *why* the Justice Department defended the law, what no one could justify to LGBT activists and allies was the language of the brief itself or the legal theories it employed to defend of the law. Even if some legal experts thought the case the brief made was fair play, it was offensive to average gay people—and they happened to be a very relevant audience in this case. This wasn't just a legal document, it was a political document, and the administration's failure to recognize it as such was a failure in leadership. Although the brief came from the Justice Department, it was Obama's Justice Department, and it should have reflected the beliefs and policies that he himself had consistently articulated both as a candidate and as president. While people sometimes pretend there's a firewall between the White House and the Justice Department, that is simply not the case. And in earnest, the White House should take an active interest in making sure the actions of every federal agency under its management—including the Justice Department—are consistent with the views and policies of the president. If there was one thing Obama had repeated over and over again since as far back as the '90s, it was that he believed same-sex spouses should have access to the same federal rights and benefits that heterosexual spouses did. While his position on marriage-related questions was sometimes convoluted, his position with regard to equal benefits never was.

But clearly defending DOMA hadn't been flagged as a potential snag, and it's hard to imagine the brief had been vetted for its political and legal implications by anyone who was deeply steeped in LGBT issues.

"It had such a buckshot approach to it, a veritable kitchen sink of anti-gay legal theories, that it seemed expressly designed to inflict maximal damage to our rights," Socarides wrote in a guest post for AMERICAblog. "Instead of making nuanced arguments which took into account the president's oft-stated support for repealing DOMA—a law he has called 'abhorrent'—the brief seemed to embrace DOMA and all its horrific consequences."[49]

Beyond incensing activists like Aravosis and Sudbay—who had stirred up a political firestorm—the brief also angered LGBT legal advocates.

In their view, senior-level appointees at the Justice Department like Attorney General Eric Holder and Assistant Attorney General Tony West had failed to take note of who at the department was staffing cases of particular importance to the LGBT community. In other words, the person who was writing marriage-related briefs for Obama's Department of Justice should have been culturally attuned to gay issues and the tone that the administration was trying to strike on them. Legal advocate Jenny Pizer, who was then director of Lambda Legal's Marriage Project, later explained to me, "What we saw in the previous administration was that there was an enormous amount of ideological staffing at work. The cases involving gay people, sexual-orientation discrimination, and mistreatment of same-sex couples were staffed mostly by people with ideological views that were not respectful of same-sex couples and the lawyering reflected that."[50]

What was even more maddening to the legal community was that the Justice Department also had fair warning. In advance of the government's *Smelt* filing, legal advocates had specifically requested a meeting with Justice Department officials in order to discuss the DOMA cases and the legal implications their arguments would have. But their outreach had been ignored.[51]

In response to the brief, four legal groups—the American Civil Liberties Union (ACLU), GLAD, Lambda Legal, and the National Center for Lesbian Rights (NCLR)—jointly issued a scathing statement saying they were "surprised and deeply disappointed in *the manner* in which the Obama administration has defended the so-called Defense of Marriage Act." (emphasis added). The release went on to state the multiple ways that the administration's brief had legally harmed and defamed LGBT people.[52]

"We disagree with many of the administration's arguments, for example that DOMA is a valid exercise of Congress's power, is consistent with Equal Protection or Due Process principles, and does not impinge upon rights that are recognized as fundamental," they said.

They also said they were "extremely disturbed" by a brand new argument the administration was making—that by not extending federal benefits to same-sex couples, the government was allowing some states to experiment with gay marriage while declining to "obligate federal taxpayers in other States to subsidize a form of marriage their own States do not recognize." The government hailed this approach as "a cautious policy of federal neutrality." Had government lawyers forgotten that LGBT Americans also pay taxes? Had they failed to consider the fact that same-sex couples were paying into a system that they were subsequently denied access to?

The legal groups took the government to task. "It is the married same-sex couples, not heterosexuals in other parts of the country, who are financially and personally damaged in significant ways by DOMA," they wrote. "For the Obama administration to suggest otherwise simply departs from both mathematical and legal reality."

In the coming weeks, as mainstream publications moved on to newer stories, Sudbay and Aravosis continued to vociferously denounce the brief and all those who defended it. They were very much aware of the potential consequences. It was the first time anyone from Obama's progressive base in DC had really gone after the White House in no uncertain terms, and it was scary territory. As a political consultant on liberal issues like immigration and labor, Sudbay prepared to lose clients over the coming months. They might fear that his presence would hurt relations with the White House. But if he had to bag groceries for a living, he told his partner of several years, at least he would have his dignity. Fortunately, he did not end up experiencing the fallout that Mixner had years earlier. Perhaps that was because his clients weren't expressly paying him to help them gain access to the White House.[53]

A couple months later, Sudbay would learn that the imbroglio had indeed reached the highest levels of government. While attending a progressive blogger conference called Netroots Nation in Pittsburgh in mid-August, he was invited to an off-the-record meeting with one of Obama's foremost advisors in the White House, Valerie Jarrett, a long-time friend of the Obamas who had followed them from Chicago to DC.

When Sudbay walked into the restaurant, Jarrett was sitting at the table with a handful of bloggers. Sudbay introduced himself. "Oh, I know who you are," she replied. As the chat wrapped up an hour later, one of the other bloggers told Jarrett, "You need to understand, we're going to push you from the left to give you space to be what you promised you would be."[54]

Since Sudbay had already trod that path, he jumped in. "I just want to say, I didn't expect to be in a fight with you over DOMA," he told her, "but we will fight you, and we will push you. It's not fun for either one of us, but this is too important and we're not going to back down."[55]

Jarrett responded that she had consulted Attorney General Eric Holder and "he told me that the brief we submitted wasn't as bad as the one the Bush administration submitted."[56]

Sudbay, who at five foot seven inches had a more unassuming presence than someone with five marathons under his belt might suggest, was shocked. They still seemed to be missing the point. "No, no, no," he said emphatically. "I expected it from the Bush administration, I didn't expect it from you—it's worse coming from you."

As he left the room, a top White House aide whom he had known for years heard the exchange and pulled him aside.

"I want to tell you something, Joe," said the aide. "The day after you broke that story—it was a Saturday—the president called me and said, get me a copy of that brief, I need to see what this is all about."[57]

The dustup had indeed sent tremors through the White House. Up to that point, most of the energy inside the building related to gay issues had been devoted to "don't ask, don't tell." Internally, President Obama had begun having serious discussions as early as April of 2009 with Defense Secretary Gates and Chairman of the Joint Chiefs Admiral Mike Mullen about overturning the policy. In his memoir, *Duty*, Secretary Gates would later write, "The only military matter, apart from leaks, about which I ever sensed deep passion on [Obama's] part was 'don't ask, don't tell.' For him, changing that law seemed to be the inevitable next step in the civil rights movement." Thanks to the president's intent, constant press inquiries on the issue, and external studies suggesting discharges could be stopped via executive order, the military's gay ban had topped the White House priority list of LGBT issues.[58]

But shortly after the DOMA uproar, a very high-level White House meeting was held the first week of July that included senior advisers Valerie Jarrett, David Axelrod, and Jim Messina; White House staff secretary Lisa Brown; Tina Tchen and Brian Bond, director and deputy director of the White House Office of Public Engagement; White House counsel Greg Craig and associate counsel Alison "Ali" Nathan from the Office of White House Counsel (the team of about twenty-five lawyers who advise the president on legal issues); and several lawyers from the Department of Justice. President Obama also stepped in for several

minutes. Discussion centered around three main goals. First, the administration needed to figure out what do about DOMA and what legal options were available. Second, going forward, the White House counsel's
office would have to coordinate better with the Justice Department and
review all legal briefs being filed on the matter. Their aim was to defend DOMA as vigorously as possible without offending or demeaning
LGBT people. And third, while the lawyers were considering how to
handle the statute itself, advisers also wanted to explore what else could
be done at different levels throughout the government to create greater
equality for LGBT people.[59]

From that point forward, for nearly two years, a weekly meeting
about LGBT concerns took place that typically included White House
LGBT appointees such as Brian Bond, Nancy Sutley, chair of the White
House Council on Environmental Quality, and Shin Inouye, White
House director of specialty media (i.e. constituency press). Also in attendance were White House officials from the Office of Cabinet Affairs,
Domestic Policy Council, and the Office of Progressive Media and Online Response. And importantly, it included the lawyers from the Office
of White House Counsel who would be researching the legal ins and
outs of DOMA. The debacle also marked the beginning of an unspoken
shift of importance in Brian Bond's role as the highest-ranking LGBT
official at the White House. Senior advisers like Valerie Jarrett would
increasingly turn to him for guidance on LGBT issues, which gave him
more clout than his lack of an "assistant" title might have suggested at
the outset of the administration.[60]

But the fury surrounding the DOMA brief also had immediate effects
outside the White House. The week after the brief surfaced, high-profile
LGBT donors, advocates, and Washington insiders started dropping like
flies from the DNC fundraiser set to take place on June 25—exactly as
Sudbay had predicted. Among them: Andy Towle of Towleroad; HRC's
field director, Marty Rouse; Alan Van Capelle, then executive director
of New York's largest LGBT group; Chuck Wolfe, then executive director of the Gay & Lesbian Victory Fund; Democratic consultant and
consummate LGBT insider, Hilary Rosen; and Stampp Corbin, a prominent Obama supporter and usual defender of the president. Mixner and
Socarides both dropped out, though perhaps that was to be expected.
And gay financial heavyweights like millionaire donors David Bohnett

and Bruce Bastian said more broadly they simply planned to stop giving to the DNC. Bastian told the *Washington Blade* that he would "continue to support certain congressmen, congresswomen and senators whom I believe will continue to fight for our rights, but I don't think blanket donations to the Democratic Party right now are justified, at least not in my book." Bohnett told veteran lesbian reporter Karen Ocamb that he was "eager to continue our substantial commitment to the DNC when we see tangible commitments with timelines to repeal DOMA, 'don't ask, don't tell,' and support for marriage equality at the federal level."[61]

The fallout caught fire in the Beltway media. Since Biden was keynoting the DNC event, *Politico*'s Ben Smith wrote, "The escalating tension sets the stage for an unusual conflict between the vice president and what has traditionally been a core Democratic group—and a wealthy one." Smith also coauthored a longer piece with Josh Gerstein titled, "President Obama fails to quell gay uproar." Many other outlets picked up on the controversy, including *The Atlantic*, *The Hill*, *National Journal*, and *The Economist*, just to name a few.[62]

On the day of the event, about 180 attendees (who paid anywhere from $1,000 to $30,400 per plate) were greeted by protesters carrying signs that read "Gay Uncle Toms" and "265 Discharged Since January 20, 2009," an accounting of "don't ask, don't tell" victims since Obama took office. The DNC put on a brave face as Vice President Joe Biden headlined the event. "I am not unaware of the controversies swirling around this dinner," Biden told the crowd, "swirling around the speed—or lack thereof—that we're moving on issues that are of great importance to you and, quite frankly, to me and to the president and to millions of Americans." DNC officials said the fundraiser ultimately netted nearly $1 million, up from $750,000 the year before.[63]

But the point had been made—the disastrous DOMA brief became a clear tipping point. Prior to the DOMA filing, the grassroots seemed to be giving the administration the benefit of the doubt. Even if activists were frustrated, they generally hoped—indeed assumed—that the administration was working on LGBT issues behind the scenes. To claim otherwise, one had to have tangible proof to the contrary. But after the filing, the burden of proof switched to the administration and the overriding assumption of grassroots activists was instead that the administration wasn't moving quickly or diligently enough to advance LGBT issues. Ironically, White House officials were becoming far more proactive at the very moment that they completely lost the trust of activists.

By June 29, when President Obama and the First Lady stood in front of attendees at the first LGBT Pride celebration ever held at the White House, a shadow had been cast over the administration. Inside the East Room, the First Couple received a warm reception as Washington advocates enthusiastically held up their cameras to snap photos. It was, indeed, totally historic to have the president recount the history of the Stonewall riots of 1969 from within the White House walls, inscribing the inception of the modern gay rights movement into the conscience of our nation. Until that time, it had been a largely invisible history, left out of school books and scrubbed from national records as the shameful and unseemly story of a degenerate group of people. But that day at the White House marked the beginning of an official remembrance with the president of the United States declaring the struggle worthy of resurrection.

"Forty years ago, in the heart of New York City at a place called the Stonewall Inn, a group of citizens, including a few who are here today, as I said, defied an unjust policy and awakened a nascent movement," Obama said, tracing the emerging desire for change among citizens who had been belittled, dehumanized, and shut out of much of America's promise.[64]

"I know that many in this room don't believe that progress has come fast enough," President Obama told about 250 attendees midway through his speech. "It's not for me to tell you to be patient, any more than it was for others to counsel patience to African Americans who were petitioning for equal rights a half century ago."[65]

"We've been in office six months now," Obama added in a matter-of-fact tone. "I suspect that by the time this administration is over, I think you guys will have pretty good feelings about the Obama administration."[66]

If in the first several months of the Obama administration, LGBT concerns had taken a backseat to issues like the economy, the wars, and health care reform, by the end of June they were certainly beginning to move more front and center.

The *Smelt* brief had not only sparked some internal soul searching and a series of meetings within the administration, it had also launched government lawyers on a serious fact-finding mission. In the White

House counsel's office, attorneys Ali Nathan, Kate Shaw, and Ian Bassin were assigned to conduct a thorough legal analysis of the Defense of Marriage Act and figure out what the administration's legal options were surrounding the law. At the Justice Department, a high-level contingent of about twenty to thirty government lawyers led by Tony West, head of the Civil Division, met with a group of attorneys that specialized in LGBT issues and family law, including representatives from the ACLU, GLAD, HRC, Lambda Legal, and NCLR. Also in attendance was Paul Smith, the Washington attorney who had argued and won *Lawrence v. Texas*, Lambda Legal's 2003 Supreme Court case overturning sodomy laws nationwide. Smith served a particularly important role. As someone who was engaged with the LGBT legal community and also a highly respected Supreme Court litigator in Washington, Smith not only knew people at the Department of Justice but also had a sense of how the hierarchy functioned at the nerve center of the enormous agency, which employed some 10,000 attorneys and 113,000 employees nationwide. In that sense, Smith was the perfect person to help bridge the gap between the LGBT legal advocates—most of whom lived outside the Beltway—and high-level Justice Department attorneys, many of whom were Washingtonians.[67]

When legal advocates met with Justice Department lawyers in the last week of June 2009, Tony West assembled a top-tier cohort of attorneys that included Deputy Attorney General David Ogden, then-Solicitor General Elena Kagan, and acting head of the Office of Legal Counsel, David Barron. This was a chance for the Justice Department to signal that it was taking the legal issues surrounding DOMA very seriously, and West had delivered. The meeting was one of four that would occur between the administration's first DOMA filing in June and the day Attorney General Holder declared the law unconstitutional on February 23, 2011.[68]

During these meetings, government lawyers were mostly in listening mode as advocates made the case for why the Justice Department should stop defending the statute. But short of that goal, legal advocates were also extremely concerned about the government's contention in the *Smelt* brief that heterosexual households were better for child welfare. In fact, nearly every independent scientific organization that had studied the issue over the last decade or so had concluded the opposite. As the American Academy of Child and Adolescent Psychiatry had stated: "There is no credible evidence that shows that a parent's sexual orientation or gender identity will adversely affect the development of the child." Additionally, between 1997–2004, the most authoritative organizations on the matter all made policy statements either rejecting the notion that LGBT parents were inferior or affirming the legal rights of same-sex parents in the interest of providing children with safe and stable family structures.[69]

As Justice Department lawyers grappled with a way forward on DOMA, lawyers in the White House counsel's office were beginning to doubt the law's constitutionality. But figuring out what to do about it would require a more thorough analysis and, inevitably, a much longer conversation within the administration. White House lawyers knew another brief in *Smelt* was due soon and their goal was for the administration to file "a placeholder" of sorts. The brief would continue to defend the law while doing the least amount of legal damage to the LGBT constituency, and it would buy them some time.[70]

Due to the administration's heightened awareness, the next DOMA brief filed by government lawyers in the *Smelt* case on August 17, 2009, was a world away from their inaugural brief. In fact, the beginning of the end of the Defense of Marriage Act began with this clarification from Justice Department attorneys:

> The government does not contend that there are legitimate government interests in "creating a legal structure that promotes the raising of children by both of their biological parents" or that the government's interest in "responsible procreation" justifies Congress's decision to define marriage as a union between one man and one woman (Doc. 42 at 8–9).[71]

It was music to the ears of the queer legal community. In the case history section of the first brief, government lawyers had cited "'defending and nurturing the institution of traditional, heterosexual marriage' because of the role it plays in 'procreation and child rearing'" as one of Congress's reasons for enacting DOMA. That rationale—of heterosexual procreation and parenting—had long been used as a cudgel by anti-gay activists in the courts. In fact, it was the centerpiece of multiple anti-gay marriage rulings in 2006 and 2007, when high courts in New York, Washington, and Maryland all denied marital rights to same-sex couples based on the notion that the government had an interest in promoting heterosexual marriage for the welfare of children. Unlike the Massachusetts and Iowa decisions, for example, those adverse decisions accepted without serious probing the claim that allowing same-sex couples to wed would somehow dissuade straight couples from marrying. Additionally, those rulings ignored the harm that was being done to the children of lesbian and gay couples, as if those children were otherwise unworthy of consideration.[72]

But the logic those courts had employed was more prejudicial than fact-based, as legal advocates had noted in their meeting at the Justice Department. In the new government brief defending DOMA, a lengthy footnote dutifully listed links to policy statements from the many organizations that supported same-sex parenting rights: the American Academy of Pediatrics, the American Psychological Association, the American Academy of Child and Adolescent Psychiatry, the American Medical Association, and the Child Welfare League of America.[73]

It was a stigma gay advocates had been fighting for years. The concept that marriage was uniquely related to procreation and raising children was at the core of legal precedents dating back to the 1970s. The Minnesota Supreme Court had rejected a right-to-marry claim by two gay men, Richard John Baker ("Jack") and James "Michael" McConnell, by noting, "The institution of marriage as a union of man and woman, uniquely involving the procreation and rearing of children within a family, is as old as the book of Genesis." When the two men appealed the ruling to the US Supreme Court, the justices refused to hear the case and summarily dismissed it in 1972 "for want of a substantial federal question." It was the equivalent of being laughed out of court. But the only transgression Baker and McConnell had committed was being wildly ahead of their time. (In fact, it wasn't until a year later in 1973 that the American Psychiatric Association officially removed "homosexuality" as a mental disorder from its *Diagnostic and Statistical Manual of Mental Disorders*, known as the "DSM.")[74]

But now, nearly four decades later, the US government was acknowledging that procreation and heterosexual parenting were not, in and of themselves, a solid rationale for restricting marital rights to heterosexual couples. Once that line of reasoning was dropped, the arguments left for the government to make in support of DOMA would grow slimmer and slimmer.

Beyond that crucial legal point, the second DOMA brief also expressly stated President Obama's position on the law. "This Administration does not support DOMA as a matter of policy, believes that it is discriminatory, and supports its repeal," read the second paragraph of the brief.[75]

On the same day as the filing, the White House press office released a statement from President Obama. It noted that his Justice Department had filed a brief, "as it traditionally does when acts of Congress are challenged," and that the brief "makes clear, however, that my Administration believes that the Act is discriminatory and should be repealed by Congress."[76]

By August of 2009, the administration was moving in a considerably more positive direction on DOMA, at least on the legal front. Had LGBT activists, gay groups, donors, and legal advocates not raised a unified voice in opposition to the first DOMA filing from the government, there's no telling how long it would have taken to effect a turnaround in the arguments. Before the outcry, legal advocates had not even been able to get the ear of Justice Department lawyers. Now, administration officials were meeting regularly both internally about LGBT issues and externally with LGBT advocates.

But the administration's attention had come a day late and a dollar short for grassroots activists, who were still not impressed. The government's defense of DOMA had become a litmus test in their view and nothing short of ceasing and desisting would satisfy them. Despite the fact that the administration had now received a wake-up call, the progress activists were seeing seemed more like concessions than proactive movement. They hungered for some real initiative on the part of the administration, both in terms of legislative advancement as well as executive action from the president. It was this chasm—between the yearning and the unmet need—that was the natural predecessor of any urgent movement for change.

COURAGE IS JUST A LACK OF OPTIONS · 4

T HE DOMA DUSTUP HAD BEEN THE PERFECT MOMENTUM builder for the upcoming LGBT march on Washington, which was set to take place on October 11, 2009. David Mixner had called on the young leaders of the movement to take up the banner of equality and freedom and they had. Just as the idea for the march had originated outside of Washington, so did the energy that fueled it. It was the same external power source that Paul Yandura and Jonathan Lewis would soon tap into to help create an insurgent force Democrats hadn't seen from LGBT activists in nearly two decades.

The last time gay activists had risen up to circumvent the inertia of the US government was during the AIDS crisis of the '80s, when scores of gay men were fighting for their lives in the face of widespread antipathy from politicians and policy makers. That period would produce what was arguably the most defining direct-action group the LGBT movement would ever see—ACT UP. And the successes of AIDS activists in the '80s served as an inspiration for the next generation of LGBT leaders who were starting to assert themselves on the national stage.

Robin McGehee was at the front of the charge to organize the 2009 National Equality March. Working alongside her as codirector was her counterpart Kip Williams, a San Francisco activist. Following the Prop 8 loss, Williams helped organize a wave of protests that swept across the state for months, including several arrestable actions in which he participated and a six-day march from San Francisco to Sacramento in March of 2009.[1]

Williams first met McGehee at a community town hall in February of 2009, during which about four hundred activists packed into San Francisco's Bill Graham Civic Auditorium to grill leaders of the No On 8 campaign on their failure. Community activists were incensed; they felt that the campaign's architects had excluded them from the process. Geoff Kors, then of Equality California, Kate Kendell of the National Center for Lesbian Rights, and campaign manager Steve Smith bore the brunt of the furor. It was emblematic of what often seemed like a continual rift between community activists and the groups that are charged with representing them. Among a number of missteps in the campaign, some would-be volunteers had been turned away—told their help was not needed. Williams was one of them. So in the weeks leading up to the election he had chosen to focus his energy instead on measures affecting undocumented immigrants and the state's prison system.[2]

But on that February night in 2009, he and McGehee waited till the drubbing was over before taking the stage to tell the audience members about two separate events they were each organizing in which participation was very much welcome. As McGehee took to the mic to rally support for her upcoming Meet in the Middle rally in Fresno, Williams stood in the wings and thought, *Who is that?* She seemed to embody the very spirit and passion that he imagined once emanated from famed activist Harvey Milk. Williams adored her from the start. Both Southerners by birth—she from Mississippi and he from Tennessee—the two became fast friends.[3]

McGehee and Williams were handpicked as codirectors of the National Equality March by Cleve Jones, who had worked on Harvey Milk's campaign for supervisor and then served as a student intern in his office in the '70s. Following Milk's assassination, Jones eventually became a movement leader in his own right. Among other things, he hatched the idea for the AIDS Memorial Quilt in November of 1985. The quilt has since grown to incorporate more than forty-eight thousand three-by-six-foot panels that commemorate individuals who were lost to the epidemic.[4]

Williams first met Jones in March of 2008 when he was doing guerilla interviews with his handheld camera in front of San Francisco City

Hall during filming of a scene from the movie *Milk*. Jones was serving as a historical adviser on the film, and Williams quizzed the longtime activist about his hopes for the movie. Jones' words proved prescient. He wanted young people to rediscover the roots of the gay rights movement, to remind them of its essence before the AIDS epidemic that so consumed activists during the '80s and the commercialism that came of age in the '90s.

"I want them to remember that we were born out of a revolutionary movement . . . the antiwar movement and the women's movement," he told Williams. "We felt that we were part of a larger revolution for peace and for social justice, and I think that much of that has been lost and it angers me and it frightens me.[5]

"If your generation of young people don't know our history," Jones continued, "you will not be prepared to fight. And I may be wrong, but history is full of examples where people who thought they were free woke up one morning and discovered they weren't free, and they had to fight or die."[6]

It was a sentiment born of a generation of gays who had been delivered by the urban-inspired freedom of the '70s only to be orphaned again by the AIDS-induced horror of the '80s. The metropolises that had wholeheartedly embraced them, it turned out, were still governed by a larger organism that systematically rejected them even as they died by the thousands. For those who escaped the plague's clutches, survival had become a part of their muscle memory. And to some, surviving meant conforming, blending in. To others, Jones and Mixner among them, surviving meant fighting.

After *Milk* made its world premiere at the Castro Theatre on Tuesday, October 28, 2008—exactly one week before the devastating Prop 8 loss—Jones began touring with the film, delivering his message about pushing and organizing and agitating for change to young people at screenings across the state. McGehee had seen the movie and was inspired to reach out to Jones in February 2009 to help spread the word about Meet in the Middle. Talking over sushi at a Palm Springs restaurant, McGehee told Jones her story and pitched him on the May 30 rally. He was in immediately.[7]

"Look," he told her, "I've got all these organizers from all across the nation and even internationally that are totally enthralled with all this

Prop 8 stuff, and we need to capitalize on that." Jones wanted to take the fight beyond California. He had not initially been enthused by the idea of a national march—they were costly endeavors and often fostered infighting as people jockeyed for speaking slots. But early in 2009, Jones began to believe the national groups were totally missing the moment. After Mixner made his call for a national rally in Washington later that year, Jones figured he had an opening and the young organizers to make it happen. At the Meet in the Middle rally on May 30, Jones officially announced, "We are going to take this campaign to Washington! We met in the middle. Next we meet on the mall!"[8]

Jones was done fighting small battles one by one. He wanted full federal equality. "Even if Prop 8 is overturned," he told the cheering crowd, "we are still second class citizens, because you know as well as I do: the most important rights granted to heterosexuals through marriage are those determined not by the states but by the federal government." Jones aspired to nothing short of full equal protection under the law in all matters governed by law in all fifty states. It may seem obvious in hindsight, but it sounded revolutionary to the young organizers he was meeting at the time. The movement had been accumulating rights and protections piecemeal—state by state, city by city, and company by company—since its inception. The federal government had been a lost cause for decades, particularly in terms of legislative remedies. But with the Democrats in full control of Congress and the Oval Office, Jones had reason to hope.[9]

From that moment on, Jones became the public face of the march; Mixner, with his organizing background, became a constant behind-the-scenes source of direction and calm; and a new generation of organizers worked the field, even if much of it was virtual. One of the toughest challenges from the beginning was finding a way to incorporate everyone who wanted to help—McGehee and Williams absolutely didn't want to recreate what they saw as the exclusionary, top-down nature of the No On 8 campaign. When Jones began forwarding them every e-mail he received about the march, his one mandate was that every e-mail got a response and everyone who wanted to help could help. It was overwhelming to say the least. Initially, the march had an executive committee of about a dozen people, but once the ball got rolling they formed a larger national steering committee of about one hundred people who took part in weekly calls. The effort also got a big assist from Join the Impact's Willow Witte, who joined the steering committee. Witte sent out organizing e-mails on behalf of the march to her list of about two hundred committed activists who had taken the lead on organizing rallies across the nation in the immediate aftermath of the Prop 8 loss.[10]

The national groups, like HRC and the National Gay and Lesbian Task Force, among others, offered little-to-no help at the outset of the enterprise. They charged that the planned march wasn't good strategy and that the organizers were politically naïve about the ways of Washington. They worried that such an event would only drain resources from other priorities. As the ever-caustic gay Congressman Barney Frank told the Associated Press on the eve of the march, "The only thing they're going to be putting pressure on is the grass."[11]

The marchers, meanwhile, accused the Washington groups of living in ivory towers while they sucked up millions of dollars of the community's money without having secured any federal rights for some thirty years. They had tired of waiting. By this point, people like Jones and Mixner had been waiting a lifetime for equality. The two men knew the power that laid in drawing a mass of protesters together. The visibility alone would spur more involvement nationwide and more actions would flow from that. Mixner, in particular, thought the administration needed to feel the heat, given Obama's tepid steps forward on LGBT rights. But it was really the younger generation of activists like McGehee and Williams who felt the fire. They refused to believe that change would have to wait for another day. They may not have known exactly what the future held for them, but they would not let it be defined by inertia.

This shared animosity between the marchers and the Washington groups left little room for constructive dialogue. Since the groups weren't pitching in, Mixner realized he would have to look elsewhere to help boost the march's momentum and profile. Mixner managed to line up nearly 150 A-list endorsements for the march, ranging from well-known LGBT movement leaders to celebrities like Oscar winners Charlize Theron and producer Bruce Cohen.[12]

Initially, McGehee was turned off by the celebrity hype—it was too HRC-esque. But when Mixner scored the support of Urvashi Vaid, the former executive director of the National Gay and Lesbian Task Force,

McGehee was duly impressed. As a young closeted lesbian attending a small Southern Baptist school in Hattiesburg, Mississippi, McGehee remembered seeing excerpts in her local paper from a speech Vaid had given at the 1993 March on Washington for LGBT Rights. She had followed up by getting the entire text of Vaid's speech, in which she asserted, "The gay rights movement is an integral part of the American promise of freedom." They were words that had inspired McGehee ever since. [13]

Though Vaid had spearheaded the 1993 effort to organize a march, this time around the Task Force wouldn't officially endorse the march until about a month before it took place. HRC also gave its blessing in a measured August statement in which Joe Solmonese said he considered the march "a starting point—not a destination" and said HRC's mission was to help participants become "citizen lobbyists" after the march was over. The word "endorse" was never used in the statement. [14]

But behind the scenes, Jones and Mixner were still taking a ton of heat from the Washington establishment. Various movement leaders were contacting them to dissuade them from going through with the march. The young organizers themselves were also sweating it out. They had been focusing mainly on drawing student activists from large campuses close to DC. It was a great strategy, one ripped straight from the playbook of Mixner's antiwar organizing days. Then Williams had the idea of contacting LGBT student groups at all the colleges within a 150-mile radius of DC and getting them to commit to bringing at least one busload of people. Unfortunately, it was already September and in order to execute in time for the October march, they would need to hire a team of organizers. Money was tight and nearly everyone working on the march was a volunteer. So a friend put Williams in touch with Paul Yandura in order to ask for some financial backing from Jonathan Lewis. [15]

Yandura had his own concerns about the march. Unlike others in Washington, he didn't think it was misguided. But even if it was successful, he wondered how that energy could be translated into a sustainable force for change. He declined to give Williams the $25,000 the organizers sought. But if the march hit its mark, he said his door would certainly be open for a follow-up conversation. [16]

About a month before the march, the steering committee convened their weekly phone call. They worried that not enough people would show up. Mixner, who was not as immersed in the day-to-day details of the organizing, kept their sights on the big picture. "You're not going to know the exact moment when they'll come, but you'll feel it building," he told them. Mixner thought the momentum was there. The march was generating a lot of stories and blog posts in the LGBT media, and he'd noticed that about sixty thousand people had "liked" the event on its Facebook page.[17]

"Can you all tell me what that means?" he asked. "Will all sixty thousand come, or is that just sixty thousand saying they liked the idea? Give me a gauge on that and then I'll be able to tell you how many I think are going to come."[18]

Of that sixty thousand, the organizers told "Mr. Mixner" (as they had taken to calling him), they thought maybe forty thousand to fifty thousand would come. It wasn't an exact science, but probably forty thousand at least, they guessed.[19]

"Well then, I think we're just fine," he said.

How could he be so sure?

"No one comes to a march alone," Mixner told them. "For every single person on that list that you think in reality is coming, add two more. If you believe in your heart that 40,000 is a solid number, then we will have a minimum of 120,000 people there. As far as I'm concerned, that's a successful march."[20]

To McGehee, it was a Field of Dreams speech—if you build it, they will come.

For the most part, Mixner had handed the organizing reins to the younger activists. Though he had taken to blogging in recent years, he didn't understand exactly how to leverage new media as an organizing tool. In the '60s, he and his associates would get a central office, work the phones, and check the mail for donations. But he realized it was a different time, and he had placed an enormous amount of trust in these young organizers. He also felt like he had as much at stake politically and personally as he had at any time since that midsummer day in 1993 when he was arrested in front of the White House. But after that September steering committee phone call, he was convinced they were going to pull this thing off.[21]

Still, many of his contemporaries assured him he was wrong. Privately, they made the case for waiting to pressure Obama until the second term, telling Mixner that pushing LGBT issues forward so soon would hurt the president and jeopardize his reelection chances. A week before the march, he received two harried calls from individuals associated with HRC—one a high-level staffer and another a board member. Neither was calling in an official capacity, but their message was the same: *You've got to cancel this. I don't know anyone who's coming. It's going to be a disaster.*[22]

They were stressful and often heated phone calls for Mixner, but he managed a chuckle. "Of course you don't know anyone who's coming— it's all young people," he said. Besides, he told them, he couldn't cancel it even if he wanted to. It wasn't his march anymore.[23]

IT WAS A GLORIOUS fall day that October 11 of 2009. People streamed onto the Capitol's West Lawn wielding their equality signs and rainbow flags. The air swelled with the energy of the thousands gathered to exercise their First Amendment rights and demand equal treatment under the law. Now. Not at some future date, at some magical hour, when it proved convenient for Washington. They wanted it now.

I stood next to Mixner as he beamed at the throng of roughly 150,000 to 200,000 marchers from his perch near the stage. He had been fighting an illness his doctors couldn't exactly place. But despite being in a wheelchair, he was practically levitating that day.

"I told you they would come," he said to me, responding to his detractors. "Never underestimate the power of people who want their freedom."[24]

The march was a huge success by anyone's standards, teeming with young people and enlisting a whole new generation of troops in the cause of freedom and equality. In their speeches, veteran LGBT leaders like Urvashi Vaid and civil rights icons like Julian Bond of the National Association for the Advancement of Colored People reminded marchers of where we had been and envisioned where we might go. C-SPAN carried the political theatre live as the fledgling rally took flight.

Mixner rose from his wheelchair to address the crowd. "Let us be clear to America—we are looking at a system of gay apartheid," he told them, commanding the podium in a black suit and dark sunglasses. "One set of laws for LGBT citizens and another set of laws for the rest of

America. Oh, no you don't!" he admonished, looking more the part of a Secret Service agent than someone who had cycled in and out of intensive care for the past few months.[25]

Lieutenant Dan Choi took the stage in his US Army dress blues and closely cropped hair—every bit the officer with the exception of a strip of ripped black tape concealing his mouth. Choi had become a minicelebrity since coming out on *The Rachel Maddow Show* on March 19, 2009. He had spoken at numerous rallies and been featured on a multitude of news segments. After tearing off the tape for his speech, Choi denounced "don't ask, don't tell."

"The era and the time for asking is over. I am not asking anymore. I am telling. I am telling. I am telling," he proclaimed, rhythmically thrusting his fist into the air, his index finger pointed to the heavens.[26]

Even megastars challenged President Obama directly from the stage. "Are you listening?" pop singer Lady Gaga yelled, declaring the event "the single most important moment" of her career. "We will continue to push your administration to bring your promise to reality."[27]

Gaga—and the march organizers—had good reason to believe Obama would be listening. The night before, Gaga had performed at HRC's annual fundraising gala where President Obama had been the keynote speaker. His scheduled appearance had been announced only a week before the event, and many activists believed it was a last-minute decision made in response to the planned march. Beyond training their sights on "don't ask, don't tell," activists were desperate to hear Obama weigh in on a November ballot initiative that sought to block Maine's same-sex couples from receiving the marital rights they had been granted just months earlier by the legislature.

Maine's marriage equality law had been set to go into effect on September 12 but was put on hold pending the outcome of a special election to be held November 3, 2009. In many ways, it felt like a replay of California's Proposition 8 all over again (though Golden State couples were already marrying by the time Prop 8 passed). Winning in Maine would be an absolute first: citizens actually affirming the right of same-sex couples to marry by popular vote. Losing would be another tragic loss for the LGBT community and a huge political setback, suggesting that only state courts and legislatures were ready and willing to legalize gay marriage. LGBT activists, anticipating a potential "People's Veto" in

Maine, had been clamoring for months for President Obama to oppose the ballot measure as he had done in writing with Prop 8 a year earlier. Obama's approval ratings were still riding relatively high in Maine at the time—58 percent—giving the president potential sway with the electorate there. The HRC event was a real opportunity for President Obama to make some sort of definitive statement about Maine's ballot measure, which would have the benefit of yielding both video and audio for potential campaign ads against the referendum.[28]

On the day Obama's HRC appearance was made public, I interviewed Mixner about the event. He said, "I'm really hoping the president comes out against the initiative in Maine. I can't see any reason why he wouldn't do it there and I'm sure HRC made that a contingency." Mixner wasn't nearly as sanguine as he sounded; he was simply applying pressure by raising the bar of expectation. He had heard from a confidant inside the West Wing that the president's decision to speak at HRC's gala was a direct result of the thousands of marchers who would be descending on Washington to express their discontent with his leadership. From HRC's perspective it was a total win. They had the most coveted political keynote in the country coming to their dinner, which would be a fundraising boon while also establishing them as one of the most powerful political groups in Washington.[29]

But the juxtaposition between the donor class and the activists was classic. It was the worker bees, the boots on the ground, that had fueled Obama's urgency. Yet it was the moneyed elites who got the benefit of seeing the president deliver a feel-good speech that was long on poetry and short on specifics. He could point to nothing concrete indicating that his administration had begun serious work on his main campaign pledge to end the military's gay ban. At that point, there still wasn't even a Senate sponsor for a repeal bill and, consequently, one hadn't been introduced. So President Obama ticked through a list of lesser accomplishments, celebrated the impending passage of hate crimes (which would come two weeks later), then recommitted himself to the cause of repeal without intimating a timeline.[30]

"I will end 'don't ask, don't tell.' That's my commitment to you," he said emphatically, as the crowd sprang to their feet for a standing ovation. It was the best he could offer in the moment. The closest he came to addressing the Maine measure was when he said, "I believe strongly in stopping laws designed to take rights away and passing laws that extend equal rights to gay couples." But notably, he never uttered the word "Maine" or referenced Washington State, where another ballot measure was aimed at overturning a robust domestic partnership measure passed by state lawmakers. Specifying a state or states would have given the statement far more teeth.[31]

HRC had done what almost any other lobby in Washington would have done—it had given cover to the most powerful entity in the country by providing Obama a platform and an opportunity to speak about his efforts on behalf of LGBT Americans. Yet the organization's leadership had failed to make any specifics—like the Maine ballot initiative, for instance, or a timeline for repeal—a condition of the speech, as Mixner had suggested. Now, when critics charged that the LGBT community was unhappy with the president or that he wasn't giving gays enough time, the White House could point to the HRC appearance as evidence that it wasn't true. For their part, HRC leaders like Joe Solmonese had endeared themselves to the White House while also being able to claim they had extracted a strong commitment from the president on ending the military's gay ban. Solmonese even sent a statement to HRC supporters urging patience and arguing that Obama's record shouldn't be judged until the end of his second term (which also assumed there would be one).

"It's not January 19, 2017," Solmonese wrote on October 9, 2009, just two days before the march. To give the President that much space was effectively giving away any leverage the organization had—HRC couldn't legitimately criticize the president for the rest of his presidency nor would the White House have cause to fear them. What's more, the president's speech occupied the most high-profile headlines in the days to come. In much of the mainstream coverage, the next day's protest had been reduced to a footnote to the story.[32]

But in many ways the very fact of President Obama's appearance signaled that the march had done its job. Mixner was fond of the saying, "Courage is just a lack of options," something one of his civil rights heroes, Fannie Lou Hamer, once told him. The march had effectively left Obama with no option but to make a bold and highly visible pledge on LGBT rights, in much the same way the DOMA brief had left activists with no choice but to make their discontent eminently clear.

For all of the movement's successes, same-sex marriage rights were revoked in Maine only a few weeks later. Obama's silence on the ballot initiative during his HRC speech was only compounded when Attorney General Eric Holder traveled to the University of Maine to address an audience of about 850 people on October 23, 2009. *The Maine Campus* newspaper noted that Holder spoke about overturning DOMA, closing Guantanamo Bay, and not prosecuting medical marijuana users. When he was asked about Maine's ballot measure, however, Holder stuck to the administration's talking points.[33]

"[The president and I] are of the view it is for states to make these decisions," Holder said, making no mention of Obama's oft-stated opposition to discriminatory laws. He was basically staying in his lane as attorney general, but the administration's continual avoidance of the issue in the weeks preceding the vote inflamed activists once again.[34]

Mixner took Holder's abstention to task on his blog on Election Day, November 3, 2009, writing that President Obama and his team were "zero help in this critical battle."[35]

"Despite repeated pleas for assistance from this community from the start of the campaign, [Obama] chose to ignore every opportunity to grant us such relief," Mixner charged. "The most we were able to get out of the White House office of communications was that he was opposed to such efforts. Try weaving that into a powerful ad or robo-calling!" As Mixner's rant suggested, the specter of Prop 8 still loomed large in the minds of advocates.[36]

Polls leading up to the Maine vote were neck and neck, with an October 20 poll showing a dead-even split—48 percent of voters supporting the measure and 48 percent opposing it. But by November 2, the same firm, Public Policy Polling, found the pro-LGBT side was slipping, with 51–47 percent now in favor of quashing equal access to marriage rights. In that poll, as Mixner cited in his post, 28 percent of Maine voters who supported Obama also indicated they would vote against marriage equality.[37]

The Holder remark, Mixner concluded, basically gave all those voters "permission to vote against our freedom."

The effort to defeat the measure was run by a young but successful Maine campaigner, thirty-one-year-old Jesse Connolly, who had a string of wins behind him. In 2004, he had delivered all four of Maine's electoral votes to the Kerry/Edwards ticket, though George W. Bush ultimately won the national election. The next year he helped defeat a referendum that sought to remove gays and lesbians from the state's human rights code. It was a ballot-box battle that had been twice waged and twice lost by LGBT activists in both 1998 and 2000, when Maine voters rejected the protections state lawmakers had added for gays in the state's nondiscrimination code. In 2006, Connolly logged another win, steering Maine Governor John Baldacci to reelection.[38]

Connolly, a straight ally whose father, Larry Connolly, had introduced Maine's first gay rights bill as a representative in 1977, knew the state's political landscape and understood the issue. The "No On 1/Protect Maine Equality" campaign had focused on several significant goals: engaging the grassroots in the campaign through regular blogger calls, deploying a robust field operation of door knockers, and waging a well-funded, muscular campaign. The effort ultimately raised $6.6 million, almost twice as much as the $3.4 million raised by the anti-gay contingent, "Stand for Marriage Maine."[39]

Despite an operation that appeared to have out-organized the opposition on nearly every level, the measure was approved by Maine voters, 53–47 percent, overturning the marital rights of same-sex couples in the state. It was a heartbreaker. The California effort to fight Prop 8, though ultimately well funded, was a sloppy campaign that required a huge course correction and the installation of a new campaign manager a little over a month before the vote. The Maine campaign, by contrast, had been a relatively coordinated effort with a seasoned campaign operative at the helm. No campaign is ever perfect and in hindsight flaws can always be found, but the Maine effort was solid, making its failure all the more frustrating.[40]

Activists felt twice betrayed by Obama. In fact, he and his team had spent the entire year dodging the issues of same-sex marriage and relationship recognition. Their reticence may not have been the decisive factor in Maine, but it certainly hadn't helped us there.

What seemed exceedingly clear by the end of 2009 was that activists were going to have to rage against the administration at every turn in order to extract concessions, like a far more friendly DOMA brief or discernible forward movement on repeal. HRC was not going to be any help in that respect. By year's end, the organization had come down decisively on the side of the administration. If anything, HRC's leadership had undermined the efforts of activists by giving Obama a pass until the end of his second term and allowing him to upstage the National Equality March.

It was these constant betrayals that made Paul Yandura and Jonathan Lewis even more certain that it was time for something unorthodox—something that would disrupt the natural order of how LGBT issues were handled in Washington and the cozy relationship between Beltway advocates and the Democratic Party. Yandura, for all his initial skepticism, had been impressed by the march organizers. He contacted Kip Williams, asking to meet with him and Robin McGehee before they left town for California. They accepted. That meeting, which took place the Monday following the march, would mark the beginning of a collaboration that unleashed an unusually efficient force for change on Washington. Yandura told the two activists he wanted to arrange for them to meet with Jonathan Lewis, who was fed up with the administration's pace on LGBT issues, among other things.

In December, McGehee and Williams flew to Florida for the meeting. McGehee felt like she had stepped on to the set of the '80s TV show *Miami Vice* as the gate opened onto the Lewis compound in Miami's swanky Coconut Grove suburb. It was a rolling multi-acre estate with structures made of coral reef slabs covered with Spanish-style terracotta roofing. Lush, native vegetation studded the grounds under a canopy of palm trees. *Where the heck am I?* she thought. *The guy who owns this place wants to talk to me about activism?* It all seemed preposterous.[41]

But McGehee and Williams would soon sense just how serious Lewis was. He was frustrated. It didn't matter which organization or person he donated to, how well connected or even well intentioned they were, nothing was happening. He had been giving money for years. Finally, the cumulative effect just got to him. One morning, he woke up angry. He was tired of excuses and hearing why things couldn't be done. He wanted action and, in his view, none of the Washington insiders were angry enough. The LGBT leaders in the Beltway were all too comfortable and close to the administration to create a revolution.[42]

As the three sat in a little wooden boathouse overlooking the water, Lewis told McGehee and Williams that he wanted people who were going to really shake things up. McGehee lamented the state of HRC, and Lewis agreed. Despite having given the group $1 million, he felt disenfranchised, just as McGehee did. She had always kept an HRC bumper sticker—the signature yellow equal sign highlighted by a blue backdrop—affixed to her car. She had always believed the group was fighting for her equality. But now that she had canvassed against Prop 8 and organized two major rallies (one statewide and one national), she began to feel that HRC had done as little as possible to help her cause. Worse yet, they didn't seem to see any value in tapping into the energy she was trying to harness to pressure the administration to make good on Obama's campaign promises.[43]

Lewis was blown away by McGehee's passion, much the way Williams had been when he first met her. He resolved to give them the money to start a group, which ultimately amounted to $440,000 by the end of 2010. No one knew exactly what the group would do, but Lewis was certain he had found the right people for the job. He wanted young firecrackers at the helm who weren't bogged down by stale Washington notions of how things should be done. He wanted something unpredictable. In his eyes, there was nothing to lose but the status quo.

ON JANUARY 13, 2010, Paul Yandura walked into the HRC headquarters in Washington, a scene that was dramatically different from the rousing meeting Lewis, Williams, and McGehee had had only weeks earlier. It was an off-the-record gathering of about twenty movement leaders—including key lobbyists, gay group representatives, and advisers to major LGBT donors like Jonathan Lewis, Tim Gill, and Jon Stryker. The meeting was billed as a legislative strategy session for the upcoming year, and Yandura couldn't believe his ears. David Smith of HRC was explaining that although they had "positive signals" from the White House on its intent to end "don't ask, don't tell," they still weren't sure if the White House would prioritize repeal in 2010 much less how they might achieve it.[44]

'If' they're going to do it . . . IF? Yandura thought. We are totally screwed.

Smith eventually distributed an eight-page memo HRC had generated detailing a 2010 lobbying campaign they had in the works with an estimated cost of $2.6–$2.9 million. As long as chief advisers to major donors are in the room, it never hurts to put a dollar amount on things.[45]

For Yandura, it was too little, too late. Throughout 2009, HRC leaders, who enjoyed the closest relationship with the administration, had been saying the White House had a plan to achieve legislative goals like ending the military's gay ban. Now the midterms were looming—which often sends Washington politicians running on any vote that seems the least bit risky—and Smith was revealing that HRC was completely in the dark. In some ways, Yandura wasn't surprised. Since September of 2009, he and the other donor advisers—who informally functioned as a group—had been requesting high-level meetings with White House staff to discuss the plan for repeal but had been rebuffed. If that plan existed, Yandura figured, the White House would not have dodged such meetings for months on end.[46]

Once Smith finished outlining the state of play, nearly everyone had a chance to speak. Aubrey Sarvis of Servicemembers Legal Defense Network, which had spearheaded the repeal effort in 2009, said that the best strategy for overturning the policy was to have repeal language included in the Pentagon's budget bill, formally known on the Hill as the National Defense Authorization Act (NDAA). If the White House stipulated that the Pentagon include repeal in its policy transmittals to the Hill, then repeal language would already be folded into the text of the bill. This would circumvent the need for adding repeal as an amendment, which would otherwise require a vote. Sarvis had essentially pushed the White House and the Pentagon on the same strategy the year before, but his advocacy had been all but ignored by the administration. Sadly, he admitted, he had no idea what the White House would choose to do in 2010, but achieving repeal without the administration's backing would be a nearly impossible task.[47]

Winnie Stachelberg of the Center for American Progress (CAP), a DC-based progressive think tank, said her organization had commissioned a series of polls and focus groups that would help test the best way to frame repeal in order to garner public support. CAP had also produced a report suggesting that Congress could repeal the policy legislatively in 2010 while allowing the military's implementation of repeal to take place over a longer period of time. This approach was gaining traction among advocates because it would secure the legislative win before the end of the year but still give the Pentagon a say in how quickly to formalize the policy change within its ranks. The military never likes to be told what to do or when to do it, and getting military buy-in was essential if the repeal effort was going to succeed.[48]

When the floor was opened for questions, Yandura asked Smith why they were all sitting around one year into the administration wondering *if* the White House would decide to engage. Less than a year ago, Solmonese had emerged from a closed-door session with Jim Messina saying there was "a plan" in place for LGBT legislation. Yet HRC had failed to warn movement leaders that they had no idea what the administration was actually doing on priorities like repeal or passing employment non-discrimination protections.[49]

Aaron Belkin of The Palm Center also expressed concern over the lack of clear White House engagement. Early in 2009, The Palm Center had produced a report arguing that the president had the authority to stop the discharges immediately during a time of war. Their approach was slightly different from SLDN's, but both groups had publicly pressured the White House to take immediate action toward overturning the policy.[50]

Pressure became a central point of contention among the advocates in the room. Smith stressed that this administration didn't like being embarrassed or attacked and wouldn't respond to such criticism. Some others agreed. Indeed, pressure might just push them to do the opposite of what activists sought. Stachelberg added that the chances of ever being louder than opponents of repeal were slim anyway. Better to focus on strategy.[51]

Some of the criticism of pressure tactics was clearly aimed at SLDN and The Palm Center. But Yandura, for one, was pleased to see that not everyone fell into the nonpressure camp. His major takeaway from the meeting was that the advocates were still sitting around waiting on marching orders from the White House. He thought any serious lobbying strategy should have been laid out in 2009 with clear benchmarks along the way. In fact, he had told Brian Bond in the fall of 2009 that if the White House formulated a plan to achieve repeal by a certain date, Jonathan Lewis and other donors would help fund whatever was needed, such as additional polling or research. Yandura was leery of funding anything unless the White House agreed to a specific strategy. He wanted to be able to hold them accountable for their end of the bargain. But now the entire effort was behind the eight ball.[52]

Everybody learned a little something from that meeting. Those closest to the White House found out that the grassroots was restless and inaction wasn't going to go over very well—a message that was surely carried back to the administration. If the National Equality March had sent a message of broad disillusionment, this meeting underscored the need for specific action. On the other side of the debate, the more activist elements in the room realized just how little collaboration had actually been taking place between the White House and the LGBT groups. They may have been meeting from time to time, but it was a one-way dialogue. The White House was calling the shots.[53]

The next day, January 14, Yandura joined Robin McGehee and Kip Williams, and two other LGBT activists—Stacey Simmons and Mark Reed—in New York for another round of talks with a very different tenor. Yandura had asked Richard Socarides to set up several meetings with some storied gay activists so McGehee and Williams could glean insights from them as they embarked on their new venture. They had several separate meetings during that mid-January trip, including one with David Mixner and two others with people who had been heavily involved in ACT UP, the revolutionary grassroots group that formed in New York in 1987 in response to government inaction on AIDS.

ACT UP stood for AIDS Coalition to Unleash Power. The organization sought to raise awareness about the deadly public health crisis that was unfolding by challenging politicians, medical professionals, and the public conscience through direct action protests and demonstrations. ACT UP was sparked, at least in part, by a speech that writer and activist Larry Kramer gave at New York's Lesbian and Gay Community Services Center. One evening in March of 1987, Kramer told the group that two-thirds of the men in the room might die within five years. "If what you're hearing doesn't rouse you to anger, fury, rage, and action, gay men will have no future here on earth," he exhorted. Some in the federal government were just starting to realize that they had willfully allowed an insidious and pernicious disease to take hold of the nation. As journalist Randy Shilts noted in his epic book *And the Band Played On*, when President Ronald Reagan finally declared AIDS "public health enemy No. 1" in April of 1987 during his first major speech on the epidemic, "36,058 Americans had been diagnosed with the disease; 20,849 had died."[54]

Kramer was outspoken, brash, and sometimes off-putting. He was often a man ahead of his time, and as such, misunderstood and under-appreciated by many of his peers. He had originally helped cofound a group known as the Gay Men's Health Crisis (GMHC) in his living room in 1981 just as a strange and nameless illness began claiming the lives of his friends. But two years later he separated from GMHC's board in disgust over what he viewed as the organization's timidity and failure to confront the crisis head on. If GMHC was too politi-cally correct, ACT UP was the antithesis. The organization was partially born of Kramer's anger, which resonated among a younger generation of gays and lesbians who amplified it throughout ACT UP's most con-sequential years in the late '80s and early '90s. Its motto, accordingly, was "Silence = Death," adopted from a logo that a small group of New York artists had originated and begun plastering all over the city in the months leading up to Kramer's pivotal speech.[55]

Ann Northrop joined the group in early 1988 after beginning work as an AIDS educator in New York. She participated in hundreds of protests but had a particular expertise in attracting press attention and communi-cating with the media after working the better part of two decades as a broadcast and print journalist. She helped democratize the group's mes-sengers by insisting that everyone be prepared to serve as a spokesperson at any given moment. Northrop, unlike Kramer, was a bridge builder by nature, though her activism was no less impassioned. She was a product of the antiwar movement, like Mixner, and also the women's movement. As a member of ACT UP, she was arrested some two dozen times for civil disobedience, including during one of the group's most high-profile actions: a 1989 protest at St. Patrick's Cathedral in New York.[56]

Northrop recounted that day to McGehee, Williams, Yandura, So-carides, and Lewis as they sat in the back room of an infamous Chel-sea diner, Moonstruck, where politicos were known to conspire. ACT UP—a truly democratic organization where absolutely everyone had an opportunity to speak their mind—had debated the action for months on end before voting to protest Cardinal John Joseph O'Connor for de-nouncing condom use as a way of preventing the spread of AIDS. They planned it meticulously and publicized the action in advance so as not to incite fear among the parishioners. On that bone-chilling December day in 1989, a glut of about 4,500 protesters flooded Fifth Avenue outside the church entrance, while undercover police officers, the police chief, and Mayor Ed Koch all took to the pews inside. As the cardinal began his homily, several dozen activists inside the church began moving into place. Northrop was among a group that laid down silently in the center aisle—an idea they had taken from a group of nuns who had performed a similar action. Some protesters chained themselves to the pews. Another group began reading a statement of complaint. But when thirty-year-old activist Michael Petrelis stood on a pew and started yelling at the cardinal, "Stop killing us! Stop killing us!" chaos ensued. Northrop thought she might be trampled to death, but the police eventually steadied the situation enough to begin arresting people and carrying the uncooperative activists out on stretchers. Most of the protesters had been removed when the cardinal continued on with mass. In a final act of rebellion, activist Tom Keane went up to take communion, as several protesters had planned to do. But when the cardinal handed him the wafer—representing the consecrated body of Christ—Keane crumpled it in his hand and let it drop to the floor.[57]

That one spontaneous act drew negative headlines worldwide for days, maybe even weeks, Northrop recalled. Public officials denounced the group and even the usually sympathetic *New York Times* editorialized against the protest, saying demonstrators had "turned honorable dissent into dishonorable disruption." ACT UP members were distraught. This time, they worried, they had gone too far and turned public opinion against them. Then one ACT UP member spoke to his mother, a suburban housewife in Connecticut. She told him that before the St. Pat's action, her friends had thought of gays as weak and wimpy. Now, she said, they viewed them as strong people who were really angry about something and ought to be taken seriously. If suburban women in Connecticut could receive that message amid the maelstrom of controversy, then the protesters had accomplished their mission. Essentially, Northrop told the budding activists before her, don't be too worried about the initial response to any one action. Just be confident that you have the moral high ground to do what needs to be done.[58]

Yandura was particularly struck by finally meeting Northrop in person. As a White House staffer in the '90s, he had carried around a clipboard with a picture of her, Michael Petrelis, and several other ACT UP members on it. If he saw them milling around the White House, he was to call the Secret Service immediately.[59]

For Socarides, the takeaway from Northrop's talk was this: just when you think you've gone too far, you've probably struck gold. The drug companies and politicians began to fear ACT UP, and that alarm went straight up to the White House. If they would take on the Catholic Church, surely they would take on anything or anyone, including the president. That gave the group enormous power, which it successfully wielded over the coming years to extract more government funding for AIDS research and quicker access to drugs.[60]

But for McGehee, meeting Larry Kramer was the most pivotal moment. He was the godfather of it all in her eyes, and in the two-plus decades since his fiery speech at New York's Lesbian and Gay Community Services Center he hadn't mellowed a bit. His apartment in the heart of Greenwich Village was filled to the gills with artwork and books and hundreds of stacked pages of a manuscript he was working on. Far from being old and frail, he was vital and engaged. As Kramer sat in his signature attire—a pair of overalls and a T-shirt—McGehee and Williams laid out their vision. They were inspired by the sense of urgency and direction ACT UP had generated during the AIDS epidemic, and they wanted to create a group that stoked similar fervor for securing full federal equality for LGBT Americans.

Kramer told them he was amazed at the number of people the young organizers had managed to assemble at the National Equality March, especially absent the backing of the national groups. He seemed equally surprised that anyone remembered him, let alone cared what he thought. He lamented the state of the movement, ranting about the irrelevance of HRC and the Task Force. *Why aren't people angry? We're second-class citizens, for God's sake. We're at war. We need an army. We need to train people. We need to be out in the streets protesting everything and everyone*, he said.[61]

Finally, Kramer stopped. He turned to Lewis and said, "Jonathan, I want to hear clearly from you, What's your goal? What's your mission? Since you're putting in the money."[62]

Lewis was resolute. "I want to organize a revolution, plain and simple," he responded. "I want to bring to the surface the anxiety and anger I feel every day—and I'm not touched by inequality, I don't even experience it myself the way others do . . . But it demoralizes me to realize we are where we are and no one cares.

"No big thing has ever happened without agitation and the associated drama," Lewis concluded. "I want our money to bring the drama that will bring the change."[63]

Kramer loved it. "If you're not firm on a name yet, why don't you call yourself ACT UP?" he offered.[64]

McGehee and Williams were stunned. On the one hand, it was incredibly validating to have Larry Kramer place so much faith in their mission. On the other, it was a heavy burden. How could they possibly be as successful as ACT UP?

Even Kramer himself expressed some skepticism that they would be able to rally people into the streets, which is exactly what they intended to do. But Kramer had also seen what a group of committed activists could accomplish, and McGehee and Williams seemed to have the fire. He wished them every success.

WHILE YANDURA, LEWIS, McGehee, and Williams were gathering intelligence for their new mission, Washington was abuzz guessing what Obama would say at his first State of the Union address on January 27, 2010. Many commentators assumed his signature health care initiative, commonly referred to as Obamacare, would get top billing. It was then on life support after a year of negotiations in the Senate had failed to yield a compromise that could attract support from even a single Republican in the Senate. Presumably that's what would be needed to advance the health care bill—one GOP vote. Massachusetts Republican Scott Brown had shaved the Democrats' Senate majority from 60 to 59 votes when he blindsided Democrats in a January 19 special election in which he claimed the vacant seat of recently deceased Senator Ted Kennedy. It would take 60 votes to beat the filibuster that was sure to come from Senate Republicans on the health reform bill.[65]

The disastrous Massachusetts election struck fear in the hearts of progressives. A Republican had won a reliably blue seat formerly held by the esteemed "Liberal Lion" of the Senate. Democrats no longer had a veto-proof majority in the chamber. And since the White House had spent the bulk of a year focusing on health care to the exclusion of nearly all legislation other than the stimulus, the rest of Obama's progressive agenda was in tatters. Whatever he had hoped to accomplish in 2010 would now be scaled back. Anything outside of health care—immigration reform, repeal of "don't ask, don't tell," legislation to curb greenhouse gas emissions—was on the chopping block.

Brown's win also placed the reality of the midterms front and center, in case anyone in Washington had actually considered contemplating policy absent the context of politics. Pundits took the loss as a signal of where the electorate might be heading in November, and it wasn't anywhere the Democrats wanted to go. Participants of the secret "don't ask, don't tell" meeting, which had taken place at HRC headquarters several days before the special election, wagered that if Brown won, all bets would be off on overturning the gay ban. Democrats would surely stay away from social issues and focus instead on jobs, which polling continually showed was a top priority for voters. Unfortunately, no one had suggested the opposite at that strategy session—that if Brown lost, repeal would certainly make the White House agenda. It just never seemed to work that way on gay issues.

The day after the secret meeting, reports had leaked that Pentagon lawyers were advising delay of repeal until the beginning of 2011 at least. The one-page memorandum, obtained by the Associated Press, had been drafted by the in-house counsel to Admiral Mike Mullen, chairman of the Joint Chiefs of Staff. "Now is not the time" for repeal, read the memo. The continuing wars in Iraq and Afghanistan "demand that we act with deliberation."[66]

Mullen had been holding internal discussions in "the tank," the Joint Chiefs' conference room at the Pentagon, in an attempt to reach a consensus among the chiefs of the five military branches on how and when to repeal the policy. Though it wasn't surprising that some Pentagon officials were advocating delay, the fact that the memo was leaked to the media suggested that the military's anti-repeal elements were trying to influence the debate and presage the outcome. Nothing in Washington is ever leaked without intention, and this was no exception. The battle lines were being drawn, and it was equally as worrisome that no one on the pro-repeal side was returning fire. In other words, if the White House didn't agree with the nature of the leaks, it should have found a way to counter them.

The next day at the press briefing, I pressed Robert Gibbs on whether the president planned to push for repeal "this year, in 2010." The discussions were ongoing, Gibbs said, but "I don't yet have a timeline." I then asked Gibbs whether the White House was "comfortable" with the leaked reports that appeared to be "a shot across the bow from the Pentagon." That yielded a noteworthy response.[67]

"I don't believe that the opinion of one person reflects the opinion of everyone in that building nor does it reflect the opinion of everyone in this building, particularly the president of the United States," Gibbs offered.[68]

Gibbs could have ducked the question entirely; instead, he fired a warning shot back at the Pentagon, or at least at whomever had leaked the memo. He clearly set the intentions of "one person" at the Department of Defense at odds with the commander in chief himself. Everyone knows who wins that fight.

But the White House was engaging in its own internal battle. Repeal had been included in an early draft of the president's upcoming speech, which was causing consternation. Some of Obama's advisors thought they should wait on the policy. They argued that the military needed more time and they might not have the votes in the Senate. An internal memo went to the president recommending that the administration hold off on repeal, maybe even until 2012.[69]

President Obama thought differently. He wanted to keep repeal in his speech. But in the days leading up to the State of the Union, few people inside the White House knew exactly what he would say.

Yet as he stood before more than five hundred members of Congress on January 27, with House Speaker Nancy Pelosi and Vice President Joe Biden seated behind him on the rostrum to his left and right, President Obama made one of his most self-assured statements of the evening.

"This year, I will work with Congress and our military to finally repeal the law that denies gay Americans the right to serve the country they love because of who they are," he said, rhythmically driving the syllables into the ether with the charge of his loosely clenched fist.[70]

Democrats, shading the right side of the chamber, sprang to their feet immediately. Even Defense Secretary Gates rose to greet the line with applause. But immediately in front of the president, Admiral Mullen and the five service chiefs sat stone faced in their dress blues and greens with their hands folded over their laps, uniformly eschewing emotion.

It wasn't until the following week that Admiral Mullen would make his own views known in no uncertain terms. During a hearing at the Senate Armed Services Committee on February 2, both he and Secretary Gates sat at a table facing the raised semicircular dais that held members of the committee, most notably Senator Carl Levin of Michigan, the committee chair, Senator John McCain of Arizona, the committee's ranking Republican member, and Senator Joseph Lieberman of Connecticut, an Independent who caucused with the Democrats. Lieberman was hawkish on foreign policy and had supported most American interventions since Vietnam, including the Iraq and Afghanistan wars. Though he had been a Democrat until he was beaten in a 2006 primary and ultimately won reelection as an Independent, Lieberman enjoyed a much stronger relationship with the military than most Democrats. Since he had also voted against enacting "don't ask, don't tell" in 1993, certain advocates had been eyeing Lieberman as a potential sponsor of repeal legislation for several years. In August of 2009, White House aide Jim Messina had approached Lieberman's chief of staff, Clarine Nardi Riddle, about having the senator take on the bill (though Lieberman wouldn't end up introducing it until March of 2010).[71]

It was the first Senate hearing on "don't ask, don't tell" since 1993, and Secretary Gates, testifying first, got straight to the point.

"I fully support the President's decision," he said in his opening statement. "The question before us is not *whether* the military prepares to make this change, but *how* we best prepare for it."[72]

Gates announced that he had already appointed a high-level working group to immediately start reviewing the policy and the issues associated with "properly implementing" a repeal of it. The group was to produce its findings and recommendations "by the end of this calendar year." Still, Gates made certain to defer to the senators, saying, "The ultimate decision rests with you, the Congress."[73]

Gates was solid. But he looked more like a man carrying out orders than someone with a predilection one way or the other. Mullen, on the other hand, took a stand. He stated his full confidence in the process that Secretary Gates had outlined. Then he got personal.

"Mr. Chairman," he said, looking at Senator Levin then dropping his gaze back down to consult his notes.

"Speaking for myself and myself only, it is my personal belief that allowing gays and lesbians to serve openly would be the right thing to do. No matter how I look at this issue, I cannot escape being troubled by the fact that we have in place a policy which forces young men and women to lie about who they are in order to defend their fellow citizens," Mullen said, his forearms placed squarely on the table before him. "For me personally, it comes down to integrity—theirs as individuals and ours as an institution."

The room—full of reporters, policy advocates, and uniformed officers—stood still for a beat, suspended in that rare moment when history breaks discernibly from the trajectory of its past. Open service had never even been a consideration of the military leadership until President Bill Clinton broached the idea in 1993. In the seventeen years since, none of the military's top brass had publicly supported letting lesbians and gays serve openly in the armed forces. Three years earlier, Mullen's predecessor as chairman of the Joint Chiefs, General Peter Pace, had laid bare the intolerance hundreds of years in the making.

"I believe that homosexual acts between two individuals are immoral and that we should not condone immoral acts," Pace told the *Chicago Tribune* on March 12, 2007, when asked about "don't ask, don't tell." It's hard to imagine how hearing such a comment affected those who were fighting to protect Pace's right to free speech even as they served their country in silence.[74]

But Admiral Mike Mullen had entirely reshaped the landscape in three short sentences. From that day forward, *not* allowing gays and lesbians to serve authentically would arguably constitute a greater breach of integrity than allowing them to do so.

Senator McCain, a Vietnam veteran and former prisoner of war, was not pleased. In 2006, he had said, "The day that the leadership of the military comes to me and says, 'Senator, we ought to change the policy,' then I think we ought to consider seriously changing it." But now, staring down at Mullen and Gates from his perch on the dais, he made it clear that, in truth, he was vehemently opposed to repeal regardless of what certain military leaders recommended. McCain directed most of his fire at Secretary Gates, saying he was "deeply disappointed" by his comments, which were "clearly biased."[75]

"It would be far more appropriate, I say with great respect, to determine whether repeal of this law is appropriate and what effects it would have on the readiness and effectiveness of the military *before* deciding on whether we should repeal the law," McCain suggested, sounding miffed. "And fortunately, it is an act of Congress and it requires the agreement of Congress in order to repeal it."[76]

In fact, Gates was happy to defer to Congress on the matter. "I would say, Senator McCain, I absolutely agree that how the Congress acts on this is dispositive," he responded.

"Well, I hope you'll pay attention to the views of over a thousand retired generals and flag officers," McCain responded, brandishing a letter of support for the policy that was signed by a cohort of retired military officers.

The remaining Republican senators on the committee pretty much followed McCain's lead, expressing discontent over the duo's stated support for repeal. Democrats, meanwhile, generally praised their statements and the process they were engaging. One concern, expressed by Senator Mark Udall of Colorado, was whether a year-long study was necessary given that multiple well-researched studies of the policy already existed. In particular, a federally funded policy think tank called the RAND Corporation had produced an exhaustive five-hundred-page study in 1993 recommending the military adopt a policy that would "consider sexual orientation, by itself, as not germane to determining who may serve in the military."[77]

Senator Lieberman also welcomed their testimony, noting his original opposition to the policy at its inception. He then asked Secretary Gates to verify that Pentagon lawyers had concluded the policy could only be overturned through an act of Congress, not via an executive order from the president.

"That is correct," said Gates.[78]

"It's up to us—in the Congress and in the Senate," Lieberman concluded. "We've got to get 60 votes to repeal 'don't ask, don't tell' or else it will remain in effect." What Lieberman seemed to be suggesting was a stand-alone repeal bill, which would require 60 votes to reach the floor for consideration because Republicans would surely filibuster the legislation.

Levin balked. "Uh . . . unless there's a provision inside the Defense authorization bill that goes to the floor," he said. If the repeal measure were attached to the Defense funding bill by the Senate Armed Services Committee, he explained, then once the bill reached the Senate floor the 60-vote burden would be on those who wanted to strip out the repeal provision.

Levin quickly caught himself—it was a little outside of the chamber's collegial etiquette to counter a fellow Senator so bluntly, especially when they agreed on the policy. But Lieberman welcomed the suggestion.

"It is with great appreciation that I accept the higher wisdom of the chairman of the committee," Lieberman said, sharing a chuckle with his friend. "I think that's a great way to go."

Both men knew that finding the 15-vote majority needed to attach repeal to the Defense bill in the Armed Services Committee would be far easier than finding the 60 votes to pass a stand-alone repeal bill in the full Senate.

GETTING EQUAL · 5

T HE WHEELS WERE IN MOTION. THE PRESIDENT HAD SAID "this year." The highest-ranking civilian official and uniformed officer in charge of the military were in agreement with the policy change. But something didn't seem right about the timetable that was beginning to materialize for repeal. And it was already becoming crystal clear that any piece of progressive legislation that failed to gain congressional approval in 2010 would be doomed indefinitely.

Secretary Gates was laying out a sweeping study that would include an unprecedented survey of the troops' attitudes about gays and lesbians, the policy itself, and how suspension of it might personally affect them. Ultimately, the survey would seek input from some 400,000 nondeployed active duty troops and reservists and another 150,000 family members of the troops. The results would be incorporated into the working group study that was due to be completed on December 1, 2010.[1]

The study and its survey posed several major problems. First and foremost: in Washington, when you don't want to do something, you study it. It's a delay tactic, plain and simple. The only difference here was that the study's announcement was set against the backdrop of the president's definitive call for repeal. Second, many LGBT Americans had an inherent distrust of government surveys and studies, especially those conducted by an entity that had been discriminating against them since its inception. But the third was the kicker: release of the study on

December 1 would fall right in the middle of the lame-duck session, leaving only one to three weeks at best to act on the legislation before the end of the session.

The so-called "lame duck" fills the gap between the midterm elections in November and the start of the new congressional session in early January. Members who have lost their election (i.e., the lame ducks) take the final votes of their careers during this window before the newly elected members claim their seats. The last day of the two-year congressional session typically fell sometime between early-to-mid December and Christmas Day. Though many Obama-era lame-duck sessions would ultimately run a bit longer, in March of 2010, anyone who knew anything about the pace and dexterity of Congress believed that there was no chance of passing groundbreaking legislation in a one- to three-week time frame. "We'll do it in lame duck," was a tongue-in-cheek phrase sometimes uttered in Washington about legislation that didn't have a chance of passing. Yet Gates was insisting that Congress wait to vote on repeal until the study was released . . . on December 1.

The other complicating factor was that the political forecast for Democrats in the midterms was already worsening. By late February, people such as political prognosticator Charlie Cook were uttering phrases like, it's "very hard to come up with a scenario where Democrats don't lose the House." If the House fell into Republican hands, the effort to repeal "don't ask, don't tell" would be dead for the next two years of the upcoming Congress and maybe longer. There was no guarantee, either, that Obama would be reelected in 2012; repealing "don't ask, don't tell" without a receptive executive would be an absolute nonstarter.[2]

But even as the storm clouds gathered for the midterms, old Washington hands were directly linking the fate of the November elections to "don't ask, don't tell." Former Bill Clinton adviser and Democratic pollster, Douglas Schoen, warned that overturning the gay ban would turn into political disaster for Democrats at the polls.

"The Obama administration's decision to repeal 'don't ask, don't tell' may well be the right decision morally, ethically and militarily," Schoen wrote on February 7, 2010, in the *Washington Post*. "But it could have a dramatic and deleterious impact on Democratic fortunes in November. . . . I fear that the Tea Party movement, social conservatives and what is left of the Christian right will use this issue to further mobilize opposition to Democratic control of the House and Senate as we approach the fall elections. The political impact could well set back the goal of achieving full civil rights for gays and lesbians."[3]

It was quite a pronouncement for many reasons, not least of which was that it lent insight into the thinking of former Clinton aides, many of whom were still firmly entrenched in the White House. It also advanced the idea that pushing too hard to advance LGBT rights would actually doom LGBT rights. So what to do then? The implication was obviously that activists should just sit on their hands and hold their breath for that miraculous day when gay rights were wildly popular and politicians begged to take votes on them.

Like many advocates, Congressman Barney Frank was starting to worry about the White House's commitment to repeal. This was noteworthy because Frank had been a vocal defender of the administration's progress on LGBT issues in the past. In fact, he had freely belittled the efforts of those who publicly criticized the White House, like when he mocked the National Equality marchers for doing little more than pressuring "the grass." But now, Frank was just about beseeching the White House to send clearer signals on a timeline for repeal. In mid-March, he told me the administration had been "ambiguous" about repeal. "I believe that the Administration should make clear that it supports legislative action this year," he said. Later that month, Frank was even more blunt, telling *Metro Weekly*'s Chris Geidner, "They're ducking. Basically, yeah, they're not being supportive, and they're letting Gates be the spokesman, which is a great mistake."[4]

Meanwhile, the Human Rights Campaign was busy prepping to host comedian Kathy Griffin for a series of activist-oriented events in Washington. Griffin, who had a sizeable LGBT following, had decided to devote an episode of her Bravo show, *My Life on the D-List*, to "don't ask, don't tell" repeal. The organization had dedicated a number of resources to setting up high-profile events that included a swanky dinner with DC A-listers, meetings with members of Congress like Representative Frank and then-Majority Whip Jim Clyburn, and a repeal rally, which they planned to hold at Freedom Plaza on March 18, 2010. It was curious placement; located on Pennsylvania Avenue in between Congress and the White House, Freedom Plaza was not the most conspicuous location. To be sure, it created a nice photo-op looking down Pennsylvania

Avenue with the Capitol dome visible in the distance. But it wasn't close enough to either branch of government to truly qualify as a protest. Servicemembers Legal Defense Network, for instance, had held several rallies in support of repeal that had taken place either right in front of the White House in Lafayette Park or right at the footsteps of Congress on the West Lawn. The point was to let lawmakers and the president know that people were displeased and wanted action.[5]

But one advantage Freedom Plaza did offer—which probably wasn't a main concern for HRC—was that it was only a several-minute walk from the White House.

Several days before the Freedom Plaza rally, Robin McGehee had flown into Washington in anticipation of her new organization's first protest. After a good bit of deliberation, members had settled on the name GetEQUAL. Their first action was planned as a simultaneous sit-in at House Speaker Nancy Pelosi's offices in Washington and San Francisco. McGehee was tasked with coordinating the DC action, while Williams joined the protest in San Francisco. The protests just happened to be on the same day as the HRC rally.

Pelosi represented one of the most progressive districts in the country and often served as the GOP's poster child for everything that was wrong with the Democratic Party. Her formidable fundraising skills made her a cash cow for the Democrats and she was also proving to be the lynchpin to Obama's agenda. When Scott Brown won the open Senate seat in Massachusetts, she didn't throw her hands up in defeat. She went to work, rallying progressive Democrats who didn't like the Senate's more conservative version of the health care bill to vote for it nonetheless. She was also a strong supporter of gay rights. But GetEQUAL felt Pelosi was paying a lot of lip service to pro-LGBT legislation without taking a lot of action. Credible sources were telling them that the employment protections bill (ENDA) had the votes to pass but Pelosi was holding it up. In fact, the day of the protests, openly gay Congresswoman Tammy Baldwin of Wisconsin told journalist Chuck Colbert that she had "counted the votes" in the House and she believed there were enough. Not everyone held the same view, but it's often impossible to know who's right until a bill actually hits the floor. GetEQUAL wanted a vote on the legislation one way or the other—at least that way they would know which lawmakers supported it and which ones didn't. The group also wanted to send a message that talk is cheap, and that even their Democratic friends wouldn't be spared if they didn't see action on LGBT bills. Once inside Pelosi's offices, the group would refuse to leave until they had a firm commitment from Pelosi on a vote for ENDA.[6]

But McGehee also had her eye on HRC's rally. No one had been challenging the big LGBT groups (or what some derided as Gay Inc.), and she found it insulting that HRC was elevating Kathy Griffin, a comedian, as a face in the fight for repeal. The policy wasn't a laughing matter. McGehee wanted to protest the rally and call it out as a big publicity stunt that accomplished next to nothing for the movement. She called Lieutenant Dan Choi and asked him to join her in DC at the house of Paul Yandura and Donald Hitchcock, where GetEQUAL would be coordinating the actions. (The Yandura-Hitchcock household in Columbia Heights would effectively become GetEQUAL's DC headquarters over the coming months.)

Choi had been telling McGehee that he was looking for what he would do next and she had invited him to join in some of the early brainstorming sessions that she and Williams organized for GetEQUAL. It wasn't Choi's first turn with a gay group. When he originally made the Rachel Maddow appearance in 2009, he was representing Knights Out, a group of West Point alums that formed to support LGBT people attending the military academy and serving in the military. After the army initiated proceedings to discharge him, Choi sought the help of SLDN, which provided pro bono legal services to service members affected by the policy. Choi was a difficult-to-manage attention getter who often went off script—like the time he attended a hearing in the House Armed Services Committee with SLDN and cornered Admiral Mullen, introduced himself, and made a plug for repeal.[7]

McGehee had been warned that making Choi a public voice for GetEQUAL could be disastrous, but she liked the fact that he was raw and unpredictable. She had also been on the receiving end of criticism for being unseasoned and unprofessional, but the entire group was an exercise in going off script. Dan Choi knew how to use the spotlight— he *was* the show, as far as she was concerned. If his dramatic flair drew unfavorable press at times, then that was just a part of the package. GetEQUAL hadn't formed to be polished; it was the gritty underbelly of the movement. Serving in Iraq under "don't ask, don't tell" was likely to wear mentally on anyone, just like being fired from your job for being gay or being deemed a legal stranger to your child might wear on you. In fact, McGehee was having problems with her own marriage and knew firsthand the real-world toll that activism could take on one's personal life. The circumstances under which LGBT Americans lived in this country were bound to have emotional consequences, and McGehee didn't want to pretend otherwise or demand that GetEQUAL activists be perfect.[8]

As soon as she invited him to join the protest, Choi suggested getting arrested at the White House. Before hopping the bus from New York to DC, he made McGehee promise that this wouldn't just be a single action but rather the catalyst for a greater sense of urgency in the movement. McGehee said she had no plans of stopping. After hanging up, she sent a cryptic text to Yandura. "Dan is coming to DC and we need some handcuffs." No explanation. On the bus ride down, Choi reached out to his friend, Captain Jim Pietrangelo, who had served in both wars in Iraq, to see if he would join the action. Pietrangelo had started in the army as an infantryman and eventually become a JAG officer by his second tour of duty. He was honorably discharged under "don't ask, don't tell" in 2004 and became a party to a lawsuit challenging the law in 2006. After a federal judge dismissed the case and the First Circuit Court of Appeals upheld the ruling in 2008, Pietrangelo appealed the case to the Supreme Court, where it was rejected in June of 2009.[9]

Once Choi arrived in DC, he spent the night before the rally going back and forth about the action. But the next morning, he decided he was prepared to get arrested. McGehee wasn't sure it was a lock, but it was go time. They had printed up fliers with Choi's picture on it telling people that following the rally, he would be heading to the White House to say, "Enough talk. We want ACTION and we want the president to publicly state that DADT will be repealed this year." A little after 12 p.m., a handful of people jumped into Yandura's SUV and headed for Freedom Plaza. It was a heady moment; Yandura cranked up the classic Civil Rights hymn, "Ain't Gonna Let Nobody Turn Me Around." Choi demanded silence. McGehee felt aflutter with a strange mix of anticipation and uncertainty. The only thing grounding her was the action plan formulating in her head. As soon as they arrived, she would zip into the crowd and distribute the fliers as quickly as possible. Once people had them in their hands, she hoped it would compel Choi to make good on his promise.[10]

Far removed from the Freedom Plaza scene, up on Capitol Hill the Senate Armed Services Committee was simultaneously holding a "don't ask, don't tell" hearing in order to gather anecdotal evidence about how the law had affected the military. Discharged Air Force Major Mike Almy told the committee he was ousted after the air force searched his private e-mails. Almy maintained that he "upheld [his] end of this law"—never disclosing the details of his private life despite being pressured to do so by his commander. "Never once in my 13-year career did I make a statement to the military that violated 'don't ask, don't tell,'" he said. When Senator McCain had the chance to speak, he asked Almy and another discharged officer, Lieutenant Jenny Kopfstein, whether they were "confused" about the policy or its "applicability" to them when they first began serving. Almy responded, "Senator, when I came in on active duty in 1993, I will admit, I think there was a lot of confusion, on a personal level, for myself, as well for the nation and the military as a whole."[11]

In fact, there was a lot of confusion at the outset of the policy. "Don't ask, don't tell" was sold as a benign way to allow lesbian and gay Americans to serve so long as they performed their duties and kept quiet about their sexual orientation. But the policy was entirely arbitrary, with some commanders fighting to keep gay soldiers and other commanders targeting them with a witch hunt. Certain commanders turned a blind eye to potential policy infractions in hopes of keeping valued members of their team. Others initiated investigations based entirely on hearsay, regardless of whether any hard evidence existed. That's not asking or telling. That's prejudice in search of a problem. Indeed, the policy's enforcement tended to ebb and flow with the needs of the military. During times of war, when the military needed as many bodies as possible, discharges fell. With the onset of peacetime, they spiked again.[12]

The press tables weren't quite as packed that day as when Gates and Mullen testified, but they were still well populated. Ever since the State of the Union, "don't ask, don't tell" had become high-stakes news. I was busy taking notes for my story and live tweeting the testimony when I got a call from John Aravosis, who had been at Yandura's home that morning. The night before, I had been alerted that something big might be coming, but I wasn't sure exactly what. "It's on," Aravosis told me.

I packed up my computer and hailed a cab to Freedom Plaza, arriving just in time to see Joe Solmonese in jeans and a white "Repeal" T-shirt introducing Kathy Griffin to the crowd of several hundred as "our friend and our hero." Attendees cheered, waving the medley of American flags, HRC logos, and "Repeal 'Don't Ask, Don't Tell'" signs that HRC staffers had distributed among them.[13]

I took my place on a riser that had been set up for the media about forty to fifty feet across from the stage so the cameras could get clean shots of Griffin with the Capitol dome in the background. That's when I saw McGehee bolting through the crowd with her fliers. She handed one to me and other members of the media, telling us we should follow them to the White House. I tweeted out that I had just arrived at Freedom Plaza, Kathy Griffin was taking the stage, and I had just been handed a flier saying that after the rally I should follow Dan Choi to the White House where he would get arrested.

Then I tweeted, "This does not sound like it was part of the HRC script." I was letting any LGBT people who followed me on Twitter know that something unusual was about to happen. But I also knew that some members of the White House press corps followed me too. They were constantly checking their Twitter feeds and might catch wind of what was about to unfold right in front of the White House. The press corps was a ready-made pool of reporters just inside the White House gates, and I hoped some of them would cover Choi's action.[14]

Choi had approached Griffin before she took the stage and asked if he could speak. She agreed. Several minutes into her scripted rally, she invited Choi to join her. He looked battle ready, sporting standard-issue fatigues, a black beret, and a steely look of determination on his face. If he had wavered earlier, it certainly wasn't evident now.

"You've been told this week and in past weeks that the president has a plan," Choi told rally attendees. "But we know the truth—we even heard Barney Frank say it and confirm it—that the president is still not fully committed to repealing 'don't ask, don't tell' this year . . ."[15]

"Our fight is at the White House. And I am asking you to send a message to the president with me, to my commander in chief—repeal 'don't ask, don't tell,' not next year, not tomorrow, but now. Now is the time!" he bellowed, inciting the crowd. "I am going to the White House right now," he said, turning to challenge Griffin. "Kathy, will you go with me?"

Griffin enthusiastically chirped, "Of course!"

Choi named a few other people, including Solmonese, who gave him a thumb's up from off stage.

Finally, he turned to the crowd. "Will you all here go with me?" he said, raising his fist in the air as he pivoted, stepped down from the stage, and minutes later started his push toward the White House with an entourage of American flags and HRC logos trailing behind him. Griffin and Solmonese stayed behind for post-rally photo-ops, but it mattered little. Their event had supplied Choi with enough troops to cause a stir. "Hey hey, ho ho, 'don't ask, don't tell' has got to go," the cohort chanted as they followed the lead of Choi and Pietrangelo.[16]

Once they reached the White House, Choi and Pietrangelo marched to what's known as the "picture-postcard zone," right in front of the White House. At that point, Choi read a statement, with Pietrangelo looking on beside him. McGehee was just a couple paces to the right of Choi, and a US Park Police officer asked her who the organizer of the protest was. Protests at the White House happen all the time—almost weekly—and the press corps and the officers tasked with patrolling the northern border of the White House on Pennsylvania Avenue become immune to them over time. But this wasn't one of the regular protest groups, nor had the Park Police been given a heads up in advance, which is common practice with any type of arrestable action. McGehee played dumb, not wanting to answer for anything before the action played out.

Choi and Pietrangelo stood on the sidewalk facing the protesters with their backs to the White House and the black, wrought-iron fence that forms its perimeter. Both men had already locked one half of a set of cuffs around each of their wrists, using their sleeves to conceal the metal band that adorned their forearm and its unattached partner. Once they were close enough to the fence, Choi gave McGehee and Pietrangelo the nod. He used his left hand to lock the handcuffs on his right arm to the fence. Then McGehee, who was still planning to join the Pelosi sit-in later that day, jumped in to help Choi affix the cuffs on his right arm to the fence. She was stopped short, however, of doing the same for Pietrangelo. As soon as McGehee finished helping Choi, the officer who had queried her earlier grabbed her hand. "You're the organizer now," he said and arrested her. It took McGehee by surprise. In her mind, Choi and Pietrangelo were committing the arrestable offense. But as she was escorted over to the police car in cuffs and they started searching her pockets, the chaos fell away for an instant. She looked at what would become an iconic image of Dan Choi standing against the fence with his arms splayed spread eagle to either side. She looked at the White House behind him and recalled putting up signs for Obama in yard after yard across the Central Valley of California. None of it added up.[17]

"We shouldn't have to be doing this," she started yelling. "We shouldn't have to be doing this!"

Though they hadn't had time to assemble a detailed media plan for the White House action, they drew a solid round of coverage that day. White House protests may be par for the course, but handcuffing one-self to the fence in battle fatigues is not. Some cable channels broke from their wall-to-wall health care coverage—which was still three days away from final passage at the time—to take video from the scene. Then-CNN anchor Rick Sanchez marveled over "how still" Choi was on the fence. "Apparently, he's had enough," Sanchez remarked. Most news outlets ran stories of the protest online. Though White House reporters were busy with the press briefing as the protest unfolded, one of them asked Gibbs about reports that Lieutenant Choi had chained himself to the fence outside.[18]

"I was wondering if the White House was given any heads-up that there would be any kind of civil disobedience like that and whether or not the president has any plans to meet with him?" the reporter asked.[19]

"No heads-up that I'm aware of," Gibbs answered, "and I don't believe there's any meeting scheduled today, no."

Naturally, the gay blogosphere ate up the entire spectacle, fueled by live tweets and posts from bloggers like Aravosis and Sudbay and reporters on the scene from the *Washington Blade* (then called the *DC Agenda*) and *Metro Weekly*. The widely read blogger and creator of The Dish, Andrew Sullivan, posted an *Advocate* photo I had taken of Choi against the fence and declared it the "Face of the Day."[20]

Between the White House protest and the bicoastal Pelosi sit-in, thirteen GetEQUAL members were arrested on March 18, 2010: seven in Washington, and six in San Francisco, including Choi, Pietrangelo, Mc-Gehee, and Williams. Most were released that day after bail was posted, though Choi and Pietrangelo were held overnight.[21]

It was quite an entrance to the national stage. GetEQUAL had ef-fectively beaten HRC at its own game, drawing attention away from its own staid rally, and put Democratic lawmakers on notice that no one was off-limits. They had arrived. And those in Washington who weren't yet convinced would start to pay closer attention as the protests un-furled. No one knew whom they would target or what they would do next. It was exactly the type of chaos politicians despise.

GetEQUAL's timing was opportune. Their agency was about to be-come imperative. As advocates working the inside game tried to move ahead on Obama's State of the Union pronouncement, it became in-creasingly clear that Defense Secretary Gates was going to stonewall. He did not want any votes on repeal before December 1.

"I do not recommend a change in the law before we have completed our study," he told reporters during a press briefing on March 25. Asked if he thought the White House shared his views, Gates responded, "You would have to ask them, but I would tell you that my impression is that the president is very comfortable with the process that we've laid out." Gates was a by-the-book Washington veteran. He would have never claimed White House sign-off unless he actually had it. Process was paramount to him. Gates believed that any actions taken before the military understood the implications of repeal would be "very risky," as he put it in the briefing.[22]

For his part, President Obama was silent. The White House seemed to have handed off the baton entirely to the Department of Defense, and Gates was now running the show on repeal. They had clearly bar-gained that if they couldn't get military buy-in, they would never be able to get the votes for repeal (the Pentagon is one of the most pow-erful and persuasive lobbies on the Hill). It was reminiscent of the way the White House had handled health care reform—stating their intent and then leaving virtually all the details to Senate negotiators. President Obama finally managed to salvage those negotiations at the last minute by interjecting himself back into the debates in early 2010. Health care reform finally crossed the finish line on Sunday, March 21, 2010. It in-volved some legislative jujitsu, with the House finally adopting a version of the bill that the Senate had passed back in December of 2009 before

Democrats lost their 60th vote. But most importantly for LGBT activists, the completion of health care reform would presumably leave space for Democrats to enact the other pieces of progressive legislation that Obama had campaigned on—*if* they had the appetite for it.[23]

That was really the big question—would Democrats try to deliver on the agenda that progressives had voted for when they gave money, time, votes, and a good chunk of heart and soul to elevate Barack Obama to the presidency? Health care was a start, but most progressives didn't think it had gone nearly far enough to reform the system. The bill had been significantly watered down in an effort to attract Republican votes, none of which ever actually materialized. So, many progressives were still in search of the change they had believed in.

It seemed, however, that they were going to have to wait a while longer for that change. With the completion of health care reform, the White House turned to the administration's next most pressing issue: surviving the midterms. And that priority didn't leave much room for passing more pieces of contentious legislation. President Obama's popularity had been plummeting since the outset of 2010 and signing health care reform into law in March hadn't helped matters. By early April his approval ratings were running the lowest of his presidency to date—around 44 percent—fueled by the public's deep skepticism of the health care law and the lagging economic recovery.[24]

Yet for all the critiques by progressives in the party, many Democrats around the country were heartened by the passage of health care reform, so much so that the Democratic National Committee's fundraising surged in March to $13.5 million—its largest monthly intake in a nonpresidential year since 2002. The White House was trying to capitalize on that momentum by sending the president to places where he still enjoyed a certain level of popularity and star power. He logged two events in Boston on April 1 and another two in Miami on April 15, for an expected haul of about $5 million altogether. Though the prospects for keeping Democratic majorities in the House following the midterms were looking especially grim, Democrats were working to put up a firewall around the Senate, which was also in jeopardy of swinging Republican.[25]

Obama's next stop was Los Angeles, where three-term California Senator Barbara Boxer was facing one of the toughest reelection challenges of her career. Similar to the stops in Boston and Miami, the president was scheduled to do two events on April 19: one for about 1,400 small-dollar donors who paid anywhere from $100–$2,500 per ticket to see Obama speak at the California Science Center, followed by a more exclusive event for some 150 high-dollar donors who paid $35,200 per couple to dine with President Obama at Los Angeles's Natural History Museum.[26]

GetEQUAL secured six tickets to the earlier event and began formulating a strategy to interrupt the president during his speech. In many ways, Senator Boxer was beside the point to the group, even though it was technically her fundraiser. They wanted to reach the president directly and this was the first opportunity they'd had to do so since their first protests in March. In their eyes, President Obama was the key to repeal. If he wanted it included as a part of the Pentagon's budget bill— the surest way to pass it—he could push to make that happen. Realistically, such a strategy would also take the blessing of Secretary Gates. But the point was, Obama needed to push the issue and they needed to push Obama. If Gates was a roadblock, then he was Obama's problem, not theirs.

In advance of the action, GetEQUAL reached out to reporters who would be in the White House pool that night to tip them off about the protest. The White House "pooler" or "pool" is the reporter or reporters who travel with the president, taking notes on his or her whereabouts and movements between venues, and providing extra details as an eye witness to the events. A typical line from a pool report might read, "AF1 wheels down at Andrews at 9:30pm," meaning the president's plane, Air Force One, landed at Andrews Air Force Base at 9:30 p.m. For one of the president's Miami fundraisers, for instance, the pool report read, "It's a neighborhood event, people having pulled chairs into driveways to watch the happenings. Palms line the looping road that runs through the neighborhood, where many homes sit behind high walls." The pool reporter's notes are then relayed to the White House press office, which distributes it to a list of roughly two thousand to three thousand other reporters who cover the White House. Pool reports are considered to be the official notes from an event, and other reporters use them to inform their own stories. The White House later distributes official texts of the president's public speeches that reporters also pull from for direct quotes.[27]

When GetEQUAL informed the White House pool that a protest by queer rights activists was scheduled to take place that night, they were hoping to encourage a mention of the protest in the pool report so it would then be relayed to other journalists who, in turn, might include it in their articles. But whether the pooler would decide to include the action in his or her notes depended entirely on how noteworthy or successful the action turned out to be.

GetEQUAL had planned a popcorn-style interruption, with each protester delivering the same chant on a loop until they were stopped. "Mr. President, it's time to repeal 'don't ask, don't tell.' Show leadership, Mr. President. I am somebody. I deserve full equality. The time to repeal is now. It is the right thing to do." As soon as one protester was silenced by security and escorted out of the venue, another would pop up and start yelling again, and so on. Of the six protesters, three were tagged with actually interrupting the president's speech: Dan Fotou, Laura Kanter, and Zoe Nicholson. The other three—David Fleck, Michelle Wright, and Laura McFerrin Hogan—were intended to provide support to the others should they be arrested or need assistance in some way. But logistical problems upset the plan from the start. Wright, Nicholson, and Hogan got stuck in traffic, and Obama's motorcade arrived early, which only exacerbated the problem. Wright and Nicholson got out of the car and hoofed it to the venue, while Hogan searched for parking. Kanter was also held up because she forgot her ID, which left Fotou and Fleck wondering where everyone was. Eventually everyone made it into the event with the exception of Hogan, which left Nicholson without her backup.[28]

The cavernous room at the California Science Center in which the speech took place is known as The Big Lab. It features an expansive concrete floor with a rectangular reflecting pool in the middle and a high arching industrial ceiling that makes the space feel like a hangar. Importantly for the protestors, there was nothing in the room that would absorb sound other than the crowd, so it was a virtual echo chamber—ideal for disrupting the president's speech. After barely making it inside, Kanter and Wright positioned themselves to the right of the stage against the wall. Fotou and Fleck stood some thirty feet in front of the podium in the space between the stage and the reflecting pool. Nicholson planted herself in the very back, behind the reflecting pool but just in front of the risers that held all the TV cameras.[29]

Obama took the stage at 6:12 p.m. "Hello California!" he yelled enthusiastically. "I am fired up!" The president ticked off some shout-outs to certain people in the audience. Then he remarked at how much he enjoyed being back "with some of the people who were there with me at the beginning—who knocked on doors and made telephone calls, who helped us win the presidency in 2008."[30]

The crowd was eating it up. It felt like a meeting of old friends rehashing the good old days when hope was the order of the day and Obama supporters were easily united under the deceptively simple banner of "Change."

But a couple minutes into the speech, as Obama began touting Senator Boxer's contributions to the state, the chanting began. "President Obama, it's time to repeal 'don't ask, don't tell,'" yelled Laura Kanter, who was the first to initiate the protest. The event was being streamed live by CNN, and though it was hard for viewers to hear exactly what Kanter was yelling, Obama's eyes began to wander a bit as her chant interrupted his cadence. A few moments later, he cupped his hand behind his ear for an instant to hear what all the shouting was about. Then he continued on with his speech.[31]

After about a minute, Kanter was removed, and Dan Fotou started up. Fotou was positioned much closer to the president, so he was visible from the stage and his cries were far more audible and difficult to ignore.

Fotou ramped up as Obama told the crowd that Boxer was "passionate about fighting for jobs—jobs with good wages, jobs with good benefits." But Obama was starting to get distracted; he and Fotou locked eyes for a moment.[32]

"It's time to repeal "don't ask, don't tell!" Fotou yelled.

Obama stopped abruptly, looked straight at his detractor, then returned, "We are going to do that!" Fire flared in his eyes momentarily, then fell away as he pointed at Fotou, saying, "Hey, hold on a second, hold on a second. We are going to do that."[33]

The crowd was equally displeased. They came to hear Obama, not his critics. Audience members spontaneously erupted into their own pro-Obama chant: "Yes, we can! Yes, we can!" People close to Fotou told him to "Shut the fuck up," while one woman shoved her fist in his face.[34]

Obama put his hand up to calm the crowd, "Guys, guys," he said. "I agree. I agree. I agree," he said to applause. "No, no, no, no, listen. What the young man was talking about was we need to pass—we need to repeal 'don't ask, don't tell,' which I agree with and which we have begun to do."

Fotou was still yelling. "Show leadership, President Obama! Repeal 'don't ask, don't tell!' It's the right thing to do!" His cries were intermittently audible on the podium mic, spiking in between Obama's words.

GetEQUAL members had decided beforehand that even if the president tried to engage them, they weren't going to be interrupted, and they weren't going to stop. At these type of events, President Obama was more accustomed to hearing a crowd member cry out, "I love you!" to which he routinely responded, "I love you back!" But faced with the occasional heckler, he typically managed to silence them with precious little effort. Obama would allow them a moment to vent and then evoke empathy for their point of view (often by agreeing with them), which usually gave them little reason to continue. Besides, heckling a man in a room full of his acolytes isn't particularly popular. The longer you yell and the more attention you attract, the less incentive there is to continue. But GetEQUAL activists didn't want to be soothed by Obama; they wanted to make it clear that they were serious, and they didn't plan on being lulled into complacency by mere assurances.

Finally, the Secret Service reached Fotou and escorted him out of the room. The president tried to get back on track.

"When you've got Barbara Boxer, who is passionate to give people all across this state a fair shake, to put the American Dream within reach for all Americans, then what we should be worried about is how are we going to make sure Barbara Boxer gets elected," he said. "And that's mostly what I want to talk about tonight."

Just as Obama headed into the familiar territory of job loss and the economy, Zoe Nicholson picked up where Fotou left off. Obama upped his decibel, trying to push past the racket. But finally, he simply stopped, leaving Nicholson an opening to land an audible blow.

"It's time for equality for all Americans!" she shouted.[35]

Obama glared at her. "I'm sorry, do you want to come up here?" Obama said, raising his hand and waving her to the stage.

Nicholson's desires were, of course, moot. Secret Service would never let her reach the stage. But in the meantime, Kanter and Fotou had been allowed to reenter the venue under the express condition that they cease and desist.

"Can I just say, once again," Obama reiterated, "Barbara and I are supportive of repealing 'don't ask, don't tell,' so I don't know why you're hollering."[36]

Fotou knew why he was hollering—the president could request to have repeal language included in the Defense authorization bill if he chose to. He let loose, cupping his hands to create a megaphone and yelling repeatedly: "Insert the language into the appropriations bill—show our LGBT servicemembers the dignity they deserve!"

The crowd started in again on a show of solidarity with the president. "Yes, we can! Yes, we can!"

Obama paused, mystified as to how to quiet the discontent that had hijacked his speech. He stepped away from the podium momentarily, leaving the TV camera frame altogether to walk over to Senator Boxer and ask whether she had voted against the gay ban in 1993. Then he returned.[37]

"Everybody," he said, raising the flat of his hand to command the attention of the crowd. "I just checked with Barbara—so if anybody else is thinking about starting a chant, Barbara didn't even vote for 'don't ask, don't tell' in the first place, so you know she's going to be in favor of repealing 'don't ask, don't tell.'"

After taking Obama off-message for nearly eight minutes, the protesters were finally removed for good.

The White House pool reports typically come in waves throughout the day, and they are usually simply numbered without a qualifier. But when the next pool report hit the inboxes of several thousand reporters at 9:30 p.m. Eastern, the subject line read: "Pool report 5—NEWS gay rights protesters interrupt." It was a flag for fellow reporters that this particular pool report might be worth a second look.

In part, the pool report read, "At 6:17, several protesters among the crowd interrupted POTUS' speech, expressing anger over the slow progress on repealing the military's 'don't ask, don't tell' policy on gay service members. The crowd tried to hush them. 'What about don't ask, don't tell?' one protester shouted . . . 'It's time for equality for all Americans!' another protester yelled at 9:22. [sic] Obama said, 'can I just say again Barbara and I are supportive of repealing Don't ask don't tell.' But protester keeps yelling. Bringing Obama's remarks to a halt."[38]

This was real-time reporting and pretty good at that. A few minutes later, pool report 6 arrived. "At 6:25 local time, POTUS has regained control of the speech," it began.

The protest was activist gold. The president of the United States is one of the most insulated people on the planet. He or she can't leave the White House without an entourage of Secret Service detail and a motorcade of anywhere from a dozen to several dozen conspicuous armored cars and police vehicles. The president may see the front page of several newspapers every morning, but the rest of the information that reaches him or her throughout the day is filtered by aides. These aides decide what's worth their boss's exceedingly limited time and energy. The select few individuals who do make it through those White House gates to meet with the president are expected to conduct themselves with a heavy dose of respect, decorum, and even deference regardless of how desperate or angry they might feel.

GetEQUAL activists hadn't just made headlines that night. They had reached beyond the media, beyond the White House handlers, to touch President Obama personally with palpable anger and discontent. Their frustration was as glaring for him during those seven minutes as his own. It was a once-in-a-term opportunity for activists fighting on any given political issue—the Secret Service would be on alert for LGBT activists in the future. But GetEQUAL had managed to use that rare opening to make their case directly to the president in no uncertain terms.

President Obama, who normally handled hecklers with the utmost cool, just couldn't get a handle on these guys—partly because it was a coordinated action emanating from different locations in the venue, partly because their passion pushed them past the point of reasonability. They simply couldn't be talked down. *Atlantic* reporter Marc Ambinder—who was often the beneficiary of direct accounts from top Obama aides—would later recount the scene following the Boxer event through the eyes of an anonymous aide who was traveling with the president. It's a good bet his source was Jim Messina.

Barack Obama was in an unusually surly mood when he climbed into a thickly armored limousine. It was April 19, and the president had just finished a high-spirited rally with Democratic financial titans in Los Angeles. His speech had been interrupted by gay-rights demonstrators frustrated that the "don't ask, don't tell" ban on gays serving openly in the military was still in place.

Obama did not like the allegation that he and his staff were deferring the issue. Indeed, the idea infuriated the man whose election had been hailed as a watershed moment for integration and inclusion. It implied that Obama, the most progressive president since Lyndon Johnson, was lying when he said publicly and repeatedly that he intended to end the ban once and for all. It implied that the commander in chief was being rolled by the military, which many gay-rights activists felt had outmaneuvered the president.

Seated in the car, painfully aware that his boss was angry, was Jim Messina, Obama's deputy chief of staff, the White House point man on don't ask, don't tell, and the target of many activists' ire. Obama uttered a curse. "Messina, I don't understand these guys. What is it about what we are doing that they don't get? If they want to protest, they should go protest someone who was against this."[39]

The account, which wasn't published until later that year, comported with what one reporter who was traveling on Air Force One that night relayed to GetEQUAL via e-mail. "Don't ask, don't tell" hadn't even been a discussion point for the president and his advisers on the way to California that day. But on the flight back, it was all they were talking about.[40]

GetEQUAL's protest at the California Science Center took place on a Monday, and it marked the beginning of a very long week for the White House. By the end of it, they would be feeling more pressure than ever before on an issue that Obama had now twice committed to accomplishing within the past year.

GetEQUAL struck again on Tuesday, chaining uniformed vets to the White House fence once again. Four former service members joined Dan Choi and Jim Pietrangelo: Cadet Mara Boyd, Petty Officer Autumn Sandeen, Corporal Evelyn Thomas, and Petty Officer Larry Whitt. Each branch of the military was represented plus nearly all the colors of the LGBT rainbow: female, male, transgender, people of varying races and ethnicities. This time, several reporters from the White

House press corps stepped outside to cover the event. The Beltway media was starting to view the repeal protests as a serious political problem for Obama and the Democrats. The Democrats needed the base to turn out in the midterms and now a once-loyal part of that base was in outward rebellion.[41]

As they had during the previous month's protest, the US Park Police closed off Pennsylvania Avenue in front of the White House in order to remove the protesters from the fence and arrest them. Being pushed back across the street from the protest still allowed most reporters to do their jobs—TV cameras and photographers could still get a decent shot from that vantage point. But this time, the Park Police took the highly unusual step of shutting down half of Lafayette Square Park, a seven-acre expanse that sits directly across Pennsylvania Avenue from the White House. Pedestrians and reporters alike were pushed back about two hundred to three hundred feet, making it difficult to get usable footage or audio of the protest. Veteran White House reporters were surprised, some were even incensed. Blogger John Aravosis, who was shooting video of the action, captured one credentialed press member challenging an officer. "If you want to kick the public out, that's fine, but let us do our job," he said. The officer simply kept shouting, "Park's closed! Back it up!"[42]

The move quickly turned into a PR blunder. *Politico* blogger Ben Smith posted the Aravosis video under the snarky headline: "Most Transparent White House Ever." After they realized they had made an error in judgment, Park Police initially tried to blame the closure on the Secret Service, while the Secret Service adamantly denied that it had anything to do with shutting down Lafayette Park. Eventually, a spokesman for the Park Police fell on his sword, telling Smith that some "young officers" had "screwed up" and pushed people further back than normal. "That has nothing to do with the Secret Service of the White House or the Administration," Sergeant David Schlosser said.[43]

It was a strong statement meant to insulate the administration from the mistake. It made me think the White House was getting particularly touchy on LGBT issues and didn't want to give gay activists any reason to get more riled up. When I walked into the briefing room on Wednesday, April 21, I was sure Robert Gibbs would call on me, expecting me to ask about the mix-up (assuming no other reporter had already done so). He would want the opportunity to distance the White House from the anger over the previous day's park closure. But to me, the transparency story was a bit of a distraction from the fact that gay rights activists had staged high-profile protests for two consecutive days. So instead of giving Gibbs the question he was prepared to answer, I planned to ask one that had nothing to do with the park closure.

My hunch proved correct. Though Gibbs often passed me over to take questions from other reporters, his focus eventually fell on me that day.

"The President was heckled pretty persistently on Monday night about 'don't ask, don't tell' repeal," I said. "Six LGBT veterans chained themselves to the White House gates yesterday—I think you actually saw it," I added, noting that Gibbs had been spotted roaming Lafayette Park during the action.[44]

"I was walking through the park at that time," Gibbs interjected.

"Were you pushed back by Park Police?" I jested.

"I will say—can I mention the Park Police?" Gibbs responded. "I think we were asked yesterday the role in which the White House played in that . . . The White House and the Secret Service did not have any role in that decision making and I think the Park Police has taken—rightly taken responsibility."[45]

Gibbs got what he was looking for—the chance to deny White House culpability. I got back to my question, once again referencing the two protests.

"All of these actions are aimed at getting repeal this year, something the White House has sort of declined to commit to since the State of the Union address," I said. "Has the White House misjudged the level of patience among LGBT and grassroots activists on this?"

Gibbs noted that the president had long believed in repeal, had committed to ending the policy during his campaign, and understood "the passion" of the people fighting for repeal.

"I don't think he's underestimated the—as you said—the patience of some," Gibbs observed. "The president wants to see this law changed, just as you've heard the chair of the Joint Chiefs and others in the military say that it's time for that change to happen."

"But," I said, "he's committed to letting the Pentagon work through its working group process until December 1, is that true?"

"Yes," Gibbs replied. "The president has set forward a process with the Joint—the chair of the Joint Chiefs and with the secretary of Defense to work through this issue."

"Before any legislative action is taken—that rules out legislative action this year?" I said.

"Well, again," Gibbs responded, "the House and the Senate are obviously a different branch of government. The president has a process and a proposal I think that he believes is the best way forward to seeing, again, the commitment that he's made for many years in trying to—changing that law."

With those final words, Gibbs began closing his briefing book and added, "Thanks guys," signaling the end of the briefing.

I had fought for those two follow-up questions—jockeying to work them in before he called on other reporters—and they had yielded fruit. Though Gibbs had not conceded that "the process" precluded legislative action this year, he had certainly implied that President Obama was more committed to the process, including its proposed timeline, than he was to guaranteeing legislative action that year.

The implication of Gibbs' response to my questions was not lost on the media. Beltway blogger Igor Volsky of ThinkProgress, a highly respected progressive blog housed at the Center for American Progress, immediately published a post titled, "Gibbs Says White House Will Wait for Pentagon to Complete DADT Review Before Pushing for Repeal." Blogger Pam Spaulding was even less sparing than Volsky in her assessment. "Robert Gibbs Finally Admits the Obama Administration Has No Intention of Pushing DADT Repeal in 2010," read her headline at Pam's House Blend.[46]

The next day, April 22, I published a story I had been working on for a couple weeks. An anonymous source had leaked information to me about a meeting that took place on February 1 in which he said White House aide Jim Messina had definitively told a group of LGBT advocates that the president would not include repeal language in his recommendations for the Defense authorization bill. My anonymous source was Alexander Nicholson, a discharged vet and executive director of Servicemembers United. He later outed himself as my source in his own postmortem book on the repeal effort, *Fighting to Serve*. But at the time, I made certain to have a second unnamed source to corroborate his account. It was partly a matter of sound journalistic practice to have a second source, but I also knew the story would get blowback and I needed to ensure it was airtight.[47]

Nicholson's story made perfect sense given Messina's reputation in Washington as Obama's F-bomb-dropping enforcer. Many progressives had grown to distrust Messina, probably because he was in charge of keeping Democrats in line, which mostly meant keeping progressives from being too publicly critical of the president. Exactly what Messina's personal convictions were was a point of disagreement—some argued he was a staunch liberal while others labeled him a sellout—but his function within the administration was never in question. His job was to keep things on schedule according to the White House plan, and that plan had proven far less aggressive than most progressives wanted it to be. When a question about the Defense bill came up with a dozen LGBT advocates during that early February meeting, just days after President Obama had pledged to work on repeal "this year," Nicholson told me that Messina snapped, emphatically saying the president wouldn't ask for repeal to be included in the legislation. "It was a definitive shut-down from Messina," he explained.[48]

HRC's David Smith had also attended the off-the-record meeting. When I reached out for a quote, he relayed a different version of events. "They were noncommittal about legislation in that meeting, but not definitively one way or the other," Smith said.[49]

Sure enough, as soon as I published the piece under the headline, "White House Sends Mixed Messages on DADT," other advocates called to refute my reporting. Lobbyist Robert Raben of The Raben Group told me, "They were, if anything, frustratingly cautious about committing to anything." Two other participants also called to add their anonymous input, and both insisted that Messina had been vague and committed to nothing. I published a follow-up story offering the alternative points of view.[50]

Nicholson, twenty-eight, was the only repeal advocate in that room who had been discharged under the policy. He played an interesting role in the repeal effort since he was neither a career LGBT advocate nor a career lobbyist at the time (nearly everyone else in that room was either one or the other). Nicholson founded Servicemembers United in 2005 with the help of some friends specifically to achieve repeal. SLDN's

Aubrey Sarvis, an army veteran who had served in the early '60s, had been cut out of the February meeting as retribution for his persistent and public advocacy that President Obama insert repeal language into the Defense bill. Sarvis, like Nicholson, was not a career LGBT advocate. He had only recently taken the helm of SLDN in 2007, though he very much understood legislative strategy after spending fourteen years working on Capitol Hill, including six serving as chief counsel for the Senate Commerce Committee.[51]

Sarvis and Nicholson served a necessary role in the mix of people who were playing the inside game—an inner circle of about a dozen LGBT advocates. The two men were not fond of each other, and most of the insiders distrusted Nicholson, in particular. In part, that was because he was willing to break rank with a fundamental rule of insider ethics: secrecy. But both Sarvis and Nicholson worked with ferocity to achieve their ends, sometimes breeching Washington protocol to advance the cause of repeal. In fact, Sarvis's omission from the high-level meeting was a signal to the others not to ruffle the administration's feathers or they too might be ostracized. Together, Sarvis's on-the-record statements and Nicholson's occasional leaks aided the legislative process in their own way. They often confirmed the worst fears of GetEQUAL and other grassroots activists, who would in turn pressure the administration from outside Washington through protests and direct actions. Democratic lawmakers and the White House would have to believe that there was a price to pay if they did not deliver in order for repeal to make the list of 2010 priorities. And Sarvis, perhaps better than anyone, understood the intricacies of using outside pressure to effect certain inside outcomes. Additionally, he and his organization commanded enough respect among both outside and inside players alike to serve dual roles that sometimes seemed at cross purposes.

Generally speaking, HRC and CAP staffers working on the Hill seemed to view grassroots activists as more of a nuisance in Washington matters than a help when it came to repeal. On the other hand, their trusted status and long-standing relationships with lawmakers and other Washington operatives gave them the ability to help redirect the course of events at crucial moments. That was especially true of Winnie Stachelberg, then a senior vice president at the Center for American Progress, and Allison Herwitt, then the legislative director for the

Human Rights Campaign. Stachelberg, an eleven-year veteran of HRC who joined CAP in 2006, often played peacemaker among the insiders and helped align the group on certain strategies. Herwitt, who before joining HRC in 2006 spent eleven years as a lobbyist for the pro-choice organization NARAL and six years working on the Hill, had the ear of certain lawmakers and the trust of their staff members at critical turning points in 2010. By all accounts of staff members on the Hill, Stachelberg and Herwitt also served as liaisons between congressional lawmakers and the White House, which was conspicuously absent on the Hill during much of the "don't ask, don't tell" battle. Stachelberg and Herwitt were creatures of Washington. They did not push the envelope in the ways that Sarvis or Nicholson did, but once everyone was marching in the direction of repeal, Stachelberg and Herwitt knew how to work within the confines of institutional Washington and the Hill to help lawmakers do their job.[52]

This group of disparate actors, who met regularly throughout 2010 about repeal, performed their own individual roles to surprisingly good effect given their strategic differences. One thing they did do well was communicate. They generally knew what one another was up to even if they didn't approve of it.

Since disagreements among them were par for the course, it was perhaps unsurprising that their views on the White House meeting varied. What actually happened that day with Messina may have been a matter of some dispute among meeting participants, but one takeaway was clear: the best thing anyone could say about the White House was that Messina had *not* committed to anything regarding legislation. In some ways, the pushback to my article said more about where the White House was than the original piece had. As Gibbs had intimated, President Obama was committed to the Pentagon's process. In fact, Secretary Gates would later write in his memoir, *Duty*, that President Obama and Rahm Emanuel "promised—unequivocally and on several occasions—to oppose any legislation before completion of the review." But even without having the benefit of that information from Gates at the time, the timeline for legislation seemed an ancillary consideration to the process for the administration.[53]

So perhaps it shouldn't have been a surprise when Defense Secretary Gates penned a stern letter the following week urging lawmakers not to vote on the policy before the Pentagon finished its study. Still, it sent shivers down the spine of pro-repeal advocates and Hill staffers in Washington because they knew waiting that long would kill the effort for the year.

"I believe in the strongest possible terms that the Department must, prior to any legislative action, be allowed the opportunity to conduct a thorough, objective, and systematic assessment of the impact of such a policy change," Gates wrote to Representative Ike Skelton, chairman of the House Armed Services Committee, who was against repeal. "Therefore, I strongly oppose any legislation that seeks to change this policy prior to the completion of this vital assessment process."[54]

The April 30 letter was cosigned by Admiral Mullen and leaked to the Associated Press's Anne Flaherty, who posted a story the same day at about 4:00 p.m. on a Friday afternoon. The leak's timing was classic— Gates and Skelton didn't need America to see the letter, they only needed lawmakers to see it. And that they did (weekends are often just two slightly less hectic days of the workweek in Washington). It ricocheted around the Hill at lighting speed. Though most of Washington was busy prepping for the weekend parties that would accompany the following night's White House Correspondent's Dinner, communications teams whipped into gear.

Most lawmakers who had a stake in repeal issued a statement within a couple hours. Speaker Pelosi called for the administration to place "a moratorium" on discharges while the study was completed. Representative Patrick Murphy, the chief sponsor of the House repeal bill, vowed to continue fighting for "full repeal this year." The White House issued a statement labeling the president's commitment to repeal "unequivocal" and saying he wanted it done "both soon and right."[55]

In his memoir, Gates describes April as a tense period between the Pentagon and the White House because he believed the president and Emanuel were beginning to relent on their commitment not to move legislation before completion of the review. But at the time, people who understood Washington machinations believed that at least one or more top White House aides had full knowledge of Gates's letter before it came to light. Perception matters on the Hill. When the Secretary of Defense speaks, lawmakers listen. The Gates admonishment was a vote killer, especially for Democrats who represented conservative areas of the country, like Senator Ben Nelson of Nebraska. If lawmakers couldn't say the Defense secretary told them it was the best way forward for the military, voting affirmatively for repeal became exponentially more risky.[56]

WHAT FOLLOWED OVER THE next month was a near miraculous recovery for repeal. Though many pro-repeal elements feared the Gates letter was a death knell, advocates and politicians persevered. It became increasingly clear to Democratic leaders in the House and the Senate that the votes simply weren't there to pass the Employment Nondiscrimination Act through both chambers. That left "don't ask, don't tell" as the last piece of LGBT legislation that had a chance of crossing the finish line before the end of the 111th Congress. Plus, a deadline was fast approaching. Both chambers were scheduled to consider the Defense authorization bill toward the end of May.[57]

And here is where a three-way dance ensued between the Department of Defense, Congress, and the White House. Gates, through his letter, had presented the Pentagon as the lead in that dance. The White House wasn't publicly challenging the secretary's assertion, which left congressional leaders with a conundrum. Were they supposed to follow the lead of the Pentagon's top civilian appointee, who reports to the president and was adamantly opposed to a vote before December 1? Should they instead follow the lead of the commander in chief of the military, the president, who had himself stated his intent to abolish the law but was now ostensibly deferring to Gates on the timetable? Or should they take the lead themselves in repealing the law that had been enacted by Congress seventeen years earlier? Passing laws is, after all, the province of Congress, not the president or a sitting cabinet member (no matter how well placed or highly regarded). If they defied Gates, they would still need his blessing in order to round up the last couple votes. If they didn't, repeal would almost certainly fall to the next Congress, which almost certainly wouldn't take it up.

Senator Carl Levin, a thirty-one-year veteran of the Senate who was chair of the Senate Armed Services Committee, seemed frustrated by the mixed signals coming from Gates and the president. On May 3, he wrote the secretary to clarify what exactly the purpose of the study was—was it to determine "whether" to repeal the law or "how" to implement repeal? The intent of the study actually had very different implications for how pertinent its completion was to taking a vote on the policy.[58]

Gates responded by revisiting his testimony from the February 2 Senate hearing on "don't ask, don't tell."

"I stated: 'The question before us is not whether the military prepares to make this change but how we . . . best prepare for it.' This remains my position and that of the Department of Defense," he wrote to Levin on May 6—an exchange that was subsequently released by Levin's office.

Levin also didn't appreciate the administration's apparent attempt to preempt congressional authority on the matter.

"We're not a rubber stamp for the president," Levin told *Congressional Quarterly* reporter Frank Oliveri on May 11, explaining that the administration couldn't dictate the timing of repeal to Congress. "He says he wants to repeal 'don't ask.' Why shouldn't we repeal it?" Levin added, referring to his letter exchange with Gates.[59]

As the chairs of most committees do, Levin took his oversight responsibilities very seriously. In meetings with repeal advocates, Levin said he had talked to Secretary Gates about various issues related to the Defense funding bill. Whenever "don't ask, don't tell" came up, he told them, he had found that Gates was never able to sufficiently explain why Congress couldn't move forward with legislative repeal even as the Pentagon produced its roadmap for how to implement that repeal. Levin was suggesting, in other words, that if the study they were producing was about *how* to change the policy and not *whether* to change the policy, then it was perfectly rational that the processes in Congress and at the Pentagon simultaneously move forward on a parallel track.[60]

In addition to Levin, Senator Lieberman, who had introduced a stand-alone Senate repeal bill a couple months earlier, and Democratic Representative Steny Hoyer, then the House Majority Leader, proved themselves to be true believers that the time for repeal had come. Like Lieberman, Hoyer was relatively hawkish on military matters and had a much better rapport with the Department of Defense and Secretary Gates than many of his more progressive colleagues in the Democratic Caucus. Hoyer, who had a number of gay staff members throughout the years, saw repeal as an issue of justice and believed LGBT equality was becoming the civil rights issue of a new day, much the way Lieberman did. As a college student, Lieberman had attended Dr. Martin Luther King Jr.'s March on Washington in 1963 and looked to it as a transformative moment in his life. His chief of staff, Clarine Nardi Riddle, had been active in the women's movement and the two of them felt a natural kinship to the rising gay rights movement. Lieberman and Hoyer both devoted multiple staff members to pushing repeal, and they would ultimately drive the issue home on the Hill with the help of other lawmakers like Speaker Pelosi and Representative Patrick Murphy of Pennsylvania and Senators Carl Levin of Michigan, Susan Collins of Maine, Mark Udall of Colorado, and Kirsten Gillibrand of New York.[61]

Everybody is a true believer retrospectively, once something has passed. They'll tell you they always knew it was going to happen—even if in truth they had doubted all along. But being a true believer in the moment requires a certain courage and steadfastness that's conspicuously absent in the halls of Congress on most days. While true believers invest themselves fully in working toward a win, everyone else on the Hill is busy subscribing to the groupthink that it can't be done, that it's too politically costly, that it must wait until another session or a second term. Washington has a way of making doubters out of people because the skeptics are so often proven right. True believers are the antidote to that conventional wisdom. And it takes a critical mass coming from all directions—activists, lobbyists, staffers, lawmakers, and policy wonks—to eventually push legislation through.

Lieberman had nearly secured the votes to attach repeal to the Defense authorization bill in committee before the Gates letter surfaced. Now he and his staff were redoubling their efforts to reach the fifteen votes necessary, a simple majority of the Senate Armed Services Committee. Representative Murphy, a young member of Congress and a veteran of the Iraq War, had done the yeoman's work of gathering about 190 cosponsors on his repeal bill in the House. He also claimed to have verbal commitments from another couple dozen members. By mid-May, Murphy had repeatedly stated that he had the 217 needed for repeal.[62]

But to lock in the final votes, advocates and lawmakers needed a compromise that put the Pentagon in charge of the timetable on implementing repeal while still allowing ample time for Congress to do its job before the end of the year. Alexander Nicholson of Servicemembers United had been pushing the idea of altering the legislation so that the policy change could go into effect as much as eighteen months after the policy was overturned by Congress. That would give the Pentagon plenty of time to finish its study. But Winnie Stachelberg of CAP came up with a twist on that plan, suggesting that the president, the secretary of Defense, and the chairman of the Joint Chiefs actually sign off on repeal—or certify it—once the military was ready for it to go into effect. That would put the military entirely in the driver's seat on timing once the bill was passed and signed into law.[63]

A final concession advocates ultimately made was to remove the nondiscrimination language, which meant that although gays would no longer be discharged once the gay ban ended, lesbian and gay service members would have no means of recourse if they suspected being discriminated against because of their sexual orientation. Nor would their rates of recruitment, retention, and promotion be tracked by the military to ensure equitable treatment. Consistent with federal law at the time, the military did not recognize LGBT soldiers as members of a minority that had been unfairly targeted, otherwise known as a "protected class" in legal terms. The Department of Defense's Military Equal Opportunity program only prohibited "unlawful discrimination against persons or groups based on race, color, religion, sex, or national origin."[64]

These compromises formed the outlines of a repeal measure that all sides might be able to support, which is where Representative Steny Hoyer and his staff stepped in to play the key role of liaison between Congress and the Pentagon. Between late January and May, Hoyer had several conversations with Secretary Gates to express his support for the idea of repealing now but implementing later. Hoyer's staff members bundled the compromises together into one amendment and on Friday, May 21, they floated the language to Senator Lieberman, Representative Murphy, and Speaker Pelosi. All were receptive. They then sent the compromise language to Liz King, the assistant secretary of defense for legislative affairs at the Pentagon. Several hours later, the White House director of legislative affairs, Phil Schiliro, called Hoyer's staff and indicated the compromise might work.[65]

Though advocacy groups had little choice but to accept the full complement of concessions at that point, none of it was popular with grassroots activists, who deeply distrusted the military. I, for one, was most concerned by the decision to remove the nondiscrimination language from the bill. It left the military to its own devices on putting equitable practices in place for the same lesbian and gay service members it had been systematically discharging for two decades. As I later noted in a column, repeal would invite lesbian and gay service members out into the open "while simultaneously affording them absolutely no legally enforceable anti-discrimination protections once they are visible."[66]

While the proposed amendment was far from perfect, at that point, not passing it would have been a disaster. A failed vote would have empowered all those lawmakers and strategists who constantly warned against tackling LGBT legislation to say, "I told you so." Warts and all, repeal was still alive. Congress had finally forced the issue. The White House and Gates followed, but less as joyous participants than as reluctant newlyweds who had been dragged onto the dance floor by their overbearing in-laws. Still, once the administration hit the floor, the orchestration was flawless.

On Monday morning, May 24, LGBT advocates from the major groups involved in repeal—CAP, HRC, Servicemembers United, SLDN, and The Palm Center—were summoned to the White House where officials briefed them on the compromise: the Pentagon study would have to be completed first; repeal would be certified by the Defense secretary, the Joint Chiefs chair, and the president; and the nondiscrimination clause would be dropped. A concurrent meeting took place in Hoyer's office on Capitol Hill where the amendment language was finalized by representatives of the Department of Defense, the White House, and staff members from the offices of Hoyer, Lieberman, Levin, Murphy, and Pelosi.[67]

Both the White House and the Pentagon publicly signaled their tepid support by issuing statements to lawmakers later that day. The administration's statement from the Office of Management and Budget noted that "ideally" Congress would have waited for the study. Nonetheless, the administration supported the vote because "the proposed amendment meets the concerns raised by the Secretary of Defense and the Chairman of the Joint Chiefs of Staff."[68]

The Department of Defense was even more halfhearted: "Secretary Gates continues to believe that ideally the DOD review should be completed before there is any legislation to repeal the 'don't ask, don't tell' law. With Congress having indicated that is not possible, the Secretary can accept the language in the proposed amendment."[69]

As lackluster as it sounded, it was enough. Lieberman's office had requested the statements so they could go back to the senators who were wavering. One by one, the fence-sitters on the Senate Armed Services Committee aired their votes to the press. On Tuesday, GOP Massachusetts Senator Scott Brown and Democratic Virginia Senator Jim Webb (a former Marine) said no. Apparently, they were not convinced of Gates's enthusiasm. On the plus side, Democratic Senators Bill Nelson of Florida and Evan Bayh of Indiana both stated publicly what they had been saying privately for weeks: yes.[70]

The Ayes stood at 14. They needed one more. By Tuesday night, Lieberman knew he had the votes. The holdouts—Nebraska's Senator Ben Nelson and West Virginia's Senator Robert Byrd (who was very ill)—both gave their private blessings. [71]

Senator Nelson issued a statement Wednesday morning saying that the Lieberman compromise "rests ultimate authority to make this change with our military leaders. I believe this is the right thing to do." 15. The final vote count in the Senate Armed Services Committee on May 27, 2010, was 16–12, the addition of Byrd gave them one more vote than necessary. Maine's Senator Susan Collins cast the sole Republican vote for repeal. The same day, the House of Representatives approved the exact same amendment 234–194.[72]

Repeal had been successfully attached to the National Defense Authorization Act (NDAA) of 2011. Pro-repeal advocates and lawmakers had found their silver bullet. Or so they thought.

WHAT EVERYONE GROSSLY underestimated was the Pentagon's will. To be sure, the Department of Defense is notorious for wielding a lot of influence on the Hill. But it seemed the Pentagon would want its projects and operations to be fully and adequately funded despite the fact that repealing "don't ask, don't tell" would be a by-product of that funding. As it turned out, Pentagon officials—Robert Gates, in particular—continued to lobby against passing the NDAA until the December report was released. That continually delayed consideration of the bill and everybody knew the longer it waited, the less likely it was to pass. Yet even after the successful vote in May, days turned to weeks and weeks to months.

As the slow grind of governing wore on, electoral politics heated up. Democrats had midterms on the brain above all else and nearly every choice they made seemed to be in service of surviving the election with the Senate still under their control. By fall, the House was all but lost.

In September, the NDAA became an avenue to score political points more than anything. Senate Majority Leader Harry Reid pledged to add an immigration measure known as the DREAM Act, which would have created a path to citizenship for foreign-born youths brought to the US as minors, as an amendment to the legislation. At the time, both repeal and the DREAM Act were viewed as dicey political issues on the Hill (though they both enjoyed majority support among American voters). Passing either one as an attachment to the Defense funding bill would have been a heavy lift. But trying to pair them together in the legislation was sure to torpedo the effort—not to mention the fact that Reid likely didn't have the votes necessary to add DREAM anyway. In the end, it was all political theatre. On September 21, Republicans predictably filibustered the NDAA and Democrats couldn't muster the 60 votes to advance the legislation to the floor for debate.[73]

Ultimately, putting the bill up for consideration was more of a symbolic gesture than anything. Repeal advocates had pushed for the vote knowing full well that waiting until after the midterms might seal the fate of repeal. Democrats, on the other hand, didn't want to head into the elections telling a key Democratic constituency that they hadn't at least tried to advance the legislation. The same went for the DREAM Act and the immigration community. Democrats on Capitol Hill would blame the failed vote on Republicans, but the manner in which Reid approached the vote doomed it from the start. That vote was more a victim of the ever-growing partisan divide and of a vacuum in leadership than of the substance itself. Bottom line, neither the White House nor the Pentagon was applying a full-court press to pass the NDAA.

If September was business as usual, Washington got a jolt to the system the following month from the judicial branch. On October 12, 2010, Federal District Judge Virginia Phillips placed a worldwide injunction on the "don't ask, don't tell" policy after ruling it unconstitutional a month earlier in a case called *Log Cabin Republicans v. United States of America*. The breadth of Judge Phillips's order was devastating, and it caught the Pentagon's leadership flatfooted. One former Department of Defense official described a moment of "pure panic" inside the building. Shifting course on a major military policy across the globe would normally require several months' worth of writing, processing, and sign-offs. Though Pentagon officials felt certain the injunction would ultimately be stayed while government lawyers appealed the ruling, the order still left the military in legal limbo for several days as leadership struggled to issue a carefully worded temporary shift in the policy.[74]

Department of Defense general counsel Jeh Johnson, an Obama appointee who played a crucial role in bridging the gap between the Pentagon and the White House on repeal, best summarized the chaos in his December 2010 testimony before the Senate Armed Services Committee.

"Monday October 11, 2010, we had a law and a policy in place . . . On Tuesday October 12, 2010, a Federal district judge in California issued an order to the Secretary of Defense to suspend enforcement of that law on a worldwide basis. Eight days later on October 20, 2010, the appellate court issued a temporary stay of the injunction while it considered whether to grant a more permanent stay . . . Thus, in the space of 8 days we had to shift course on the worldwide enforcement of the law twice, and in the space of a month faced the possibility of shifting course four different times."[75]

The cataclysmic ruling marked the beginning of Secretary Gates's born-again style conversion on repeal. Following the order, Gates realized it was only a matter of time before the courts overturned the discriminatory law outright. That epiphany would soon transform him into a steadfast and urgent supporter of repeal.

As the election loomed, White House officials became consumed with damage control. Tea Party activists were on a tear while Democrats' enthusiasm simultaneously plummeted. The administration was trying to jump-start its base after failing to pump out major legislative wins for its progressive constituencies, including advocates for LGBT equality, the environment, immigration, labor, and reproductive rights. On October 26, White House officials invited about a dozen "don't ask, don't tell" repeal advocates to a closed-door strategy session. The meeting included top aides Valerie Jarrett and Jim Messina and a fifteen-minute drop-in from the president. It was likely intended to signal a good-faith effort on the part of the administration to pass repeal. But the discussion started with HRC's Joe Solmonese noting the sense on the Hill was that the White House wasn't very engaged in the repeal effort—in other words, lawmakers and their aides hadn't heard much if anything from the president and his staff about passing repeal. It got worse when Nathaniel Frank, an academic expert on the policy who formerly had worked for The Palm Center, suggested that the perception among LGBT activists was that the White House hadn't prioritized the issue.[76]

Jarrett rejected the notion out of hand, saying it absolutely wasn't true. Messina, the bad cop in the room, shot back at Frank, "You're criticizing us." Frank responded, "I'm not criticizing you." He said that while he couldn't tell the administration how to work with Congress to successfully pass repeal, "all that matters is that this White House understands that this issue will continue to dog the administration until it's resolved."[77]

That was received even more poorly. "You're threatening us!" charged Messina. Frank, who was now in Messina's crosshairs, said he hadn't intended to threaten the administration, he was only trying to underscore "the perception that people have that this hasn't been a priority."[78]

When President Obama stopped by, the meeting did produce one valuable piece of information. Aubrey Sarvis asked President Obama directly if he thought Defense Secretary Gates could ever support repeal. "Yes, I think he can," the president said. Some advocates in the room took that as a sign that the Pentagon's working group study would have positive results when it was finally released, which turned out to be exactly right.[79]

Though repeal had languished for months, it got a huge boost heading into December when the Pentagon's report on implementing repeal was released on November 30. The study had been part of a process that Obama and Gates had agreed upon in moving toward repeal. And to the president's great credit, the Department of Defense's "Comprehensive Review of the Issues Associated with a Repeal of 'Don't Ask, Don't Tell,'" authored by general counsel Jeh Johnson and US Army General Carter Ham, gave an unequivocal green light to changing the policy. The 250-page report concluded that the risk of repealing the gay ban "to overall military effectiveness is low." After surveying 400,000 active-duty troops and receiving 115,052 responses, the data showed that 67 percent of service members said repeal would have either "a positive or no effect" at all on unit readiness and 22 percent said the effect would be "equally positive as negative;" only 12 percent anticipated a negative impact.[80]

The day the report went public, Secretary Gates urged the Senate to pass the legislation "before the end of this year" lest repeal be forced by "judicial fiat." After Gates saw the report and realized that repeal was in fact achievable with minimal disruption to the force, he told every reporter he could find that his "greatest fear" was that a judge would have the final say on when and how the policy would end. By contrast, legislative repeal, which Gates had once begrudgingly accepted, now provided Pentagon officials with all kinds of controls over the timeline for implementing the change in policy. Gates was no dummy. He didn't want the courts dictating anything to the military in the midst of two wars. After delaying legislative action at every turn for most of the year, Gates was now a fervent supporter.[81]

His appeals were the type of game-changer that would have locked in those final votes a few months earlier, but they had emerged too late in the session to single-handedly reverse course on the legislation. The bill was now at the mercy of the political gridlock that was swallowing Washington whole. If it failed to pass before the end of 2010, the repeal measure didn't stand a chance of moving forward during the next Congress. The midterms had been the rout everyone expected. Democrats managed to hold on to the Senate but Republicans would control the House come January. In other words, a failed vote in December would mean that Barack Obama—the hope-and-change candidate, the yes-we-can president—had fallen short of leveraging historic Democratic majorities in Congress to score this major legislative win for a key progressive constituency.

LGBT Americans were not the only group who felt frustrated with Obama's inaction during his first two years in office. Labor unions had been dealt a blow when legislation that would have made it easier for workers to form unions, commonly known as "card check" by its detractors, was pronounced DOA in early 2009. By the summer of 2010, meanwhile, environmentalists had watched Democrats scrap a climate bill that aimed to curb carbon emissions. Comprehensive immigration reform, admittedly complicated but also an Obama campaign promise, never got off the ground. Its little brother, the DREAM Act, would ultimately log an important but unsuccessful vote. Health care reform finally passed but not before the administration bargained away a public option (which would have allowed Americans to choose a government-run plan) and blindsided reproductive rights advocates with a compromise that many believed would pave the way for future restrictions on abortion access. Following the midterms, many progressives were mourning the remains of an agenda that had been largely bypassed and would now be lost to the upcoming Congress.

But the final act for "don't ask, don't tell" wasn't over yet. The tag-team wins of the pivotal court ruling and the definitive Pentagon report set the stage for the harried course of events that would unfold in the month of December.

LAME DUCK · 6

THE LINE TO GET A PICTURE TAKEN WITH THE PRESIDENT AND first lady at White House holiday parties runs like clockwork. Marines systematically process a queue that's about 250 couples deep over the course of roughly ninety minutes, ensuring that each attendee secures a pictorial keepsake of their executive encounter that is guaranteed to impress friends and family on whatever mantel it lands. Once they reach their photo destination, every guest and their plus-one write down their names on a card and hand them to their uniformed escort, who then advises them to walk stride-for-stride beside her or him approximately five paces until they hit the mark where they are announced to the first couple.

My plus-one—my comrade in arms Joe Sudbay—had agreed to come only after I had begged him. After witnessing the administration's persistent reluctance to move forward on LGBT issues, Sudbay was no fan of Obama. And as a committed jean and fleece wearer, he was generally nauseated by the pomp and circumstance surrounding most Washington events. But I had insisted. This was the president we had poked and prodded and schemed about for two years to no avail. If we were going to leave the first half of his presidency empty handed on repeal, then at the very least, we should have a picture to memorialize our efforts.

Naturally, what one might say to the president during the only ten unscripted seconds you might ever be afforded with the leader of the free world is a question that weighs on people's minds. Anyone who doesn't arrive at the White House with clear intent for that fleeting moment usually solidifies their thinking during the thirty minutes it takes for them to trace the line that snakes around the ground floor corridor through to the Map Room before delivering its attendees to the Diplomatic Reception Room, where a picture of George Washington presides over a garland-laced, bulb-studded mantel flanked by two meticulously dressed Christmas trees.

As Joe and I discussed our options, I decided I'd revisit my request from the previous year for a one-on-one interview, which President Obama had yet to grant any reporter from an LGBT outlet. Joe, on the other hand, decided to simply say, "It's great to see you again, Mr. President." It may have sounded like an innocuous greeting, but Joe intended to remind the president of a memorable meeting they'd had a couple months earlier.

Joe had faced off with the president in October during a five-person blogger interview in which the president first intimated that his position on same-sex marriage was beginning to move in the direction of full equality. They were the first on-the-record questions Obama had taken from someone representing the LGBT constituency since he had become president, and Joe had handled it like a pro. To be sure, I had hoped for the distinction of being the first LGBT media member to fire a question or two at Obama after attending two years of briefings with press secretary Robert Gibbs and carving out a space for myself in the White House press corps. But in truth, Sudbay had been in a much better position to pressure the president, especially on same-sex marriage. Free from the constraints of presenting himself as a more dispassionate journalist, he was able to make a deeply personal appeal to the president on the matter of marriage equality. He was also in a committed relationship with a partner of four years, which helped fuel a certain personal urgency on the matter.

"Since you've become president, a lot has changed," Joe began on October 27, 2010. "So I just really want to know, what is your position on same-sex marriage?" he implored. "People in our community are really desperate to know . . . And part of it is that you can't be equal in this country if the very core of who you are as a person and the love—the person you love is not—if that relationship isn't the same as everybody else's."[1]

"I think it's a fair question to ask. I think that I am a strong supporter of civil unions," Obama said. "But I also think you're right that attitudes evolve, including mine. And I think that it is an issue that I wrestle with and think about because I have a whole host of friends who are in gay partnerships."[2]

It was the first time the president had used the word "evolve" in relation to his stance on same-sex marriage. Obama aides who were in the room later described the exchange as "intense" specifically because Sudbay had offered up raw emotion. Perhaps they had become accustomed by then to people taking a more legalistic, separate-but-equal approach to probing President Obama's marriage position.[3]

My own suspicion was that President Obama went to that interview ready to make news on gay marriage simply by dropping the word "evolve." It is, after all, a term politicians embrace as they prepare to reverse course on a previously held position. It also puts the public on notice that sooner or later, change is gonna come. Of course, the public's response to that signal can also have bearing on just how soon or how late that change actually arrives.

It seemed likely that the White House wanted the news on Obama's evolution to spread to their base in time for the upcoming midterms without drawing too much national attention too quickly. They probably bargained that the blogger interview would reach progressive activists but wouldn't rise to the level of mainstream news—as in, no headlines would grace the covers of daily newspapers across the nation or traditional news outlets like the *New York Times* or *USA Today*. They bargained right. While the LGBT media and more niche sites like Huffington Post and *Politico* jumped on the fact that Obama's barometer was moving on same-sex marriage, his shift didn't seem to have a massive mainstream impact until a couple of months later.[4]

But none of that undermined the importance of Joe Sudbay speaking his truth to the president face to face. Those moments—when a president actually hears something unadulterated and unfiltered by his aides from someone who's willing to express real urgency and disappointment—are few and far between. Sudbay had also pressed Obama on "don't ask, don't tell," but it was marriage that stole the spotlight. If the progressive blogger meeting was part of an effort to excite the Democratic base, it failed miserably. But whatever the administration's intentions in setting up the interview, Sudbay had managed to make an impression on Obama.

So at the holiday party on December 7, when Joe settled upon saying, "It's great to see you again, Mr. President," it was a subtle reminder of the candid exchange they had shared a couple months earlier.

When Sudbay and I reached the Diplomatic Reception Room, our attendant marine announced us to the president and first lady. "This is Kerry Eleveld and her guest, Joe Sudbay." I had been told to greet the president first as Joe spoke to Mrs. Obama before we switched, posed for the picture, and went on our merry way, surrendering our spaces to the next guests who would perform the same perfunctory ritual moments later.

"Hello, Mr. President. Happy Holidays," I said, shaking the president's hand and matching his wide, toothy, grin with one of my own. "I'd still like to do that sit-down with you I mentioned last year." Not that I expected him to have any recollection of our previous year's interaction, but I wanted to remind him that my request had been a year on the table.

"We need to do that," he responded, picking up his head to scan the room for his deputy press secretary Bill Burton. "Where's Bill at?" he added, hoping to make a note of it.

Burton didn't materialize right away so, as scripted, I moved to the first lady. "Merry Christmas," I said. "You know, seeing you is really the highlight of the evening. We see him all the time," I joked, gesturing to the president, only half kidding. Mrs. Obama gave me a warm, earnest look that any Midwesterner would recognize.

"That'll be our little secret," she retorted playfully as we turned to take our places.

But as I pivoted to tuck myself between President Obama to my left and Joe to my right for our photo, I realized something had gone terribly awry. The president was glaring at Sudbay, wagging his index finger as he forcefully enumerated all the work he had put into passing the repeal of "don't ask, don't tell," an effort that was currently stalled in the lame-duck session and looked almost certain to perish.

"I've done everything I said I would do," the president was saying, referring to his last encounter with Joe in October, "and I still need the sixtieth vote. I got a thousand-page report, and I got the secretary of defense, the chairman of the Joint Chiefs, and . . . ."[5]

It was more than a little uncomfortable. Joe was frozen. And I suddenly found myself in the odd position of searching for something to say that could smooth the ruffled feathers of a man whom I had spent the past year admonishing and occasionally disparaging in the series of weekly columns I wrote alongside my regular reporting.

"It's never enough, is it, Mr. President?" I said, looking up at him. The sound of my voice interrupted the president's cadence. He glanced at me momentarily, seemingly a little annoyed by the reminder that other people were in the room. "No, it's not," he said. Then he turned back to Joe, took one more breath as if to reload for another round, and proclaimed, "We have to take this picture." Obama turned on a dime and flashed a big cheesy grin. Poof, it was over.

Joe didn't utter another word before we were summarily ushered out. He had simply greeted the president as planned and, as soon as they started shaking hands, Obama unloaded. The picture had been snapped so quickly after Obama turned that Sudbay's hands were still held out in front of him—apparently ready to ward off the president—rather than around the backs of his neighbors like the rest of us. In the aftermath, I busily snapped shots of Joe's ashen face and kept joking, "I can't take you anywhere." In truth, I, too, was stupefied. As we walked away from the White House, we kept recounting the scene to each other, trying to make sense of it.[6]

NEITHER ONE OF US would begin to understand the full implications of what had just happened in that room until a couple of hours later. That night, we both started getting reports that Senate majority leader Harry Reid planned to take a vote the next day on the NDAA—the bill to which "don't ask, don't tell" repeal was attached. That vote was going down in flames and the president—and everyone else—knew it. We didn't have the votes to pass the Defense bill through the full Senate.

What Joe and I had just witnessed was the president of the United States coming unglued for the briefest of moments as he made a case for why the following day's defeat shouldn't be laid at his doorstep. That's when I knew that all the activism—all the arrests at the White House gates and the interruptions at Obama's speeches and fundraisers—had paid off. In that moment, the president was directing his own bit of damage control at the one person in his midst whom he knew would be rallying the LGBT masses against him the following day.

My source who alerted me to the impending vote—a key senate staffer whom I had come to trust implicitly—told me that the vote was scheduled for the next day but added that White House officials didn't intend to lobby undecided lawmakers who were needed to pass the bill. If the White House wasn't even making phone calls, it meant they had already written off the vote.

As I rushed to type up a brief story indicating that Majority Leader Reid intended to take the vote, my source called back and said that White House officials were, in fact, going to make calls. Still, this entire episode seemed more of a symbolic exercise than a real effort to pass "don't ask, don't tell." The legislation didn't have the support, but Majority Leader Reid didn't want to be tagged with not taking the vote. The White House, meanwhile, didn't want activists to accuse them of not caring enough to pick up the phone. Everyone was covering their butts on a vote that they had stalled until the last possible moment in the session and still weren't truly prioritizing. It was frustratingly reminiscent of the failed September vote, and it was also our last chance.

LGBT advocates wanted and needed a vote, but in order for that vote to succeed, it needed to be a priority of the White House. In this case, that meant not rushing the vote before Republicans were prepared to vote for it.

Unfortunately, the White House agenda had been made clear time and again by press secretary Robert Gibbs at the briefings over the last several weeks. With almost annoying predictability, when asked what the White House wanted to focus on during the lame duck session, Gibbs had dutifully recited their two major priorities: their intention to extend the Bush-era tax cuts to middle-class Americans and to ratify a new version of the Strategic Arms Reduction Treaty (START) with Russia. A third nonnegotiable for lawmakers was a budget bill to keep the government funded.[7]

Achieving tax cuts and START was incredibly ambitious for a lame-duck session. Not only were lawmakers who had been voted out of office more or less biding their time until the sun finally set on their term, but it was also typically a slow time legislatively—a time when symbolic votes were often taken and certain smaller pet projects sometimes saw the light of day. Historically, major priorities had not been left until lame duck. It was simply not an effective strategy. But the deep political polarization that steadily worsened during Obama's presidency often meant that lawmakers weren't able to make the compromises necessary to pass legislation until a deadline forced their hand.

The White House had waited until the last second to lay out exactly what it wanted to walk away with before the session officially closed. The president and his aides never seemed to come out swinging until they were undeniably and almost irreversibly backed into a corner. It was a pattern that had become all too familiar during Obama's first couple years in office even on the issue they had elevated as their holy grail: health care reform. The White House had continually avoided telling congressional negotiators what exactly the president wanted in the bill right up until reform was circling the drain at the beginning of 2010. This pattern offered a valuable lesson for LGBT activists: this White House was often inert until they were left with absolutely no other choice but to take action.[8]

Even if Gibbs didn't include the NDAA among the White House's priorities for lame duck, he knew better than to shoot down the possibility of passing "don't ask, don't tell" repeal during press briefings. That would have incensed activists, who were more than ready to attack the administration on the issue. But Gibbs only mentioned repeal as a potential lame-duck win when he was asked about it directly—questions Gibbs was receiving regularly from both me and another gay reporter who had joined me in the briefing room, Chris Johnson, from the *Washington Blade*.[9]

The perception that repeal was more of an afterthought for Democrats than a serious priority—a notion that was corroborated for me by reports from staff members of key Senators—was confirmed when Majority Leader Reid announced the Senate floor schedule for the week of December 6. He enumerated tax cuts, START, and the government budget bill plus votes on the DREAM Act and some other extraneous bills. Nowhere did he mention "don't ask, don't tell" repeal or the Defense authorization bill.[10]

Reid said the Senate should be able to complete the priorities he had laid out in time to adjourn by his target date, December 17.

"That should give us ample time to do those things before we leave here," he summarized from the Senate floor. "That's the plan, we hope we can execute it."[11]

Senator Levin, perhaps a little shocked by the omission of Defense, asked Reid to say something about the legislation. Oh yeah, "We're also trying to figure out a time to move forward on the defense authorization bill," Reid added.

It was not a good sign to say the least. Reid's language mirrored that of the White House, which was also being reinforced by my sources on the Hill. Not only did it appear that repeal only had a slim chance of getting a vote, but it also signaled that the Democratic leadership wasn't particularly invested in trying to secure those votes. Yet Senator Levin surely had a stake in passing the legislation, with or without repeal. He did not want the distinction of being the first Armed Services Committee chairman in half a century to fail to fully fund the Department of Defense.

All of these factors led me to publish an unusually frank column in *The Advocate* on Monday, December 6. "I have to level with you," I wrote, "'Don't ask, don't tell' repeal is most likely dead. Goodness knows, I hope to be wrong, but nothing short of a December-induced miracle on 34th Street could resurrect it now."[12]

Declaring the effort's defeat wasn't something I took lightly. But as all the politicians postured and bloviated, I felt obligated to translate the subtext of what I thought was really happening to readers throughout the country. Otherwise, I was afraid activists would keep reading occasional quotes from Gibbs and Reid and others without being prepared for the disappointing endgame we were slowly but surely headed toward.

After I posted word of the effort's probable demise, several of my sources contacted me to say they agreed with my analysis and appreciated the piece. Reid's communications director, Jim Manley, however, wasn't one of them. Although I had ultimately laid blame for the state of play on the White House, I had also skewered Reid's weekend performance on the Senate floor. Manley called to assure me that "don't ask, don't tell" repeal was most certainly a key issue for Senator Reid.

"Look, this is a priority for the Majority Leader," Manley emphasized, clearly annoyed with the tone of my article.

I was not reassured in the least. I wanted to put lawmakers on notice that they would not escape scrutiny and even backlash when the effort finally went south. The only thing Manley's call convinced me of was that no one wanted to be remotely associated with what I had described in the column as an "epic failure" in leadership during the two-year period that had amounted to "the best opportunity that history has ever presented to advance LGBT equality bills."

No one, including President Obama. So four days after Reid had forgotten to mention repeal in his vote schedule from the Senate floor, two days after my phone call with Manley, and one day after Sudbay and I had our brush with Obama at the White House, a spot opened up in the calendar to take a vote on the Defense authorization bill to which repeal was attached. When they scheduled the vote for December 8, Democrats knew they didn't have the sixty senators necessary to beat a GOP filibuster. But they also didn't want to walk away from the session without giving it a shot. That would have been a blatant sign that repeal didn't matter. Long before that early December vote came to pass, I couldn't find anyone who believed Senate Democrats and the White House had properly lined up the votes for the legislation. Now they seemed to be rushing a vote in order to check a box.

Nonetheless, by Wednesday afternoon of December 8 the White House went on record in an effort to make it clear to the public that President Obama had done his part even if the measure failed.

"The President has been reaching out to Senators from both sides of the aisle to reiterate his desire to see Congress pass the National Defense Authorization Act, including a repeal of 'don't ask, don't tell', during the lame duck," White House spokesperson Shin Inouye told me and other reporters.[13]

Ultimately, the vote was delayed another day, but that mattered little. As expected, the Defense funding bill went down to defeat on December 9 by a vote of 57–40, garnering only one GOP senator: Susan Collins. Three senators didn't cast a vote and a newly elected Senator from West Virginia, Joe Manchin III, will always hold the distinction of being the sole Democrat to vote against the legislation.[14]

The repeal effort for the year appeared to finally be lost. The Defense authorization bill is a particularly complicated piece of legislation that usually requires at least a month or two of debate and negotiation before Congress passes it, even without a controversial rider. There simply wasn't enough time left to shepherd the mammoth bill to the president's desk by Reid's preferred date, December 17.

It was over, I thought. Finally, the clock had run out. Finally, the lame-duck timing that some of us had been warning against had snuffed out whatever embers of hope had remained for repeal. It was dead for at least the next two years, if not longer. To be honest, as crushed as I was, a piece of me also felt relieved that the charade was finally over. I had been sounding the alarm bells for months, as had other LGBT bloggers and reporters and some advocacy groups like SLDN, Servicemembers United, and GetEQUAL. I was exhausted from trying to tell a story that most Washington insiders didn't want to be told and many LGBT activists didn't want to accept.

In the briefing room, leading up to the vote, fellow members of the White House press corps had been asking me what I thought the odds were for passing repeal. I was telling them 10 percent. When they asked why, I explained there just didn't seem to be the will or the time to debate the Defense authorization bill and so, what originally seemed like a silver bullet for repeal, had backfired.

Time of death: Dec. 9, 2010, approximately 4:04 p.m. Eastern.

But at 4:24 p.m., as I was fleshing out my story, I received a cryptic e-mail from a Senate staffer:

"4:30 pm—Lieberman, Collins, Udall just called a press conference in Senate press gallery."

Was it good news?

"No . . . but it will reveal how the fight will go on," was the response.

Senator Mark Udall of Colorado, who was on the Senate floor lamenting the partisan politics to which repeal had fallen victim, was the first to publicly mention that another effort was afoot.

Minutes later he would leave the Senate floor to join Senators Lieberman and Collins as they announced their intent to introduce a stand-alone "don't ask, don't tell" repeal bill, something that had really never been seen as an option before. In fact, most people assumed repeal didn't stand even a remote chance of passing unless it was attached to some other pressing priority—a time-tested method for passing things through the Senate that might not otherwise stand a chance alone. But now, after months of lobbying, repeal had developed a momentum all its own. Lieberman and Collins and other Senators were invested in the bill, had spent time on the bill, and desperately wanted to see it pass.

During the press conference, both Lieberman and Collins lambasted Majority Leader Reid for rushing the vote that day. Republican Senators had signed a pledge saying they wouldn't vote on any other pieces of legislation until they got a tax vote. They were as desperate to solidify tax cuts for the richest 2 percent of Americans as Democrats were for the middle class. So calling the vote on the Defense bill before the tax cuts had been finalized ensured its failure.[15]

Lieberman, who had been making heroic efforts to serve as a mediator between Reid and Republicans in those final days, had been saying for weeks that he was "confident" they had the 60 votes necessary to pass repeal. In fact, it was a strategy he and his staff had developed to push Reid to take a vote during lame duck. That way, the Majority Leader wouldn't be able to claim that repeal didn't have enough support for a vote.[16]

As he stood at the podium in the Senate press gallery, Lieberman charged that Reid had doomed repeal by calling the vote on the larger Defense bill too early. Sixty or more Senators, he said, "were committed and asked that the vote on the Defense authorization bill be held up until after the tax vote." Of course, Reid's staff was arguing that Republicans were holding the Defense bill hostage in order to force the tax vote. Both positions held some merit, but the bottom line was that both sides were content to sacrifice "don't ask, don't tell" repeal on the way to achieving their ends on taxes.

"We have suffered a setback," Lieberman noted in his signature monotone cadence, "but the reality remains that sixty—and I think maybe more than sixty—members of the Unites States Senate have made clear that they support the repeal of 'don't ask, don't tell.' And while that is the case—and it is the case—we're not going to give up."[17]

"So it ain't over till it's over. And insofar as the efforts to repeal 'don't ask, don't tell,' it ain't over," Lieberman concluded before stepping away from the podium.

Lieberman's staff knew that if at the end of the day Washington headlines read, "'Don't Ask, Don't Tell' Is Dead," the effort would indeed be impossible to revive. So as soon as they realized Reid was going to call the vote without negotiating with Collins, essentially consigning it to failure, they hastily arranged a press conference. Just before the press conference was scheduled to begin, Lieberman's legislative director Todd Stein contacted Collins's staff to ask if she would cosponsor a freestanding repeal bill. She agreed, as long as the legislation read exactly the same as it had before. In that moment, "don't ask, don't tell" repeal suddenly became a bipartisan bill, a status it had failed to achieve in the Senate since its introduction in March. The stand-alone measure Lieberman and Collins introduced later that day was something Lieberman's staff had only discussed as a Plan B internally and with Representative Hoyer's office. They felt that publicly discussing it prior to the press conference that day—even with LGBT advocates— would have prematurely signaled defeat on the preferred method of passing repeal, the NDAA.[18]

After the news conference, I revised the odds of passing repeal up to 20 percent. One White House correspondent looked at me perplexed by the fact that my probability computation had risen rather than plummeted after the disastrous Defense authorization vote garnered only fifty-seven senators.

"Now that it's not weighted down by a Defense bill that would take weeks to debate," I explained, "it's actually got a shot."

STILL, EVEN WITH SUPPORT from Lieberman, Collins, and Udall, the prognosis for the stand-alone bill wasn't good. There continued to be no evidence that it was a critical part of the White House "to-do" list. The West Wing was focused on START. The president had met with General Colin Powell for a photo-op to discuss the merits of the treaty and take questions from reporters—the type of visibility that materializes when someone has real skin in the game.[19]

By Monday, December 13, Gibbs seemed quite certain that, after tax cuts, the debate on START would be next. If, as Reid had said a number of times, he was aiming to recess by the end of the week, there simply wouldn't be time for a vote on the stand-alone repeal bill. The tax bill hadn't passed, ratifying START would likely take a few days, and Congress had yet to pass a budget bill for the coming year.[20]

"If the legislative effort fails, are there other options on the table?" I asked Gibbs during that Monday briefing. "I mean, this is a distinct possibility now," I added.[21]

"Well, I should say this," he responded resolutely, "I think it's a distinct possibility that 'don't ask, don't tell' will be repealed by the end of this year and that's where our effort is focused."

He sounded uncharacteristically confident, but I wasn't entirely persuaded. Gibbs had to sound certain. In the event of failure, the White House needed to be able to make the case that they made an honest effort but that Republicans had blocked the bill.

The outlook brightened slightly when the tax bill passed on Wednesday. Senate Democrats and Republicans agreed to extend Bush-era tax cuts across the board to both middle-class Americans and the country's wealthiest income earners. What's more, three Senate Republicans went on record saying they would support the stand-alone repeal bill in the wake of the tax vote: Senators Scott Brown of Massachusetts, Lisa Murkowski of Alaska, and Olympia Snowe of Maine.[22]

Additionally, House Majority Leader Steny Hoyer had found a way to pass the stand-alone repeal bill through the House that would render it a "privileged" resolution in the Senate, meaning the measure could bypass days of procedural hurdles that might have complicated its path once it reached the Senate. That same Wednesday, the House voted 250–175 to pass the legislation, significantly ratcheting up pressure on the Senate to act. But finding time in the Senate calendar was still the kicker.[23]

By Thursday, the same Robert Gibbs who had professed the likelihood of passing repeal earlier that week, seemed a little less sure of himself.

"I believe we have the votes," he told me during the White House brief. "It's clear that whether it's Senator Brown or Senator Murkowski or Senator Snowe or others, there is an effort to get this done if we have time to."[24]

If we have time to? That sounded much less definitive, but it was a prognosis echoed by Senator Reid. "I don't know if I'll bring it [up for a vote] before Christmas," Reid told reporters, adding that he could call the Senate back for post-holiday votes. Before he turned his attention to "don't ask, don't tell" repeal, he wanted to pass the $1.1 trillion budget bill to fund the government that he had been negotiating for months.[25]

Everyone had assumed the budget bill was on course for passage over the weekend. Reid said he had the votes, including nine Republicans. But when the bill finally surfaced, it included about $8 billion of "earmarks"—a Washington term for special projects that go specifically to a certain lawmaker's district. Though the previous year's budget had also come in at $1.1 trillion, the atmospherics in Washington had changed drastically after Tea Party voters demonstrated a new urgency around fiscal responsibility.[26]

GOP Minority Leader Mitch McConnell, who had supported the bill prior to the midterms and was getting more than $100 million in earmarks for his district, did an immediate one-eighty on Reid and started railing against the measure. It was one of those unusual moments in Washington when nearly everyone goes to bed one night thinking the momentum is heading one way and then wakes up the next morning to a completely different reality. At around 8:00 p.m. Thursday evening, Senator Reid called a press conference to concede defeat on the budget bill and pull it from the floor.[27]

But the demise of the budget bill meant good things for passage of "don't ask, don't tell" repeal. Reid suddenly needed to fill the gap in the schedule as he pieced together a new deal on the budget. And just like that, there was new hope for repeal. Reid's office began contacting Lieberman, other pro-repeal lawmakers, and LGBT advocates Thursday night to inform them that the Majority Leader had filed for a vote on repeal. On Saturday, December 18, US Senators would have one final chance to weigh in on the possibility of eradicating systemic, government-directed discrimination in the military.

At the White House on Friday, Gibbs seemed pretty sure of himself on "don't ask, don't tell," which finally struck me as a good sign.

"I think you can see certainly the path for important victories in the repeal of 'don't ask, don't tell' and in the ratification of the new START treaty," Gibbs said in an off-camera briefing.[28]

In some ways, it wasn't so much what he said that day as the way he said it. He spoke with a subtle but rare candor on almost everything, which yielded more complete sentences than usual. Perhaps Gibbs was just sensing the end of a long, grueling lame-duck session, but he seemed confident that he could finally envision a conclusion to this three-ring circus. And at long last, he was including repeal among his list of probable wins without prompting from journalists.

I stayed in the briefing room that day as I typed the day's quotes into a quick story titled: "Gibbs Bullish on DADT." By the time I finished posting the piece, Gibbs had reemerged to do a TV interview about what he expected to be the administration's lame-duck successes. All the reporters had vacated the room by then—having gone back to their desks to tap out prognostications about the bitter end of the session. It was just me, some camera hands, and Gibbs, who was being interviewed remotely. I sat there taking in the spectacle with the distinct realization that I might not frequent that room too many more times since I would be switching jobs in January to work at a new LGBT advocacy organization called Equality Matters. When the interview wrapped, it occurred to me that I might never catch Gibbs in such an unguarded moment again.

So as he headed for the sliding door that separates the briefing room from the White House press aides, I approached Gibbs, stuck out my hand and said, "This might sound a little strange, Robert, but thank you for calling on me over the past couple years."

As frustrated as I had been on numerous occasions in that room—either because of the nonanswers Gibbs had tossed my way or, worse yet, the many times he had passed me over for a question—I always respected the fact that he had indeed continued to call on me. I might have suffered some two-week dry spells in between opportunities, but whether I was allowed to voice an inquiry at all was entirely in the hands of the press secretary commanding the podium. And as loathe as Gibbs seemed to call on someone who was bound to ask a question for which, nine times out of ten, he would have no satisfactory answer, he never shut me out altogether.

Gibbs and I had developed a respect for one another and for the give and take in which we had both reluctantly engaged. And over the course of that extended encounter, perhaps we had even developed a strange affinity for each other, or at least I had for him.

Gibbs, who was surely caught off guard by my unjournalistic advance, took my hand, tilted his head toward me slightly, and graciously affirmed, "Of course, of course," with the slight embarrassment of someone who ever so briefly just broke from character. Those were the last words I ever spoke to Robert Gibbs face to face.

I WENT TO BED THAT night filled with anxious anticipation; nothing in Washington was ever a sure thing, and I knew repeal could evaporate just as mystically as the budget bill had. Though most of my sources were cautiously optimistic that the key Republicans—Senators Susan Collins, Olympia Snowe, Scott Brown, and Lisa Murkowski—would pull through on repeal, I had gotten word on the Democratic side that Senator Joe Manchin was still a "no" and Senators Kent Conrad and Jim Webb were on the fence. If we lost three Democrats in total, we would need to pick up at least five Republicans to reach the sixty mark for a win.

Lieberman and his staff members, who had been continuously lobbying senators and their aides on a daily, sometimes hourly basis, were near certain they had it won. But nothing is a lock until the roll is called and the votes are cast. "This is not a done deal in any way," warned one of my confidants in the Senate.[29]

Saturday, the day of the vote, just happened to be a gloriously sunny day. As I approached the Capitol with laptop, press badge, and recorders in hand, the Capitol dome practically looked transcendent glistening in the sunshine. I had trod that path any number of times and rarely thought much of it, but I found myself stopping in my tracks as if to pay homage to a moment that had yet to pass and that, no matter the outcome, would reverberate for a long time to come.

After snapping a quick shot of the Capitol, I called Joe Sudbay and continued walking toward the security entrance on the Senate side. "Got anything?" I fired—our standard greeting to each other in the waning days of the session. I sort of doubted he would have any news; Joe and I had been communicating constantly on repeal and, by that point, were nearly functioning with a single brain. Though we never revealed sources, we shared nearly all intel with each other in those final months with the mutual understanding that if it was worth relaying, it was solidly sourced. For the most part, I had called Joe for grounding—sort of like eating comfort food when you're not really hungry. What he said that day was inconsequential. I just needed to know he was in my bunker before I got sucked into the maelstrom of floor speeches and vote counting and last-minute maneuvering that would be pulsing through the bullpen of reporters in the Senate press gallery.

After passing through the Capitol building metal detectors and taking the elevator three floors up to the press room, I scurried around looking for an open cubicle within earshot of a TV. Although the Senate chamber was accessible just off the press gallery, no electronics were allowed in it. So reporters spent most of their time typing away at cubicles, relying on televised footage and only entering the chamber occasionally to catch firsthand the drama of an impassioned floor speech or particularly contentious and historic votes.

It was the same Senate press gallery in which I'd had my run-in with an irascible Senator John McCain three months earlier following the first failed repeal vote in September. He wasn't testy originally—far from it. He and his compatriot, Senator Lindsey Graham, had run up to the press gallery immediately after the vote to exult over their success in blocking the repeal measure to the forty or so reporters who had gathered to grab quotes for their stories. But when they waded into the territory of whether the "don't ask, don't tell" policy had ever been invoked to investigate the personal lives of service members—their e-mails, relationships, and off-duty activities—things went downhill pretty quickly.

Graham was the one who first spiked my heartbeat when, in the course of an answer, he declared, "People in the air force are not breaking into rooms finding out if you're gay. That's not going on."[30]

I immediately felt uncomfortable with the blanket insinuation that people's private lives were not being intruded upon in the course of "don't ask, don't tell" investigations. Author and researcher Nathaniel Frank had documented abuse of the policy in hundreds of cases in his book on "don't ask, don't tell," *Unfriendly Fire: How the Gay Ban Undermines the Military and Weakens America*. Nonetheless, I was inclined to let it pass. How the policy was being prosecuted in the military wasn't really the story of the day—the fact that the vote had failed and the repeal effort was on life support was the matter at hand.[31]

But McCain wouldn't let it rest.

"The regulations are, we do not go out and seek to find out someone's sexual orientation," he said, stretching Graham's fib. "We do not!"[32]

That was it. Two senators were spewing lies to a group of mainstream reporters who may or may not have known the truth. More importantly, they were trouncing all over people who were risking their lives for this country even as their livelihoods were being threatened. Not to mention the cost of the policy for the thirteen thousand service members who had already been discharged.[33]

"But senator, that's not the way it plays out," I said flatly.

He turned to where I was seated about two feet away from him and glared at me. Uh oh.

"That is the fact! That is the fact," McCain shot back. "Now ma'am, I know the military very well, and I know what's being done. And what is being done is, that they are not seeking out people who are gay. And I don't care what you say, I know it's a fact."[34]

"It's not what I say . . . " I offered, struggling to remain even-tempered.

"I don't care what you say, and I don't care what others say!" he interrupted. "I've seen it in action. I've seen it in action. I have sons in the military, I know the military very well. So they are not telling you the truth."

Actually, I had personally witnessed hearings at the Senate Armed Services Committee—on which McCain served—where a discharged service member testified about his personal e-mails, among other things, being compromised in the course of an investigation. McCain himself had questioned former Major Mike Almy, who was kicked out after the air force searched his e-mail and discovered correspondence that suggested he was gay. But Almy never "told," so to speak; he never declared that he was gay, even under questioning by his superiors.[35]

"Senator, just to make sure, just to make sure about this . . . " I said, wanting to get McCain on record as clearly as possible.

"Just to make sure," he responded. "We do not go out and seek out and find out . . . "

"Private e-mails are not being searched?" I pressed. "Private e-mails are not being searched?"

McCain rebuffed, "We do not go out and find out whether someone is gay or not."

"There are documented cases of that," I replied.

"They do not, they do not, they do not," McCain protested. "You can say that they are, you can say that pigs fly, it's not true!"

Graham stepped in. "Bring him to my office, I'd like to see him," he said, referring to the discharged officer I had referenced, Almy.

I had posed as many follow-ups as I felt comfortable asking when reporter Chris Geidner, then with *Metro Weekly*, jumped in to back me up. "It is the case of Mike Almy, Senators," said Geidner, repeating the charge several times.

"Bring them to our office," McCain said defiantly, adding in a sing-song tone, "It is not the policy, it is not the policy, it is not the policy, it is not the policy!"

September 21, 2010, had been a particularly disheartening day, and the verbal lashing from Senator McCain left me even more disconcerted. I was worried, too, that I had damaged any semblance of objectivity I had maintained up to that point in front of a room full of my colleagues, some of whom knew me as a gay reporter and others who didn't.

But a small smile swept across my face when a friend contacted me a couple hours later to say they were getting ready to post video of the exchange. Cameras were not allowed in that portion of the press gallery, but someone had clearly violated protocol. I didn't ask questions, though I was somewhat concerned that I would come off as disrespectful in the footage. Fortunately, McCain's temper trumped my inquisition, making me look notably stoic by comparison. Despite the anger that had welled up within me in that moment, I came across as persistent but measured. And I was right—or at least my inquiry was anchored in fact—which never hurts. McCain did not fare so well. Though he may have been correct about the initial intent of the policy, in practice, the military had applied it much differently.

Once the story posted that day, several progressive blogs picked it up immediately. Sudbay wrote a piece for AMERICAblog titled, "When Kerry Eleveld Wouldn't Let John McCain Lie About DADT." It went viral and was covered by programs like *Countdown with Keith Olbermann* on MSNBC—a silver lining to an otherwise dismal day.[36]

That altercation hung in my mind as I sat in the press gallery nearly three months later taking in the floor speeches from the TV near my cubicle. To be honest, I was pretty scattered that day and entirely fried from the past several months, which had felt like a pitched battle—sometimes against the administration, sometimes against the Senate Democratic leadership, and occasionally against Republicans. One of the only things that seemed harmonious in those final weeks was how desperately all the LGBT activists wanted and, in some cases, *needed* a positive outcome on "don't ask, don't tell." LGBT advocates in Washington did not always agree on strategy nor did they all trust each other, but finally we were all of one mind. Every single one of us realized that our chances for a major advancement on repeal would be dead for the rest of Obama's first term and perhaps as much as a decade or more if the legislation failed to move before year's end. Now all we could do was watch and wait for the verdict of a vote that would inevitably alter the course of the march toward equality no matter what its outcome.

As I listened to the floor speeches, I did my best to tweet out some of the juicier moments to my followers. Senator Ron Wyden, a Democrat from Oregon who was two days away from undergoing surgery for early stage prostate cancer, took the floor. The announcement of his medical condition several days earlier had prompted questions about whether he would miss Saturday's vote, thereby leaving repeal one vote shy of the critical sixty mark. But he made it that day, and his remarks offered a glimpse of the historic nature of the day.

"Let me just say briefly, Mr. President, why it was so important for me to be here today," Wyden said, addressing the Senate President presiding over the floor debate. "'Don't ask, don't tell' is wrong. I don't care who you love, if you love this country enough to risk your life for it, you shouldn't have to hide who you are. You ought to be able to serve."[37]

Senator Lieberman, the glue that held the repeal coalition together in an otherwise corrosive Senate climate, was also on the floor that morning even though it was the Sabbath—a demonstration of his personal commitment to repeal given the fact that he's an observant Jew. Lieberman had walked five miles to the Capitol that morning in keeping with Jewish tradition that prohibits the use of automobiles during Shabbat. I never doubted that he would be there, but his dedication was impressive nonetheless.[38]

Things were looking good. There were no last-minute red flags from my sources and Democrats were sounding distinctly resolute in their floor speeches. Then Senator McCain took the floor.

"Now, I am aware this vote will probably pass today in a lame-duck session, and there will be high fives all over the liberal bastions of America," McCain groused, looking particularly grim. "But don't think that it won't be at great cost," he warned, delivering a final dose of the paranoid prophecy he had specialized in over the course of the debate. "I hope that when we pass this legislation that we will understand that we are doing great damage, and we could possibly and probably . . . harm the battle effectiveness which is so vital to the support, to the survival of our young men and women in the military."[39]

I had been specifically waiting to hear McCain speak, and his grudging acceptance of repeal was all the confirmation I needed that the vote would be a success. He knew we had it, reporters knew we had it, anyone with a pulse knew we had it. But hearing it from McCain—who had been instrumental in opening up time in the Senate floor schedule through his crusade against Reid's budget bill—felt like sweet justice.

All that was left to do now was hold my breath. As the voting began around 11:35 a.m., I started ticking down the list of must gets. Democrats Webb and Conrad: yes. Republicans Brown, Murkowski, and Snowe: yes. Even freshman GOP Senator Mark Kirk—who had not been a main target—voted our way. It was a done deal.

Some strange hybrid of relief and exultation flooded my body. Tears filled my eyes. Journalists aren't supposed to cry—it defies objectivity—and, as a rule, we are a rather jaded bunch. But for the last year, I had gone to bed every night and awoken every morning wondering, what question can I ask, what story can I write, what truth can I reveal that will help clear the path for repeal. And surely none of my counterparts in the gallery had any illusions about my investment in the outcome of that vote.

Final tally: 63–33. Six Republicans voted for repeal.[40]

This was only the cloture vote—the 60-vote hurdle that determined whether or not the bill would advance to consideration for final passage. But it was the vote that *mattered*—if we could get 60 to advance it, getting the 51 votes to finally pass the measure was a sure thing.

I tried to focus. Must. Post. Outcome. I reread the lede I had crafted in an expectant state not long before the vote commenced—I had been unwilling to jinx it by writing the words hours earlier, which is what I should have done. In fact, several hours before I had asked one of my editors in Los Angeles, Andrew Harmon, to construct a short piece in case the vote failed. "I can't bear to write it," I told him. "Too bleak."

Republicans could have delayed the final vote on the legislation for another day according to Senate procedure, but their leadership obviously concluded that stalling gained them nothing other than an abbreviated holiday break given the decisive numbers. The Senate press gallery sent out word that the vote on final passage would proceed at around 3:00 p.m.

I joined a dozen other reporters in the Senate chamber to witness the watershed moment that would finally actualize repeal. As many times as I had reported from the press gallery and entered the chamber to watch floor speeches, I had never actually watched a vote take place in real time.

An unlikely assortment of advocates looked on from separate corners of the expanse: members of the LGBT groups that had fought for repeal, Obama administration officials, House and Senate aides, and LGBT journalists. But I hardly took note of them from my perch in the balcony. Hanging over the rail for optimal bird's-eye view, I was more fascinated with observing the demeanor of different Senators as they recorded their roll call vote. Most of them would casually approach the Senate clerk and either give the high sign or a thumb's down as they made eye contact with her. Sometimes they would engage her in a brief exchange to relay their position. She called off the entire list of senators in alphabetical order for every vote, but their vote was not finalized until they had personally interacted with the clerk.

As the Senators milled about, cycling to and fro, one caught my eye in particular. Lindsey Graham of South Carolina strode over the plush blue carpeting toward the platform where the clerk was standing. He caught her eye as he approached, lifted his arm, turned his thumb toward the ground and began zealously pumping his arm up and down. The animated gesture seemed so excessive and disdainful inside a chamber where everything and everyone commenced with such civility, such collegiality. It was both ridiculous and unnecessarily hostile at the same time.

But no amount of contempt could erase the fact that the final numbers posted at 65–31 in favor of extinguishing the odious law—14 votes more than needed. The policy that had taken four months to enact after President Bill Clinton first announced it in 1993, had finally been undone in Congress by seventeen years of sustained activism. I had been lucky enough to witness the culmination of those efforts, the labor of so many who had come before me. But especially the work of former Army Captain Michelle Benecke and attorney Dixon Osburn, who had the vision to cofound SLDN in 1993, and the literally thousands of service members whose military careers had been ruined by the policy and who lent their stories to the cause.[41]

I floated through the rest of the day in a hazy, dreamlike state. Some mainstream reporters who had been covering "don't ask, don't tell" as a part of their beat shot me congratulatory glances and nods from across the room. Elated e-mails flooded my inbox. Key lawmakers offered interviews. A couple news outlets requested to speak with me. My concentration was shot. I performed the rest of my tasks that day with minimal effectiveness and went out that night to share a celebratory drink with some friends.

The next morning I awoke to the strangest feeling. A pervasive stillness had settled into me, welcome but unexpected. After nearly fifteen years of continuously searching for the next interview to land, the next story to break, and the adrenaline pushes that invariably accompany the chase of any tale worth telling, I felt no need to call anyone, plot my next advance, or even contemplate what remained unreported, undiscovered.

I made a cup of coffee and stood on the balcony of my fourth floor apartment, looking south over the city that had consumed me—from the Capitol dome to the Washington monument and everything in between—for nearly two years.

I didn't wake up chasing a story that day. It had been written.

THE LEGAL ADVANCE · 7

PRESIDENT OBAMA HAD LOGGED A MAJOR VICTORY WITH "don't ask, don't tell" repeal. But LGBT activists were not about to let the administration sit on its laurels. Now that their first major equality goal had been achieved, they were ready to lobby for marriage equality. Regardless of whether Obama and his aides were ready for renewed pressure, they just couldn't escape it.

In fact, even as grassroots activists and advocates on the Hill had been relentlessly pushing forward on repeal legislation in 2010, LGBT legal advocates had been quietly advancing their bid to dismantle the Defense of Marriage Act. Over the course of 2010, a distinction began to develop in the way the Obama administration's political operatives and its lawyers tackled the issues of DOMA and same-sex marriage. It was an unspoken division—one that was simply a product of a person's function and corresponding responsibilities—but it would continue to influence the way the administration handled the two issues in 2011 and 2012.

On one hand, the attorneys at the Justice Department and in the White House counsel's office knew that the Defense of Marriage Act would keep dogging them because they would have to keep responding to the cases that legal advocates were pushing forward. They had deadlines to meet, briefs and arguments to deliver, and the unrelenting call of a legal system to answer to. Certainly, government lawyers did not all agree on what to do about DOMA, but they knew they couldn't just press snooze on it indefinitely until they felt better situated to deal with the law.

The political operatives, on the other hand, weren't grappling with something so tangible as the grind of the legal system. They were dealing with the much more nebulous area of political rhetoric and posturing regarding same-sex marriage. And unlike government lawyers, they seemed to have the sense that with the right communications strategy, perhaps they could minimize the president's exposure on the topic and skirt the issue—at least until after the 2012 campaign. Sure, DOMA was tricky and perhaps unavoidable as it moved through the courts. But Obama had a firmly stated policy stance in favor of overturning it, something they continued to make clear at every possible turn. Ideally, that would suffice, keeping LGBT activists at bay and buying President Obama enough time to spare him the complication of reexamining his civil unions stance before the next election.

There were two problems with that theory. First, it completely ignored the fact that the culture, the judicial system, and the states were slowly but surely accepting and advancing same-sex marriage. Eventually, those forces were going to penetrate Washington and force the hands of politicians, regardless of whether they were ready for it. Second, President Obama had won the 2008 election on the idea that he represented a new day and a different kind of politician. He was supposed to be ahead of the times—the leader of a new era in America—not comfortably following the pack. Even if the complexities of DOMA and state ballot measures were somewhat murky for the general public, same-sex marriage was a simple concept. You were either for everyone's freedom to marry or against it. Obama was against it. No amount of posturing could blur that truth. And for the first time for progressives, embracing marriage equality was really becoming a question of morality, not politics. In other words, the president's marriage stance, which was originally forged during his 2004 bid for the US Senate, was beginning to seem both antiquated and immoral to progressives by 2010.

Conservatives had long framed the marriage question as a moral one, and in their view, restricting the institution to heterosexual couples was the right moral stance. Many progressives, meanwhile, had viewed the question instead as a political one—what's palatable enough to make a

Democratic politician electable by the general public? Throughout the first few presidential election cycles of the new millennium, the people who were most passionate about the issue of same-sex marriage were Christian conservatives (who typically made up around 25 percent of the electorate) and, increasingly, LGBT voters (who roughly accounted for 4 to 6 percent of the electorate). Those were losing numbers for the marriage equality side. Many progressives, gays included, had ceded the issue to conservatives, at least insofar as presidential politics were concerned. More people on the right were animated by it—enough so that a politician's marriage stance alone might dictate their vote.

But the number of Democrats who felt strongly about giving everyone the freedom to marry began to change as more people began to see the real harms being done to their neighbors, their friends, and their family members. It wasn't so much a strategy of any one particular group as it was an emergent force that started to take hold as LGBT people became more visible and vocal about their lives. The protests that ensued following the passage of Prop 8 were a sign of visible anguish among LGBT activists and their allies. On top of that, headlines about inequities became more prominent even as public awareness mounted. Stories about people like New Jersey's Lieutenant Laurel Hester, a cancer-stricken Ocean County retiree who made a desperate effort to transfer her pension funds to her domestic partner in the final days of her life, reminded Americans that discrimination wasn't simply a theoretical matter. Real people were being hurt, and in many cases, irreparably. The more media attention the injustices got, the more Americans cared. And the more they cared, the more media attention the injustices got.[1]

At the same time, LGBT Americans just kept coming out, more and more of them, and at even younger ages. Pioneering activist Harvey Milk would have been proud. He had exhorted gays and lesbians in the '70s to come out of the closet, to tell their stories, and to do it over and over again.

"Gay people, we will not win their rights by staying quietly in our closets," Milk told a massive throng of more than 250,000 marchers on June 25, 1978, at a San Francisco Gay Freedom Day Parade. "We are coming out! We are coming out to fight the lies, the myths, the distortions! We are coming out to tell the truth about gays! For I'm tired of the conspiracy of silence."[2]

The greater movement took Milk's advice to heart and continued to rediscover its urgency as the AIDS epidemic took hold. By 1994, a *Newsweek* poll found that 53 percent of people said they knew someone who was lesbian or gay; in 2008, *Newsweek* found that number had risen to 78 percent of respondents. And everyone who knew somebody was more likely to support laws that protected and equalized treatment for LGBT Americans. A Public Religion Research Institute poll released in 2013 found that people who had "a close friend or family member" who was lesbian or gay were almost twice as likely to support same-sex marriage as those who didn't (63 to 36 percent).[3] Nothing demonstrated this better than the divide between President George W. Bush and Vice President Dick Cheney, whose daughter Mary is gay. In 2004, Bush publicly backed a constitutional amendment banning same-sex marriage during his reelection campaign. But when Cheney was asked about the issue that year during a vice presidential debate, he famously responded, "Freedom means freedom for everyone."[4]

Meanwhile, the issue that had once uniquely ignited the right caught fire on the left. In 2004, for instance, Pew Research Center found that 36 percent of voters "strongly opposed" same-sex marriage while just 11 percent "strongly favored" it; by 2008, voters who strongly opposed marriage equality had dropped to 30 percent while a growing number, 14 percent, strongly favored it; and by 2012, those numbers were dead even, with 22 percent of voters both strongly opposing it and strongly favoring it.[5]

The switch in sentiment among much of Obama's base—from seeing marriage equality as a political issue that simply needed to be finessed to viewing it as one of moral urgency that must be rectified—was a real problem for the president and his political team, and they knew it. Obama had won the presidency based on the proposition that he was a forward-thinking leader of a new American era, yet his marriage position was completely at odds with that political persona. He was now on the wrong side of a generational debate, favoring tradition over progress. The politician who got elected in 2008 was never going to be able to sell that to the voters he needed in 2012—especially not the young, who had turned out at record rates in 2008 and voted overwhelmingly in his favor.[6]

2010 would not be any kinder to the administration than 2009 had been, even though the White House started out with a big win. On

April 15, 2010, President Obama announced that he would expand hospital visitation rights to same-sex couples. Any hospital that took Medicare or Medicaid—the vast majority across the country—would have to "respect the rights of patients to designate visitors" or risk losing government funding. The rule actually benefited any patient who wasn't married and wanted to choose someone other than a relative or spouse as a primary caregiver. Obama had been talking for years about securing equal rights for same-sex couples, and he often specifically mentioned hospital visitation. But until April 2010 he had little to show for it. The inspiration finally came after the *New York Times* ran a story about Janice Langbehn, who had been kept from the bedside of her dying partner of eighteen years, Lisa Pond. The Washington State couple was on vacation in Florida with their three adopted children when Pond, thirty-nine, collapsed of a brain aneurysm and was rushed to Miami's Jackson Memorial Hospital. Despite the fact that Langbehn and Pond had brought their Washington State power-of-attorney documents, Langbehn was barred from visiting Pond for nearly twenty hours with one exception: she was allowed into the hospital room for five minutes while a priest delivered Pond's last rites.[7]

Lambda Legal brought a lawsuit against the hospital on behalf of Langbehn. When the Florida state judge dismissed the case in September of 2009, the *New York Times* ran a follow-up story in which Langbehn said, "I don't think I will feel complete vindication until all hospitals in the U.S. allow people to decide their own circle of intimacy and who should be there after surgery, during a routine hospitalization, or at the time of death."[8]

Obama chief of staff Rahm Emanuel had a habit of bringing something into the White House in the morning and expecting it to be fixed by 5:00 p.m. That's the spirit in which he handed the article to lawyers in the White House counsel's office one morning. It took a bit longer than one day, but they got it done. It was the perfect issue for Emanuel, who was ever mindful of the greater electorate. On one hand, the LGBT community considered it a huge win—many partners lived in fear of the horror Janice Langbehn, Lisa Pond, and their three children endured. Yet on the other, it wasn't nearly as controversial as taking on same-sex marriage. One *Newsweek* poll in December 2008, for instance, found that while only 39 percent of Americans supported same-sex marriage, 86 percent of respondents favored hospital visitation rights for gay partners.[9]

But the two big legal cases that had been launched in 2009—the *Gill* case challenging DOMA and the *Perry* case against Prop 8—would start yielding results in 2010 that pressured the administration to move beyond carve-outs like hospital visitation. On July 8, 2010, a federal district judge in Boston, Joseph Tauro, ruled in *Gill* that DOMA was unconstitutional and said same-sex couples should be entitled to the same federal benefits as heterosexual couples.

Tauro actually considered two separate cases challenging DOMA— *Gill* and *Commonwealth of Massachusetts v. US Dep't of Health & Human Services*—both of which were filed in Massachusetts, part of the First Circuit. The *Gill* case had been brought by GLAD on behalf of seven married same-sex couples and three widowers who were denied benefits like Social Security survivor payments, health coverage for spouses of federal employees, and the ability to file joint tax returns. The second case, filed in July 2009 by the attorney general of Massachusetts, Martha Coakley, was the first challenge to DOMA by a state. It claimed that the federal law was unconstitutional because it interfered with the state's authority "to define and regulate the marital status of its residents." Not only did this inequity have federal consequences for the sixteen thousand same-sex couples who had married in the Bay State since 2004, it also impacted state programs. The Commonwealth, for instance, couldn't cover same-sex spouses who would have otherwise qualified within its joint federal-state Medicaid program, MassHealth, which offered health care coverage to low- and moderate-income residents. Instead, it had to set up a separate program solely with state funds.[10]

In reviewing the law, Judge Tauro could find no legitimate purpose for the federal government to shut married same-sex couples out of the benefits and protections provided under 1,138 provisions of federal law. He also concluded that DOMA had been motivated by animus. And because "'animus alone cannot constitute a legitimate government interest,'" Tauro wrote, channeling a previous US Supreme Court decision, "this court finds that DOMA lacks a rational basis to support it."[11]

The Tauro ruling was important in part because it drew heavily from *Romer v. Evans*, a precedent-setting Supreme Court ruling for gay rights in 1996 that very much laid the groundwork for future

LGBT wins. In that decision, authored by Justice Anthony Kennedy (the court's frequent swing vote), the Supreme Court overturned a Colorado constitutional amendment blocking any jurisdiction within the state from enacting pro-gay measures, such as nondiscrimination protections. Justice Kennedy's decision in *Romer* appeared as if it had flowed from a pen intent on vanquishing a federal statute that didn't yet exist—DOMA. "It is at once too narrow and too broad," he wrote of the Colorado measure. "It identifies persons by a single trait and then denies them protection across the board." But US lawmakers were undeterred. They overwhelmingly approved DOMA just four months after that Supreme Court ruling struck down Colorado's Amendment 2, and President Bill Clinton signed it into law on September 21, 1996. Still, the ruling would not go unnoticed. Nearly fifteen years later, Judge Tauro's decision overturning DOMA was infused with the spirit of Kennedy's words in *Romer*.[12]

Justice Kennedy was particularly worthy of appeal and consideration precisely because he had penned the majority opinion for both major LGBT victories that had come through the Supreme Court—*Romer v. Evans* (1996) and *Lawrence v. Texas* (2003). So when the initial decision invalidating Prop 8 came down on August 4, 2010, the presiding federal judge, Vaughn Walker, also devoted considerable attention to the analysis Justice Kennedy had written. The closely watched Prop 8 case (aka *Perry*) filed by Ted Olson and David Boies was the first federal court trial in the nation to consider the validity of state bans on same-sex marriage. But the Olson-Boies legal team had the benefit of using legal arguments informed by state challenges dating back to the very first successful trial in Hawaii in 1996, which followed a win from the Hawaii Supreme Court in 1993. What resulted in the 2010 California trial ruling was a devastating blow to the notion that there was any motivation other than prejudice for prohibiting same-sex marriages.[13]

The comprehensive 136-page opinion included a 55-page "Findings of Fact" section that reflected Walker's painstaking examination of whether the government had any reasonable interest in excluding same-sex couples from marriage. Proponents of Proposition 8 presented only two expert witnesses in support of their case. One of them, David Blankenhorn, testified that society benefited from retaining marriage just for heterosexual couples. But Blankenhorn then admitted that "[same-sex] marriage would benefit same-sex couples and their children, would reduce discrimination against gays and lesbians and would be 'a victory for the worthy ideas of tolerance and inclusion,'" as Judge Walker wrote in his opinion. Walker ultimately determined that Blankenhorn lacked sufficient scholarly background to make him a credible expert on the matter in question, meaning that his testimony constituted merely "inadmissible opinion."[14]

Their second witness, Kenneth Miller, a professor of government at California's Claremont McKenna College, asserted that gay and lesbian Americans have demonstrated some measure of political power. It was a contention that might undermine the argument of Olson and Boies that sexual orientation should qualify as a protected class, meaning that any law using sexual orientation as a classification should be viewed with more suspicion by the courts. But Miller also admitted to having scant knowledge of the LGBT experience and conceded that gays had endured a history of "severe prejudice" and "widespread and persistent" discrimination. While Miller may have been an expert on ballot initiatives, it became clear that he knew precious little about LGBT politics. Once again, Walker concluded that the purported expert's opinions were "entitled to little weight."[15]

Meanwhile, the team of lawyers challenging Proposition 8 presented eight lay witnesses and nine expert witnesses—seventeen in total. Their testimony essentially debunked every unfounded claim that anti-gay proponents had employed for years to advance "traditional marriage." In fact, Walker found, the *tradition* of marriage had changed considerably throughout the years. It was once a gendered institution that promoted and maintained certain roles for men (to provide for the family) and women (to raise children); yet it is now considered "a union of equals." It also once excluded interracial couples from marrying, yet that prohibition has ended.

"Race and gender restrictions shaped marriage during eras of race and gender inequality," Walker observed, "but such restrictions were never part of the historical core of the institution of marriage."[16]

The ruling also lanced the notion that the state had an interest in promoting heterosexual marriage by restricting same-sex marriage. Like the decisions of the Massachusetts, Iowa, and other state high courts that had affirmed same-sex couples' equality rights, Walker concluded, "Proponents presented no reliable evidence that allowing same-sex couples to marry will have any negative effects on society or on the institution of marriage," he wrote. In fact, during oral arguments, when Judge Walker repeatedly pressed the proponents' attorney Charles Cooper on how allowing same-sex marriages would harm the interest of promoting "naturally procreative unions," Cooper responded, "Your honor, my answer is: I don't know."[17]

Judge Walker also dispensed with the idea that heterosexual parents are better for children. "Indeed, the evidence shows beyond any doubt that parents' genders are irrelevant to children's developmental outcomes," he wrote, referring to the testimony of psychologist Michael Lamb, who had studied developmental psychology since the '70s. Lamb testified that more than one hundred peer-reviewed studies have shown that children raised by same-sex parents are just as likely to be well adjusted as those raised by opposite-sex couples. He also cited policy statements from the American Psychological Association and seven other professional organizations in support of his claim.[18]

And in so far as the state has an interest in promoting stable households, Walker continued, "evidence shows that Proposition 8 undermines that state interest, because same-sex households have become less stable by the passage of Proposition 8."[19]

Walker was wholly unimpressed by the case the defense had put forward, and he wasn't shy about saying so. The proponents' presentation "was dwarfed by that of plaintiffs," he observed, ruling that Proposition 8 violated the Fourteenth Amendment's Due Process and Equal Protection Clauses of the US Constitution.

"Moral disapproval alone," Walker concluded, "is an improper basis on which to deny rights to gay men and lesbians." It was a distinct nod to Justice Sandra Day O'Connor's concurring opinion in *Lawrence*, which had invoked Kennedy's articulation of this point in *Romer*.[20]

By the time Walker was finished, he had referenced Justice Kennedy's decisions in *Romer v. Evans* and *Lawrence v. Texas* no less than twelve times. As some commentators noted, the opinion read like a love letter to the most important vote on the Supreme Court. Justice Kennedy was the bridge between the court's cohorts of reliably liberal- and conservative-leaning justices—four on each side. Whichever way Kennedy leaned, he typically took the weight of the court with him.

The sweeping ruling in favor of the fundamental right of same-sex couples to marry sparked a firestorm of media interest. Judge Walker had officially planned to release the decision around 2:00 p.m. Pacific time on August 4, but a copy of it leaked nearly an hour early and lit up the Internet within minutes. It could not have arrived at a better time. LGBT advocates were hungry for a victory after Hawaii's Governor Linda Lingle had vetoed a civil unions bill in July and lawmakers in both New York and New Jersey failed to pass marriage bills the previous winter.[21]

The White House issued a bare bones statement about Walker's decision: "The President has spoken out in opposition to Proposition 8 because it is divisive and discriminatory. He will continue to promote equality for LGBT Americans." That was it. The unceremonious communication was a clear sign the White House didn't want to engage. But one statement alone would not satisfy journalists. The ruling was too big and unequivocal. LGBT advocates were elated. And reporters increasingly understood what an enormous bind President Obama was in on gay marriage.[22]

The Wednesday news cycle was already winding down by the time the ruling hit on the East Coast. But the following morning on MSNBC's *The Daily Rundown*, Savannah Guthrie and Chuck Todd kicked off an interview with top White House adviser David Axelrod by grilling him about the president's marriage position.

"I think the American public could be forgiven if they're a little confused about where the president stands on all of this," Guthrie began. "He has said he opposes same-sex marriage. He has said during the campaign he didn't mind what California voters were trying to do, trying to [pass] Prop 8. Yesterday, though, the White House comes out and says, well, the president has spoken out against Prop 8 in the past. He said he would work to repeal the federal Defense of Marriage Act, but that the Justice Department, since he's been president, has actually litigated on behalf of that law. So let's just forget all of that in the past and ask you, where does the president stand today? Does he still oppose same-sex marriage?"[23]

Axelrod raised a brow at the mention of Obama not minding the passage of Proposition 8 and tried to correct the record. "The president opposed Proposition 8 at the time," he noted. "He felt that it was mean-spirited, and he opposed it at the time."[24]

Axelrod then tried to assure his interrogators that the Walker ruling hadn't influenced the president's opinion on the matter one bit. "The president does oppose same-sex marriage, but he supports equality for gay and lesbian couples, and benefits and other issues," Axelrod said. "He supports civil unions, and that's been his position throughout. So nothing has changed."

Perhaps nothing had changed inside the White House, but outside everything was changing. Public opinion was evolving at warp speed, a federal judge had just eviscerated every major argument against same-sex marriage, and Ted Olson and David Boies were doing a victory lap on TV screens across America. There was a palpable feeling that things were on the move and even Axelrod's stoic delivery couldn't convince Guthrie otherwise.

"But David," she responded, "can I just say, I'm looking at an interview right here that Jake Tapper of ABC did back in June of 2008, where Tapper asks him, 'Does it bother you what California's doing?' And the president responds, 'No.'"

Guthrie was right. That's exactly what Obama had said on June 16, 2008, during an on-camera interview. Obama was endorsing the idea that marriage should be decided "at a state and local level," as he put it. The implication was that he was prepared to accept Proposition 8 if that was what Californians wanted. But in so doing, he was inherently endorsing the right of the majority to vote on the rights of a minority.[25]

Axelrod wasn't incorrect about Obama's stance on Prop 8. Obama had sent that letter in 2008 to the LGBT Democratic club in San Francisco saying he opposed the measure. But he had talked out of both sides of his mouth on the issue, and the contradictions were finally catching up to the White House. The topic had become too urgent. Journalists sensed the tide was turning, and they had moved beyond simply throwing out a perfunctory question on LGBT equality here and there.

Chuck Todd took one more pass at clarifying the point.

"Well, David, how about let's clear this up—does the president support states trying to go their own way on same-sex marriage? Do you think it's appropriate for a state to ban it and appropriate for other states to decide it's OK?" asked Todd.

"Well," Axelrod responded, "he does believe that marriage is an issue for the states, and he did oppose Proposition 8."

Wait, let's get this straight: Obama wants the states to decide except for when he opposes the outcome? The answer might have been amusing if the whole interview hadn't been so telling. On the issue of same-sex marriage, the White House was in a bubble, immune to the changing world outside it. Axelrod's assurance that "nothing has changed" may have been an exercise in wishful thinking, but the fact that he even thought he could sell it also revealed how completely out of touch White House officials were.

WHILE THE WALKER ruling was roiling the administration's political operatives, the Tauro ruling on DOMA had greater implications for the administration's lawyers. They now faced the question of whether they should appeal the decision of a federal district court judge to the First Circuit Court of Appeals. The answer to their dilemma would come down to one fundamental question: Was the Defense of Marriage Act constitutional? It was a weighty consideration. Answering "no" would suggest the administration should stop defending the law even though the president has a constitutional obligation to uphold laws duly enacted by Congress. Answering "yes" meant the president's Justice Department would continue to defend a law that blocked the federal government from providing the one thing Obama had repeatedly and consistently advocated for: equal benefits for same-sex spouses.

Not everyone was of like mind on the matter, to put it mildly. The decision would involve a rigorous internal debate about the consequences of either course along with a sometimes contentious back and forth between the attorneys at the White House counsel's office and those at the Department of Justice, not all of whom were in agreement either.

By the time of the Tauro ruling in July, the White House lawyers who had been assigned to investigate DOMA had concluded the law was unconstitutional.

They had arrived at that conclusion partly because they decided that laws affecting gays and lesbians should be reviewed under a more rigorous standard of review known as "heightened scrutiny," which is one of several "equal protection" tests judges use to review the constitutionality of laws. The lowest and easiest of these tests for a law to pass is called "rational basis" review. It means that attorneys simply have to come up with some conceivable legitimate reason for a law's existence—no matter how implausible or far-fetched that reason may seem—and some logical connection between that reason and the law in question. On an issue like food safety, for instance, lawmakers might pass a law requiring food service workers to always wash their hands when they return to their work stations. It's a broad law, in that it affects a lot of people, but lawmakers conceivably have a legitimate interest in promoting public health and the law is rationally related to that end goal. So it would withstand rational basis review. Generally speaking, if attorneys can posit some legitimate public purpose and then find a "rational" connection between that purpose and the law, the law will satisfy the rational basis standard of review.[26]

But, when laws allocate advantages or disadvantages based on historically suspicious criteria such as race or sex, the courts assess the constitutionality of those laws using a more rigorous standard. "Strict scrutiny," which is used for laws that classify based on race or national origin, for example, is the most difficult test of whether a law passes constitutional muster. There are also mid-level tests known as "intermediate scrutiny" and "heightened scrutiny," used for classifications based on sex, for instance, which aren't as demanding as strict scrutiny but are still much harder to pass than the rational basis test.

In order to survive strict scrutiny, a law must serve a "compelling" governmental interest and be narrowly tailored to advance that interest with the fewest extraneous effects possible. Intermediate scrutiny, a slightly less rigorous test, requires that a law be closely related to an "important" public purpose. Imagine the food safety example with a twist. In this case, lawmakers decided that men are typically messier than women and aren't as meticulous about their personal hygiene. So they passed a law requiring male workers, but not female workers, to wash their hands when they return to their work station. Because the law uses a classification based on sex, the courts would be suspicious of that and therefore apply an intermediate scrutiny standard of review. Under that test, the law would likely be found unconstitutional even though it could conceivably serve a public good. That's because it's overly broad—meaning it affects all male food service workers—and it relies on gender stereotypes that don't necessarily have any basis in fact.

But perhaps the most important thing to remember about rational basis review versus the more stringent forms of review is this: in rational basis, the burden of proof falls on the party challenging the law or policy to show that it's not rationally related to any legitimate governmental interest; in the more demanding forms of review, such as heightened scrutiny or strict scrutiny, the burden of proof shifts to the government to demonstrate that a law in fact advances either an important or a compelling public purpose and that it does so in the least intrusive way possible. So if DOMA were reviewed under rational basis, the burden would fall on LGBT advocates to prove it was unconstitutional. But under heightened scrutiny, the burden would fall to government lawyers to prove the law's constitutionality, and they would have to find an important purpose for DOMA and also argue that it served that purpose while having the fewest negative consequences possible. It's a much higher bar.

The idea here is that, when a law uses a suspicious classification to single out an unpopular minority for unfavorable treatment, courts should carefully check the motivations behind that law. The US Constitution established a system of governance that sought to balance the individual freedoms and equality guaranteed by the Bill of Rights with the greater public good. The more rigorous constitutional tests are an acknowledgment that majority rule is valid only to the extent that it does not persecute minorities. Or put another way, restricting the equal rights of disfavored minorities is only constitutional when it's justified by a sufficiently urgent public need. A *heightened scrutiny* or *strict scrutiny* test forces government lawyers to explain whether a law has an adequate purpose and is not simply advancing discrimination or maintaining a biased status quo. If the motivations for the law do not justify singling out a minority, then the law is deemed unconstitutional.

The White House lawyers studying DOMA believed that heightened scrutiny should be the standard of review when considering laws that affect lesbian and gay citizens, even though the vast majority of judges to date, including Judge Tauro, had only applied the rational basis test. Once heightened scrutiny was applied to DOMA, the team of White House lawyers also concluded that a reasonable argument could not be made in defense of the law, rendering it unconstitutional. But now they had a legal dilemma that cut both ways: the president had taken an oath of office to uphold the Constitution and if he concluded that a law was unconstitutional, arguing otherwise in court might violate that oath; on the other hand, he was constitutionally charged with faithfully executing the nation's laws. So what were they to do when these two obligations—upholding the Constitution and faithfully executing the laws—were at odds?[27]

Even if the law was unconstitutional, they needed to consider the institutional consequences of not defending it. Would it become too easy for future presidents to trod the same course, thereby undermining the rule of law? What if the next president was a staunch conservative who decided to stop defending the Affordable Care Act (aka Obamacare) simply because she didn't like it or thought it was bad policy. "There was a deep recognition that this could be a slippery slope," said one former White House official. They had to find some limiting principle that would serve as the trigger for when to stop defending.[28]

It wasn't actually unprecedented for presidents to deem a law unconstitutional and stop defending it, but it was certainly rare. After White House lawyers were initially assigned to research DOMA, they quickly gathered a binder of cases where the Justice Departments of previous presidents had sent a letter to Congress saying that the administration was dropping its defense of a law. Sending that letter was part of a statutory protocol mandated by Congress. Nearly every president in recent memory—Jimmy Carter, Ronald Reagan, George H. W. Bush, and Bill Clinton, among others—had done so. But in some of those instances, the Supreme Court had already found fault with a law that just happened to still be on the books. *Simkins v. Moses H. Cone Memorial Hospital*, for instance, called into question a 1946 law allowing federal funding for hospitals that practiced racial discrimination so long as they also provided "separate but equal" facilities. In 1963, President Kennedy's Justice Department joined a private class action lawsuit against such hospitals, but Kennedy's action was very much in keeping with the Supreme Court's 1954 ruling *Brown v. Board of Education*, which held that "separate but equal" facilities are unconstitutional.[29]

In the case of DOMA, one federal district judge had ruled the law unconstitutional. Additionally, in 2009, two federal appellate judges who were overseeing employee grievance procedures had concluded that DOMA did not bar lesbian and gay employees of their court from receiving spousal health benefits for their partners. Those judges ordered the federal government to provide the health benefits, but the Obama administration ignored the orders. Still, neither the Supreme Court nor any federal appeals court panel had yet opined on the law or its legal underpinnings in any sort of definitive way. For the moment, then, there was no clear precedent that the administration could invoke in dropping its defense.[30]

Still, the more White House attorneys studied examples of previous administrations declining to defend a law, the more comfortable they became with the prospect of ending the government's defense of DOMA. The history proved that doing so did not represent an irresponsible proposition. And at no time did they consider not *enforcing* the law. If the administration stopped defending DOMA, it would still enforce the law, which meant the federal government would continue to deny benefits to same-sex couples. That would give another body, such as the House of Representatives, the opportunity to step in and continue defending the law and leave the ultimate say on its constitutionality up to the Supreme Court. That way the president wouldn't be unilaterally scrapping the law, he would simply be sending a strong signal that he believed it was unconstitutional.

But they still had to come up with some principle for guiding the administration's decision on whether to continue defending DOMA, and they settled on this: they would defend only as long as reasonable arguments could be made in support of the law. If no reasonable arguments could be made for DOMA in light of the appropriate constitutional test, it was time to stop defending.[31]

This is where the standard of review (*rational basis* vs. *heightened scrutiny*) became critical to the thinking for the White House lawyers. Heightened scrutiny is a standard that, once applied to sexual orientation classifications, makes any anti-gay law very difficult to defend. In fact, some lawyers believed that DOMA was constitutional by rational basis standards but clearly unconstitutional under heightened scrutiny. So one's view of the law partially came down to whether one believed sexual orientation-based laws should be viewed as presumptively "suspect"—meaning they required a more rigorous standard of review.

The four factors used to determine whether laws classifying on a particular basis warrant the most stringent level of scrutiny, *strict scrutiny*, are the following: (1) whether that classification has been used historically to discriminate against a particular group; (2) whether the classification involves traits that are obvious and/or readily changeable (e.g. the color of one's skin); (3) whether a group so classified and historically abused remains vulnerable in the political process; and (4) whether the trait in question affects an individual's ability to contribute to society. To the White House lawyers investigating DOMA, anti-gay classifications absolutely called for a higher standard of review once these four factors were applied. But the problem was that the Supreme Court had not applied this four-part test in the two big LGBT-equality wins, *Romer v. Evans* and *Lawrence v. Texas*. *Romer* used rational basis review and left open whether heightened scrutiny would one day be required in future cases. *Lawrence* relied on a history of strict scrutiny cases to inform its analysis but never explicitly stated what level of review had been applied.[32]

In *Gill*, Judge Tauro had little choice but to use the rational basis test instead of heightened scrutiny. His trial-level court was governed by the precedent set by the First Circuit Court of Appeals, which had already embraced rational basis as the proper test for sexual orientation classifications in a 2008 case challenging "don't ask, don't tell" (*Cook v. Gates*). Consequently, that was the standard that Justice Department lawyers arguing the Massachusetts DOMA cases had used, too.

But the government lawyers preparing to appeal Tauro's rulings in the two DOMA cases knew the briefing to the First Circuit Court of Appeals would be a definitive escalation in the administration's defense of the law. The panel of judges in the First Circuit might revisit the question of what standard of review should be used. It was their prerogative to do so. What would government lawyers say then—did they really want to go on record arguing that heightened scrutiny shouldn't apply to discrimination against lesbians and gays? It was a catch-22 in the eyes of some government lawyers: arguing for rational basis review would be legally incorrect, but if they intended to keep defending the law, rational basis was the only standard of review under which reasonable arguments could be made in DOMA's defense.

The dilemma for the administration would not stop with whether to appeal *Gill*. The government would soon be facing additional challenges to the law from LGBT legal advocates, who were steadily ramping up the pressure. In particular, lawyers at GLAD, led by Mary Bonauto and the organization's legal director Gary Buseck, had a new DOMA case in the works that would present another broad-based challenge to the law. But this time, it would be in a circuit where there was no precedent for standard of review. Arguing the law in a circuit that had no precedent would require government lawyers to make a case for which level of scrutiny should be applied to DOMA.

Following the Tauro decision on July 8, 2010, legal advocates met once again with a high-powered contingent of about twenty-five Justice Department attorneys on August 10, 2010. This time, the advocates put on the full-court press for why heightened scrutiny should apply to laws discriminating against LGBT Americans. They walked through the four factors, reminding Department of Justice lawyers of the case they would have to make if they argued against applying heightened scrutiny. Advocates couldn't imagine Obama's Justice Department arguing that gays hadn't endured a history of discrimination. They'd be laughed out of court. Advocates also couldn't imagine Department of Justice lawyers suggesting that being gay somehow limits one's ability to contribute to society. That would be flat-out homophobic. Nor could they make the absurd argument that gays can or should change their sexual orientation in order to escape discrimination. And while they could make an argument that gays had some political power, as one witness had tried to do in support of Prop 8, that would mean deliberately overlooking the number of times LGBT rights had been taken away at the ballot box in the last decade alone. That's not what political power looks like.[33]

In the minds of LGBT legal advocates, there was only one possible outcome if you applied the four factors honestly: heightened scrutiny. Reaching a different conclusion was both intellectually disingenuous and legally inaccurate. Doing so would also force many of the Justice Department's top appointees—including Attorney General Eric Holder and Assistant Attorney General Tony West, both of whom were men of color—to turn their backs on the very same constitutional principles that had slowly but surely helped transform the national landscape for black Americans.[34]

When advocates had first made the case that the administration should stop defending the law in the summer and fall of 2009, Justice Department lawyers probably found it somewhat far-fetched. But just one year later, the power dynamic had shifted substantially. Government lawyers were now facing tough decisions. And in that August 2010

meeting, advocates suggested that the government could not indefinitely duck the question of whether heightened scrutiny should apply
to LGBT-related cases. The mutual understanding in the room was that
LGBT advocates would soon file a case that would force the US government to take a stand. If they argued for rational basis—that gays had
experienced no history of discrimination, that they couldn't make a full
contribution to society, and so on—their arguments would be untenable
by any reasonable standard. But if they opted for heightened scrutiny,
the Defense of Marriage Act would likely never pass constitutional muster under that test. In other words, it would be impossible to come up
with any reasonable arguments to defend it.[35]

In their dialogue with government lawyers, LGBT legal advocates
had argued all along that heightened scrutiny was the proper test under
which to review DOMA and, therefore, many also concluded that the
government should cease its defense because DOMA was clearly unconstitutional. The White House lawyers assigned to DOMA had also
reached that view by the fall of 2009, but they spent much of 2010
wrestling with the legal and institutional implications of not defending
it. Some lawyers in the White House counsel's office continued to argue
that the administration had a duty to defend the law. But advocates had
more work to do in convincing lawyers at the Justice Department, which
was even more divided. While the twenty-five some odd lawyers who
work in the White House are all appointed by the president, the Justice
Department is filled with career government lawyers who defend laws
under successive presidents (Republican and Democratic alike) regardless of their own political leanings or personal views.[36]

During the August 2010 meeting with legal advocates, some of the
toughest questions came from career Department of Justice lawyers,
like Edwin Kneedler, who were much more institutionally prone to
defending under almost any circumstance. Kneedler, a deputy solicitor
general, had served about thirty-five years at the agency and had argued
more than one hundred cases at the Supreme Court. The Office of the
Solicitor General within the Justice Department is charged with arguing the government's side of cases at the Supreme Court and, among
other things, deciding which cases to appeal when the government loses
in lower federal courts (such as with the Tauro ruling in *Gill*). The solicitor general's office is also a mix of political appointees and career

departmental lawyers; it is led by the solicitor general (a presidential appointee), one principal deputy (another appointee), and three career deputies (one of whom was Kneedler).[37]

At the time, the acting solicitor general was Neal Katyal, an Obama appointee who had originally served as the principal deputy but assumed the responsibilities of solicitor general when Elena Kagan left the position in May 2010 to be appointed to the Supreme Court. White House lawyers and some Justice Department attorneys had been engaged in a back and forth with Katyal and Kneedler about whether to defend. They struggled to make headway. Kneedler was one of the strongest proponents of the institutional rule that the Department of Justice always defends laws duly enacted by Congress. Katyal concurred.[38]

Before making a decision about how to proceed on *Gill*, the solicitor general's office rounded up memos on the matter from different divisions within the Justice Department. In their memos, both the Civil Rights Division (headed by Thomas Perez) and the Civil Division (headed by Tony West) concluded that heightened scrutiny should apply in the absence of a binding precedent for rational basis review. The Civil Rights Division went on to say that, even under rational basis review, DOMA was indefensible and the Justice Department should not appeal Judge Tauro's ruling. But the Civil Division disagreed on that point. Since the administration had already made an argument defending DOMA under rational basis review and the case was in a circuit where the precedent was clear, the Civil Division concluded that the administration should continue to defend DOMA in the First Circuit and appeal the *Gill* ruling.[39]

Lawyers at the White House also prepped a memo. They reasoned that DOMA was unconstitutional under heightened scrutiny and that anti-gay legal classifications likely had to be considered "suspect" if the traditional four-factor analysis were applied. In their memo, they also tracked the history of presidents who had declined to defend certain laws and concluded that doing so would not be a breach of either tradition or constitutional obligation if President Obama concluded that the law was unconstitutional.[40]

Ultimately, the Justice Department decided to continue defending the law. On October 12, 2010, Assistant Attorney General Tony West filed a "Notice of Appeal" with the US District Court of Massachusetts in the matter of *Gill v. Office of Personnel Management*.

But LGBT legal advocates weren't finished either. One month later, on November 9, they made good on their promise, filing two separate cases in the Second Circuit, which had no precedent for what legal test should be used to review laws affecting gays.

In Connecticut, GLAD filed *Pedersen v. Office of Personnel Management*, a case involving several plaintiffs that once again challenged the federal government's denial of health, pension, and tax benefits to married same-sex couples and widows.

That same day, in New York, attorney Roberta "Robbie" Kaplan with the law firm Paul, Weiss, Rifkind, Wharton & Garrison, filed a case in conjunction with the ACLU on behalf of Edie Windsor, a gutsy Manhattan widow who decided she had been wronged when the federal government sent her a bill for $363,000 in estate taxes after her spouse and partner of more than forty years, Thea Spyer, died. Despite their lawful Canadian marriage, which New York recognized, the feds had treated the two women as perfect strangers. But if the federal government had recognized them as spouses, Windsor could have inherited Spyer's estate without triggering any tax at all.

The coordinated filings were nothing short of a frontal assault on the law that would finally force the administration off the fence on rational basis versus heightened scrutiny. Government lawyers could no longer hide behind precedent to avoid taking a position on what standard of review should be applied to laws affecting gay and lesbian Americans. It was a decision that would reach straight up to the president himself.

WHEN I WALKED into the Oval Office to interview President Obama on December 21, 2010, Congress had repealed "don't ask, don't tell" just three days earlier and LGBT legal advocates had been patiently pressing forward their legal advance on DOMA. The administration was now facing two Second Circuit challenges to the law.

Obama was responding to the request I had made directly to him at the White House holiday party, but it was a long time in coming. My interview was the first one-on-one the White House had granted to a journalist representing an LGBT outlet, though they had given a number of interviews to other constituency media. The Spanish-language outlet Univision, for instance, and the African American magazine *Ebony* both ran exclusive interviews in the first year of Obama's presidency. President Obama had also taken questions from numerous constituency press reporters at nationally televised White House press conferences, but never from an LGBT outlet.[41]

The only LGBT media access they had granted to the president was when they included Joe Sudbay among the progressive bloggers who interviewed Obama just before the 2010 midterms. And in many ways, that had been an act of desperation by the administration to stoke progressive enthusiasm before Election Day.

I was convinced that the communications team had largely shielded the president from LGBT press access for two reasons. First, President Obama was regularly getting heckled by LGBT activists who were making very specific demands about "don't ask, don't tell" repeal, and he had not found a good way of assuaging those activists. It didn't matter whether he was giving speeches in Los Angeles, New York, or Miami, queer activists showed up and made their presence known, just as GetEQUAL activists had at Obama's fundraising event for Senator Barbara Boxer in Los Angeles. Second, Obama was increasingly having trouble painting himself as pro-equality while he was still clinging desperately to his separate-and-unequal support for civil unions.

To make matters worse, shortly after he was elected in 2008, a candidate questionnaire dating back to 1996 surfaced in which Obama, then running for Illinois state senate, had written: "I favor legalizing same-sex marriages, and would fight efforts to prohibit such marriages." The questionnaire had come from *Outlines* newspaper, an LGBT publication in Chicago that later merged with the *Windy City Times*. The timing of the news release, January 13, 2009, was as good as possible for Obama—the election was over. But it was awful in terms of overall news exposure. If it had been released at any point prior to Election Day, the questionnaire would have attracted a ton of press attention and dogged Obama for the rest of the race. Many people already suspected that Obama's civil unions stance was simply a political calculation. It's one thing for politicians to make political calculations—they all do it and voters more or less accept that it's a part of the game. It's another thing to get caught doing it. It's a little like trash-talking on the field—it's all good till the ref hears you.[42]

Marriage was simply not a good topic for President Obama. He had no good answers for where he had been on the matter or where he was now, and he certainly wasn't willing to speculate on where he was going until he got there. Nonetheless, "don't ask, don't tell" repeal was a huge win for both the administration and the LGBT constituency. After all the grief Obama had taken from LGBT activists, the White House wanted President Obama to take a victory lap. It was one of the best opportunities he'd had in two years to focus media attention on something that was a major advancement for both LGBT Americans and the progressive base alike.

When my press contact called to offer me the interview, he originally said they would only give it to me on the condition that I limit my questions to "don't ask, don't tell" repeal. No way, I said, as I stood in front of my cart at the grocery store. No self-respecting journalist would agree to those terms. "And besides, I would be skewered," I added. "The constituency has been waiting to hear from Obama for two years, and all I ask about is 'don't ask, don't tell?'" We went back and forth a couple times and finally I said, "The only way I'll take it is if I write in the intro paragraph that I was restricted to asking questions about repeal as a condition of the interview." They didn't take to that idea. We hung up, and I began mulling over which loaf of bread to buy and whether I had just blown my chance to interview a sitting president. Perhaps they would shop around for another journalist who would accept their terms.

But my press contact called back about ten minutes later. The interview was mine, he said. "You'll have ten minutes and you can ask about anything, but certainly we hope you'll focus on 'don't ask, don't tell,'" he added. I assured him that I would be remiss if I didn't ask the president about the greatest legislative advancement in the history of the movement.

Ten minutes. It was precious little to work with given that I would be trying to cover the first two years of his term that had already elapsed and the next two years on the horizon. Even more worrisome, my sense was that they were telling me they would shut down the interview at any moment if they didn't like the way it was going. The subject they were most concerned about was marriage. No one had asked the president directly about that 1996 questionnaire since it surfaced. Sudbay had brought a copy of it to his interview in the Roosevelt Room but opted not to use it. He made the right choice. His personal appeal to the president on marriage equality was far more effective, in my opinion, than antagonizing him in front of a room full of people in his own home. But now I faced the same conundrum—should I box in the president on the very question he and his aides were most afraid of? I was convinced they would end the interview immediately.

The bigger question, though, was how best to represent the concerns of LGBT Americans. Indeed, while Obama's marriage stance was a topic that many Americans were focused on, it wasn't the most important topic to many in the incredibly diverse LGBT community. For many, workplace protections were the number one issue. Contrary to popular belief, a 2013 study of poverty patterns by the Williams Institute, for instance, found that poverty rates among the lesbian, gay, and bisexual population were often higher than that among the general population. But the results varied considerably by gender, region, and race. Poverty rates among female same-sex couples, for instance, were higher than that among married different-sex couples, while male same-sex couples had lower overall poverty rates than both in the data. Lesbians and gays in California fared much better overall in the data than those in national surveys, likely due to greater acceptance, stronger employment protections, and more supportive communities. African Americans in same-sex couples had poverty rates at least twice that of different-sex married African Americans. African American men in same-sex couples were more than six times more likely to be poor than white men in same-sex couples, and African American women with female partners were three times more likely to be poor than white women with female partners.[43]

Additionally, transgender individuals typically had a much harder time getting and keeping jobs than the general population. A 2013 study by the Movement Advancement Project found that more than 44 percent of transgender individuals were underemployed and, on average, 40 percent of transgender individuals said they faced discrimination on the job. Transgender individuals and those who do not conform to traditional gender stereotypes have often been the most stigmatized and marginalized members of the LGBT community. Consequently, for many of them, job protections—not marriage—were the number one concern.[44]

At the time, I couldn't imagine hurling a contentious marriage question at the expense of talking about workplace fairness. Asking Obama about his previous marriage stance was a totally legitimate inquiry and delivering a well-crafted gotcha question about the questionnaire likely would have attracted lots of media attention. But it wouldn't have an immediate impact on LGBT rights and elevating marriage above all else didn't seem fair to the constituency as a whole. It didn't matter what kind of marriage question I asked in that moment, I concluded, I wasn't going to single-handedly convince the president to change positions. Sudbay had ably trod that territory just a few months earlier.

I felt I had to incorporate a reference about employment protections into the transcript, even though the legislation would clearly be stalled now that Republicans would be assuming control of the House. Then I resolved to focus on something that the president could tangibly make a difference on through his executive authority—the Defense of Marriage Act and, more broadly, standard of review. Those were two areas where he, in his individual capacity as president, could help significantly change the landscape for LGBT Americans. I desperately hoped to do two things. First, push him on issues where he alone had the authority to act. And second, get some sense of his road map for moving equality forward over the next two years. That way the community could hold him to account if he missed those milestones. Though LGBT activists had spent the first two years pushing President Obama and Congress to act on legislation, they would no longer be able to lay responsibility for legislative inaction at the doorstep of the White House. It would be too easy for the administration to blame House Republicans for letting something like the Employment Nondiscrimination Act—or any other pro-equality bill—languish.

I decided not to waste time dwelling on the past by bringing up the 1996 questionnaire. I'd let the president take his victory lap on the historic bill he was about to sign into law the following day. I guessed that "don't ask, don't tell" would take about five minutes of the interview. Obama would talk long on overturning the gay ban because it was the reason they had granted the interview in the first place. Then I would nudge him a bit on the freedom to marry. After all, if gays would soon be able to make the ultimate sacrifice on the battlefield in full view of their countrymen, shouldn't they also be able to commit their lives to the person they loved? That would take about two minutes or so, I predicted, which would leave me a couple minutes to mention workplace protections and then ask about the courts and DOMA. Perhaps his press shop would give me a few extra minutes, but it seemed unlikely. When I had interviewed Obama as a candidate, they had adhered very closely to the time limit in both instances.

The first ten minutes ended up going almost exactly as I anticipated.

"Mr. President," I began, "you're on the verge of signing legislation that is arguably one of the greatest advances for LGBT civil rights. What does it mean to you personally? And if you were to put it on a continuum of your accomplishments as president, where do you think it will rank in the history books?"[45]

"I am incredibly proud," he said, "And part of the reason I'm proud is because this is the culmination of a strategy that began the first week I was in office."[46]

The president was off and running. I had purposely asked a broad question because I knew it would take me a minute or two to regain my faculties. Interviewing a president in the Oval Office is a bit terrifying. You're totally on his turf—the president sits in that office every day, and he holds all the power there. President Obama was seated to my right in a mahogany chair, and there were about four to five other people in the room: the stenographer, who records the interview and puts out the official transcript, including the start and stop time; the official White House photographer; a Secret Service officer; and two communications people, who were sitting on the golden-brown couch across from where I was seated. Basically, everyone there knows the room and the protocol better than you do, and they're all there to make sure things go well for the commander in chief.

Obama used the opportunity to talk about his approach to getting repeal done—first by getting Secretary Gates and Admiral Mullen on board, then by engineering a study that would prove attitudes among the enlisted soldiers were far more progressive than their superiors thought.

"Things don't always go according to your plans," he told me, "and so when they do—especially in this town—it's pleasantly surprising."[47]

The narrative he relayed was indeed part of what happened, though it was not the full story. The person whom I had witnessed wagging his finger at Joe Sudbay just a couple weeks earlier at the holiday party was not the portrait of a man who thought things were going according to plan. The president had certainly played a positive and pivotal role in ending the gay ban—especially in convincing the military leadership that repeal could be implemented with minimal disruption. In that sense, he had indeed helped engineer a critical cultural shift at the Pentagon. But in truth it was the activists, key lawmakers, and the courts that made repeal an imperative in the waning days of the 111th Congress. Still, that moment was not the time to quarrel over the past, and even if it had been, I couldn't spare the seconds. The president deserved credit, and repeal was a victory for everyone involved.

"This is one of those issues," Obama continued, "where you know individual people directly that are going to be impacted and you know it helps shift attitudes in a direction of greater fairness over the long term. I think when people look back 20 years from now," he added, "they'll say this was one of the more important things that I've gotten done since I've been president."[48]

I checked my two recorders on the table next to me—we were about five minutes in now. "Given what you've just said, Mr. President, do you think it's time that gays and lesbians should be entitled to full marriage rights?"

The president noted that he had been making a lot of headlines lately—the lame-duck session had turned out to be unusually productive between ratifying START, extending the Bush-era tax cuts for another two years, and overturning "don't ask, don't tell."

"I'm not going to make more news today," he said. "Like a lot of people, I'm wrestling with this. My attitudes are evolving on this." It was the second time he had alluded to his evolution on marriage equality—the first was with Sudbay two months earlier when he said, "Attitudes evolve, including mine." So a pattern was now developing. This would clearly be his new position on marriage moving forward.

One more push. "Can you imagine a time when you would get there?" I asked. "You say 'evolving,' and that sort of assumes that you get somewhere."

"I'm going to stick with my answer," he responded.

I glanced at my recorders again. A little over seven minutes had elapsed.

"I know one of the things that people were interested [in]—especially gay and transgender Americans—was passing employment nondiscrimination protections. But looking forward, it looks like most legislation, pro-LGBT, will be stalled in Congress," I said. "So as you look to much of the action that's going to be happening in the courts—do you think that gays and lesbians and transgender people should have a heightened scrutiny status?"

Before answering the question, the president worked in a point about changes he could make "administratively" to continue advancing LGBT equality without Congress. "My ability to make sure that the federal government is an employer that treats gays and lesbians fairly, that's something I can do, and sets a model for folks across the board," he offered.

"But DOMA," I started to protest, would stand in the way of equal benefits for LGBT government workers.

The president saw where I was headed and cut me off before I completed the question, turning back to my original query about the courts.

"I think that if you look at where Justice Kennedy is moving, the kind of rational review that he applied in the Texas case was one that feels right to me," he said. "Even if he was calling it 'rational review,'" Obama noted, "certain groups may be vulnerable to stereotypes, certain groups may be subject to discrimination, and that the court's job historically is to pay attention to that."

I certainly wasn't capable of debating a former constitutional law professor on the point, but this much I knew: this was the type of heightened scrutiny-light that had frustrated legal advocates for years because it failed to explicitly protect LGBT Americans from all sorts of discriminatory laws. Obama's answer suggested to me that he wasn't particularly close to dropping his administration's defense of DOMA.

Ten minutes had passed by now but the communications people allowed the interview to continue. I returned to "don't ask, don't tell" and nailed down a time frame on how long implementation of repeal would take. "Months . . . not years," the president said in response. I also asked President Obama whether he would find a way to remedy the nondiscrimination mandate that had been dropped from the repeal legislation. He wouldn't give a definitive answer on that, which in political terms, usually means "no."

At fifteen minutes in, the press handlers told me my next question would be the last.

"It's a lot of pressure," I uttered, almost involuntarily, upon hearing the news (mercifully, the stenographer never included that in the official transcript). It was likely the last question I would ever ask of President Obama, given their track record on granting interviews. What most worried me was that I still didn't have a clear idea that the administration had any specific action plan on LGBT issues moving forward. Other than saying he would "continue to look for ways administratively" to advance the cause of equality, the president had given me nothing concrete.[49]

I paused for a moment, searching my head for the best question, and decided to ask the most overarching question possible in order to open the floor for President Obama to say whatever he wanted about the next two years of his presidency.

"Big-picture question about LGBT people and where the movement is headed," I said, still searching for the words. "You're sitting in the midst of a time that's of great change. You're not quite willing to go there on same-sex marriage yet. What do you see as something that moving forward would be one of the biggest possible advancements for LGBT people—potentially in the course of your presidency in the next two years?"

The floor was his. President Obama started by making a distinction between the things he wanted to see happen and things that could actually happen. He wanted Congress to pass workplace protections and repeal DOMA but conceded, "I think that's not going to get done in two years."

I listened for a couple minutes but heard nothing substantive. At one point I interjected, "I think people wonder what *can* happen" since passing legislation seemed unlikely.

The president got a little exasperated. "I understand, Kerry," he responded. "I'm trying to answer your question, and you keep on coming back at me."

I apologized. That was my cue to shut up and let him talk. He talked for a few more minutes, referencing cultural change and saying he would look for ways to "continually speak out" about equality in order to "chip away" at the attitudes of legislators and bring more change. He was making the case for using his bully pulpit to advance equality.

"I'm confident that these other issues will get done," he concluded. "And as I said, there are things that we can continue to do administratively that I think will send a message that the federal government, as an employer, is going to constantly look for opportunities to make sure that we're eliminating discrimination."

It all seemed soft to me. Well intentioned, yes, but nothing one could hold onto. Then, before I even realized what I was doing, I added, "What about not defending DOMA?" The press people were not happy, and I was later reprimanded for not adhering to the "last question" protocol. But the president graciously entertained my final inquiry.

"As I said before," he responded, "I have a whole bunch of really smart lawyers who are looking at a whole range of options. My preference wherever possible is to get things done legislatively," he said. "That may not be possible in DOMA's case. That's something that I think we have to strategize on over the next several months."

Eureka. It was by far the most illuminating answer President Obama had given about the road map ahead.

The president and I posed in front of his desk for a quick photo before I shook his hand and thanked him for the interview. Then my press contact, Shin Inouye, escorted me from the Oval Office back to the briefing room. I remarked at the president's answer on DOMA, but Inouye assured me it was nothing.

I was convinced it was something, even though at the time I didn't have the benefit of knowing all the work legal advocates had put into changing the administration's position on defending the law. Obama's wording was notable particularly because it was an absolute departure from what Robert Gibbs and Justice Department spokespeople had been saying for nearly two years about DOMA. Their standard line was that the Justice Department was doing what it typically does—defending the laws duly enacted by Congress. Up to this point, no one in the administration had so much as whispered anything different, at least not publicly.

But now, President Obama himself was saying that he had "smart lawyers" surveying the options on DOMA. It was cause for real optimism on an issue that had broad implications for same-sex couples across the country. So many of the inequities and instabilities that LGBT households faced were a result of the law, which robbed same-sex spouses and even their children of safety nets like health care, Social Security, and pension benefits. The president's response suggested that his administration might actually shift from serving as a roadblock in the effort to vanquish DOMA to finally becoming a partner in that fight.

NEW YORK STATE OF MIND · 8

I WALKED AWAY FROM THE WHITE HOUSE ON THE NIGHT OF the interview totally spent and slept for most of the following week, taking occasional breaks for meals. The four months leading up to the repeal of "don't ask, don't tell" had felt like a pitched battle, day in and day out. Never in my life had I felt such an intense mix of sheer relief and utter exhaustion than I did after repeal passed. The interview, which had used up the last of my reserves, was my final hoorah as Washington correspondent for *The Advocate*. In January of 2011, I started with Equality Matters, a division of the progressive media watchdog group, Media Matters for America. Over the next year, I would occasionally attend press briefings, but my main charge was to write long-form investigative and opinion pieces about politics and the LGBT movement. In essence, I was trading in my journalist hat for more of an advocacy role, at least for a year.

Before ever setting foot in the new organization, I resolved to devote the next year to pushing the administration on DOMA and marriage equality. After that, I would either shift the focus of my writing to other issues or get another job entirely. But with every fiber of my being, I believed that Obama would benefit politically from supporting same-sex marriage, not to mention the fact that it was "the right thing to do," as Obama himself was fond of saying. So I would do whatever I could to convince the administration that Obama had no choice but to embrace marriage equality.[1]

The political upsides of supporting the freedom to marry may seem obvious in retrospect, but at the time it was a very contentious issue, even among LGBT activists. In fact, at the outset of 2011, I attended a retreat organized by Paul Yandura on behalf of Jonathan Lewis that included LGBT activists ranging from McGehee, Aravosis, and Sudbay to media mavens like Dan Savage (the popular sex advice columnist and cocreator of the pro-LGBT "It Gets Better" campaign) and Michelangelo Signorile (an author and progressive radio host at SiriusXM) to more political types like Richard Socarides and Chad Griffin (then the board president of the American Foundation for Equal Rights, which had mounted the legal challenge to Proposition 8). Even at this retreat of some twenty-five people—many of whom were viewed as the lefties of the LGBT political movement—there was a debate about whether endorsing same-sex marriage would sink Obama's reelection effort. In the end, nearly every attendee favored pushing the president, regardless of its effects on his political prospects.

But as confident as I was about the politics, many Beltway operatives were certain of exactly the opposite. If Obama endorsed marriage equality before the 2012 election, they worried the move would be political suicide. It would alienate independent voters and, some argued, religious black voters. The belief was hard to shake; it arose from the very public political drubbing LGBT Americans had been subject to over the past decade. In Washington, even at the beginning of 2011, the smart money was still on the notion that gay issues and especially marriage equality were a political liability. "Don't ask, don't tell" repeal was viewed as both a miracle and a fluke by many Washington political operatives.[2]

Of course, the same crowd had also contended that passing repeal would be a drag on Obama's reelection chances, even if it was the right thing to do. They had also been dead wrong. Repeal had ultimately been far more popular with a large swath of voters (along with bolstering Obama's leadership cred) than the White House's signature achievement of 2010—health care reform. In fact, repealing the gay ban was so noncontroversial that pollsters all but quit asking the question once Congress passed the bill, unlike health care reform, which continued to be a hot-button topic. After repeal was finally implemented in September of 2011, CBS News revisited the question once more and found 68 percent of voters still favored allowing open service—entirely consistent with how it had polled over the previous several years. Even among Republicans, more favored open service (48 percent) than did not (41 percent), and of those who opposed it, only 12 percent felt "strongly" about it. Health care reform, on the other hand, continued to be a net negative for Democrats, at least in terms of public perception. A Kaiser tracking poll released that same month, for instance, found that more Americans had an unfavorable view of the law (43 percent) than a favorable one (41 percent). In other words, political experts had been entirely mistaken about which White House-backed measure would be more controversial.[3]

Upon passage of repeal, much of America had more or less yawned and gone about the business of celebrating the holidays. The only people who had truly paid attention to the accomplishment were LGBT advocates and Obama's progressive base. Unlike health care reform, which had inspired protests across the country and served as a galvanizing event for the Tea Party movement, repeal inspired no such backlash. It was uniformly celebrated by progressives and a virtual nonissue for conservatives. In the next election cycle, no member of Congress was targeted or lost their seat based on their vote to overturn "don't ask, don't tell." Public opinion had been shaped by seventeen years of LGBT activism on the issue, so public reception of repeal was never dependent on messaging from the White House in the way that health care reform was. Repeal proved to be a net positive for President Obama, and it cost the Democrats nothing.[4]

But once repeal was old news, Washington's political elite ignored the example set by "don't ask, don't tell" repeal and adopted marriage as the new gay landmine. Many of Washington's LGBT political operatives agreed. It was true that Americans hadn't yet come down on the matter decisively one way or the other. But to me, accepting the notion that endorsing marriage would doom Obama felt like a lingering piece of internalized homophobia. Many gay Americans had been told most of their lives that they were dirty and maybe a little deranged. The high-profile and virulent anti-gay politics of the past decade had only reinforced that concept, and it was admittedly difficult for many LGBT Americans to believe anything had or could change.

Of course, some queer Americans weren't all that persuaded that having the freedom to marry was the holy grail of equality. They were understandably worried about getting and keeping jobs and would much rather have seen employment nondiscrimination protections enacted at the federal level. Still others didn't give a damn who had to pay a political price. They wanted politicians—and this president in particular—to do the right thing on same-sex marriage no matter what.

I didn't fit perfectly into any of those camps. I believed we were at the tipping point politically—that LGBT issues and even marriage equality were becoming winning issues. I also knew that marriage, given its celebrated place in our society, held incredible symbolic importance. Even if we were afforded federal rights and benefits through some other means, it would never carry with it the dignity of the word "marriage." Though I deeply wanted to see some moral courage from the president on the matter, I also thought it was critical to LGBT Americans overall that President Obama be reelected. He was not perfect, but he was clearly better than any Republican candidate was going to be on our issues. If Obama hadn't embraced the freedom to marry by the end of the year, I reasoned, there was no way his campaign would allow him to switch positions in 2012. It would be too close to the election. Though I didn't necessarily see myself as a partisan Democrat (they were too reliably wish-washy on progressive issues I cared about), I was certainly closely associated by then with the LGBT movement. So anything I penned about marriage equality and Obama in 2012 could potentially be a political liability for the president—something I wanted to avoid if I could.

Little did I know in January how close the administration was to dropping its defense of DOMA. LGBT legal advocates met with Justice Department lawyers two more times—once on September 10, 2009, and again on January 10, 2011. The mood was tense in that final meeting even though the terrain wasn't exactly new. Advocates had advanced their position since last fall, and the administration now had no choice but to respond. The government's brief in *Windsor* was due later in January, but there was still a rift within the Justice Department about what to do. Now that the government had to make a case for what standard of review should apply to laws involving lesbians and gays, the Civil Division—which had previously argued for continuing the government's "rational basis" defense in the First Circuit—concluded that heightened scrutiny was the proper standard of review. And just like the lawyers in the White House counsel's office, they did not believe DOMA was constitutional under that test. The solicitor general's office, however, adamantly believed the government should continue defending the law. Attorney General Eric Holder and President Obama would have to weigh in.[5]

A trial lawyer with the Justice Department phoned Robbie Kaplan, the attorney representing Edie Windsor, to ask if she would grant the government a month-long extension on the brief. Kaplan didn't immediately agree, but Assistant Attorney General Tony West called her back.[6]

"Robbie," said West, "we're literally deciding what position to take. Are you telling me, you won't give me an extension?"[7]

Kaplan was dubious about their intensions. She agreed, but not without dropping a little nugget for West to chew on.

"You know what, Tony," she said, "when you and the president are deliberating on this, I'll be praying for you."[8]

On February 23, Kaplan would find herself on the phone again with West. The ACLU's James Esseks, director of the organization's LGBT and AIDS project and cocounsel on the *Windsor* case, was also on the line when West delivered the news that the Justice Department had concluded it could not defend the constitutionality of the Defense of Marriage Act.

For Esseks, it was mind blowing. He had been litigating marriage cases for a decade and wasn't used to winning. In fact, Esseks and Kaplan had collaborated on a 2006 marriage case in New York in which the state's high court ruled that gays did not have a constitutional right to marry. Esseks had also worked on the successful marriage case in California in which the state's Supreme Court struck down the state's marriage ban in May 2008 only to have the ruling reversed by voters at the ballot box in November. But now the US government was saying that a federal statute violated the Constitution and that government discrimination against gay people should be presumed to be unconstitutional. Esseks knew it would be transformative for every part of the LGBT rights movement. It was like feeling the earth shift underneath his feet in real time.[9]

Kaplan was taking the call from a family vacation in the Caribbean. Tears filled her eyes when she heard what West had to say. After she got off the phone, she immediately called Edie Windsor to inform her that the government was taking their side in the case—a milestone in their journey that would eventually culminate at the US Supreme Court.[10]

Just two months after the legislative victory on repealing "don't ask, don't tell," the administration was plowing ahead on dismantling DOMA. In Holder's letter informing Congress that the Justice Department would no longer defend the law, he made the case for using a higher standard of review. "The President and I have concluded that classifications based on sexual orientation warrant heightened scrutiny and that, as applied to same-sex couples legally married under state law, Section 3 of DOMA is unconstitutional," he wrote.[11]

It was a lawyer's decision, not a politician's. The politics had upsides and downsides no matter what the administration decided. In this case, LGBT activists would be elated while conservative politicians and legal scholars would cry foul. The battle on DOMA was far from over; the Republican-led House of Representatives would step in to continue defending the law. But after much deliberation by warring factions within the administration, Attorney General Holder and President Obama had clearly concluded that they didn't want to make a legal argument to the Supreme Court about DOMA that they didn't actually believe in. As LGBT legal advocates had suggested, it was the morally correct decision to make the legally correct argument, even it if posed institutional or even political problems down the road. And President Obama, every bit the constitutional law scholar, had been unable to turn his back on the Constitution of the United States as he understood it.

It was one of the boldest—if not the boldest—executive actions he had taken at that early stage of his presidency, and it would ultimately have a stunning impact on the trajectory of LGBT equality when the case reached the Supreme Court in March of 2013. Even so, it still didn't buy the president much time or space on marriage equality, which was becoming more urgent by the week for the progressive base in the lead-up to the 2012 election cycle.

Public opinion on gay marriage had shifted dramatically within the first two years of Obama's presidency, and by early 2011, that trajectory was impossible to ignore.

Obama's religious reasons for rejecting same-sex marriage no longer seemed "moral" to many in the progressive base, with the exception of some religious African Americans. The polls reflected that movement. In May of 2011, after fifteen years of tracking gay marriage, Gallup found for the first time that a majority of Americans, 53 percent, now supported the right of same-sex couples to legally marry. It was one of a handful of credible polls that had found majority support for same-sex marriage over the last nine months. Support in the Gallup poll was highest among Democrats (69 percent) and young people ages eighteen to thirty-four (70 percent). But among blacks support lagged. During all of 2011, Pew Research Center found that only 36 percent of non-Hispanic blacks favored same-sex marriage while 49 percent of non-Hispanic whites did.[12]

Still, marriage equality was progressing. As the statistician Nate Silver wrote in the *New York Times* in April of 2011: "One way to read the trends of the past few years is that we have passed an inflection point wherein it is no longer politically advantageous for candidates to oppose same-sex marriage."[13]

In some sense, the president's preference for wrapping his objections to same-sex marriage in religious garb was a miscalculation of the way progressive and even centrist Democrats understood religion and morality. His progressive base in particular tended to view morality more through the lens of social justice and the Golden Rule than through one of rigid religious doctrine. When gay marriage is filtered through this lens, progressives are more likely to support it than to oppose it.

"God is in the mix—that kind of argument is harder to make with this volatility," observed John Green, a political scientist and senior adviser at the Pew Research Center, in an article I reported in the spring of 2011. "Part of it is because public opinion is changing, but there are also many people who support progressive causes for traditional religious reasons, whether it's a matter of social justice or caring for the poor or caring for their neighbor."[14]

It was a double hit. Much of Obama's base was growing increasingly impatient with his stance on marriage and, worse yet, his justification for not supporting equality was beginning to sound obsolete at best and offensive at worst.

ON JUNE 23, 2011, Obama gave a key speech in New York to the DNC's Gay and Lesbian Leadership Council. As it turned out, Obama addressed the crowd of about six hundred the very night before the New York State legislature would vote on whether to legalize same-sex marriage in the Empire State. Though advocates were anxiously anticipating the vote—the third such effort on marriage since 2007—the outcome was anything but certain.

It was high drama. The self-declared "fierce advocate" who didn't support marriage equality was swooping into New York to fundraise on the eve of an historic vote. New York would be the biggest state to legalize same-sex marriage since California had done so fleetingly in 2008. It would also singlehandedly double the percentage of Americans living in marriage equality states.

"What Will Obama Tell the Gays Under the Shadow of Lady Liberty?" I wondered in the headline of a piece I published just a couple of days before his speech. "As he heads into the 2012 election cycle," I wrote, "it's becoming increasingly difficult for him to have it both ways on same-sex marriage—to carry the magic mantle of hope and change, to appeal to the better angels of our nature, while literally falling behind the trend lines on supporting something as fundamentally American as the expression of our liberty."[15]

I hopped the train to New York to watch the fireworks and ended up witnessing the worst speech I would ever see Obama give. Rather than rising to the task of bridging the gulf between his stated position and the anticipation that permeated the room that night, he seemed to shrink from it. It seemed like he didn't want to be in the room, and neither did anybody else after Obama failed entirely to acknowledge the momentous nature of the vote that was about to proceed. No one, myself included, had expected Obama to come out in full support of marriage equality that night. It would have seemed like little more than a fundraising ploy at the $1,250-plus per plate dinner. But the president certainly had the oratory skills to mark the moment without fully endorsing the freedom to marry—to note the importance of the vote and to revel in an emerging movement. Yet instead of making an effort to lift up the audience and give them hope, he chose to stick to the well-worn promises he had been trotting out since 2004.

"I believe that gay couples deserve the same legal rights as every other couple in this country," he said, carefully avoiding the terms *marriage* and *civil unions*. The crowd embraced the line at first, figuring that

Obama was about to gesture to the impending vote. But it turned out to be a drive-by mention rather than a real engagement with the topic.[16]

Instead the crowd was left hanging as he turned to a recitation of the rights he had helped secure, starting with hospital visitation. "Nobody should have to produce a legal contract to hold the hand of the person that they love," President Obama said. Then he mentioned the limited set of benefits he had ordered federal agencies to extend to gay couples, continuing to tick down the list of his administration's accomplishments.

Discussing the rights he had secured for LGBT Americans was fine— as a starting point. After all, these were the necessary set of legal boundaries that distinguished one from two, bound in marriage. But it missed the point. Heterosexual couples didn't count the sanctity of their lifelong commitments to each other by the bundle of rights that came with them. It seemed that few people knew much of anything about the stream of legalities that flowed from a trip down the aisle.

This was a turning point for the crowd. They wanted something more than a sterile accounting of benefits. They didn't want Obama the realist of 2004 anymore; they wanted Obama the idealist, and to some extent they wanted his blessing.

"How about marriage?" yelled Joy Tomchin, a real estate developer, budding film producer, and a regular Democratic donor. "How about marriage?" she repeated, standing up from her chair.[17]

"Marriage!" yelled another person, followed spontaneously by several others.

Within about three seconds, Secret Service officers surrounded Tomchin. "Sit down, right now," one officer said sternly. Tomchin had attended without any intention of protesting the president. But the more he avoided the elephant in the room, the angrier she got. It just burst out. In that instant, Tomchin and a handful of other attendees held up a mirror for the president. He couldn't even say the word, they had to say it for him. But now she feared the Secret Service would eject her. She sat down.[18]

"I heard you guys," Obama responded. "Believe it or not, I anticipated this," he said, eliciting a hearty laugh and some cheers from the room. It seemed there was more backing for the president than for the hecklers for a second. But once again, Obama pivoted away from marriage just as quickly as he had stumbled into it.

"Where was I?" he said. "That's why we're going to keep on fighting until the law no longer treats committed partners, who have been together for decades, like they're strangers."[19]

This was the type of missed connection that continually hung in the air that night. Obama was trying to sell LGBT donors on the fact that he was with them in the fight. Yet he couldn't endorse the very thing they yearned for: some resolution in a battle that had been fought one too many times in Albany, a battle that was crying out for a champion at the national level.

Obama's final words fell flat.

"With your help, if you keep up the fight, and if you will devote your time and your energies to this campaign one more time, I promise you we will write another chapter in that story," he pledged in a solemn tone. "And I'll be there . . . right there with you," he concluded, stumbling toward the finish line of his speech.[20]

There was nothing soaring in his farewell. Instead of bellowing out the lines like the captain of a team steeling for a tough game, Obama seemed to be soberly asking the crowd to shoulder the burden of the struggle while he stood safely on the sidelines. The implicit message was that he would do his part in the next term. Several progressive commentators in the Beltway media took that to mean that if he were reelected he would come out for marriage equality. But a second term was far from a sure thing. Most of Obama's progressive base was demoralized and the economy was still struggling, both of which posed severe challenges for Obama among the broader electorate. If Obama was asking LGBT Americans to wait a bit longer and support him in the meantime, it was a sizeable request.[21]

I, for one, didn't care what he might be promising in the future. "Queer Americans quite simply don't need the promise of inspired leadership next term, we need the promise of it now," I wrote after the event.[22]

At that point, it felt like we had scraped and clawed for every advance we had gotten from his administration. I was tired of the suggestion by many in Washington that we should be enthused about some halfhearted hint at the hope for tomorrow—that somehow if we just bided our time, everything would magically fall into place later. We had settled for that in 2008, but times had changed drastically since then.

And the only people who hadn't wrapped their minds around that reality, it seemed, were sitting in the White House.

WHAT THE MARRIAGE movement needed was exactly what Governor Andrew Cuomo was providing in the state of New York. Some Gotham gay activists didn't trust Cuomo. They believed he was responsible for anti-gay tactics that were wielded during his father's 1977 campaign for mayor of New York against Ed Koch (Koch ultimately won). Yet at precisely the moment that President Obama was trying to steer clear of marriage equality, Cuomo had decided to make it a top priority for his administration. And although it's easy to think of New York as a state dominated by one of the largest and most progressive cities in our nation, statewide politics are actually balanced out considerably by the much more conservative citizens in the mostly rural areas north of the city.[23]

There was no question that supporting a push on marriage equality was a risky political calculation for Cuomo. But on March 9, 2011, he called about a dozen LGBT advocates to the state capitol to strategize about passing same-sex marriage before the end of his first legislative session as governor. At the time, he was soaring in the polls with a whopping 77 percent favorability rating among New Yorkers, 57 percent of whom said he was doing an excellent or good job, according to a Siena College poll released in mid-February. In March, after only three months in office, Cuomo would accomplish the near-impossible feat of delivering an on-time budget that shored up the state's $10 billion projected deficit without raising new taxes. For the first time since 2007, the Siena poll noted, New Yorkers were more optimistic than pessimistic about the state's direction.[24]

Cuomo arguably had more political power at that point than he would ever have again as governor. And perhaps more so than other first-time governors, Andrew Cuomo—the son of New York's forceful fifty-second governor, Mario Cuomo—was familiar with the dysfunction and political stalemates that typically paralyze Albany. The younger Cuomo and his team were ever mindful that Governor Eliot Spitzer's scorched earth approach to Albany politics in 2007, his first year in office, had all but ruined his ability to govern before he was forced to resign over a personal scandal in 2008. So the question was, what do you do with the power you have? Because you might never have it again.

Cuomo settled on legalizing same-sex marriage, making him the third consecutive Democratic governor of the Empire State since 2007 to take a stab at passing marriage legislation. Governor Spitzer, who forged new ground among national Democrats when he made a 2006 campaign pledge to sign marriage equality into law, first introduced a marriage bill in 2007. Spitzer's well-meaning but ultimately ineffective successor, Governor David Paterson, tried to bring the legislation home in 2009, but it failed in the Democratically controlled Senate by a startling vote of 38–24. Paterson, who had a rather charming reputation for going off-script, once told me, "One of the reasons we need same-sex marriage is because the statistics for heterosexual marriage are so bad; that might be a way to upgrade some of the success rates." Unfortunately, eight of his Democratic colleagues in the state senate didn't agree, and no Republican senators were willing to take a risky vote in favor of a bill they knew was doomed.[25]

For New Yorkers and especially LGBT New Yorkers, the Democrats' inability to push a marriage bill through the senate was starting to feel like a horrific version of *Groundhog Day*. But the stinging vote on December 2, 2009, marked a turning point in strategies for marriage equality advocates. First, they needed Republican support. Democrats alone would not do the trick even if they had majority-control of the senate chamber (the Democratically controlled assembly, which had passed marriage equality three times since 2007 without a hitch, wasn't at issue). Second, the equality groups—the Empire State Pride Agenda, Freedom to Marry, Human Rights Campaign, Marriage Equality New York, and Log Cabin Republicans—needed to scrap the turf wars that sometimes consumed them and form a united front. Third, advocates needed to oppose the election of anyone and everyone in the senate who had voted against the freedom to marry. It hadn't mattered to lawmakers that a poll released in June of 2009 by Quinnipiac University found 51 percent of state voters supported same-sex marriage while 41 percent opposed it. Voting "no" was still considered the politically safe bet at the time. That had to change.[26]

The silver lining of the failed vote was that marriage equality advocates now had a target list and a new attitude. They formed a coordinated bipartisan effort that included a mix of wooing Republicans and threatening the reelection campaign of any candidate that opposed same-sex marriage. In the spring of 2010, wealthy philanthropist and LGBT donor Tim Gill jump-started a political action committee (PAC) called Fight Back New York with a $30,000 donation. The PAC, devoted solely to unseating senators who voted against marriage equality, ultimately took in more than $800,000 that year from over 1,500 donors, including gifts as small as $1.00. Fight Back New York's largest three donors ended up being Gill at $122,000, billionaire philanthropist Jon Stryker at $83,000, and Jonathan Lewis at $50,000. The three men had a history of funneling their donations to many of the same LGBT efforts over a handful of years, though their giving philosophies also diverged at times.[27]

But in this case, the donor list was perhaps less important than who was targeted by those contributions: two senate Democrats and one senate Republican. All had voted against the same-sex marriage bill and all would lose their election to a pro–marriage equality challenger. Instead of attacking the senators' marriage votes, Fight Back New York found each candidate's Achilles heel and blew it up for voters to see. In the case of Queens Democrat Senator Hiram Monserrate, for instance, the calculus was simple. The disgraced senator had been convicted of assaulting his girlfriend and was under investigation for misusing taxpayer funds. Fight Back New York flooded the district with about one hundred thousand mailers painting him as a criminal, reaching some sixteen thousand households in a special election that drew a little under sixteen thousand voters. Monserrate lost by a landslide to his main competitor, Democrat José Peralta, 65 to 27 percent. Later that year, Fight Back New York would also contribute to the fall of Buffalo Democrat, Senator Bill Stachowski, to his primary challenger, Tim Kennedy, and Queens Republican Senator Frank Padavan's loss to his Democratic rival in the general election, Tony Avella.[28]

As liberal donors played their part, conservative funders also stepped up, proving same-sex marriage was a bipartisan issue. In September of 2010, billionaire hedge fund manager Paul Singer, former Republican National Committee Chair Ken Mehlman (now a partner at the global investment firm KKR), and Silicon Valley venture capitalist Peter Thiel organized a fundraiser on New York's West Side that raked in

$1.5 million for the cause of marriage equality. That money went to the American Foundation for Equal Rights, which was funding the legal challenge to Proposition 8 and counted Mehlman as a Board member.[29]

At the event, Singer talked movingly about paging through the wedding album of his gay son and son-in-law, who had married in Massachusetts, as he sat alongside the two men.

"No moment better encapsulated for me the contribution to societal stability than that moment of normalcy in leafing through that album," Singer, who was usually quite press shy, told the crowd of some two hundred mostly conservative attendees.[30]

But that was just the beginning of the statement pro-equality conservatives would make on the matter. Once they realized Cuomo was serious about passing a marriage bill, Singer and Mehlman teamed up again to funnel another million-plus to the New York effort; $425,000 came from Singer personally with another $650,000 donated by a handful of other conservative donors. The money went toward media campaigns and field organizing coordinated by New Yorkers United for Marriage (the coalition that was formed by the LGBT organizations).[31]

Mehlman, who publicly disclosed that he was gay in 2010, was reviled by some LGBT activists (particularly Democrats) for his role in the GOP's 2004 effort to reelect George W. Bush by driving anti-gay voters to the ballot box through marriage referenda. During a post–coming out interview I conducted with him, Mehlman said he regretted not being in a better place personally to argue against the strategy when he was managing President Bush's reelection campaign. But he also noted that since he couldn't change the past, he was trying to right some of his wrongs by focusing on the difference he could make in the future. As the RNC's former fundraiser-in-chief, Mehlman had a lot of connections at his disposal, and he began putting them to work on LGBT issues and marriage equality.[32]

Even against that backdrop, Cuomo's gamble was gutsy. The counter argument for his administration in March of 2011 was very attractive politically: *We're doing well, it looks like we're going to deliver an on-time budget for the first time in God knows how long—we could do marriage next year, or we could do it in 2013. Why rock the boat? Let's see where the polling goes over the next couple years and then weigh how crucial it is to our reelect.*

But instead of saving what many considered a tangential battle for a safer day, Cuomo took it on, charging his right-hand man and closest political confidant, Steve Cohen, with getting it done. Cohen spent the next few months aligning the LGBT advocates working on the issue, courting Republican lawmakers and twisting the arms of Democrats who might defect on the vote. In some ways, one of the biggest hurdles was convincing both caucuses that the effort could in fact succeed. There's a lot of money floating around Albany, and both sides could fundraise heavily off the issue from people who either passionately supported or opposed marriage equality. In that sense, a number of lawmakers had an interest in not settling the issue. And certainly no Republicans wanted to vote for the bill and then have it fail. Any Republican who cast a "Yay" vote was bound to face a tough reelection, and there's no reason to fall on your sword to no good end.

The night before that historic vote in Albany, as Obama delivered a lackluster speech that would reportedly bring in $750,000 in campaign donations, New York's Capitol halls were packed with protesters, advocates, legislative staff, journalists, and politicians who had inhabited the same pressure cooker for nearly a dozen days on end. Amid the sweaty bodies and stale air, the governor's staff, marriage allies, and some Republican lawmakers were balancing the timing of the marriage vote with the precision of a tightrope walker. They knew the bill would have to be brought to the floor for a vote literally the moment the language was finalized or else the opportunity might vanish as quickly as it appeared. Votes in Albany tend to fall apart the longer they sit. Lawmakers who are ready to take a courageous stand sometimes get cold feet. And in this case, Republicans controlled the state senate and a good number of GOP caucus members were still adamantly opposed to taking the vote at all.[33]

But marriage advocates also understood that the vote couldn't proceed before a final round of measures were passed that addressed property taxes, rent control, and college tuition hikes, among other things—it was a package advocates had simply taken to calling "the big ugly." The marriage vote had to be last so lawmakers couldn't say they voted against it because other measures were more pressing. So throughout Thursday night and into the early morning hours of Friday, the governor's staff continued slowly and methodically drafting and redrafting a series of amendments for the marriage legislation in order to stall the bill's completion until the following day.

On Friday, June 24, 2011, at about 10:30 p.m., the bill finally passed the Republican-led senate by a vote of 33–29. It was the final vote of the session. Senate majority leader, Dean Skelos, had not only allowed the bill to come to the floor, he had also given his blessing to every member of the GOP caucus to "vote their conscience" after GOP senators had privately debated the issue behind closed doors for nine hours. In the end, four Republican senators—James Alesi, Mark Grisanti, Roy McDonald, and Stephen Saland—voted in favor of the freedom to marry. It was the first time a Republican-controlled chamber in any state in the nation had approved same-sex marriage legislation.[34]

Two major celebrations took place that night along with countless other moments of elation that undoubtedly unfolded in private residences across New York. Just past midnight, after Governor Cuomo signed the marriage bill and the legislative session officially came to a close, politicos of every stripe streamed into the governor's mansion for one of the most buoyant send-offs to a legislative session in recent memory. It was a diverse crowd—elected officials from both sides of the aisle, staffers, people from the senate and the assembly, members who voted in favor of marriage equality, and even those who voted against it. The festivities were infused with a sense that Albany was finally working the way a government should work. Perhaps it was the ability of lawmakers to agree to disagree on the contentious bill while letting it move forward anyway, or maybe it was simply a sense of pride in getting everything done, but nearly everyone seemed to be delighting in what the state government had accomplished after a grueling couple of weeks.

After about a half hour, it dawned on Steve Cohen, Cuomo's point person on marriage equality, that one person in particular was missing: the governor. Cohen knew that when the crowds swelled and Cuomo wanted a moment alone, he would sometimes duck off to a private space behind the main area on the first floor of the mansion. That's where he found the governor.

Cuomo embraced Cohen with some mix of relief and awe. "We really did something special," he told Cohen. "We're going to remember this the rest of our lives. This is something our fathers would never have believed we could accomplish."[35]

Both men had grown up with very successful and commanding fathers. To Cohen, who had managed the process obsessively ever since that March meeting with advocates, the accomplishment captured the essence of what government service is supposed to be about. It wasn't just that they had gotten something difficult passed, it was that they got something passed that would have a real impact on people's daily lives. Something that would make their parents proud. In the five years that Cohen had worked for Cuomo, first in the attorney general's office and then the governor's office, this was the moment he would never forget.[36]

Back in the city, I joined hundreds of revelers as they gathered in Greenwich Village outside the Stonewall Inn, the birthplace of the modern gay rights movement where, in 1969, a group of gay and transgender activists had finally rebelled against the police officers who routinely raided the establishment. Stonewall wasn't the first gay rights protest to ever take place, but it became the rallying cry in a struggle to beat back queer oppression that would be forever memorialized by the LGBT community every year in June. On that magical Friday night, New York's Gay Pride Parade was just thirty-six hours away from filling the streets with festivity.

The Stonewall Inn's signature red neon sign hung in the darkened window, its emblazoned letters announcing themselves anew amid a crowd that had known them as home through decades of ups and downs. People with tambourines, noisemakers, and the most basic of all sound machines—their voices—erupted into spontaneous chants, formed dance circles, and greeted complete strangers with the welcoming glances of old friends. We were all winners in that grand lottery—none of us more enabled than the other, none of us more empowered, none of us luckier or more blessed. Personally, I had never come close enough to marrying someone to know the shape of either its terror or its bliss. But I was no longer blocked from broaching that threshold by the whimsy of a handful of judges who knew nothing of me or my life or the dreams that would rush my heart over the course of a lifetime. It was the completion of a journey that had begun five years earlier for me, when I had covered the New York court ruling that rendered me and all my LGBT peers second-class citizens in the state. The little piece of my heart that ripped open that day had been restored.

The electricity of Sinatra's city that never sleeps pulsed through the sweet summer air that evening, but it was a newer rhythm of Jay-Z's "Empire State of Mind" that bounced from the pavement and wafted into the sky as people belted out the chorus. New York, as ever, reinvigorated with the sense of possibility that rises from the streets to greet all who migrate there.

I saw a number of familiar faces that I had known either through the journalism world or from covering LGBT politics in the city. But I never expected to cross paths with Jonathan Lewis that night. I practically bumped straight into him as I was weaving my way through the crowd. We weren't particularly close friends, but we were comrades in arms from very different worlds who shared a mutual respect for one another. We looked at each other, startled for a moment to be face to face, then spontaneously embraced. Lewis smiled broadly and, as we began to move past each other, suddenly clutched my forearm and said, "Remember this. Always remember this moment." Then he held up his phone and snapped an impromptu shot of us.

When I later reflected on that chance meeting, I wondered how often someone like Jonathan—who has donated to many, many political causes—ever has the opportunity to see something he poured thousands of dollars into actually come to fruition in such a palpable, meaningful way. And to savor that sweetness amid a crush of people enveloped in some sort of exquisite euphoria. Not many, I guessed. Not many.

THE EVOLUTION · 9

THE SUCCESSFUL NEW YORK MARRIAGE VOTE UNLEASHED A media flurry of not so flattering comparisons between Governor Cuomo and President Obama. At the *New York Times*, Nate Silver suggested that if President Obama lost the 2012 election, Democrats would likely crave a more aggressive leader in their 2016 nominee.

"The type of leadership that Mr. Cuomo exercised—setting a lofty goal, refusing to take no for an answer, and using every tool at his disposal to achieve it—is reminiscent of the stories sometimes told about with President Lyndon B. Johnson, who had perhaps the most impressive record of legislative accomplishment of any recent president," Silver wrote on June 25, 2011. "It's also a brand of leadership that many Democrats I speak with feel is lacking in President Obama."[1]

Silver was joined by the *Times'* sharp-tongued columnist Maureen Dowd, who wrote, "For the president, 'the fierce urgency of now' applies only to getting checks from the gay community, not getting up to speed with all the Americans who think it's time for gay marriage. As with 'don't ask, don't tell,' Obama is not leading the public, he's following."[2]

Dowd's sentiment was echoed by *Washington Post* columnist Dana Milbank who wrote, "The president is once again 'leading from behind.'" It was a phrase one of Obama's aides had used to describe the president's slow approach to taking military action in Libya that ultimately helped rebels oust the country's brutal dictator, Muammar Gaddafi. But as soon as the phrase first surfaced in a *New Yorker* article in May of 2011, the characterization was embraced by the media as a catchall for the president's leadership style. "Leading from behind," which had come from within, now made White House aides bristle. As the article had noted, it wasn't the type of campaign slogan that inspired confidence for 2012, especially as someone like Governor Cuomo was being hailed for his brand of leadership on securing marriage rights for all New Yorkers.[3]

But Andrew Sullivan of The Dish wasn't as quick to criticize the president. He challenged other commentators' comparisons between Cuomo and Obama in a post titled, "A President, Not a Governor," at his blog, which was then housed on The Daily Beast website.[4]

Sullivan—who is gay and had argued for legalizing gay unions in his 1996 book *Virtually Normal*—suggested that Obama's silence on the issue was actually helping the cause of marriage equality by letting the debate simmer at the state level.

"The genius of federalism is that it allowed us to *prove* that marriage equality would not lead to catastrophe, that it has in fact coincided with a strengthening of straight marriage, that in many states now, the sky has not fallen," Sullivan wrote on June 29. "Obama's defense of federalism in this instance is not a regressive throwback; it is a pragmatic strategy."[5]

Some gay advocates in Washington started touting Sullivan's argument even as mainstream outlets were almost universally panning what they viewed as the president's misguided political calculation. This worried me. Sullivan wasn't making a moral argument for or against the freedom to marry; he was saying that Obama's neither-here-nor-there positioning was actually advancing the cause of marriage equality. Sullivan had been a conservative-leaning pioneer on the freedom to marry, but now he was providing high-profile cover to President Obama and all the advocates who worried that pushing him on marriage would hurt his reelection.

I feared the sentiment might take flight among advocates unless someone provided an equally public counterpoint, so I queried The Daily Beast to see if I could write a response. They were happy to engage the debate.

Sullivan's logic, I wrote on July 6, "is founded on two misguided assumptions: (1) that if Obama came out for same-sex marriage, the debate at the state level would somehow grind to a screeching halt and

(2) that Obama's position exists outside that deliberation, magically affecting neither the content nor the outcome of the debate."[6]

Perhaps most important, I added, Sullivan's thesis "fails to anticipate the presidential effect on a landmark case at the U.S. Supreme Court," which might come as early as 2012. "At that point, the marriage-equality movement will need every potential arrow in its quiver: including public opinion, state wins, and yes, the support of our nation's chief executive." While the polling already showed majority support for marriage equality, I argued that a presidential imprimatur would substantially accelerate that trend.[7]

As the public debate raged on, internal debates at the White House that had been stewing throughout the year continued. Top aides to President Obama like David Plouffe and Stephanie Cutter had indicated to Democratic operatives early in 2011 that they believed President Obama would fully embrace marriage equality. They just weren't sure whether he would do so before or after the 2012 election. Meanwhile, some consultants had been suggesting to White House aides that the president would benefit from coming out for marriage equality before the next election. This issue, much like "don't ask, don't tell," had become a broader progressive issue, they argued, not just an LGBT issue. If the president was going to end up there anyway, they added, he should do it sooner rather later. The closer it got to the election, the more political the move would look.[8]

One Democratic consultant suggested dropping the news during a wide-ranging mainstream interview with someone like PBS talk show host Charlie Rose. The president's aides could make sure the marriage question got asked and then President Obama could simply answer the right way.[9]

Former RNC chairman Ken Mehlman had been offering similar advice. Mehlman had been Obama's classmate at Harvard Law School in the early '90s and the two shared a mutual respect for each other. During the final months of the effort to repeal "don't ask, don't tell," White House aides had asked Mehlman to talk to nearly a dozen Republican Senators who were still on the fence about repeal. Though he had retired from politics as a profession, Mehlman had made a personal commitment to do what he could for the cause of LGBT equality.[10]

Following the repeal victory, the president invited Mehlman to the White House for lunch in early 2011. They discussed a number of topics, including same-sex marriage. Mehlman told the president that he saw marriage equality as having more upsides than downsides, both from a policy and a political perspective.[11]

Politically speaking, the polling on marriage was getting better all the time. But to Mehlman, the polling was less important than the context. People, in his view, don't vote on issues, they vote on attributes. Issues are simply the lens through which voters view a candidate's character.

George W. Bush, for instance, won the 2000 election in part because of his commitment to education reform. It wasn't that voters necessarily understood every aspect of how his plan would work or the aggregated data about which kids were being left behind and how that would change. But the issue reinforced the voters' sense that Bush was a uniter who wanted to make things better for everyone—of him being a "compassionate conservative."

Mehlman believed one of the key attributes that helped Obama win in 2008 was that voters viewed him as a fair-minded guy who would stand up for his beliefs. A perfect example of this was Obama's 2008 speech on race in the wake of revelations that his former pastor, Reverend Jeremiah Wright, had given some racially inflammatory sermons. In that speech, titled "A More Perfect Union," Obama addressed head-on the racial divisions that often permeate our national discourse and used his own personal narrative as "the son of a black man from Kenya and a white woman from Kansas" to help bridge the divide. It was a defining moment in the campaign and a speech that many Americans found commonality with even if they didn't agree with all of Obama's sentiments.[12]

Coming out for marriage equality, Mehlman counseled, would remind voters that Obama's a guy who stands on principle even if some voters didn't entirely agree with him.

Beyond the question of Obama's qualities as a leader, Mehlman argued that attitudes on the issue itself had clearly shifted in favor of same-sex marriage. The polls now showed majority support for marriage equality. And in terms of how important the issue was to voters, the people who strongly supported the freedom to marry were now more energized by the issue than those who strongly opposed it.

It was an ideal trifecta: a winner on attributes, overall support, and salience. Mehlman argued that Obama should come out in favor of same-sex marriage soon to make it clear that the president's change in position wasn't just a politically motivated calculus.[13]

Following his conversation with the president, Mehlman continued to discuss the issue with Obama adviser David Plouffe throughout the spring and summer of 2011. And while the White House wrestled with the issue behind the scenes, the press repeatedly gave President Obama opportunities to complete his evolution, especially after the New York vote.

"Do you believe that marriage is a civil right?" NBC's Chuck Todd asked the president at a midday news conference on June 29.[14]

Obama danced around the question. Saying "yes" would suggest that same-sex couples had a constitutional right to marry nationwide. The answer would not only signal a change in his position, it would contradict his long-held contention that marriage was a matter for the states to decide. On the other hand, flatly denying that marriage was a civil right would invite fury from the left. So instead, President Obama did what he had been doing for the last few years. He ticked through a list of his administration's accomplishments, reiterated his support for the debate that had played out in New York the previous week, and ended by saying, "I think we're moving in a direction of greater equality and I think that's a good thing."[15]

Laura Meckler of the *Wall Street Journal* followed up on Obama's assertion that it was a positive development that so many states were moving toward equality. "Does that mean that you personally now do support same-sex marriage?" she asked.[16]

President Obama shut that down immediately. "I'm not going to make news on that today," he said to laughter from the press corps. "Good try, though." It was a signal to other reporters that they shouldn't waste their breath asking because they wouldn't get anywhere.

But Meckler wasn't dissuaded. "I'm sorry," she said, "I know you don't want to say anything further on the same-sex marriage issue, but what you said before really led me to believe that that's what is in your personal mind. And I'm wondering what's the distinction you're drawing."[17]

"Laura, I think this has been asked and answered," he said curtly. "I'll keep on giving you the same answer until I give you a different one, all right?"[18]

Obama's trusty fallback of "not making news today" was wearing dreadfully thin. Moving forward, he couldn't continually stanch the marriage question throughout the election cycle without damaging his candidacy. On the campaign trail, "this has been asked and answered" wouldn't win him any points with voters even if it bought him a temporary pass with reporters in the East Room. Come 2012, the president would have to address the question without deflecting, especially when he was talking more directly to voters at forums and debates.

But whatever he might have projected externally, the New York marriage win had taken a toll on him personally and the drubbing he was still taking in the press didn't help matters. In a series of September 2011 meetings with his top aides, chronicled by journalists Mark Halperin and John Heilemann in their book *Double Down*, Obama began seriously pondering his 2012 reelection by reflecting on his regrets from his first few years in office. The list read like a scrap heap of prime progressive issues. He lamented their failures on climate change, immigration reform, poverty, closing Guantanamo Bay, and, finally, gay marriage.

"'Look,' he said, 'everybody here probably knows that I've long since evolved on this issue,'" Halperin and Heilemann reported. "I haven't been comfortable for some time with where I am publicly. I don't want to keep ducking it."[19]

During those meetings, President Obama told his advisers that he wished the press would just ask the marriage question a different way. Instead of asking what he thought about marriage equality, he wanted to be asked how he would have voted if he were a state legislator in New York. As he explained, he was a state legislator once, and if the press had asked him that, he didn't think he could lie.[20]

Of course, when you're president of the United States, if you really want someone to ask that question, you can make it happen. The truth was that it was exactly the type of inquiry the president's aides had been trying to insulate him from for years. But now their boss was growing restless, and the last thing they wanted was for him to spontaneously switch positions under the questioning of some random reporter. Controlling those questions, however, was becoming an increasingly difficult proposition at the very same time that the president's answers were ringing more and more hollow.

Obama's own dysphoria was punctuated by yet another unsettling revelation: internal campaign polling came back late in 2011 showing that the only motivating issues for young voters aged eighteen to thirty were the environment and same-sex marriage. It was a critical piece of Obama's voting coalition—66 percent of voters under thirty had chosen Obama over Senator John McCain in 2008—and the president was currently failing them on both counts.[21]

In light of polling and the president's own frustrations, it was time to find a way to lay the groundwork for Obama to revise his position. In fall of 2011, Plouffe asked Mehlman to get more specific about how Obama might announce his evolution to being pro–marriage equality. In devising a strategy, Mehlman drew from a wealth of public data, private data, personal experience, and ongoing conversations he was having with both AFER, the group behind the Proposition 8 lawsuit, and the New York–based group Freedom to Marry, which had conducted an exhaustive review of polls, focus groups, and academic research on the marriage issue from across the country. In a detailed e-mail to Plouffe on November 10, 2011, reported in full by Jo Becker in *Forcing the Spring*, Mehlman advised the White House to do it during an interview that included the president, First Lady Michelle Obama, and a female interviewer. He suggested discussing the fact that they, as a family, had been talking about same-sex marriage, and that as a country, we should be encouraging people to make lifelong commitments to one another.[22]

Specifically, Mehlman suggested the president say, "I fully understand that some will agree, while others will disagree, with where our family has come down on this. Thankfully in America we can talk about these complex issues with civility, decency, and respect . . . As Michelle and I have been thinking through what we teach Sasha and Malia about America's greatness and how we've constantly enlarged the circle and expanded freedom, we no longer feel we can make an exception that treats our gay friends differently just because of who they love."[23]

While Mehlman was corresponding with Plouffe, the president of Freedom to Marry, Evan Wolfson, was making a similar pitch to White House adviser Valerie Jarrett, who had emerged as the moral conscience of the West Wing on LGBT matters. Jarrett, who was often the only woman in the room at key White House meetings (not to mention the only woman of color in the room), felt a deep personal connection to the issue and had been involved in multiple meetings with LGBT advocates. She seemed to view this as a legacy issue in which the politics of the moment couldn't be neatly cleaved from the president's place in history. Not everyone agreed with Jarrett. Plouffe and David Axel-rod, the 2008 campaign manager and chief strategist respectively, were much more data driven and the numbers still gave them pause. Steph-anie Cutter, the 2012 deputy campaign manager, wanted the numbers to work but was more prone to seeing the upsides of Obama coming out for marriage. But her boss, 2012 campaign manager Jim Messina—the man who would ultimately be responsible for the fate of Obama's reelection—was the most nervous of all. And in politics, fewer people get in trouble for being cautious than they do for being aggressive. All of the advisers were desperate to see the president win a second term, but their road map to getting there sometimes diverged.[24]

The politics of the upcoming election year weren't about to make their deliberations any easier. Minnesota's Republican-controlled legislature, spoiling for a fight with its Democratic governor, Mark Dayton, had by-passed him in spring of 2011 to approve a ballot measure banning same-sex marriage for consideration in November 2012. In the first couple months of 2012, three more states would solidify marriage fights at the ballot box. Gay advocates in Maine submitted enough signatures in January to ensure consideration of a measure that would legalize same-sex marriage—the first such attempt to proactively petition voters for the right to marry. In February, state lawmakers in both Washington and Maryland passed bills legalizing gay marriage, prompting promises from anti-gay activists in both states to overturn the laws via referendum in November.[25]

The fifth marriage showdown of the year was set to take place even sooner, during a May 8 primary election in North Carolina, the only southern state left without a constitutional amendment banning same-sex marriage (though it was already prohibited by state law). Defeating a marriage amendment in the South was a long shot to be sure. The prospect was made even more difficult by the fact that the spring pri-mary would include GOP presidential candidates, which would likely generate higher turnout among the state's more conservative voters. But the proposed amendment was especially draconian, banning not only gay marriage but also any form of legal union for same-sex couples (civil unions, domestic partnerships, etc.). That's where LGBT advocates saw a glimmer of hope. While a majority of Tar Heel voters still opposed same-sex marriage, a January 2012 Public Policy poll found that a solid majority (57 percent) supported some form of legal recognition for gay couples, whether it was marriage or civil unions; only 40 percent were against recognizing any type of partnership whatsoever. So defeating the measure would require getting more voters to the polls and ensuring that they understood what they were voting for. Indeed, as people started to realize the scope of the measure, support had begun to tick down from 61 percent in October 2011 to 56 percent by January.[26]

LGBT advocates from the Coalition to Protect All North Carolina Families, which led the effort to defeat the measure, asked officials at the Democratic National Committee to commit resources to their campaign—mainly in the form of money and recorded robocalls. Advocates hoped to avoid a repeat performance of Maine in 2009 when Obama for America, an extension of the DNC, sent "get out the vote" e-mails to Democratic supporters but failed to provide any information about the issues on the ballot, including the measure that ultimately repealed same-sex marriage rights there. The Tar Heel activists also asked for President Obama to weigh in against the North Carolina measure specifically, which was something he had failed to do in Maine. Jeremy Kennedy, who was heading up the North Carolina effort, took the extra step of making those requests public in an *Advocate* article reported by Andrew Harmon. If the DNC and the White House opted not to lift a finger, at least people would know their help had been formally sought.[27]

North Carolina held particular importance to Democrats in 2012. In 2008, Obama had squeaked out a victory there, besting Senator John McCain by less than half a percentage point. It was the first time the state had voted Democratic in a presidential election since 1976. Obama's campaign team, heavily invested in trying to take it again, had decided to hold the Democratic convention in Charlotte in hopes of reenergizing the state's Democratic voters.[28]

The North Carolina marriage battle was something the Obama campaign would have rather avoided, but they were reassured by the fact that the vote would be over months before the September convention. Still, one more marriage consideration would be added to their plate for the year, marking six marriage fronts altogether. Freedom to Marry launched an initiative in mid-February called "Democrats: Say I Do" that sought to add a pro–gay marriage plank to the Democratic Party platform. In 2008, the platform had stopped short of endorsing marriage equality, saying instead, "We support the full inclusion of all families, including same-sex couples, in the life of our nation, and support equal responsibility, benefits, and protections." It also denounced the Defense of Marriage Act and "all attempts to use this issue to divide us."[29]

The proposed 2012 language would add, "We support the full inclusion of all families in the life of our nation, with equal respect, responsibilities, and protections under the law, including the freedom to marry . . . and oppose discriminatory constitutional amendments and other attempts to deny the freedom to marry to loving and committed same-sex couples."[30]

Freedom to Marry had approached the issue carefully—letting top party officials and White House aides know in advance that they planned to launch the campaign. Still, it was an aggressive push of the kind that inside-the-Beltway groups would likely have never made. But Freedom to Marry, by virtue of its New York home, was less prone to let party doctrine set its agenda. And unlike the Human Rights Campaign or the National Gay and Lesbian Task Force, both of which focused on LGBT issues more broadly, Freedom to Marry was a single-issue organization, which meant that they would be judged solely by their success on that one issue, much like the repeal organizations. If multi-issue organizations failed in one area, they could always say they were focusing on a different issue. Single-issue organizations did not have that luxury.[31]

Finally, it didn't hurt that the group's founder and president, Evan Wolfson, had been championing marriage equality ever since he wrote a thesis on it in 1983 during his third year at Harvard Law School. It was titled, "Samesex Marriage and Morality: The Human Rights Vision of the Constitution." Gay marriage was still an eccentric notion back then and, to some, the subject may have seemed as foreign and esoteric as something out of George Orwell's *1984*. But it became Wolfson's life work. He founded Freedom to Marry in 2003 as a way to help push the conversation out of the courtroom and into the public sphere.[32]

Wolfson and his team had set two interrelated goals for 2012: (1) push the president to support marriage equality; and (2) score some marriage wins at the ballot box. Pushing the platform language seemed a natural extension of a discussion that the Democratic Party had been having about same-sex couples since at least 2000, when a line about supporting "full inclusion of gay and lesbian families in the life of the nation" had first been added. Endorsing same-sex marriage was also now in alignment with the views of about two-thirds of Democrats. Perhaps most importantly, it gave the group a vehicle for forcing a public conversation about same-sex marriage that would pressure the president without directly attacking him.[33]

Despite the planning that went into alerting Democratic Party officials, the group had little idea just how quickly the concept would take off once they introduced it in February. As one might imagine, not everyone welcomed the push with open arms initially, including some Party officials and LGBT advocates. But within a month of its launch, it had gained the support of House Minority Leader Nancy Pelosi, twenty-two Democratic senators (nearing half the caucus), and the chair of the Democratic convention, Los Angeles Mayor Antonio Villaraigosa. When Villaraigosa was asked on March 7 whether he thought the Democratic platform should include marriage equality, he responded, "I do. I think it's basic to who we are. I believe in family values and I believe that we all ought to be able to have a family and marry if you want to."[34]

Later that day, in a conference call with reporters, campaign chief Jim Messina faced questioning from CNN's Jessica Yellin about Obama's marriage position, the convention, and the plank.[35]

Messina ducked. "There's a process," he responded, adding, "There's not even a delegate platform committee yet."[36]

But the worst of it came on March 25, when journalist George Stephanopoulos questioned David Plouffe about the matter on ABC's Sunday talk show *This Week*.

"Now, the president has said he's evolving on the issue of gay marriage, but he's still opposed," Stephanopoulos noted. "Does that mean that he's going to fight the inclusion of this plank in the Democratic platform?"[37]

Plouffe put forth an all-star hits of dodges, saying he didn't have "anything to add," there wasn't even a platform committee yet, and that the president had made "groundbreaking progress" for LGBT Americans. Stephanopoulos finally offered, "But why can't he say what he believes on this issue?"[38]

Plouffe paused momentarily. "Well, George, he has said what he believed."

But it really didn't matter what the president was saying anymore. No one was taking him at his word, especially not the journalists covering the White House and the campaign. That Obama and his advisers had not yet settled on a way to end the endless questioning they were enduring on same-sex marriage was a testament to just how profound the pressure is to get it right when you're working to reelect a president, especially the first African American president of the country. It also indicated just how impossible it is to turn the corner on conventional wisdom once it's settled comfortably into Washington's psyche.

Obama and his advisers had weathered the embarrassment in New York; they had ignored routine counsel from consultants and operatives on the outside; they thus far seemed to be ignoring polling showing that marriage equality was one of only two issues that would drive young voters to the polls; they had not budged on the issue even though consistent polling showed that solid majorities of both Democrats (65 percent) and independents (57 percent) supported same-sex marriage and even though polling showed that the people who were now most motivated by that issue alone were those in favor of marriage equality. And maybe most stunning, they didn't yet seem to understand that after seventeen months of saying he was "evolving," no one believed that the president hadn't already arrived at a destination.[39]

It's unclear what the downsides of coming out for marriage were, although surely there were some. But overall, Obama's aides had become so granular in their thinking—focusing on what it would mean voter-by-voter in North Carolina, in Ohio, in Florida—that they couldn't see the big picture. The president's brand was in shambles. Forget about leading from behind, he didn't seem authentic and he had almost entirely turned a blind eye to the progressives who elected him. Even he must have recognized this on some level as he lamented his first-term failings during those fall 2011 meetings with his inner circle.[40]

What seemed to be lost on them in between the data points was that LGBT equality had become more than a set of issues. You couldn't just check off the boxes on "don't ask, don't tell" and DOMA anymore and declare victory. Americans had come to think of the problem more holistically—it was a human rights issue, not a special interest. As Frank Bruni of the *New York Times* had pointed out, Americans on average then believed that about 25 percent of the population was LGBT. The fact that exit polling usually put us at closer to 3–6 percent of voters suggested just what an integral part of the country's consciousness we had become.[41]

It was like America woke up one morning and suddenly couldn't imagine itself without us. We were so much more than the sum of our political parts. And being willing to finally dignify our love as a commitment equal to that of any other couple was the last step in fully embracing our humanity.

But with just a handful of months to go before the Democratic convention, President Obama and his aides still didn't have a specific date or interview planned. It had been an ongoing topic of conversation in the White House for more than a year. But in April of 2012, their dilemma on LGBT issues would be compounded.

FOR MONTHS, THE White House had been pondering an executive order that would prohibit federal contractors from discriminating against workers on the basis of their gender identity and sexual orientation. Advocates had been trying to pass a federal law prohibiting bias against LGBT workers for nearly forty years, since the mid '70s. But with Republicans in control of the House in 2012, it was once again a lost cause. Still, some kind of antidiscrimination measure was absolutely essential. At the time, a patchwork of only sixteen states had laws protecting LGBT workers from being fired on the basis of either their gender identity or sexual orientation, leaving LGBT residents in the rest of the country unprotected. Many advocates had thrown their weight behind the executive order, thinking it was the movement's last best chance for a win before Election Day.[42]

Politically, it seemed like a total winner. A whopping 90 percent of Americans actually believed that such discrimination was already banned by federal law, and another 73 percent of likely 2012 voters supported providing the protections to LGBT workers. The Center for American Progress (CAP) and HRC had both conducted polling on the issue in 2011 with very similar results. It was also something the groups had been asking for since the earliest days of the administration. In a document called "A Blueprint for Positive Change" that was prepared for the Obama transition team in 2008, HRC asserted: "When the federal government hires private companies to perform government functions with public funds, it can and should expect the contractors to adhere to the same civil rights standards as the government would if it were doing the work." But the executive order had been largely overshadowed by bigger issues in the first few years of the administration. Now, though, with same-sex marriage seemingly at a standstill, advocates were prepared to introduce the issue again.[43]

Within the federal government, workplace protections already existed by 2012 for lesbian, gay, bisexual, and transgender employees. Building upon President Clinton's 1998 executive order that covered gay and lesbian federal employees, President Obama issued a directive that gender identity be written into the government's Equal Employment Opportunity guidelines, which was completed in 2010. The transgender protections weren't as strong as an actual executive order, which carries the force of law, but the guidelines were now considered official government policy.[44]

The executive order we now sought would have extended LGBT protections to some 28 million federal contract workers, or approximately 22 percent of the nation's workforce. Nothing to sneeze at.

Jonathan Lewis and Paul Yandura, who could find no good reason for Obama's lack of action on workplace protections, had taken on the LGBT nondiscrimination order as a pet project in 2012. Yandura enlisted the help of many of the same players who had a hand in waging the outsider campaign against "don't ask, don't tell." In mid-March, Yandura held what he called a "war room" meeting that included his partner, Donald Hitchcock, Joe Sudbay, John Aravosis, Tico Almeida from a recently formed group Freedom to Work, and Heather Cronk and Charles Butler of GetEQUAL. Yandura also recruited me.

At that meeting, we talked about different ways to achieve the executive order, how to build pressure for it by placing certain stories with the LGBT media, and how to educate the mainstream media about it. We knew that Valerie Jarrett had written a memo recommending the president sign the order, that the Departments of Labor and Justice had expressed support for such an action, and we had even heard conflicting reports about whether a draft of the executive order already existed. But our biggest hurdle by far was getting the White House press corps interested in the order when marriage equality was the hot LGBT topic of the day. In fact, many members of the press, just like the general public, believed federal protections already existed for LGBT workers. As GetEQUAL's Heather Cronk had learned on multiple occasions, simply convincing reporters that the protections did not exist was an uphill battle.

In an effort to facilitate that education, GetEQUAL designed an action to catch the attention of White House reporters at the annual White House Easter Egg Roll on April 9. Tickets to the event had been offered to the group by the White House LGBT liaison, Gautam Raghavan, who had replaced Brian Bond when he moved over to the DNC halfway through 2011. Raghavan had no idea how the group would end up using the invitation. GetEQUAL resolved to have their lead organizer in New Mexico, Jarrod Scarbrough, fly in to attend the event with his partner, Les Sewell, and their eight-year-old daughter Alegra Scarbrough. It was personal for Scarbrough and his family. Scarbrough worked for United Healthcare, a federal contractor, and he had nondiscrimination protections under New Mexico law. But the family was relocating to Florida, where those protections would be lost. The president could alleviate that problem with the stroke of a pen, and Scarbrough and Sewell hoped to ask President Obama, face to face, to take action.[45]

Momentum for the executive order began building around the end of March. On March 28, HRC finally released a poll it had commissioned in November of 2011. Like the CAP polling, HRC found that 73 percent of Americans supported the executive order and even 60 percent of conservatives favored the policy. On April 3, seventy-two congressional members led by New Jersey Representative Frank Pallone released a letter urging the president to sign the order. And the April 9 Easter Egg Roll was a hit. Even though Scarbrough and Sewell never actually got the chance to speak with Obama, their presence fueled a round of more than a dozen stories in LGBT and mainstream media alike, including pieces written by White House correspondents David Jackson of USA Today and Kristen Welker of NBC.[46]

But the big breakthrough came when the president's aides invited several Washington LGBT groups to the White House on April 11 to deliver some bad news. Perhaps White House officials hoped to ease the pressure that was beginning to mount, or perhaps they felt a sense of obligation to level with some of their staunchest allies. But whatever their intent, it was a trap of their own making.

When representatives from HRC, the Task Force, CAP, and Freedom to Work arrived, they were told the executive order was being put on hold indefinitely. It was an initiative that advocates had been talking about with the White House for months. Ironically, the Obama aide who delivered that news was also the insider who had been the greatest champion of the stalled effort, Valerie Jarrett. The snub was a total blow to LGBT advocates, especially given how much public support the order had.

Worse yet, it seemed that LGBT nondiscrimination was one of the only issues that Obama wouldn't address in an executive order. For months, Obama had been championing his We Can't Wait campaign, which the White House had rolled out in October of 2011 in an effort to rally middle-American voters over the coming election year. The idea of the campaign was that America couldn't wait for Congress to do its job, so President Obama had to make use of his executive powers to move the nation forward. Over the coming year, the White House would announce nearly fifty new initiatives designed to help boost the economy and create more jobs.[47]

By April of 2012, they had already announced plans to provide $2 billion in federal grants to start-up businesses, invest $4 billion in making buildings more energy efficient, accelerate transportation grants, make it easier for students to repay their loans, and provide resources to help vets transition into the private workforce. But now, even as he worked to expand opportunity for other Americans, President Obama was explicitly saying that ending discrimination against LGBT workers could indeed wait. The baffling announcement—at what was supposedly an off-the-record meeting—was given sizeable space in all the major news outlets, including the *Wall Street Journal, New York Times,* and *Washington Post.* "The dispute opened up an unexpected election-year rift between the president and a loyal political constituency that has scored historic victories from his White House," wrote Peter Wallsten of the *Post.*[48]

Both Joe Solmonese of HRC and Winnie Stachelberg of CAP went on record expressing their disappointment. Hearing publicly from two usual allies of the administration was a sign of just how bad the breach was.[49]

The White House likely figured it would take one twenty-four-hour hit of bad coverage for the executive order before some other campaign news item would replace it. But once again the administration had underestimated the resonance LGBT issues now had with the broader public. The president's refusal to codify into law such a basic

American principle as workplace fairness seemed to touch a mainstream nerve, not to mention the fact that it served as an instant educational tool for the very demographic we most needed to help spread the word: reporters.

All the major news outlets posted stories that Wednesday (which also appeared in their print editions on Thursday). Our next goal was to fuel another cycle of stories for Friday. We needed a media hook so we concocted our own We Can't Wait campaign as a direct counterpoint to the White House slogan. The key to capturing the press corps' interest was to make sure the campaign went directly after the president and the White House and was well funded, preferably by a well-known donor with deep pockets. In the press release, we included the fact that Jonathan Lewis was donating $100,000 to the effort. It also had to read like a declaration of war. To that end, we quoted Tico Almeida of Freedom to Work in the release, urging, "This is a political calculation that cannot stand." We made sure that charge was prominently placed in the release and then got it into the hands of NBC's White House reporter, Kristin Welker, who had expressed interest in the story. When press secretary Jay Carney called on Welker at the news conference that day, the fireworks started.[50]

At first mention of the order, Carney began turning the pages of his briefing book to a written statement they had prepared in advance. Welker noted that the president supported workplace non-discrimination policies, so "why not sign this executive order?" she asked.[51]

Carney began reading: "Thank you for the question. The president is dedicated to securing equal rights for all LGBT Americans. And that is why he has long supported an inclusive employment non-discrimination act, which would prohibit employers across the country from discriminating on the basis of sexual orientation and gender identity."[52]

After all the talk of executive orders, the White House was now trying to pin their failure to address workplace discrimination on Congress. Carney said they were seeking a "legislative solution to LGBT employment discrimination" and finished by drawing a direct analogy between ENDA and "don't ask, don't tell" repeal.

"I would make the comparison here that pursuing that strategy, the passage of ENDA, is very similar to the approach the President took for the legislative repeal of "don't ask, don't tell," Carney concluded.[53]

The comparison was bogus. First of all, when Democrats controlled both chambers of Congress in 2009–2010, repeal actually stood a chance of passing. That was no longer the case, so any sort of legislative action on LGBT issues—nondiscrimination protections included—would have been next to impossible. Second, while people legitimately disagreed about whether the president had the authority to halt discharges via executive order, no one questioned his ability to prohibit federal contractors from discriminating against LGBT people. It was an executive action ripped straight from the playbook of President Franklin Delano Roosevelt, who delivered the civil rights movement one of its first major advances of the twentieth century when he signed an order in 1941 prohibiting defense contractors from discriminating based on race. FDR had done so under pressure from civil rights leaders like A. Philip Randolph, who had been threatening to stage a march on Washington. FDR's order was ultimately built upon over the years by Republican and Democratic presidents alike until 1965 when President Lyndon Johnson signed Executive Order 11246, banning contractors from discriminating against "any employee or applicant for employment because of race, creed, color, or national origin."[54]

What is important to understand is that Johnson's executive order exists alongside Title VII of the Civil Rights Act of 1964, which bans discrimination among private employers nationwide. The 1965 executive order actually provides extra protections to employees of federal contractors. So the order and the law work in concert with each other: both are legally binding, and attorneys bring lawsuits on behalf of clients using whichever seems most applicable to their particular situation. LGBT advocates wanted the executive order in order to provide basic protections for millions of LGBT workers but also to potentially jumpstart a legislative effort, much the way Roosevelt's 1941 order had.

But despite how absurd the White House's position may have seemed to everyone else in the room, Carney stuck to the talking points in his briefing book, saying the president was "deeply committed" to passing legislation. Finally Welker said, "Tico Almeida, who's the president of Freedom to Work, has issued a statement saying, 'This is a political calculation that cannot stand.' Is this a political calculation?"[55]

"Absolutely not," Carney responded.

By now, several other reporters were ready to jump in, including LGBT journalists Chris Geidner of *Metro Weekly* and Chris Johnson of the *Washington Blade*. They weren't buying the analogy for a minute. Geidner, a lawyer-turned-journalist, asked Carney whether President Obama believed that Executive Order 11246 from 1965 and Title VII of the Civil Rights Act were "redundant." The White House press shop either hadn't anticipated that question or didn't understand why comparing passage of ENDA to "don't ask, don't tell" repeal was useless.

"I haven't had that discussion with him, Chris," Carney answered. "What I do know for a fact is that this president is absolutely dedicated to securing equal rights for LGBT Americans."

All in all, questioning on the executive order consumed almost ten minutes of the briefing, an even better showing than we had hoped for.[56]

The next day, the Friday edition of the *New York Times* carried an editorial titled, "The Sin of Omission," playing off the fact that President Obama was churning out executive orders left and right on other issues even as he decided that addressing LGBT discrimination was a bridge too far.[57]

"It is unclear why Mr. Obama declined to do the right thing here," the *Times'* editorial board wrote. "His hesitation to ban gay bias by government contractors, like his continued failure to actually endorse the freedom to marry, feels like a cynical hedge."[58]

At the end of those three days, no less than fifty-six stories had been written about the president's refusal to sign the executive order. Along with all the major dailies, broadcast outlets like MSNBC and CBS wrote stories; numerous Beltway blogs like AMERICAblog and ThinkProgress and political outlets like Huffington Post, *Politico*, *Slate*, and *The Atlantic* covered it; the Tribune News Service picked it up too, which meant that it ran in local papers across the country, including in Los Angeles, Chicago, Boston, Minneapolis, Baltimore, and Orlando, among others. It had blown well past the twenty-four-hour news cycle into a mini-firestorm that would last for weeks. In fact, the controversy started to take on a life of its own. Those of us working to keep the story alive just fanned the flames here and there.[59]

Over the next week, Chris Johnson of the *Washington Blade* questioned Carney again on the matter; the largest Latino advocacy group, the National Council of La Raza, called on Obama to issue the executive order; and Democratic members of Congress began to break ranks with the president, a somewhat unusual move during a presidential election year. Senator Jeff Merkley of Oregon, the lead sponsor of the ENDA bill in the Senate, issued a statement saying he was "deeply disappointed" by the White House's failure. Openly gay Representative Jared Polis of Colorado told *Roll Call*, a Capitol Hill newspaper, "They certainly have a lot of explaining to do in the LGBT community."[60]

On April 30, the story was elevated from the realm of political reporting into mainstream culture when Jon Stewart dedicated a segment to it on *The Daily Show*. The program aired a video clip of Jay Carney saying that the White House hoped to build support for a "legislative solution" and followed it with a clip of Obama saying, "We can't wait for an increasingly dysfunctional Congress to do its job." The president's refusal to act on this particular issue was a disastrous message for Obama to be sending to the ever-important demographic of eighteen- to twenty-nine-year-old voters who also happened to be some of Jon Stewart's most avid fans.[61]

By the time Vice President Joe Biden walked on to the set of *Meet the Press* on Friday, May 4, the White House had weathered an entire month of blistering criticism on gay issues. Biden, playfully called "Uncle Joe" by some, was known for a genial loquaciousness that reporters loved but often gave his aides heart palpitations. In an election year, talking off the cuff is a particularly dangerous quality in a vice president. The interview, to be taped Friday and broadcast Sunday, would be Biden's first to air after Obama officially kicked off his reelection campaign on that Saturday, May 5. In advance of the interview, Biden's handlers and White House aides reportedly devoted more than a dozen hours of prep time to screening him on everything from domestic issues to economics to foreign policy. But the one matter they overlooked, according to *Double Down*, was also the one that had consistently drawn both headlines and sharp questioning for the past month: LGBT rights. Their perpetual blind spot was about to trip up the carefully planned rollout of their campaign.[62]

When Biden brought up the GOP's social policies during the interview, the show's host, David Gregory, took the opening to ask Biden if he was "comfortable" with same-sex marriage. Biden hedged a bit, noting that he was merely the vice president and "the president sets the policy." But he didn't stop there. "I am absolutely comfortable with the fact that men marrying men, women marrying women, and heterosexual men marrying women are entitled to the same exact rights," he said.

"All the civil rights, all the civil liberties." Far from scripted, Biden then engaged in a series of free associations on the topic, touching on everything from Obama's other LGBT advances to cultural change to the popular pro-gay sitcom *Will & Grace* and, finally, to a Los Angeles fundraiser he attended at the household of a gay couple with two adopted children. Biden recounted telling the two men, "I wish every American could see the look of love those kids had in their eyes for you guys. And they wouldn't have any doubt about what this is about."[63]

It was every bit a heartwarming embrace of the power of love and family, gay or otherwise. And a press secretary's nightmare.

Later that day, Igor Volsky of the blog ThinkProgress got a call from a friend of his working on the campaign. After swearing Volsky to secrecy, his friend informed him that Biden had more or less just endorsed marriage equality. Though Volsky didn't have the benefit of seeing the exact transcript, as soon as he hung up, he wrote up an entry and planned to post it immediately after the clip aired on Sunday. The headline—"Joe Biden Endorses Same-Sex Marriage"—didn't leave any doubt as to what had just happened.[64]

Volsky proceeded to dutifully sit on the information all weekend, even as he thought it dubious the story wouldn't leak out ahead of time. He spent one of the most sleepless weekends of his twenty-six years on the planet checking the Internet every hour or so for any hint of the news. But it held. Within minutes of Biden's utterance on Sunday morning, Volsky dropped a partial transcript into his piece, momentarily scanned his Twitterfeed for other stories, then hovered his finger over the "post" button. *Had Biden really "endorsed" same-sex marriage?* Volsky wondered. He hadn't actually used the words, "I support." But if he wanted to be first, Volksy had to make a call. Right then. *Biden implied it,* he thought. *That's how it will be interpreted. If I'm going to freak out about this I may as well do the right thing.*[65]

He posted, tweeting out the link immediately after. Within minutes, several other outlets were up with similar stories, though some headlines used caveats like "appears to" or "seems to" endorse gay marriage. Volsky stuck with his headline. It became the site's most trafficked post to date at the time.[66]

Before the show had even ended, however, the Obama campaign launched a sustained push to walk back Biden's statement. David Axelrod took to his twitter account, suggesting that Biden's remarks reflected exactly what President Obama had been saying all along.

"What VP said—that all married couples should have exactly the same legal rights—is precisely POTUS's position," he wrote, using the acronym for the president of the United States. The vice president's office was also feverishly making the case to reporters that Biden and the president were on the same page. Biden's aides circulated a clarification statement to reporters reading, "The vice president was expressing that he too is evolving on the issue, after meeting so many committed couples and families in this country."[67]

It was preposterous. The campaign's response infuriated LGBT Americans who were heartened to hear the vice president of the United States finally acknowledge their love as no less worthy than anybody else's. In hindsight, it's hard to believe that the campaign had the entire weekend to prepare for Biden's statement and still mismanaged the response so badly. They had basically gone from trying to keep the LGBT constituency "happy enough" until after the election to emphatically reminding everyone that the president still opposed marriage equality and so did his vice president, regardless of what he had said about it.

But Biden wasn't the only one in Obama's administration to go off script. On Monday morning, Secretary of Education Arne Duncan was asked on MSNBC's *Morning Joe* whether he believed same-sex marriage should be legal.

"Uh . . . Yes, I do," he said with a quick grin, after hesitating for only a millisecond. There was no walking back that kind of statement.[68]

The genie was out of the bottle. Biden wasn't an outlier. What everyone in Washington had already known was finally coming to light: Obama was surrounded by people who were ahead of him on the issue. Only now, they weren't going to lie about it. It didn't take a visionary to imagine a steady trickle of similar pronouncements over the coming months from administration officials who would be asked the same question at random, whenever reporters could find an opening.

At Monday's brief, Carney faced a swarm of marriage questions. No less than forty-four of them to be exact. It was the dominant theme of the brief. But the worst of it for the administration wasn't the sheer volume, it was the tone. In so many words, reporter after reporter accused the president and his aides of lying to the American people.[69]

"Jay, the president has raised millions of dollars from LGBT donors," noted CNN's Jessica Yellin, "many of whom say that they believe in a second term the president will come out in support of gay marriage. So doesn't he owe them—or owe voters in general—his direct response . . . will he or won't he support gay marriage in a second term?"[70]

ABC's Jake Tapper followed up: "Why not just come out and say it and let voters decide?"

NBC's Chuck Todd: "So help me out there. He opposes bans on gay marriage but he doesn't yet support gay marriage?"

NPR's Mara Liasson: "It's pretty rare when somebody runs for office saying, in effect, I'm getting ready to change my mind."

Carney repeatedly said he had "no update" and continually reminded reporters that Obama's record on LGBT rights was "extensive and considerable and unparalleled." At one point, he actually offered, "The next time the President has a news conference, if you want to ask him that, you're certainly welcome to."

The next news cycle included reporting from the *Washington Post* that "about one in six of Obama's top campaign 'bundlers' are gay," which shed further light on just how difficult the president's equivocation was becoming. If Obama wanted to ensure their support, he would have to change his tune—and quickly. The following month, Obama was scheduled to address a seven-hundred-person LGBT fundraiser in Los Angeles. The prospect must have been daunting given how uncomfortable his speech to LGBT donors in New York had been.[71]

By Tuesday, some Democratic strategists who were gay but also not particularly prone to publicly criticizing the White House on LGBT issues started delivering some sobering straight talk. Hilary Rosen, a consultant and CNN pundit with close ties to the White House, told *Politico* the issue had become "a distraction" for the campaign. "The biggest issue isn't whether he's for it or not," Rosen said. "The biggest issue is giving the right wing a chance to keep it on the front pages." In the same article, Steve Elmendorf, a Democratic strategist also close to the White House, said, "He should have moved on it last year. Now, you're going to continually be in a position on the trail and in debates where you're going to be asked the question."[72]

Amid the media firestorm, the results of North Carolina's marriage referendum vote materialized, and they couldn't have inspired confidence among White House aides. The Obama campaign had tepidly waded into the battle in mid-March, issuing a statement through a North Carolina spokesperson that the president "opposed divisive and discriminatory efforts to deny rights and benefits to same-sex couples. That's what the North Carolina ballot initiative would do." Yet voters resoundingly endorsed the measure on Tuesday, banning any form of union between same-sex couples by a margin of 61–39 percent.[73]

But by then the writing was on the wall. The issue had snowballed into a boulder. The platform fight loomed. Four states would settle marriage battles in November. Major LGBT donors had once again begun to close their wallets. An adviser to a major donor told the *Post*'s Peter Wallsten that although the top twelve LGBT donors in the country had already "maxed out" to the president's campaign, they had not yet given any money to pro-Obama Super PACs, like Priorities USA. "And if there is the expectation that they're going to," said the unnamed adviser, "then there will have to be some concrete actions in fairly short order to demonstrate this administration's desire to keep them included in this campaign."[74]

It wasn't simply a matter of whether Obama was uncomfortable facing donors anymore. It had reached the point where it was getting difficult for donors to sit in a room with Obama and feel good about themselves. Public perception had now outstripped even their own expectations—despite their millions and, in some cases, billions of dollars. It was often easy for LGBT donors to rationalize why their own rights should take a back seat to the effort to reelect President Obama. But at a certain point, you start to feel like you're being had, no matter how much money is at your fingertips.

Donors weren't the only ones balking. The issue had reached a fever pitch among both reporters and voters. Every time the president answered a question about his views on same-sex marriage in the next seven months—and it would most definitely be asked—he would look like a guy running for cover. As David Mixner had once told me, "Courage is just a lack of options." For all their planning and polling and plotting, the campaign had run out of options.

WHEN I FIRST BEGAN seeing reports surface on the morning of Wednesday, May 9, that President Obama was going to change his marriage position, it almost seemed too good to be true. As desperate as the situation was, the campaign's top aides had consistently turned a blind eye to more than a year's worth of mounting evidence that their negligence could undermine the president's reelection. But as rumors of the historic shift continued to circulate, the White House did nothing to correct the narrative. No tweets. No clarifying statements. It must be real.

As a recovering "breaking news" reporter without anywhere to direct my spike in adrenalin, I resolved to watch the 2:00 p.m. ABC interview from a treadmill at the gym. Walking at a steady clip, I watched President Obama tell ABC's Robin Roberts exactly what many of us had been waiting for him to say for years.

The president explained that he had "hesitated" on gay marriage, in part because he thought "civil unions would be sufficient." But he added that he'd had a change of heart over the course of many conversations with friends and family and neighbors.

"When I think about members of my own staff who are incredibly committed, in monogamous relationships, same-sex relationships, who are raising kids together. When I think about those soldiers or airmen or marines or sailors—who are out there fighting on my behalf—and yet, feel constrained, even now that 'don't ask, don't tell' is gone because they're not able to commit themselves in a marriage," he said. "At a certain point, I've just concluded that—for me personally, it is important for me to go ahead and affirm that—I think same-sex couples should be able to get married."[75]

He did it. He really did it. At first, it felt almost anticlimactic; I must have still been in a state of disbelief. But as I exited the gym into the lobby the tears came fast, without warning, as the enormity of what just happened pulled me to the floor for a few moments. Nearly everything I had hoped to accomplish in Washington had happened—just not at all how I had envisioned it. And certainly not without a price. I had come to Washington a journalist who intended to document history through even-tempered reporting, but along the way I had become a frustrated activist. Impatience was what the job had called for, in my estimation, and it would take leaving Washington and a couple years of writing before I was able to rediscover my center of gravity.

But in that moment, I felt an overwhelming sense of relief. The president's final evolution was everything we could have hoped to deliver to the movement. It fell far short of the equality of opportunity and safety and dignity that so many LGBT Americans still craved and deserved. But from a political standpoint, given how close we were to the presidential election, it was the best we could have done. It would have a profound impact at the ballot box in 2012, where marriage equality activists prevailed in each of the four states, and enormous implications for the Supreme Court cases that eventually came in 2013 and 2015.

And for the first time since I had relocated to Washington, I began to wonder what you're supposed to do when you win. Certainly, there was so much more work to be done, but on a personal level, I felt as if I had made the contribution I could make. I had not begun covering LGBT issues in 2006 so I could advance them; I started covering them so I could report. Period. And covering the White House had initially seemed like a win in and of itself, at least journalistically. But like so many Americans, the more I bore witness to the injustices that LGBT Americans suffered, the more impossible it became to be dispassionate. The 2008 election had delivered an unprecedented chance to right some of those wrongs. But as time wore on in those first couple years, I felt like I was watching the opportunity of a lifetime surrender to the whims of politics, and I had been drawn into the fray. On May 9, 2012, I was finally released.

But it wasn't only people who had brought external pressure on the administration who felt validated by the president's words. LGBT officials who had toed the line inside the White House walls were equally jubilant.

Brian Bond, who served as the highest-ranking LGBT official at the White House for the first two and a half years of the administration, had borne the brunt of activist impatience, especially throughout the administration's defense of DOMA and the fight to overturn the military's gay ban. He was now heading up constituency outreach at the DNC and had been instrumental in helping the campaign get a hold of outside polling on marriage for comparison against their internal numbers. Bond watched Obama's interview in the office of DNC executive director and former White House political director, Patrick Gaspard. He cried and went numb as the president made history. Bond had always trusted that Obama would one day come out in support of marriage equality. He'd held political jobs in the past where he felt like he was being used, but he had never felt that way about working in the Obama White House. Still, there was a difference between believing in something and seeing it actually come true. Bond and Gaspard embraced, and as Bond walked out of Gaspard's office, he was struck by all the young DNC staffers—"the kids"—assembled around the TV screens to watch the president. That moment would stay with him forever.[76]

Back at the White House, Gautam Raghavan had taken on the role of being the administration's liaison to the LGBT community after Bond left halfway through 2011. For about nine months, the thirty-year-old had talked to the community about everything from health care to immigration issues. When the president's position on marriage came up, Raghavan, who had married his partner in September of 2010, would steer the conversation toward DOMA and how the president's decision to stop defending it would have much greater legal and policy implications than his symbolic support for marriage equality. But in the last few months, it seemed, nearly every discussion Raghavan had participated in with LGBT advocates and citizens had turned back to one thing: President Obama's marriage position. It was undeniable—people wanted to hear from the president. Now Raghavan found himself on the second floor of the West Wing, where about twenty of his colleagues who also handled constituency outreach were crammed into the office of Jon Carson, director of the Office of Public Engagement. Carson's office windows looked south, where the towering profile of the Washington Monument would have been visible but for a concrete security wall that blocked most of it from view.[77]

The moment they were about to witness was historic, Carson told them, and they should all take this opportunity to drink it in.[78]

Raghavan, who had learned of the interview that morning, stood just outside the office doorway so he could access his phone and a computer. Immediately following the broadcast, he would need to circulate the transcript to key LGBT leaders so they had word directly from the White House. Everywhere he looked, TVs were tuned into ABC, as the West Wing collectively paused to take in the president's words. But it wasn't until Raghavan heard them himself that he realized how powerful it would actually be for him and millions of Americans to hear the president of the United States reaffirm their relationships. Raghavan broke down. The first call he placed from within the White House was to his husband to share the moment.[79]

THE SAME PRESIDENT who had once confessed his progressive failures to his inner circle in the fall of 2011 would go on to reengage nearly every constituency he seemed to have left behind in his first two years in office: single women, immigration activists, environmentalists, and LGBT Americans. Beyond endorsing same-sex marriage, President Obama used his executive power to grant deportation relief to hundreds of thousands of immigrant youth, known as DREAMers, who were brought to the United States as children; broker a compromise that sought to ensure contraception would be covered for all women under the Affordable Care Act, regardless of their employer; and further delay the construction of an oil pipeline called the Keystone XL that environmental activists vehemently opposed.

The 2012 Democratic convention was nothing short of a celebration of third-rail politics—all the issues Democrats had been afraid to push too hard publicly for years for fear it might cost them in national elections. The Democratic platform included the most emphatic statement of support to date for LGBT families and same-sex marriage. "We support the right of all families to have equal respect, responsibilities, and protections under the law. We support marriage equality and support the movement to secure equal treatment under law for same-sex couples," it read in part.[80]

I initially tried to count the number of times marriage equality was mentioned from the stage but lost track. It was pervasive. Meanwhile, DREAM activist Benita Veliz became the first undocumented youth to address a Democratic convention; and Sandra Fluke, the darling of the reproductive rights movement after House Republicans excluded her from a hearing on insuring birth control, delivered a prime-time message from the DNC stage.

On Election Day, President Obama reassembled the voting coalition that had lifted him up in 2008, once again winning solid majorities of single women, minorities, and young people. Gay marriage, the goblin that had struck fear in the hearts of Democrats ever since 2004, helped the president get reelected rather than hurting him—boosting both his bottom line and his vote share. Following his marriage announcement, NPR reported that Obama's fundraising spiked, jumping from nearly $3.5 million May 6–8 to $8.8 million May 9–11. And in polling conducted in eight battleground states for Project Right Side,

Ken Mehlman's new conservative pro-LGBT group, Obama's gay marriage stance was found to be a "motivating factor for nearly 3 out of 4 Obama voters," with 73 percent of them saying it made them "more likely" to vote for him. The same survey found that 58 percent of independent voters in battleground states also supported marriage equality. Likewise, the president's embrace of marriage equality surely helped deliver the wins in all four of the states considering marriage measures at the ballot box in 2012. While Minnesota parted ways with some thirty of its predecessors to defeat the anti-gay marriage amendment to its state constitution, citizens in Maine, Maryland, and Washington voted to affirm the right of same-sex couples to marry.[81]

In his second term, Barack Obama would never have as much power as he'd had in the first two years of his presidency and, for some progressives, he would never fully become the president they hoped he would be. But on LGBT equality, he eventually did right. That effort was boosted in part by his own wishes, but much of the credit is due to LGBT activists who wouldn't settle for less and wouldn't settle for later. Had advocates failed to push forward a repeal vote in the spring of 2010 that the Department of Defense was actively lobbying against, the repeal bill would have never been in position to be passed during the lame-duck session that December. And that one major legislative victory in the final hours of the 111th Congress opened the door for the groundbreaking advances in LGBT rights that unfolded over the next several years. Had repeal failed, how much harder would it have been for the administration to stop defending the Defense of Marriage Act in the courts when it was still actively defending "don't ask, don't tell"? And how could a president who was still discharging qualified women and men from our military because of whom they loved declare himself a believer in the freedom to marry?

Good intentions only go so far in Washington, even when they belong to the commander in chief. On the other side of that intention, there has to be a hammer. In politics, that very real and relentless pressure comes in the form of money or votes or both. LGBT activists had effectively blended the power of public opinion that had been more than fifty years in the making with the elixir of wealth to nudge the ever obstinate world of Washington into modernity.

In the process, they not only charted a new course toward their own freedom; they also helped free the president, giving him the space he needed to speak out in support of their rights.

As he stood at the rostrum during his second inauguration, Obama sounded like a man who had rediscovered himself, a man renewed by the power of the people's contract with their fundamental freedoms— the unalienable rights of life, liberty, and the pursuit of happiness.

"For history tells us that while these truths may be self-evident, they've never been self-executing," he explained, "that while freedom is a gift from God, it must be secured by His people here on Earth."[82]

He talked of our citizenry's commitment to each other's health and well-being, of our interconnectedness, and of how our collective past now informs our collective future.

"We, the people, declare today that the most evident of truths—that all of us are created equal—is the star that guides us still; just as it guided our forebears through Seneca Falls, and Selma, and Stonewall," he said, putting LGBT equality on a platform alongside women's suffrage and civil rights. "It is now our generation's task to carry on what those pioneers began." Our journey as a nation would not be complete, Obama said, "until our gay brothers and sisters are treated like anyone else under the law—for if we are truly created equal, then surely the love we commit to one another must be equal as well."[83]

In that speech, Barack Obama, our country's first black president, did something that perhaps only he could have done—he made gay rights the descendent of our nation's greatest and most hallowed movements for equality. He told America that its promise would not be fulfilled without the inclusion of its lesbian, gay, bisexual, and transgender citizens. It was an unequivocal affirmation of our humanity delivered by the most authoritative voice in the country.

This was the guy we had elected in 2008. This was the guy we had been waiting for. And this, it seemed, was the guy he'd always wanted to be.

CONCLUSION

PRESIDENT OBAMA PRESIDED OVER A TIPPING POINT IN THE history of LGBT rights—a time when Congress passed its first-ever pieces of pro-gay legislation, when government-sanctioned discrimination against gays in the military and same-sex couples began to crumble, when a sitting president declared all love equally sacred and the voters went from rejecting marriage equality at the ballot box some thirty times prior to 2012 to ratifying it by popular vote in three consecutive states that same year.

But the president did not do it alone. The forces that helped move him and his administration in the direction of progress contained the classic elements of every struggle for freedom and equality: societal pressure, a moral dilemma, and a group of people who were deemed unreasonable because they refused to engage the political system in accepted and ordinary ways.

Of all the progressive constituencies who had helped elect Obama in 2008, LGBT activists were the first to aggressively pressure the Democratic administration during Obama's first term. DREAM activists—young, passionate, and irrepressible—came the closest to matching grassroots gays in style and tone, and they were ultimately more successful than Beltway immigration groups in achieving first-term results. While comprehensive immigration legislation backed by Washington immigration groups never got a vote in the 111th Congress, the fact that the DREAM Act—which would have created a pathway to citizenship for young undocumented immigrants brought to the United States as minors—even logged a Senate vote was due solely to the fervent activism of DREAMers. They mounted large-scale protests and challenged President Obama directly and repeatedly, just as LGBT activists had. In 2012, President Obama would finally take executive action to provide temporary legal status to the young immigrants, an absolute testament to the efforts of DREAM activists. The program, called Deferred Action for Childhood Arrivals (DACA), helped pave the way for President Obama to provide further deportation relief in 2014 for up to five million DREAMers and parents of US citizens and legal residents, though the programs were stalled by a legal challenge from conservative lawmakers. Another progressive cause, the environmental movement, eventually adopted many of the same direct-action tactics leveraged by gay rights activists and DREAMers, and they too got results. The environmental movement succeeded in both stalling approval of the Keystone XL pipeline and making marked second-term gains toward the reduction of carbon emissions. It was another example of President Obama becoming increasingly proactive over time on an issue—climate change—which he seemed to care deeply about.[1]

But what really separated LGBT rights activists from the other movements was that they moved incredibly quickly, organizing actions to help set up passage of "don't ask, don't tell" repeal while Democrats still had majorities in both chambers of Congress. It sounds simple in retrospect, but going after the president you helped bring into office at the very moment when nearly every powerful Democratic entity in Washington is counseling patience was completely unconventional. It drew derision from the Beltway's Democratic establishment and even many of its LGBT institutions, which had run the movement virtually unchallenged since the mid '90s. But the singular achievement of passing repeal before the close of the 111th Congress was well worth the struggle. Vanquishing the military's gay ban broke the logjam on LGBT rights and became the difference between Barack Obama's presidency being simply an important milestone in the movement for equality versus a monumental turning point in history.

I covered Obama as a candidate and then as president for nearly five years. What I witnessed during that time were the contortions of a shrewd and cautious politician grappling with his conscience as he came face to face with activists who were no longer willing to subordinate their equality. Not to the cause of Democrats—a party that was LGBT-friendly in theory but had proven anemic in actuality. Not even in support of a man who epitomized the kind of integration and acceptance gays hoped to one day achieve themselves.

What was clear to anyone who had a view to the White House was that activists' continual prodding frustrated President Obama and his aides. In the president's eyes, his administration was taking reasonable steps toward advancing LGBT equality on a pragmatic timeline, one that had to take into account other concerns such as the economy, health care reform, and the wars in Iraq and Afghanistan.

Pragmatism, however, is a losing proposition in any civil rights struggle. And it was that friction—between the pragmatism of a politician and the urgency of a movement—that prompted the president and his aides time and again to move faster in advancing gay rights than they had initially intended. It was that friction that produced more progress for LGBT activists than any other single progressive constituency in Obama's first term and set the nation on course to eventually embrace LGBT Americans as full citizens.

At the time of its passage, "don't ask, don't tell" repeal was arguably the most pristine progressive legislative win of Obama's first two years in office in terms of both public perception and substance. Health care reform, despite right-wing reports to the contrary, had been a centrist piece of legislation that deeply disappointed many progressives due to its lack of a public option (a provision that would have allowed consumers to choose a government-run insurance plan over a private plan). In actuality, passing the Affordable Care Act was still a huge achievement, but it wasn't all that progressives had hoped for at the time. President Obama had other big wins, to be sure, like passing Wall Street reform and the $787 billion stimulus package in the wake of the 2008 financial crisis, but both were controversial at the time and both had vocal detractors from both sides of the aisle. And certainly expanding the children's health insurance program to millions of low-income children and enacting the Lilly Ledbetter Fair Pay Act for women were popular accomplishments. But they were so popular that they cruised through Congress within the first couple weeks of when Obama took office. Neither involved the extended full-court press that passing repeal required.[2]

Ending the gay ban marked the unqualified completion of a high-profile campaign pledge that advanced a fundamental American right: at work, you should be judged by your ability to do the job, nothing else. In its wake, the president would go on to either advance or achieve nearly every single priority of the LGBT community coming into his presidency. Every new win drew more praise from progressives and exposed the fact that virulent homophobia animated only a small and increasingly marginalized segment of the population. Doing the right thing just got easier and easier.

There were the major victories beyond overturning the military's gay ban. After the administration ended its defense of DOMA, government lawyers joined LGBT legal advocates in 2013 in making a forceful argument against the constitutionality of the law at the US Supreme Court. Administration lawyers also authored a brief in *Hollingsworth v. Perry*, the challenge to Proposition 8, at the high court in 2013. In it, they argued for the expansion of marriage equality to more states (though they stopped short of asking the court to overturn marriage bans nationwide). But it was the Supreme Court decision gutting DOMA in *United States v. Windsor*, released on June 26, 2013, that helped crush anti-gay marriage bans across the country. When the Supreme Court originally heard the case on March 27, 2013, a mere nine states plus the District of Columbia had legalized same-sex marriage. But the *Windsor* decision, authored by Justice Anthony Kennedy, overturned a critical section of DOMA and unleashed a domino effect of court rulings in its wake. By the time the second marriage equality case—*Obergefell v. Hodges*—reached the Supreme Court two years later, same-sex marriage was already legal in 36 states. In that case, President Obama's Justice Department filed a "friend of the court" brief arguing for the right of same-sex couples to marry in all fifty states. The decision in *Obergefell*, issued on June 26, 2015, finally struck down gay marriage bans nationwide.[3]

Beyond the ripple effect the *Windsor* ruling unleashed in the states, a string of changes also flowed from federal agency after federal agency, lending some insight into just how intrusive DOMA had been on the lives of same-sex couples and their families. Within days of the decision, the federal government immediately began extending benefits to same-sex spouses that were previously only available to heterosexual spouses. In July, Department of Homeland Security Secretary Janet Napolitano announced that US Citizenship and Immigration Services would begin reviewing visa petitions filed on behalf of a same-sex spouse "in the same manner as those filed on behalf of an opposite-sex spouse." A month later, Secretary of State John Kerry said US embassies and consulates abroad would follow the same visa policy, even if you lived in a country that didn't legally recognize your marriage. The Department of Defense also announced in August that it would begin extending benefits to same-sex spouses of service members and civilian employees. Since many service members lived in states where they could not legally marry, the Pentagon leveled the playing field by allowing gay service members leave time in order to travel to a jurisdiction where they could legally tie the knot. And finally in August, the Treasury Department and IRS ruled that legally married same-sex spouses would be treated as married for federal tax purposes, regardless of whether they resided in a state that didn't recognize their marriage. Similar announcements came from the Departments of Labor and Education regarding recognition of same-sex marriages for the purposes of pension plans and federal student aid applications.[4]

Beyond the reaches of DOMA, other major wins included ending the twenty-two-year-old HIV travel ban, which prevented persons with HIV from entering the United States. The '80s-era law had been repealed legislatively under President George W. Bush, but the rule change wasn't successfully implemented until the fall of 2009 under President Obama. As for employment protections, President Obama ultimately did about as much as he could do without the help of Congress. In July of 2014, he finally issued an executive order that prohibited federal contractors from discriminating against LGBT employees. The president also strengthened protections for transgender workers in the federal government via executive order in his second term, an action that built upon his 2010 addition of transgender workers to the federal government's Equal Employment Opportunity (EEO) policies.[5]

Another big win for the transgender community came in June of 2010, when Secretary Hillary Clinton's State Department revised the rule for changing the gender marker on an individual's passport, dropping the requirement that one present proof of gender reassignment surgery. In 2013, the Social Security Administration adopted a similar policy, making it possible for transgender individuals to update their Social Security records by presenting either a passport or a birth certificate that reflected their proper gender, or certification from a physician confirming their gender transition. As basic as this sounds, these changes significantly improved the lives of transgender Americans, especially those who lived in states that had outdated or discriminatory policies. Having an official document that accurately reflects the way one presents to the world makes life substantially easier for transgender individuals while also making their domestic and international travel far safer.[6]

Then there were a series of smaller regulatory changes that slowly began to eradicate systemic discrimination. The Department of Health and Human Services, under the leadership of Secretary Kathleen Sebelius, initiated a number of pro-LGBT policy changes. They included ending the Bush-era practice of allowing health care workers to refuse service to LGBT individuals for religious or moral reasons; launching a review of the policy of not allowing gay and bisexual men to give blood donations; announcing plans to begin collecting public health data on LGBT individuals in federal health surveys (which would help secure more government funding for providing health services to LGBT Americans); and issuing state guidance on covering LGBT families through federal welfare programs. The department also awarded nearly $15 million in grants to create a model program for supporting LGBT and questioning youth in the foster care system and to establish two first-ever national resource centers—one for LGBT elders and another for LGBT refugees.[7]

At the Department of Education, Secretary Arne Duncan announced in June of 2011 that gay-straight alliances (or GSAs) had the right to form in public schools as a matter of federal law under the Equal Access Act. The Reagan-era statute required public schools to provide equal access for extracurricular clubs.[8]

In 2011, the Veterans Administration issued a new health directive to all its facilities, ordering them to respectfully deliver health care to both transgender and intersex veterans.[9]

In another first, the Department of Housing and Urban Development (HUD) released a study that revealed widespread discrimination against same-sex couples who applied for housing in the private rental market in fifty different metropolitan areas. The study found that "heterosexual couples were favored over gay male couples in 15.9 percent of tests and over lesbian couples in 15.6 percent of tests."[10]

And at the Department of Justice, Attorney General Eric Holder was quick to recognize same-sex marriages that were performed legally, even in states like Utah and Michigan where bans were struck down, marriages took place, and then a stay was issued on the original ruling while further litigation ensued. "These families should not be asked to endure uncertainty regarding their status as the litigation unfolds," Holder said of Utah's 1,300 newly married same-sex couples, just days after the Supreme Court stayed the December 20, 2013, ruling.[11]

In many ways, taken together, it was like the federal government finally began to recognize lesbian, gay, bisexual, and transgender people as citizens of this country. Because the government had systematically denied our existence, LGBT Americans had suffered discrimination in virtually every policy area controlled by the government. In turn, that resulted in public policies that completely failed LGBT individuals and yielded a less vibrant, less unified nation. The history of HIV/AIDS in this country demonstrates that whenever the government turns a blind eye to the people who are living within its borders, the whole country suffers, whether from higher costs or from dangerous health outcomes. When the federal government failed to develop an urgent public health response to HIV and AIDS in the '80s, it allowed the disease to blossom into an epidemic that eventually penetrated every race, ethnicity, gender, and socioeconomic class of the nation. Were it not for the relentless and unapologetic agency of HIV/AIDS activists, who knows how much longer it would have taken to develop effective treatments for the disease.

What was striking is that most of these policy advances—big and small—would have been deemed "heavy lifts" by Washington hands at the beginning of the Obama administration. But that was mostly because Washington was so wildly out of step with most of the American public after the total stagnation on LGBT equality that had gripped the Beltway during the Bush years. The anti-gay marriage amendments that swept the nation between 2004–2010 managed to capitalize on the one gay rights issue that many Americans still feared: marriage equality. But not all LGBT issues were created equal. With the exception of marital rights, by 2009, vast majorities of Americans believed that LGBT citizens should be treated fairly in most areas of their lives, including employment, military service, housing, health care, and other issues. Yet these distinctions were lost on Washington.

But if the mentality of the Bush years had a crippling effect on the early Obama White House, President Clinton's legacy had an even more profound impact. Ultimately, two of the key issues that had haunted President Clinton's first two years in office—the military's gay ban and health care reform—also hexed President Obama. Yet while Clinton suffered bruising defeats on both "liberal" causes and relied on centrism to win a second term, Obama didn't have that option. He initially tried to move to the middle as Clinton had in the '90s on both issues—first by making a sustained yet unsuccessful bid to build bipartisan support for health care reform, and second by not passing repeal before the midterms. Yet Democrats still took a beating at the polls. Obama and his aides had wildly underestimated the importance of public opinion on both fronts. Following the midterms, the White House was left with little choice but to reckon with the American public's quickly shifting views on LGBT equality. Once they did, they were able to help effect remarkable change—and build a successful progressive reelection campaign in 2012.

Public opinion was, in fact, one major point of divergence between the civil rights movement and the gay rights movement. While popular attitudes lagged behind the pace of the laws on racial equality, they raced ahead of the laws on LGBT equality. When President Harry Truman gave the order to desegregate the US Armed Forces in 1948, for instance, a Gallup poll found that 63 percent of Americans still supported keeping black and white soldiers separate. It was almost the mirror opposite of ending the military's gay ban, which the vast majority of Americans supported by the time it finally happened.[12]

The same is true for attitudes on interracial and same-sex marriage. When the 1967 Supreme Court ruling *Loving v. Virginia* overturned laws in sixteen states that prohibited marriages between people of differing races, about 70 percent of Americans still opposed such marriages. At the time of the ruling, interracial marriage was already legal in thirty-four states even though it was very unpopular among the public at large. By contrast, public opinion was prologue to the marriage equality revolution that quickly swept the nation following the *Windsor* ruling. More than half the country already supported same-sex marriage by the time a key portion of DOMA was overturned, yet only nine states had legalized it.[13]

What this all meant in the early years of Obama's first term was that the public was a resource in waiting for gay rights activists who wanted the country's laws and lawmakers to catch up with American culture. Once Obama and his administration got fully on board, the momentum was unstoppable.

Six months into his administration, President Obama and the First Lady hosted the first LGBT Pride reception ever to be held at the White House. At the time, LGBT activists across the nation were already beginning to mobilize against an administration that they regarded with suspicion and already felt betrayed by. Yet to a mostly adoring crowd of a couple hundred LGBT people gathered in the East Room, Obama asserted, "I suspect that by the time this administration is over, I think you guys will have pretty good feelings about the Obama administration."[14]

He was right. Many if not most LGBT Americans who supported Barack Obama in the 2008 election now have pretty fond feelings for the president. But when President Obama uttered those words, the timeline he was counting on was the day he assumed he would be leaving office, January 19, 2017. He was too competitive not to count on winning a second term. It was a timeline grassroots activists never accepted, and thank goodness they didn't. But on that June day in 2009, whether one believed Obama was staying true to his campaign promises was a matter of perception. He believed he would deliver. Grassroots gays felt he was already failing to do so.

The story of President Obama's marked LGBT rights accomplishments is one where everyone turned out to be right, or at least partially so. President Obama was correct in the sense that he absolutely believed his administration would ultimately do the right thing no matter how long it took. Grassroots activists were also right to believe that the administration needed a relentless, outside-the-Beltway push to reach the many goals Obama had committed to on the campaign trail. Repealing "don't ask, don't tell," had to be an unequivocal imperative for the administration and lawmakers, otherwise it would have easily been pushed into the next congressional calendar. And although most

Washington-based LGBT advocates were too friendly with the administration to create that imperative, those advocates were also right to believe the movement still needed a robust inside game on Capitol Hill in order to finish the job legislatively. Every one of these groups—the grassroots, Washington advocates, and administration officials—needed each other to make it work. None of them would have been singularly successful without the others.

But for all the gains that were made during Obama's presidency, the struggle for full equality is far from over. America is still getting comfortable with same-sex marriages and still discovering all the ways in which LGBT citizens continue to be subjected to discrimination. The latest effort by anti-gay forces to perpetuate homophobia and bigotry is to assert that providing equal rights to LGBT individuals encroaches on the religious liberties of other Americans. It's a ruse. No one is suggesting that people shouldn't be able to practice their faith as they see fit. They absolutely should. But they should not be able to invoke that faith as a justification for discriminating against people with whom they disagree.

This is not a new concept. The US Supreme Court and the federal government established a framework for addressing racial discrimination and other forms of intolerance through a series of rulings and laws, particularly in the '50s and '60s. Unfortunately, while most of those laws and legal precedents protect people on the basis of race, color, religion, sex, national origin, and disability, none of them explicitly provide protections on the basis of sexual orientation or gender identity. The one important caveat to the lack of those protections is that courts have increasingly viewed discrimination against transgender individuals in the workplace as sex discrimination and therefore covered by Title VII of the Civil Rights Act of 1964.[15]

But for the most part, gay, bisexual, and transgender individuals must rely on a woefully inadequate patchwork of laws to protect them from discrimination. Some of those laws cover LGBT residents across the board in housing, public accommodations, and the workplace, while others only cover them in the workplace. Some of those laws protect gays and bisexuals but not transgender residents. Some of them are statewide and others only apply to specific jurisdictions within a state. But none of them are national, and under federal law, LGBT Americans are still not deemed a protected class despite their long history of discrimination. It is sometimes easy for people on the coasts to forget the need for federal protections, but it remains ever so apparent to those who reside in the middle and southern regions of the country.

Achieving the freedom to marry nationwide has been a profound affirmation of our dignity and will go a long way toward providing stability to LGBT families across the country. But the next step on the way to realizing full equality for lesbian, gay, bisexual, transgender, and queer Americans is to enact civil rights legislation that protects them in all areas of their lives. That will be the challenge of the next president of the United States and federal lawmakers in congressional sessions to come, regardless of political philosophy or party identity. Because providing these fundamental freedoms is not a gay cause or a liberal cause, it is quite simply an American cause. It's a call to basic fairness that will be led and pushed by a new generation of citizen activists. And that generation will not settle for anything less for the people they know simply as their brothers and sisters, their moms and dads, and their best friends for life.

ACKNOWLEDGMENTS

I WROTE THIS BOOK BECAUSE I WAS CONVINCED THAT I HAD witnessed something extraordinary over just a handful of years. So I would first like to thank the citizen activists for being the spark that produced the combustible moment that literally unfolded around me in Washington DC. For a political journalist, this is the stuff dreams are made of.

I would also like to thank the people who gave me the early green light to relocate to Washington from New York when I asked to go in 2009: then editor-in-chief of the *Advocate*, Jon Barrett, and Here Media's CEO, Paul Colichman. Additionally, thank you to Richard Socarides and David Brock for giving me a platform from which to write after I left the *Advocate*, and Matthew Breen, current *Advocate* editor-in-chief for giving me a column while I reported this book.

When it finally came time to start shaping the narrative that unfolds on these pages, David Domke helped me workshop my ideas, find the book ends for the story from start to finish, and envision the through line. Without his early edits to my proposal, I am quite certain this project never would have gotten off the ground.

Also critical to my early inspiration was my agent Will Lippincott, who always believed I had a story to tell and provided the steady guidance that every first-time author hopes for. He has made the right call at every turn and I have been fortunate to have him at my side throughout this project. I would also be remiss if I did not thank the team of editors who helped me mold my manuscript into a compelling narrative: Tim Bartlett, who saw the proposal's potential from the very start and gave this book life; Alex Littlefield, who helped me make sense of an initially clunky manuscript and made me believe this book could be important; and Katy O'Donnell, who smoothed the rough edges of the prose from beginning to end with irrepressible enthusiasm. And finally, to my publisher, Lara Heimert, who brought the book across the finish line beautifully and without whom none of this would have been possible. This group of seasoned professionals along with the greater team at Basic Books are directly responsible for making *Don't Tell Me to Wait* the book it became.

More generally, I would like to thank both my sources and my readers. A reporter is only as good as her sources and I appreciate the time that so many gave generously to help me tell this story, not to mention those who have informed my work throughout the years. In that respect, one person in particular stands out: Jenny Pizer at Lambda Legal. To the extent that I have been able to grasp any of the intricate legal issues surrounding LGBT rights and make them digestible to my readers, Pizer has been the reason.

Another person who has continually offered me the benefit of his knowledge about progressive activism and the ways of Washington is Joe Sudbay. I am grateful for both his friendship and his insights. When we first met on March 3, 2009, I could not possibly have imagined how instrumental he would become to my reporting.

Which brings me to my readers—without them, a reporter isn't worth much. So thank you to all the readers who have followed my work and continued to place their faith in me throughout the last decade. My hope was always to bring you the best of the stories that I had the great good fortune to report on, and you are the very reason that I finally had a chance to synthesize that reporting into one distinct narrative. I hope you have found reading it as inspirational as I found reporting it.

I would also like to thank the many LGBT journalists, authors, and bloggers who welcomed me into the fold and offered me help and guidance at different junctures as I learned to report on a movement that was entirely new to me when I started on the beat in 2006: Karen

Ocamb, David Mixner, Mike Signorile, Paul Schindler, Trenton Straube, Sean Kennedy, Pam Spaulding, Sean Bugg, Randy Shulman, John Aravosis, Dan Savage, Lisa Keen, Kevin Naff, Lou Chibbaro Jr., Rex Wockner, Ann Northrop, and Larry Kramer.

Thank you to Susan Rasky, posthumously, my professor at UC Berkeley's Graduate School of Journalism who stoked my love of political reporting and taught to me to view journalism as a civic service. She very much molded the reporter I became.

To my many siblings— Rob, Julita, Lisa, Wendy, Jenny, John, Kristina, and Matt—thank you for the interest you have taken in my work. I so appreciate your support for both me and the cause. To my mom, Lynn Eleveld, thank you for the many gifts you have given me. And many thanks also to my father, Robert Eleveld, and his partner, Michele McIsaac, who have delighted in my every professional accomplishment, no matter how big or small. You began encouraging me early and often to write a book. Turns out, you were on to something!

And finally, to my love, Laura Janowitch, who has walked alongside me every step of this journey. Thank you for keeping me grounded and believing in me.

NOTES

NOTES TO INTRODUCTION

1. On nine hundred marriages, "Gays Rush to San Francisco to Wed," *BBC News*, February 15, 2004, http://news.bbc.co.uk/2/hi/americas/3488005.stm; on couples camping, Simone Sebastian and Tanya Schevitz, "Marriage Mania Grips S.F. as Gays Line Up for Licenses," *San Francisco Chronicle*, February 16, 2004, http://www.sfgate.com/news/article/Marriage-mania-grips-S-F-as-gays-line-up-for-2795629.php; on bouquets, Heather Knight, "The Flowering of Love," *San Francisco Chronicle*, February 21, 2004, http://www.sfgate.com/news/article/The-flowering-of-love-Strangers-from-Midwest-2820653.php; on four thousand marriages, Howard Mintz, Mary Anne Ostrom, and Mike Swift Mercury, "Path to the Altar: Stories of People in Same-Sex Marriage Fight," *San Jose Mercury News*, June 15, 2008, http://www.mercurynews.com/ci_9593246?source=rss.

2. "Saddleback Presidential Candidates Forum," CNN, August 16, 2008, http://www.cnn.com/TRANSCRIPTS/0808/16/se.02.html.

3. Ibid.

4. On Prop 8's cost, "Proposition 8: Who Gave in the Gay Marriage Battle?" *Los Angeles Times*, http://projects.latimes.com/prop8/.

5. Remarks by the president on the Supreme Court decision on marriage equality, White House, June 26, 2015.

6. On pushing the envelope, Kerry Eleveld, "Obama Explains Why He's the Best Candidate for LGBT Americans," *The Advocate*, October 27, 2007, http://www.advocate.com/news/2007/10/27/obama-im-most-inclusive -gay-issues; see also Kerry Eleveld, Obama on marriage: "Attitudes Evolve, Including Mine," *The Advocate*, October 27, 2010, http://www.advocate .com/news/daily-news/2010/10/27/obama-marriage-times-are-changing.

7. On marriage polling, Nate Silver, "Gay Marriage Opponents Now in Minority," *New York Times*, April 20, 2011, http://fivethirtyeight.blogs.nytimes .com/2011/04/20/gay-marriage-opponents-now-in-minority/?_php=true& _type=blogs&_r=0; see also Frank Newport, "For First Time, Majority of Americans Support Legal Gay Marriage," Gallup, May 20, 2011, http://www.gallup .com/poll/147662/first-time-majority-americans-favor-legal-gay-marriage.aspx.

NOTES TO CHAPTER 1

1. Mary Anne Ostrom, "Hillary Clinton Campaigns in Fresno," *Mercury News*, October 23, 2007, http://www.mercurynews.com/news/ci_7255714?nclick _check=1; Jason A. Bezis, "Fresno County—Voted Twice for Obama," Cal-PolitiCal, December 16, 2012, http://calpolitical.blogspot.com/2012/12/fresno -county-voted-twice-for-obama.html.

2. Author interview with Robin McGehee, August 19, 2013.

3. On executive committee, Michael Petrelis, "Names of All 16 Members of No on 8's Executive Committee Made Public," The Petrelis Files, January 21, 2009, http://mpetrelis.blogspot.com/2009/01/names-of-all-16-members-of-no -on-8s.html; on funding, "Proposition 8: Who Gave in the Gay Marriage Battle?" *Los Angeles Times*, http://projects.latimes.com/prop8/; on Mormons, Stephanie Mencimer, "Of Mormons and (Gay) Marriage," *Mother Jones*, April 5, 2010, http://www.motherjones.com/print/43171; see also Jesse McKinley and Kirk Johnson, "Mormons Tipped Scale in Ban on Gay Marriage," *New York Times*, November 15, 2008, http://www.nytimes.com/2008/11/15/us /politics/15marriage.html.

4. On McGehee, author interview with Robin McGehee, August 19, 2013; on robocalls, Ben Smith, "Still Using Obama on Prop. 8," *Politico*, November 4, 2008, http://www.politico.com/blogs/bensmith/1108/Still_using_Obama_on_Prop_8 .html.

5. On McGehee, ibid.; on Obama's speech, "Transcript: Illinois Senate Candidate Barack Obama," *Washington Post*, July 27, 2004, http://www .washingtonpost.com/wp-dyn/articles/A19751-2004Jul27.html.

6. On Rove, Adam Nagourney, "'Moral Values' Carried Bush, Rove Says," *New York Times*, November 10, 2004, http://www.nytimes.com/2004/11/10 /politics/campaign/10rove.html?_r=0; on turnout, Lisa Trei, "Why Bush Won in 2004," Stanford News Service, November 17, 2004, http://news.stanford .edu/pr/2004/polls-1117.html; on terrorism, Paul Freedman, "The Gay Mar-

riage Myth," *Slate*, November 5, 2004, http://www.slate.com/articles/news_and
_politics/politics/2004/11/the_gay_marriage_myth.html; on Bush's vote share,
Karl Rove, *Courage and Consequence: My Life as a Conservative in the Fight*
(New York: Simon & Schuster, 2010), 376–377.

7. On bundling, Jeffrey Schmalz, "Gay Areas Are Jubilant over Clinton,"
New York Times, November 5, 1992, http://www.nytimes.com/1992/11/05
/nyregion/the-1992-elections-the-states-the-gay-issues-gay-areas-are-jubilant
-over-clinton.html.

8. "Nominee Clinton Describes Vision of 'New Covenant,'" CQ Almanac,
accessed November 19, 2014, http://library.cqpress.com/cqalmanac/document
.php?id=cqal92-845-25178-1106424.

9. On ballot measures, "History of State Constitutional Marriage Bans,"
Human Rights Campaign, accessed November 19, 2014, http://www.hrc.org
/resources/entry/state-constitutional-marriage-bans#_ftnref1.

10. On the delegate count, David Corn, "Citing Delegate Math, the Obama
Camp Tells Clinton: You Will 'Fail Miserably,'" *Mother Jones*, February 29, 2008,
http://www.motherjones.com/mojo/2008/02/citing-delegate-math-obama
-camp-tells-clinton-you-will-fail-miserably; see also "Election 2008 Results: Democratic Delegate Count," *New York Times*, accessed May 14, 2015, http://politics
.nytimes.com/election-guide/2008/results/delegates/; on LGB voters, "Hunter
College Poll Finds Clinton Has Support of 63% of LGB Likely Voters," The
City University of New York, accessed November 19, 2014, http://www1.cuny
.edu/mu/forum/2007/11/29/hunter-college-poll-finds-clinton-has-support-of
-63-of-lgb-likely-voters/.

11. On rankings, Chris Bowers, "Partisan, Political Blogosphere Traffic Rankings," MyDD, February 27, 2005; see also Jennifer Deleo, "The 20 Best Political Web Sites," *PC Magazine*, August 28, 2008, http://www.pcmag.com/article2
/0,2817,2329081,00.asp.

12. "Poll: Black Support Helps Clinton Extend Lead," CNN, October 17,
2007, http://www.cnn.com/2007/POLITICS/10/17/poll.blacks.democrats/.

13. Lynn Sweet, "Sweet Home Obama, Campaign Launches Gospel Tour
in S.C.," *Chicago Sun-Times*, October 19, 2007, http://blogs.suntimes.com
/sweet/2007/10/sweet-blog-extra-sweet-home-ob.html.

14. Richard Leiby, "Donnie McClurkin, Ready to Sing Out Against Gay
'Curse,'" *Washington Post*, August 29, 2004, http://www.washingtonpost.com/wp
-dyn/articles/A42982-2004Aug28.html.

15. On past statements, Sarah Wheaton, "Obama's Gospel Tour," *New York
Times*, October 19, 2007, http://thecaucus.blogs.nytimes.com/2007/10/19
/obamas-gospel-tour/; on the blog post, John Aravosis, "Obama to Do Gospel
Tour with Radical Right Singer Who Crusades Against "the Curse of Homosexuality," AMERICAblog, October 20, 2007, http://americablog.com/2007/10
/obama-to-do-gospel-tour-with-radical-right-singer-who-crusades-against-the
-curse-of-homosexuality.html.

16. Earl Ofari Hutchinson, "Obama Should Repudiate and Cancel His Gay Bash Tour, and Do It Now," Huffington Post, October 20, 2007, http://www .huffingtonpost.com/earl-ofari-hutchinson/obama-should-repudiate-an_b _69244.html.

17. David A. Bositis, "Politics and the 2004 Election," The Joint Center for Political and Economic Studies, 2004, http://www.jointcenter.org/publications1 /publication-PDFs/NOP-pdfs/nop-Politics.pdf, 10–11.

18. Ann Sanner, "Gay Group to Obama: Drop Singer from Tour," *Associated Press*, October 23, 2007.

19. On HRC's budget, "Salaries of HIV, LGBT Leaders," *Washington Blade*, March 26, 2009, http://web.archive.org/web/20090402004849/http:// washblade.com/2009/3-27/news/national/salaryChart.jpg.

20. On the Task Force's budget, ibid.; on the controversy, Kerry Eleveld, "House Leaders May Strip Gender Identity from ENDA," *The Advocate*, September 28, 2007,http://www.advocate.com/news/2007/09/28/house-leaders-may-strip -gender-identity-enda; see also Kerry Eleveld, "ENDA to Be Separated into Two Bills: Sexual Orientation and Gender Identity," *The Advocate*, September 29, 2007, http://www.advocate.com/news/2007/09/29/enda-be-separated-two-bills-sexual -orientation-and-gender-identity; on HRC support, Andrew Miga, "Gay Rights Group Supports Job Bias Ban," Associated Press, November 6, 2007; on the vote count, "Final Vote Results for Roll Call 1057," Office of the Clerk, US House of Representatives, November 7, 2007, http://clerk.house.gov/evs/2007/roll1057.xml.

21. Don Frederick, "Obama's Link to Gospel Singer Sparks Controversy," *Los Angeles Times*, October 22, 2007, http://latimesblogs.latimes.com/washington /2007/10/obamas-link-to-.html.

22. Pam Spaulding, "More Obama Campaign Miscalculations," Salon, October 26, 2007, http://www.salon.com/2007/10/26/obama_mistakes/.

23. On Obama's quote, Kerry Eleveld, "Obama Explains Why He's the Best Candidate for LGBT Americans," *The Advocate*, October 26, 2007, http://www .advocate.com/news/2007/10/27/obama-im-most-inclusive-gay-issues.

24. Barack Obama, "World AIDS Day Speech," Saddleback Church, December 1, 2006.

25. On Eleveld's response, author recording of interview with Barack Obama, October 26, 2007.

26. Katharine Q. Seelye, "Obama's Gospel Concert Tour," *New York Times*, October 29, 2007, http://thecaucus.blogs.nytimes.com/2007/10/29/obamas -gospel-concert-tour/comment-page-4/.

27. Peter Hamby, "Obama Supporter: 'God Delivered Me from Homosexuality,'" CNN, October 29, 2007, http://politicalticker.blogs.cnn.com/2007/10/29 /obama-supporter-god-delivered-me-from-homosexuality/comment-page-13/.

28. Author interview with John Aravosis, July 10, 2013.

29. On Clinton's interviews, Eric Resnick, "Clinton Sticks with Civil Unions After N.J. Report," *Gay People's Chronicle*, February 29, 2008, http://www

.gaypeopleschronicle.com/stories08/february/0229081.htm; see also Kevin Naff, "An Interview with Hillary Clinton," *Washington Blade*, February 11, 2008; on Obama's ads, Kerry Eleveld, "Obama Makes Gay Ad Buys in Ohio, Texas," *The Advocate*, February 28, 2008, http://www.advocate.com/news/2008/02/28 /obama-makes-gay-ad-buys-ohio-texas; "Open Letter from Barack Obama to the LGBT Community," The Bilerico Project, February 28, 2008, http://www .bilerico.com/2008/02/open_letter_from_barack_obama_to_the_lgb.php.

30. On Clinton's interview, Mark Segal and Sarah Blazucki, "Clinton Talks, Obama Balks," *Philadelphia Gay News*, April 4, 2008, http://www.sgn.org /sgnnews36_14/page2.cfm; on the editorial, Tracy Baim, *Obama and the Gays: A Political Marriage* (Chicago, Prairie Avenue Productions, 2010), 102.

31. John Wright, "Obama Talks . . . " *Dallas Voice*, April 11, 2008, http:// www.dallasvoice.com/obama-talks-1024340.html.

32. On Obama's quote, Kerry Eleveld, "Obama Talks All Things LGBT with *The Advocate*," *The Advocate*, April 10, 2008, http://www.advocate.com /news/2008/12/23/obama-talks-all-things-lgbt-the%C2%A0advocate?page =full; on constituency press interviews, Kerry Eleveld, "All Politics Is Local," *The Advocate*, April 21, 2008, http://www.advocate.com/news/2008/04/21/all -politics-local; on addressing black audiences, Jason Horowitz, "Obama Addresses Homophobia, Anti-Semitism and Xenophobia Among Black Americans," *New York Observer*, January 20, 2008.

33. Kerry Eleveld, "Obama Talks All Things LGBT with *The Advocate*," *The Advocate*, April 10, 2008, http://www.advocate.com/news/2008/12/23/ obama-talks-all-things-lgbt-the%C2%A0advocate?page=full.

34. On pickup, Nedra Pickler, "Obama: Repeal of 'Don't Ask' Possible," Associated Press, April 10, 2008.

35. Lisa Leff, "Backers of Calif. Gay Marriage Ban Ready to Submit Petitions," Associated Press, April 21, 2008.

36. In re Marriage Cases, 183 P.3d 384, 400 (Cal. 2008), http://www.courts .ca.gov/documents/S147999.pdf.

37. Sarah Wheaton, "Reaction to Gay Marriage Ruling," *New York Times*, May 15, 2008, http://thecaucus.blogs.nytimes.com/2008/05/15/reaction-to -gay-marriage-ruling/comment-page-2/?_r=0.

38. On deferring to states, *United States v. Windsor*, 570 U.S. ___, 133 S.Ct. 2675, 2692 (2013).

39. On the editorial, "A Victory for Equality and Justice," *New York Times*, May 17, 2008, http://www.nytimes.com/2008/05/17/opinion/17sat1.html; on the statements, Robert Barnes and Ashley Surdin, "California Supreme Court Strikes Bans on Same-Sex Marriage," *Washington Post*, May 16, 2008, http://www.washington post.com/wp-dyn/content/article/2008/05/15/AR2008051500589.html; see also Justin Ewers, "McCain Supports Efforts to Ban Gay Marriage," *U.S. News & World Report*, June 27, 2008, http://www.usnews.com/news/campaign-2008/articles /2008/06/27/mccain-supports-efforts-to-ban-gay-marriage.

40. On the statement to reporters, author review of official campaign state-ment received via e-mail from Tommy Vietor on May 15, 2008; on statement sent to LGBT advocates, David Mixner, "Obama's Statement on California Supreme Court Decision," DavidMixner.com, May 15, 2008, http://www.davidmixner.com/2008/05/breaking-news-o.html.

41. On Obama's line, "TRANSCRIPT: Jake Tapper Interviews Barack Obama," *ABC News*, June 16, 2008, http://abcnews.go.com/WN/Politics/story ?id=5178123; on the blog, Sara Whitman, "Shut the Hell up," The Bilerico Proj-ect, June 18, 2008, http://www.bilerico.com/2008/06/shut_the_hell_up.php.

42. Brian Leubitz, "Barack Obama Opposes Prop 8, That Anti-marriage Amendment," Calitics, June 29, 2008, http://www.calitics.com/showDiary .do?diaryId=6307.

43. On the Houston GLBT questionnaire, "Barack Obama's Presidential Candidate Screening Questionnaire from 2008. From the Houston GLBT Po-litical Caucus PAC," posted by *Metro Weekly*, http://issuu.com/metroweekly /docs/houston_glbt_political_caucus?e=2755234/2969675; on the spokesper-son, author correspondence with Obama campaign spokesperson, June 30, 2008.

44. On the flip-flop, "Barack Obama's Changing Positions: Everyone's Been Listening to Him," John McCain Campaign press release, July 8, 2008, http:// www.presidency.ucsb.edu/ws/?pid=91551.

45. Kerry Eleveld, "Obama Explains Why He's the Best Candidate for LGBT Americans," *The Advocate*, October 27, 2007, http://www.advocate .com/news/2007/10/27/obama-im-most-inclusive-gay-issues.

46. On Warren/Prop 8, Amy Sullivan, "Inaugural Pastor: The Two Faces of Rick Warren," *Time*, January 18, 2009, http://content.time.com/time/nation /article/0,8599,1872453,00.html.

47. On Chico's marriage stance, Baim, *Obama and the Gays*, 99; on Obama trying to understand, author interview with Tracy Baim, May 12, 2014.

48. Author interview with Tracy Baim, May 12, 2014.

49. Baim, *Obama and the Gays*, 117–118.

50. Baim, *Obama and the Gays*, 118.

51. Ibid.

52. On being a firebrand, Joel Roberts, "Here's What Jesus Wouldn't Do," *CBS News*, September 8, 2004, http://www.cbsnews.com/news/heres-what -jesus-wouldnt-do/; on "selfish hedonist," Jennifer Skalka and Ofelia Casillas, "Keyes Takes Jabs at His Own Party," *Chicago Tribune*, September 1, 2004; on Obama's deception, Nicole Ziegler Dizon, "Obama Says His Beliefs Say No to Gay Marriage," *Chicago Sun-Times*, September 25, 2004.

53. After several days of criticism: "Alan Keyes Lights 'Em Up," *Chicago Tribune*, September 14, 2004, http://articles.chicagotribune.com/2004–09–14 /news/0409140262_1_keyes-campaign-officials-keyes-comments-alan-keyes.

54. David Mendell, "Obama Would Consider Missile Strikes on Iran," *Chi-cago Tribune*, September 25, 2004.

55. Baim, *Obama and the Gays,* 142.

56. On the meeting, Baim, *Obama and the Gays,* 1517; on their concerns, ibid., 1518; on Munar, ibid., 1624.

57. On their appreciation, author interview with Tracy Baim, May 12, 2014; on the advisory group, Baim, *Obama and the Gays,* 1518.

58. On tens of thousands, Jessica Garrison and Dan Morain, "Same-Sex Marriage Total at 11,000," *Los Angeles Times,* October 7, 2008, http://articles .latimes.com/2008/oct/07/local/me-gaymarriage7.

59. On Hardball, "Hardball College Tour: Barack Obama," *NBC News,* April 2, 2008, http://www.nbcnews.com/id/23925495/ns/msnbc-hardball _with_chris_matthews/t/hardball-college-tour-barack-obama/#.VPI62 ihGHtA; on the flier, Cynthia Laird, "Prop 8 Backers Use Obama in Ad," *Bay Area Reporter,* October 30, 2008, http://www.ebar.com/news/article.php?sec =news&article=3450.

60. Seth Hemmelgarn, "No on Prop 8 Admits Mistakes," *Bay Area Reporter,* March 5, 2009, http://ebar.com/news/article.php?sec=news&article=3769.

61. On the crowd, "240,000 Pack Grant Park for Election Rally," *ABC 7 Eyewitness News,* November 5, 2008, http://abc7chicago.com/archive/6489707/.

62. "Transcript: 'This Is Your Victory,' Says Obama," CNN, November 4, 2008, http://edition.cnn.com/2008/POLITICS/11/04/obama.transcript/.

63. Kerry Eleveld, "Change Comes from the Middle of the Country," *The Advocate,* November 5, 2008, http://www.advocate.com/news/2008/11/06 /change-comes-middle-country.

64. On the protests, Associated Press, "In California, Protests over Gay Marriage Vote," *New York Times,* November 9, 2008, http://www.nytimes.com/2008 /11/10/us/10protest.html.

65. On Join the Impact, author interview with Willow Witte, April 16, 2015; see also, Claire Cain Miller, "Gay-Rights Advocates Use Web to Organize Global Rally," November 14, 2008, *New York Times,* http://bits.blogs.nytimes.com/2008 /11/14/gay-rights-activists-use-web-to-organize-global-rally/?apage=2.

66. On Warren's message, "Pastor Rick's News and Views 10/23/2008 Part 3 (Prop 8)," Saddleback Church, October 23, 2008, http://www.saddleback .com/blogs/newsandviews/index.html?contentid=1502.

67. Sunlen Miller, "Obama Defends Rick Warren Pick," *ABC News,* December 18, 2008, http://abcnews.go.com/blogs/politics/2008/12/obama-defends-r/.

68. On Socarides/Zeleny, author interview with Richard Socarides, August 23, 2013.

69. On Socarides' worry, ibid.

70. Jeff Zeleny and David D. Kirkpatrick, "Obama's Choice of Pastor Creates Furor," *New York Times,* December 19, 2009, http://www.nytimes.com /2008/12/20/us/politics/20warren.html?_r=0.

71. Ibid.

72. Ibid.

73. Neal Conan, "What Happened with Gay Bishop's Invocation?" NPR, January 19, 2009, http://www.npr.org/templates/story/story.php?storyId=99557462.

74. Ibid.

75. Michael Jensen, "Developing: HBO Says They Aren't to Blame for Not Including Gene Robinson in Concert Special," AfterElton.com, January 18, 2009, http://www.afterelton.com/blog/michaeljensen/developing-hbo-not -blame-exclusion-gene-robinson; Kerry Eleveld and Ross Von Metzke, "HBO Blames Obama Transition Team for Robinson Blackout," *The Advocate*, January 17, 2009, http://www.advocate.com/news/2009/01/17/hbo-blames-obama -transition-team-robinson-blackout.

76. Ibid.

NOTES TO CHAPTER 2

1. On the disagreement, author interview with Jonathan D. Lewis, June 3, 2013; author interview with Paul Yandura, June 3, 2013.

2. On Democracy Alliance, Thomas Edsall, "Rich Liberals Vow to Fund Think Tanks," *Washington Post*, August 7, 2005, http://www.washingtonpost. com/wp-dyn/content/article/2005/08/06/AR2005080600848.html; on Lewis /Soros, Ryan Grim, "Peter Lewis Leaves Democracy Alliance, the Liberal Donor Network," Huffington Post, March 21, 2012, http://www.huffingtonpost. com/2012/03/21/peter-lewis-democracy-alliance_n_1368551.html; on donations, author interview with Jonathan D. Lewis, June 3, 2013.

3. On the $1 million, ibid.; on the plaque, viewed and photographed by the author, May 2014.

4. On the investment, author interview with Jonathan D. Lewis, June 3, 2013.

5. On the enemies list, ibid.; see also "Statement of Information: Hearings Before the Committee on the Judiciary, House of Representatives, Ninety-third Congress, Second Session, Pursuant to H. Res. 803, a Resolution Authorizing and Directing the Committee on the Judiciary to Investigate Whether Sufficient Grounds Exist for the House of Representatives to Exercise Its Constitutional Power to Impeach Richard M. Nixon, President of the United States of America. May–June 1974," GovDocs, https://archive.org/details/statementofinfor08unit.

6. On Yandura's initiation, author interview with Paul Yandura, May 21, 2013; on the security clearance, Marlene Cimons, "Clinton Ends Prohibition of Security Clearances for Gays," August 5, 1995, *Los Angeles Times*, http:// articles.latimes.com/1995-08-05/news/mn-31708_1_security-clearances.

7. On the CNN producer/Clinton's response, Clarence Page, "Clinton, When Asked, Should Not Have Told," *Chicago Tribune*, December 23, 1999, http://articles.sun-sentinel.com/1999-12-23/news/9912220885_1_president -clinton-gays-clinton-s-critics.

8. On Nunn, Donna Cassata, "Nunn Emerges as Power Player as White House Tries to Lift Gay Ban," Associated Press, January 30, 1993; on the

compromise, Paul F. Horvitz, "'Don't Ask, Don't Tell, Don't Pursue' Is White House's Compromise Solution: New U.S. Military Policy Tolerates Homosexuals," *New York Times*, July 20, 1993, http://www.nytimes.com/1993/07/20 /news/20iht-gay_1.html; on gay groups, Sam Howe Verhovek, "Gay Groups Denounce the Pentagon's New Policy," *New York Times*, July 21, 1993, http:// www.nytimes.com/1993/07/21/us/gay-groups-denounce-the-pentagon-s-new -policy.html.

9. On meeting Clinton, author interview with Paul Yandura, May 21, 2013.

10. On HRCF contribution, "Guide to the Human Rights Campaign Records, 1975–2005," Cornell University Library, http://rmc.library.cornell.edu /EAD/htmldocs/RMM07712.html.

11. On pressing Dean, Author interview with Paul Yandura, May 21, 2013.

12. Matt Stoller, "Where's the Strategy on Gay Issues for 2006?" MyDD .com, April 22, 2006; see also Lou Chibbaro Jr., "Prominent Dem Slams Party on Gay Rights," *Washington Blade*, April 27, 2006.

13. Author review of Paul Yandura's affidavit, June 18, 2008, page 3, *Hitchcock v. DNC Services Corp., et al.*, No. 2007 CA 003040 B (D.C. Super. Ct.); Lou Chibbaro Jr., "Gay Dems lead GOP Counterparts in Fundraising: Democrats Say Gays Raised $10–18 Million for 2000 Campaigns," *Washington Blade*, October 31, 2003.

14. Lou Chibbaro Jr., "Dean Fires Dems' Gay Outreach Chief," *Washington Blade*, May 3, 2006.

15. Ibid.

16. On wooing Evangelicals, Kerry Eleveld, "Gotta Have Faith," *The Advocate*, August 14, 2007, http://www.advocate.com/politics/commentary/2007 /08/14/gotta-have-faith?page=full; on the outreach desks, author review of Paul Yandura's affidavit, June 18, 2008, page 5, *Hitchcock v. DNC Services Corp., et al.*, No. 2007 CA 003040 B (D.C. Super. Ct.); see also Lou Chibbaro Jr., "Prominent Dem Slams Party on Gay Rights," *Washington Blade*, April 27, 2006; on Daughtry, Dan Gilgoff, "Helping Democrats Find a Way to Reach the Religious," *New York Times*, October 20, 2007, http://www.nytimes.com /2007/10/20/us/20religion.html?_r=0.

17. On Democrats' success, Laurie Goodstein, "Religious Voting Data Show Some Shift, Observers Say," *New York Times*, November 9, 2006, http:// www.nytimes.com/2006/11/09/us/politics/09relig.html?_r=0; on favoring Bush, "Election Results: 2004 Election Season," CNN, accessed May 14, 2015, http://www.cnn.com/ELECTION/2004/pages/results/states/US/P/00/epolls .0.html.

18. On merit, Joshua Lynsen and Lou Chibbaro Jr., "DNC Lawsuit Ensnares Lesbian Activist," *Washington Blade*, January 17, 2008; on embarrassing e-mails, Kevin Naff, "Democrats' Gay Problem—Embarrassing E-mails Reveal What DNC Really Thinks of Gay Media—and Voters," *Washington Blade*, January 18, 2008; on testifying, Mary Ann Akers, "Howard Dean's

Gay Headache," *Washington Post*, March 20, 2008, http://voices.washington post.com/sleuth/2008/03/howard_deans_gay_headache.html; on the offer, "Hitchcock Says No to $100,000 Offer," PageOneQ, August 22, 2008, http://pageoneq.com/news/2008/Hitchcock_says_no_to_100_0822.html; on the settlement, author interview with Paul Yandura, May 21, 2013.

19. Andrew Belonsky, "The Gays, the Dems, Some Serious Trouble, and Dough," Huffington Post, January 14, 2008.

20. Author interview with Paul Yandura, May 21, 2013; author review of nonpublic joint contribution report of Jonathan D. Lewis and Peter B. Lewis, dated November 23, 2008.

21. On turnout, Paul Taylor and Mark Hugo Lopez, "Six Take-Aways from the Census Bureau's Voting Report," Pew Research Center, May 28, 2013, http://www.pewresearch.org/fact-tank/2013/05/08/six-take-aways-from-the -census-bureaus-voting-report/.

22. On meeting Obama, author interview with Jonathan D. Lewis, June 3, 2013.

23. Author interview with Paul Yandura, May 21, 2013.

24. Ibid.

25. Author interview with Jonathan D. Lewis, June 3, 2013.

26. On passing over John Berry, Kerry Eleveld, "Gays Shut Out of Cabinet," *The Advocate*, December 18, 2008, http://www.advocate.com/news/2008/12/18 /gays-shut-out-the%C2%A0cabinet; on Berry's appointment, "Director of the Office of Personnel Management: Who Is John Berry?" AllGov, March 5, 2009, http://www.allgov.com/news/appointments-and-resignations/director-of-the -office-of-personnel-management-who-is-john-berry?news=838443.

27. Kerry Eleveld, "Gay Man to Be Tapped as Deputy Director of Obama's Public Liaison Office," *The Advocate*, January 8, 2009, http://www.advocate.com /politics/2009/01/08/brian-bond-be-tapped-deputy-director-obamas-public -liaison-office.

28. On Berry's appointment being a breakthrough, Kerry Eleveld, "Taking Back the Workplace," *The Advocate*, April 3, 2009, http://www.advocate.com /politics/2009/04/03/history-making.

29. On Clinton appointments, "A Record of Progress for Gay and Lesbian Americans," Clinton-Gore Administration, http://clinton2.nara.gov/WH /Accomplishments/ac399.html; on thirty-seven appointees, Kerry Eleveld, "Obama's First 100 Days Prove Inclusive," *The Advocate*, April 29, 2009, http://www.advocate.com/politics/2009/04/29/obamas%C2%A0first-100 -days%C2%A0prove-inclusive; on 90 percent, Jeff Krehely, "Polls Show Huge Public Support for Gay and Transgender Workplace Protections," Center for American Progress, June 2, 2011.

30. On hate crimes, Ann Scales, "Clinton Moves Against Hate Crimes," *Boston Globe*, November 11, 1997; see also "S.1529—Hate Crimes Prevention

Act of 1998," Congress.gov, https://www.congress.gov/bill/105th-congress/senate-bill/1529.

31. On 618 civil servants, "Sexual Orientation and the Federal Workplace," US Merit Systems Protection Board, accessed September 30, 2014, http://www.mspb.gov/netsearch/viewdocs.aspx?docnumber=1026379&version=1030388&application=ACROBAT; on first protests, Neil Miller, *Out of the Past: Gay and Lesbian History from 1869 to the Present* (New York: Vintage Books, 1995), 343.

32. On the signs, "Ernestine Eckstein in Picket Line/Kay Tobin Lahusen (1965)," New York Public Library Digital Gallery, Image ID: 1605756, accessed September 30, 2014, http://digitalgallery.nypl.org/nypldigital/id?1605756; "Remembering Gay Rights Activist Frank Kameny (1925–2011)," The Smithsonian, accessed September 30, 2014, http://www.smithsonianmag.com/smithsonian-institution/remembering-gay-rights-activist-frank-kameny-1925-2011-105187020/?no-ist; on the 1975 policy change and 1998 executive order, "Sexual Orientation and the Federal Workplace," US Merit Systems Protection Board, accessed September 30, 2014, http://www.mspb.gov/netsearch/viewdocs.aspx?docnumber=1026379&version=1030388&application=ACROBAT.

33. On Gibbs, "Press Briefing by Press Secretary Robert Gibbs," White House, May 12, 2009; on the report, "How to End 'Don't Ask, Don't Tell,'" The Palm Center, May 2009, http://www.palmcenter.org/files/active/0/Executive%20Order%20on%20Gay%20Troops%20-%20final.pdf.

34. US Department of Defense, Secretary Robert Gates interview with *Fox News*, March 29, 2009, http://www.defense.gov/transcripts/transcript.aspx?transcriptid=4390.

35. On first discussion, Robert M. Gates, *Duty: Memoirs of a Secretary at War* (New York: Knopf, 2014), 333.

36. On the ad, Leo Shane, "SLDN: End 'Mixed Signals' on Gays in the Ranks," Stars and Stripes, April 27, 2009; on the blog post, Aubrey Sarvis, "Stand by Your Word, Mr. President: End 'Don't Ask, Don't Tell,'" Huffington Post, May 28, 2009, http://www.huffingtonpost.com/aubrey-sarvis/stand-by-your-word-mr-pre_b_191759.html?; on the poll, "Washington Post-ABC News Poll," conducted April 21–24, 2009, *Washington Post*, http://www.washingtonpost.com/wp-srv/politics/polls/postpoll_042609.html

37. On Solmonese: Kerry Eleveld, "Obama's First 100 Days Prove Inclusive," *The Advocate*, April 29, 2009, http://www.advocate.com/politics/2009/04/29/obamas%C2%A0first-100-days%C2%A0prove-inclusive.

38. Ibid.

39. On watching a replay, author interview with Richard Socarides, August, 23, 2013.

40. On Emanuel's counsel, Greg Sargent, "Book: Rahm 'Begged' Obama for Days Not to Pursue Ambitious Health Reform," *Washington Post*, May 14, 2010,

http://voices.washingtonpost.com/plum-line/2010/05/book_rahm_spent
_week_aggressiv.html.

41. On Rahm, background author interview with progressive advocate, October 24, 2013. On the Blue Dogs, Michael Tomasky, "Who Are the Blue Dogs?" *New York Review of Books*, December 3, 2009, http://www.nybooks.com/articles /archives/2009/dec/03/who-are-the-blue-dogs/; see also, Naftalie Bendavid, "'Blue Dog' Democrats Hold Health-Care Overhaul at Bay," *Wall Street Journal*, July 27, 2009, http://www.wsj.com/articles/SB124865363472782519.

42. Author interview with Richard Socarides, August, 23, 2013.

43. Richard Socarides, "Where's Our 'Fierce Advocate'?" *Washington Post*, May 2, 2009, http://www.washingtonpost.com/wp-dyn/content/article/2009 /05/01/AR2009050103401.html.

44. Sheryl Gay Stolberg, "As Gay Issues Arise, Obama Is Pressed to Engage," *New York Times*, May 6, 2009, http://www.nytimes.com/2009/05/07/us /politics/07obama.html?_r=0.

45. Ibid.

46. On favoring Obama, author interview with David Mixner, August 4, 2013; on the cadre, Kerry Eleveld, "Obama Picks Up LGBT Supporters from Edwards," *The Advocate*, February 1, 2008, http://www.advocate.com/news /2008/02/01/obama-picks-lgbt-supporters-edwards.

47. On $3 million, Howard Fineman, "The Inner Circle," *Newsweek*, October 25, 1992, http://www.newsweek.com/inner-circle-200104.

48. On the arrests, Cindy Loose, "Former Clinton Adviser Arrested in Gay-Rights Protest at White House," *Washington Post*, July 31, 1993; on Rahm, David Mixner, *Stranger Among Friends* (New York: Bantam Books, 1996), 313–314; on losing clients, author interview with David Mixner, August 4, 2013.

49. David Mixner, "March on Washington for Marriage Equality," David-Mixner.com, May 20, 2009, http://www.davidmixner.com/2009/05/march-on -washington-for-marriage-equality-2009.html.

50. Ibid.

51. On resigning, author interview with Robin McGehee, August 19, 2013; see also Amy Graff, "Collateral Damage: Young Casualty of Proposition 8," SFGate, November 21, 2008, http://blog.sfgate.com/sfmoms/2008/11/21 /collateral-damage-young-casualty-of-prop-8/.

52. On the march, Joe Garofoli, "Prop. 8 Opponents Take Their Case to Fresno," *San Francisco Chronicle*, May 31, 2009, http://www.sfgate.com /politics/article/Prop-8-opponents-take-their-case-to-Fresno-3296860.php; on Milk's assassination, "Harvey Milk," *New York Times*, accessed May 14, 2015, http://topics.nytimes.com/top/reference/timestopics/people/m/harvey _milk/index.html.

53. Garofoli, "Prop. 8 Opponents Take Their Case to Fresno."

54. Author review of video footage of Meet in the Middle 4 Equality, YouTube, accessed April 3, 2015, https://www.youtube.com/watch?v=9X1yf8ZdK1c.

NOTES TO CHAPTER 3

1. Monica Davey, "Iowa Court Voids Gay Marriage Ban," *New York Times*, April 3, 2009, http://www.nytimes.com/2009/04/04/us/04iowa.html ?pagewanted=all&_r=0.

2. On timing, author review of personal work e-mails.

3. Kerry Eleveld, "White House Responds to Iowa," *The Advocate*, April 3, 2009, http://www.advocate.com/news_detail_ektid77464.asp.

4. Nan Hunter, "Powerful Pam Shames the White House on Iowa Marriage Decision," Hunter of Justice, April 6, 2009, http://hunterofjustice.com /2009/04/powerful-pam-shames-white-house.html.

5. On the exchange, author review of personal work e-mails.

6. On Vermont, Keith B. Richburg, "Vermont Legislature Legalizes Same-Sex Marriage," *Washington Post*, April 7, 2009, http://www.washingtonpost .com/wp-dyn/content/article/2009/04/07/AR2009040701663.html.

7. On Obama's decisive steps, Susan Page and Mimi Hall, "Road Toughens After Obama's First 100 days," *USA Today*, April 30, 2009, http://usatoday30 .usatoday.com/news/washington/2009–04–27-next-100-days_N.htm.

8. Kerry Eleveld, "White House Office of Missed Opportunity," *The Advocate*, April 7, 2009, http://www.advocate.com/politics/2009/04/07/presidential -office-missed-opportunity.

9. Abby Goodnough, "Maine Governor Signs Same-Sex Marriage Bill," *New York Times*, May 6, 2009, http://www.nytimes.com/2009/05/07/us/07marriage .html.

10. Kerry Eleveld, "Gibbs Asked About Maine at White House Press Briefing," *The Advocate*, May 6, 2009, http://web.archive.org/web/20090508101446/ http://www.advocate.com/news_detail_ektid82715.asp; see also, "Press Briefing by Secretary of State Hillary Clinton and Press Secretary Robert Gibbs," White House, May 6, 2009.

11. "Press Briefing by Press Secretary Robert Gibbs," White House, May 12, 2009.

12. On separate but equal, "Barack Obama in 2007 Democratic Primary Debate on GLBT Issues," On the Issues, accessed April 3, 2015, http://www .ontheissues.org/Archive/2007_HRC_LOGO_Barack_Obama.htm.

13. Kerry Eleveld, "Gibbs Questioned on DOMA Repeal," *The Advocate*, May 18, 2009, http://www.advocate.com/news_detail_ektid84566.asp.

14. Author review of video footage.

15. John Aravosis, "Gibbs Questioned on Timeline for DOMA Repeal," AMERICAblog, May 18, 2009, http://americablog.com/2009/05/gibbs -questioned-on-timeline-for-doma-repeal.html.

16. On the first credentialed reporters, author correspondence with Lou Chibbaro Jr., April 7, 2015; author correspondence with Lisa Keen, April 7, 2015.

17. On Gill being filed, "Gill et al. v. Office of Personnel Management et al.," GLAD, accessed May 1, 2014, http://www.glad.org/work/cases/gill-v -office-of-personnel-management.

18. On passage, H.R. 3396—Defense of Marriage Act, Congress.gov, accessed April 6, 2015, https://www.congress.gov/bill/104th-congress/house-bill/3396.

19. On the 1975 ruling, *Sosna v. Iowa*, 419 U.S. 393 (1975); on Lawrence, *Lawrence v. Texas*, (02–102) 539 U.S. 558 (2003).

20. On Goodrich, "Goodridge et al. v. Dept. Public Health," GLAD, accessed April 4, 2015, http://www.glad.org/work/cases/goodridge-et-al-v-dept -public-health/.

21. On Olson/Boies, Jo Becker, "A Conservative's Road to Same-Sex Marriage Advocacy," *New York Times*, August 18, 2009, http://www.nytimes .com/2009/08/19/us/19olson.html?pagewanted=all&_r=0.

22. On debating the lawsuit, Lisa Leff, "Gay Groups Call Federal Marriage Suit Premature," Associated Press, May 27, 2009; see also, Jim Carlton, "Federal Suit Divides Gay-Marriage Backers," *Wall Street Journal*, May 28, 2009, http:// www.wsj.com/articles/SB124343841198058745.

23. Kerry Eleveld, "Gibbs Grilled on Obama's Marriage Position," *The Advocate*, May 27, 2009; "Press Briefing by Press Secretary Robert Gibbs," White House, May 27, 2009.

24. Ibid.

25. On the two rulings, Carol J. Williams, "Rulings on Gay Couples' Spousal Benefits Question the Defense of Marriage Act," *Los Angeles Times*, February 6, 2009, http://articles.latimes.com/2009/feb/06/local/me-marriage-act6; see also Robert Pear, "Obama on Spot over a Benefit to Gay Couples," *New York Times*, March 12, 2009, http://www.nytimes.com/2009/03/13/us/politics /13benefits.html?hp=; on the benefits, Jeff Zeleny, "U.S. to Extend Its Job Benefits to Gay Partners," *New York Times*, June 16, 2009, http://www.nytimes .com/2009/06/17/us/politics/17gays.html; see also "Fact Sheet: Presidential Memorandum on Federal Benefits and Non-Discrimination," The White House, accessed June 12, 2014, http://www.whitehouse.gov/the-press-office/fact -sheet-presidential-memorandum-federal-benefits-and-non-discrimination.

26. Kerry Eleveld, "Madam Secretary," *The Advocate*, January 10, 2011, http:// www.advocate.com/print-issue/cover-stories/2011/01/10/madam-secretary.

27. On before the presidential memorandum: Kerry Eleveld, "Clinton Ready for Equal Treatment at State?" May 22, 2009, http://web.archive.org /web/20090526214047/http://www.advocate.com/news_detail_ektid85471. asp.

28. "Press Briefing by Press Secretary Robert Gibbs," White House, June 17, 2009.

29. On a number of questions, Kerry Eleveld, "Press Corps Fixates on LGBT Concerns," *The Advocate*, June 18, 2009, http://web.archive.org/web /20090620234317/http://www.advocate.com/news_detail_ektid91594.asp.

30. Brian Williams, "Taking the Hill: Inside Congress," *NBC News*, June 2, 2009, http://www.nbcnews.com/id/30892505/#31094378.

31. Ibid.

32. David Badash, "Obama: Gays, Not Gay Marriage, Have a Friend in the White House," The New Civil Rights Movement (blog), June 4, 2009, http://thenewcivilrightsmovement.com/obama-gays-not-gay-marriage-have-a-friend-in-the-white-house/marriage/2009/06/04/3117.

33. *Smelt v. United States*, Case No. SACV-09–286 DOC (MLGx) (C.D. Cal. June 11, 2009), available via Scribd.com, accessed April 5, 2015, https://www.scribd.com/doc/16355867/Obama-s-Motion-to-Dismiss-Marriage-case.

34. On Aravosis's hopes to collaborate, author interview with John Aravosis, July 10, 2013.

35. On 2004, Barack Obama, "Letter to the Editor: Obama on Marriage," *Windy City Times*, February 11, 2004, http://www.windycitymediagroup.com/gay/lesbian/news/ARTICLE.php?AID=4018; on 2008, Barack Obama, "Open Letter from Barack Obama to the LGBT Community," Bilerico.com, February 28, 2008, http://www.bilerico.com/2008/02/open_letter_from_barack_obama_to_the_lgb.php.

36. Ibid.

37. On cocktail parties, "Obama Chic: Inside the White House Cocktail Parties," *Fox News*, March 19, 2009, http://www.foxnews.com/story/2009/03/19/obama-chic-inside-white-house-cocktail-parties/; on tamping down expectations, Kerry Eleveld, "Obama's First 100 Days Prove Inclusive," *The Advocate*, April 29, 2009, http://www.advocate.com/politics/2009/04/29/obamas%C2%A0first-100-days%C2%A0prove-inclusive.

38. On hate crimes stalling, author interview with Joe Sudbay, August 2, 2013, background author interview with second meeting participant, July 19, 2013, and background author interview with third meeting participant, June 13, 2014; on Judy Shepard, Jon Barrett, "Judy Shepard Meets with Obama," *The Advocate*, May 20, 2009.

39. On David Smith's comments, Kerry Eleveld, "LGBT Leaders Lobby for Openly Gay Appointees," *The Advocate*, December 16, 2008, http://www.advocate.com/news/2008/12/16/lgbt-leaders-lobby-openly-gay-appointees?page=0,1; on HRC's blueprint, author review of personal work e-mails received on December 19, 2008, see also, "Call on President-Elect Obama to Restore Our Trust and Take Real Action on Equality," December 22, 2008, Queers United, http://queersunited.blogspot.com/2008/12/call-on-president-elect-obama-to.html.

40. On a first for "lesbian, gay, bisexual, and transgender," "Commemorating the Fourth Anniversary of the Shepard-Byrd Hate Crime Prevention Act," US Department of Justice. Accessed June 6, 2014. http://blogs.justice.gov/main/archives/3358.

41. Author interview with Joe Sudbay, August 2, 2013.

42. Ibid.

43. John Aravosis, "Obama Defends DOMA in Federal Court. Says Banning Gay Marriage Is Good for the Federal Budget. Invokes Incest and Marrying Children." AMERICAblog, June 12, 2009, http://americablog.com/2009/06 /obama-defends-doma-in-federal-court-says-banning-gay-marriage-is-good -for-the-federal-budget-invokes-incest-and-marrying-children.html.

44. *Smelt v. United States*, Case No. SACV-09–286 DOC (MLGx), at 18 (C.D. Cal. June 11, 2009).

45. On the AP, Linda Deutsch, "DOJ Moves to Dismiss First Fed Gay Marriage Case," Associated Press, June 12, 2009; on blogs, Ben Smith, "Justice Defends DOMA," *Politico*, June 12, 2009, http://www.politico.com/blogs /bensmith/0609/Justice_defends_DOMA.html; see also, The Daily Dish, "Obama's Gratuitous Insult to Gay Couples," *The Atlantic*, June 12, 2009, http://www.theatlantic.com/daily-dish/archive/2009/06/obamas-gratuitous -insult-to-gay-couples/200575/; on arrival of the Solmonese statement, author review of personal work e-mails received on June 12, 2009; on the legal groups, "LGBT Groups Decry Obama Admin's Defense of DOMA," GLAD, June 12, 2009, accessed on April 5, 2015, http://www.glad.org/current/news-detail /lgbt-legal-advocacy-groups-decry-obama-administrations-defense-of-doma/.

46. On blindsiding, background author interview with a former White House official, June 1, 2014; on the Bonauto/Barnes meeting, author interview with Mary Bonauto, civil rights project director at GLAD, August 12, 2014.

47. Chris Johnson, "Activists Angry over Justice Department's Defense of Gay Marriage Ban," *Southern Voice*, June 19, 2009.

48. Kerry Eleveld, "The Other Side of Justice," *The Advocate*, June 12, 2009, http://web.archive.org/web/20090711153702/http://www.advocate.com /news_detail_ektid90000.asp.

49. Richard Socarides, "The Decision to Defend DOMA, and Its Consequences," AMERICAblog, June 14, 2009, http://americablog.com/2009/06 /choice-to-defend-doma-and-its.html.

50. Author interview with Jenny Pizer, March 21, 2014.

51. Background author interview with legal advocate, May 28, 2014; background author interview with legal advocate, June 2, 2014.

52. On the statement, "LGBT Legal and Advocacy Groups Decry Obama Administration's Defense of DOMA," Gay and Lesbian Advocates and Defenders, June 12, 2009, accessed June 9, 2014, http://www.glad.org/current/news-detail /lgbt-legal-advocacy-groups-decry-obama-administrations-defense-of-doma/.

53. Author interview with Joe Sudbay, August 2, 2013.

54. On Jarrett's quote, ibid; on the other bloggers' comments, ibid.

55. On Sudbay's quote, ibid.

56. On Jarrett's quote, ibid.

57. Ibid.

58. On "don't ask, don't tell" consuming most of the energy, background author interview with a former White House official, June 1, 2014; on April meetings, Robert M. Gates, *Duty: Memoirs of a Secretary at War* (New York: Knopf, 2014), 333; on Gates' memoir, ibid., 298; on being a top priority, background author interview with a former White House official, June 1, 2014.

59. On the meeting participants, background author interview with a former White House official, August 28, 2014; on the goals, background author interview with a former White House official June 1, 2014, and background author interview with a former White House official, August 28, 2014.

60. On meeting participants, background author interview with a former White House official June 1, 2014, and background author interview with a former White House official, August 28, 2014.

61. On dropping like flies, Jim Burroway, "Two More Boycotting DNC Fundraiser," *Box Turtle Bulletin*, June 18, 2009, http://www.boxturtlebulletin .com/2009/06/18/12272; see also, Kerry Eleveld, "View from the Hill: The Dems," *The Advocate*, June 19, 2009, http://www.advocate.com/politics /2009/06/19/view-hill-dems, and Karen Ocamb, "Will Gays Divorce the Dems?" Huffington Post, June 19, 2009, http://www.huffingtonpost.com/karen -ocamb/will-gays-divorce-the-dem_b_217613.html.

62. On Ben Smith, Ben Smith, "Gay Figures Pull Out of Biden Fundraiser," *Politico*, June 16, 2009, http://www.politico.com/blogs/bensmith/0609/Gay _figures_pull_out_of_Biden_fundraiser.html; on other media, Josh Gerstein and Ben Smith, "President Obama Fails to Quell Gay Uproar," *Politico*, June 18, 2009, http://www.politico.com/news/stories/0609/23868.html; see also, Sam Youngman, "President Extends Olive Branch to Gays, Lesbians with Benefits Directive," *The Hill*, June 18, 2009, https://thehill.com/homenews/administration /47181-president-extends-olive-branch-to-gays-lesbians-with-benefits -directive; John Mercurio, "Obama Keeping Friends at Arm's Length," *National Journal*, June 17, 2009, http://www.nationaljournal.com/njonline/obama -keeping-friends-at-arm-s-length-20090617; "How Far Can They Be Pushed?" *The Economist*, June 17, 2009, http://www.economist.com/blogs/democracyin america/2009/06/how_far_can_they_be_pushed.

63. On the fundraiser protesters, speeches, and money raised, Kerry Eleveld, "DNC Fundraiser Nets $1 Million," *The Advocate*, June 16, 2009, http://web .archive.org/web/20090629052949/http://www.advocate.com/news_detail _ektid93604.asp.

64. Remarks by the president at LGBT Pride month reception, White House, June 29, 2009.

65. Ibid.

66. Ibid.

67. On the White House lawyers, background author interview with a former White House official, June 1, 2009; on the DOJ meeting, background author interview with legal advocate, May 28, 2014, background author interview with

legal advocate, June 2, 2014, background author interview with legal advocate, June 5, 2014; on DOJ attorneys/employees, "About the Office," US Department of Justice, accessed June 9, 2014, http://www.justice.gov/oarm/about-office; see also, "Overview," US Department of Justice, accessed June 9, 2014, http://www.justice.gov/jmd/2013summary/pdf/fy13-bud-summary-request-performance.pdf#summary.

68. On the attendees, background author interview with legal advocate, May 28, 2014, background author interview with legal advocate, June 2, 2014, background author interview with legal advocate, August 15, 2014.

69. On the American Academy of Child and Adolescent Psychiatry, "Gay, Lesbian, Bisexual, or Transgender Parents," American Academy of Child and Adolescent Psychiatry, accessed June 10, 2014, http://www.aacap.org/aacap/Policy_Statements/2008/Gay_Lesbian_Bisexual_or_Transgender_Parents.aspx; on the organizations, "Professional Organizations on LGBT Parenting," Human Rights Campaign, accessed May 2, 2014, http://www.hrc.org/resources/entry/professional-organizations-on-lgbt-parenting.

70. On White House lawyers doubting, background author interview with a former White House official, June 1, 2014; on the goal of the brief, background author interview with a former White House official, June 1, 2014.

71. *Smelt v. United States*, Case No. SACV-09–286 DOC (MLGx), at 6 (C.D. Cal. August 17, 2009).

72. On the first brief, *Smelt v. United States*, Case No. SACV-09–286 DOC (MLGx), at 6 (C.D. Cal. June 11, 2009); on the New York, Washington, and Maryland decisions, *Hernandez v. Robles*, 855 N.E.2d 1 (N.Y. 2006), *Andersen v. King County*, 138 P.3d 963 (Wash. 2006), *Conaway v. Deane*, 932 A.2d 571 (Md. 2007); see also, Anemona Hartocollis, "New York Judges Reject Any Right to Gay Marriage," *New York Times*, July 7, 2006, http://www.nytimes.com/2006/07/07/nyregion/07marriage.html?pagewanted=all&_r=0; Curt Woodward, "State Supreme Court Upholds Washington Gay Marriage Ban," Associated Press, July 26, 2006; Lisa Rein and Mary Otto, "Maryland Ban on Gay Marriage Is Upheld," *Washington Post*, September 19, 2007, http://www.washingtonpost.com/wp-dyn/content/article/2007/09/18/AR2007091802177.html; Dahlia Lithwick, "Rational Lampoon," *Slate*, July 26, 2006, http://www.slate.com/articles/news_and_politics/jurisprudence/2006/07/rational_lampoon.single.html.

73. On the footnote, *Smelt v. United States*, Case No. SACV-09–286 DOC (MLGx), at 6 (C.D. Cal. August 17, 2009).

74. On the Minnesota Supreme Court, *Baker v. Nelson*, 191 N.W.2d 185, 186 (Minn. 1971); on the Supreme Court rejection, *Baker v. Nelson*, 409 U.S. 810 (1972); on 1973, "LGBT–Sexual Orientation," American Psychiatric Association, accessed April 6, 2015, http://www.psychiatry.org/lgbt-sexual-orientation.

75. *Smelt v. United States*, Case No. SACV-09–286 DOC (MLGx), at 2 (C.D. Cal. August 17, 2009).

76. Ben Smith, "Obama Underlines DOMA Opposition," *Politico*, August 17, 2009, http://www.politico.com/blogs/bensmith/0809/Obama_underlines_DOMA_opposition.html.

NOTES TO CHAPTER 4

1. On organizing the protests, author interview with Kip Williams, September 25, 2013; see also Seth Hemmelgarn, "March to Sacto in March," *Bay Area Reporter*, January 1, 2009, http://www.ebar.com/news/article.php?sec=news&article=3608.

2. On the town hall, Seth Hemmelgarn, "No on Prop 8 Admits Mistakes," *Bay Area Reporter*, March 5, 2009, http://ebar.com/news/article.php?sec=news&article=3769.

3. On Williams' impression of McGehee, author interview with Kip Williams, September 25, 2013.

4. On Cleve Jones's history with Harvey Milk, author interview with Cleve Jones, December 29, 2014; on the quilt, "The AIDS Memorial Quilt," AIDSQuilt.org, accessed April 7, 2015, http://www.aidsquilt.org/about/the-aids-memorial-quilt.

5. "Interview with Cleve Jones," YouTube, uploaded March 13, 2008, accessed April 7, 2015, https://www.youtube.com/watch?v=27yj4Ad9yb4.

6. Ibid.

7. On McGehee meeting Jones, author interview with Robin McGehee, August 19, 2013.

8. On Jones' quote to McGehee, ibid.; on Jones announcing the march, "Meet in the Middle—Cleve Jones," YouTube, uploaded May 31, 2009, accessed April 7, 2015, https://www.youtube.com/watch?v=GsI4vFDXqKQ.

9. On Jones' quote, ibid.; on full equal protection, author interview with Cleve Jones, December 29, 2014.

10. On the challenges, author interview with Robin McGehee, August 19, 2013, and author interview with Kip Williams, September 25, 2013; on Witte's assist, author interview with Willow Witte, April 16, 2015.

11. On little to no help, author interview with Cleve Jones, December 29, 2014, author interview with Robin McGehee, August 19, 2013, and author interview with Kip Williams, September 25, 2013; on Barney Frank, Andrew Miga, "Frank Says D.C. Gay Rights March Misses Mark," Associated Press, October 10, 2009.

12. On endorsements, David Mixner, "Massive Number of LGBT Leaders Endorse National Equality March," DavidMixner.com, September 2, 2009, http://www.davidmixner.com/2009/09/massive-number-of-lgbt-leaders-endorse-national-equality-march.html.

13. On Vaid's speech, "Speech at the 1993 March on Washington for LGBT Rights," UrvashiVaid.net, accessed June 13, 2015, http://urvashivaid.net/wp /?p=97.

14. On the Task Force, Joe Jervis, "NGLTF on the March on Washington," Joe.My.God, June 8, 2009, http://joemygod.blogspot.com/2009/06/ngltf-on -march-on-washington.html; see also Joe Jervis, "Reversal: Task Force Endorses National Equality March," Joe.My.God. September 3, 2009, http://joemygod .blogspot.com/2009_08_30_archive.html; on HRC, "HRC Endorses March on Washington," *Seattle Gay News*, October 2, 2009, http://www.sgn.org/sgnnews37 _40/mobile/page20.cfm.

15. On taking heat, author interview with Cleve Jones, December 29, 2014, and author interview with David Mixner, August 4, 2013; on Williams' idea and approaching Yandura, author interview with Kip Williams, September 25, 2013.

16. On Yandura's thinking and declining to donate, author interview with Paul Yandura, May 21, 2013; author interview with Robin McGehee, August 19, 2013; and author interview with Kip Williams, September 25, 2013; see also, Andrew Harmon and Kerry Eleveld, "The Rise of GetEqual," *The Advocate*, June 1, 2010, http://www.advocate.com/society/military/2010/06/01/rise -getequal?page=full.

17. On Mixner's comment, author interview with Robin McGehee, August 19, 2013; on sixty thousand likes, author interview with David Mixner, August 4, 2013.

18. Ibid.

19. Ibid.

20. Ibid.

21. On having a lot at stake, ibid.

22. On the calls, ibid.

23. Ibid.

24. Author review of notes from October 11, 2009; see also, Advocate .com Editors, "The March Is On," *The Advocate*, October 11, 2009, http://www .advocate.com/news/daily-news/2009/10/11/march?page=0,1.

25. On Mixner's speech, "National Equality March Rally: David Mixner Speaks," YouTube, uploaded October 11, 2009, accessed April 8, 2015, https:// www.youtube.com/watch?v=o5kySGYZl4U; see also, Kerry Eleveld, "Text of Mixner's Speech," *The Advocate*, October 11, 2009, http://www.advocate.com /news/news-features/2009/10/11/text-david-mixners-speech.

26. "National Equality March Rally: Lt. Dan Choi Speaks," YouTube, up-loaded October 11, 2009, accessed April 8, 2015, https://www.youtube.com /watch?v=H-eUfCA2gJo.

27. "National Equality March Rally: Lady Gaga Speaks," YouTube, up-loaded October 11, 2009, accessed April 8, 2009, https://www.youtube.com /watch?v=mRNsl_0AZOs.

28. On the ballot initiative, Associated Press, "Voters in Maine Will Decide Fate of Same-Sex Marriage Law," *New York Times*, September 2, 2009, http://www.nytimes.com/2009/09/03/us/03maine.html?_r=1; on the poll, "The 42nd Pan Atlantic SMS Group Omnibus Poll, Fall 2009, Election 2009 Issue," Pan Atlantic SMS Group, accessed May 7, 2014, http://www.panatlanticsmsgroup .com/resource/d/26729/OMNIBUSFall2009.pdf.

29. On Mixner's quote, Kerry Eleveld, "Pressure Mounts on Obama Speech," *The Advocate*, October 5, 2009. http://web.archive.org/web/20091009142520 /http://www.advocate.com/News/Daily_News/2009/10/Pressure_Mounts _on_Obama_Speech/; on the West Wing confidant, author interview with David Mixner, August 4, 2013.

30. On no sponsors, Kerry Eleveld, "Sen. Reid: No sponsors for DADT," *The Advocate*, June 15, 2009, http://web.archive.org/web/20090711150930 /http://www.advocate.com/news_detail_ektid90581.asp; see also, Kerry Eleveld, "White House Talks DADT Repeal with Lieberman," *The Advocate*, October 12, 2009, http://www.advocate.com/news/daily-news/2009/10/12/white -house-talks-dadt-repeal-lieberman.

31. On Obama's remarks, "Remarks by the President at the Human Rights Campaign Dinner," White House, October 11, 2009, http://www.whitehouse .gov/the-press-office/remarks-president-human-rights-campaign-dinner.

32. John Aravosis, "HRC: Obama Gets Until 2017 to Keep His Promises, and Don't Criticize Him Until Then," AMERICAblog, October 9, 2009, http:// americablog.com/2009/10/hrc-obama-gets-until-2017-to-keep-his-promises -and-dont-criticize-him-until-then.html.

33. On Holder's speech, Dylan Riley, "U.S. Attorney General Eric Holder Speaks at UMaine," *The Maine Campus*, October 23, 2009, http://mainecampus .com/2009/10/23/u-s-attorney-general-eric-holder-speaks-at-umaine/?ref=hp.

34. On Holder's quote, ibid.

35. David Mixner, "Maine, Obama and the LGBT Community," DavidMix-ner.com, November 3, 2009, http://www.davidmixner.com/2009/11/maine -obama-and-the-lgbt-community.html.

36. Ibid.

37. On polls leading up, "Tied in Maine," Public Policy Polling, accessed May 8, 2014, http://publicpolicypolling.blogspot.com/2009/10/tied-in-maine.html; on slipping, "Gay Marriage Still Close," Public Policy Polling, accessed May 27, 2014, http://www.publicpolicypolling.com/pdf/2009/PPP_Release_ME_1102.pdf.

38. On defeating the anti-gay ballot initiative, Katie Zezima, "Maine May Consider, for a Third Time, a Gay Bias Question," *New York Times*, July 27, 2005, http://www.nytimes.com/2005/07/27/national/27maine.html?pagewanted =print&_r=0.

39. On money raised, Peter Quist and Nadeanne Haftl, "2009–2010 Ballot Measure Overview," National Institute on Money in State Politics, accessed May 7, 2009, http://www.followthemoney.org/press/ReportView.phtml?r=486.

40. On being sloppy, David Fleischer, "Finding 4: No On 8's Biggest Mistake," *The Prop 8 Report*, accessed May 29, 2014, http://prop8report.lgbt mentoring.org/read-the-report/findings-overview/findings-1–7-prejudice /finding-4-princes-delay-avoidance.

41. On McGehee, author interview with Robin McGehee, August 19, 2013.

42. On Lewis, author interview with Jonathan D. Lewis, June 3, 2013; see also, Andrew Harmon and Kerry Eleveld, "The Rise of GetEqual," *The Advocate*, June 1, 2010, http://www.advocate.com/society/military/2010/06/01/rise -getequal?page=full.

43. Author interview with Robin McGehee, August 19, 2013, and author interview with Jonathan D. Lewis, June 3, 2013.

44. On Smith's comments, author interview with Paul Yandura, May 21, 2013; author review of Yandura's notes from the meeting, dated January 13, 2010; background author interviews with two LGBT advocates, January 14, 2010; see also, Kerry Eleveld, "LGBT Advocates Hold Urgent DADT Meeting," *The Advocate*, January 15, 2010, http://www.advocate.com/news/daily -news/2010/01/15/lgbt-advocates-hold-urgent-dadt-meeting.

45. Author review of a detailed HRC memo from Joe Solmonese regarding their repeal strategy, dated January 2010.

46. Author interview with Paul Yandura, May 21, 2013; author review of Yandura's notes following a donor adviser meeting, dated January 13, 2010.

47. On Sarvis, author interview with Paul Yandura, May 21, 2013; author review of Yandura's notes from the meeting, dated January 13, 2010.

48. On Stachelberg, ibid.

49. On Yandura's question, ibid; on the plan, Sheryl Gay Stolberg, "As Gay Issues Arise, Obama Is Pressed to Engage," May 6, 2009, *New York Times*, http:// www.nytimes.com/2009/05/07/us/politics/07obama.html?_r=0.

50. On Belkin, author interview with Paul Yandura, May 21, 2013; author review of Yandura's notes from the meeting, dated January 13, 2010.

51. On pressure, ibid; background author interviews with two LGBT advocates, January 14, 2010; on Smith and Stachelberg, author interview with Paul Yandura, May 21, 2013; author review of Yandura's notes from the meeting, dated January 13, 2010.

52. On telling Bond, author interview with Paul Yandura, May 21, 2013.

53. Author interview with Paul Yandura, May 21, 2013; author review of Yandura's notes from the meeting, dated January 13, 2010; background author interviews with two LGBT advocates, January 14, 2010; see also, Kerry Eleveld, "LGBT Advocates Hold Urgent DADT meeting," *The Advocate*, January 15, 2010, http://www.advocate.com/news/daily-news/2010/01/15/lgbt -advocates-hold-urgent-dadt-meeting.

54. On Kramer's speech, Jason DeParle, "Rude, Rash, Effective, Act-Up Shifts AIDS Policy," *New York Times*, January 3, 1990; on Reagan, Randy Shilts,

And The Band Played On (New York: St. Martin's Press, 1987), 596; see also, Susanne M. Schafer, "President Calls for Moral Approach to Teaching About AIDS," Associated Press, April 1, 1987.

55. On starting GMHC, Randy Shilts, *And The Band Played On*, 90; on quitting GMHC, ibid, 275–277; on Silence = Death, "Silence = Death," ACT UP—New York, accessed April 8, 2015, http://www.actupny.org/reports/silencedeath.html.

56. Author interview with Ann Northrop, August 22, 2013; see also, "Meet Ann Northrop," Gay USA, accessed April 8, 2015, http://www.gayusatv.org/site/northrop.html.

57. On the protest, author interview with Ann Northrop, September 13, 2013; see also, Jason DeParle, "111 Held in St. Patrick's AIDS Protest," *New York Times*, December 11, 1989, http://www.nytimes.com/1989/12/11/nyregion/111-held-in-st-patrick-s-aids-protest.html; see also, David Handelman, "Act Up in Anger," *Rolling Stone*, March 8, 1990, http://www.rollingstone.com/culture/features/act-up-in-anger-19900308.

58. On the editorial, *New York Times*, "The storming of St. Pat's," December 12, 1989; on Northrop's advice, author interview with Ann Northrop, September 13, 2013.

59. Author interview with Paul Yandura, May 21, 2013.

60. Author interview with Richard Socarides, August 23, 2013.

61. Author interview with Robin McGehee, August 19, 2013; author interview with Kip Williams, September 25, 2013; author review of Paul Yandura's notes from the meeting, dated January 14, 2010.

62. Author interview with Paul Yandura, May 21, 2013.

63. Author review of Paul Yandura's notes from the meeting, dated January 14, 2010.

64. Author interview with Robin McGehee, August 19, 1015, and author review of Paul Yandura's notes from the meeting, dated January 14, 2010.

65. On Brown's win, Michael Cooper, "GOP Senate Victory Stuns Democrats," *New York Times*, January 19, 2010.

66. Associated Press, "Pentagon Lawyers Urge Further Delay in Repeal of Ban on Openly Gay Troops," January 14, 2010.

67. Kerry Eleveld, "Gibbs: DADT Discussions Continue, No Timeline Yet," *The Advocate*, January 15, 2010, http://www.advocate.com/News/Daily_News/2010/01/15/Gibbs_DADT_Discussions_Continue/.

68. Ibid.

69. On the early draft, Roxana Tiron, "Sen. Levin Asked to Hold Off on Hearing on 'Don't Ask, Don't Tell' Policy," *The Hill*, January 25, 2010; on the memo, background author interview with a former White House official, February 3, 2014, and review of author's reporter notes from March of 2010.

70. "Remarks by the President in the State of the Union Address," White House, January 27, 2010.

71. On eyeing Lieberman, background author interview with LGBT advocate, August 24, 2011; on Messina, author interview with Clarine Nardi Riddle, chief of staff to Senator Lieberman, April 7, 2014.

72. "Hearing of the Senate Armed Services Committee," Federal News Service, February 2, 2010, accessed April 9, 2015, http://www.defense.gov/qdr /HEARING_OF_THE_SENATE_ARMED_SERVICES_COMMITT1.pdf.

73. Ibid.

74. "Joint Chiefs Chairman Gen. Peter Pace Calls Homosexuality 'Immoral,'" Associated Press, March 13, 2007.

75. On McCain 2006, "Hardball's College Tour with John McCain," *Hardball with Chris Matthews*, NBC News, October 18, 2006, http://www.nbcnews .com/id/15330717/ns/msnbc-hardball_with_chris_matthews/t/hardballs -college-tour-john-mccain/#.VSa6CyhGHtA.

76. "Hearing of the Senate Armed Services Committee," Federal News Service, February 2, 2010.

77. National Defense Research Institute, "Sexual Orientation and U.S. Military Personnel Policy: Options and Assessment," RAND Corporation, 1993, http://www.rand.org/content/dam/rand/pubs/monograph_reports/2009 /RAND_MR323.pdf.

78. "Hearing of the Senate Armed Services Committee," Federal News Service, February 2, 2010.

NOTES TO CHAPTER 5

1. On the survey, William H. McMichael, "Pentagon Sends Out Survey on Gay Troops," *Navy Times*, July 7, 2010, http://archive.navytimes.com/article /20100707/NEWS/7070312/Pentagon-sends-out-survey-gay-troops.

2. On Cook's forecast, Chris Cillizza, "Charlie Cook: 'Very Hard' to See How Democrats Keep House," *Washington Post*, February 22, 2010, http:// voices.washingtonpost.com/thefix/house/charlie-cook.html.

3. "How to Change 'Don't Ask, Don't Tell,'" *Washington Post*, February 7, 2010, http://www.washingtonpost.com/wp-dyn/content/article/2010/02/05 /AR2010020501926.html.

4. Kerry Eleveld, "Frank Revises Statement Regarding White House Position on DADT," *The Advocate*, March 15, 2010, http://www.advocate.com/news /daily-news/2010/03/15/frank-revises-statement-re-white-house-position -dadt; Chris Geidner, "The Politics of Repeal," *Metro Weekly*, March 26, 2010, http://www.metroweekly.com/2010/03/the-politics-of-repeal/.

5. On the episode, Hank Stuever, "Kathy Griffin's 'My Life on the D-List' Trip to Washington Falls Flat on Humor," *Washington Post*, July 13, 2010, http://www .washingtonpost.com/wp-dyn/content/article/2010/07/12/AR2010071202817 .html.

6. Chuck Colbert, "As Pro-gay Provision Stripped from Health Reform, Pressure Grows for Votes on ENDA, DADT," Keen News Service, March 19, 2010, http://www.sdgln.com/news/2010/03/19/pro-gay-provisions-stripped-health-reform-pressure-grows-votes-enda-dadt#sthash.vUzebwc7.dpbs.

7. On Choi's history with gay groups, Gabriel Arana, "The Passion of Dan Choi," *The American Prospect*, December 2013, https://prospect.org/article/passion-dan-choi; on Choi/Mullen, Kerry Eleveld, "Lt. Choi Attends Defense Testimony," *The Advocate*, May 13, 2009, http://web.archive.org/web/20090525141936/http://www.advocate.com/news_detail_ektid83992.asp.

8. On McGehee's thinking, author interview with Robin McGehee, August 19, 2013.

9. On Pietrangelo, Mark Thompson, "Dismay over Obama's 'Don't Ask, Don't Tell' Turnabout," *Time*, June 9, 2009, http://content.time.com/time/nation/article/0,8599,1903545,00.html.

10. On the flier, author review of the original flier; on the car ride, author correspondence with Paul Yandura, February 9, 2014, and author interview with Robin McGehee, August 19, 2013.

11. On the hearing, "Hearing Before the Committee on Armed Services, United States Senate, One Hundred Eleventh Congress, Second Session," US Government Printing Office, Senate Hearing 111–546, March 18, 2010, http://www.gpo.gov/fdsys/pkg/CHRG-111shrg57495/html/CHRG-111shrg57495.htm.

12. On times of war, Ann Scott Tyson, "Sharp Drop in Gays Discharged from Military Tied to War Need," *Washington Post*, March 14, 2007, http://www.washingtonpost.com/wp-dyn/content/article/2007/03/13/AR2007031301174.html.

13. On the rally, "Kathy Griffin at Gay Rally in DC (Part 1): Speaks Against "Don't Ask Don't Tell," YouTube, uploaded March 18, 2010, accessed April 9, 2015, https://www.youtube.com/watch?v=V0YPlohBxtk.

14. On texts, author review of personal tweet log, dated March 18, 2010.

15. "Kathy Griffin @ Repeal DADT Rally Pt 3," YouTube, uploaded March 18, 2010, https://www.youtube.com/watch?v=t99ASaqVkr4.

16. "DC Rally for Gay Soldiers Against DADT w/ Kathy Griffin, Dan Choi, Tom Goss," YouTube, uploaded March 19, 2010, https://www.youtube.com/watch?v=QAqAZB70mcs.

17. On the action, author interview with Robin McGehee, August 19, 2013; see also, Kerry Eleveld and Andrew Harmon, "Choi Arrested at White House Gates," *The Advocate*, March 18, 2010, http://www.advocate.com/news/daily-news/2010/03/18/dan-choi-protests-front-wh.

18. On CNN, "Rick Sanchez on Dan Choi's Arrest," YouTube, uploaded March 18, 2009, https://www.youtube.com/watch?v=tbYQ8oxqFg4&feature=youtu.be.

19. "Briefing by White House Press Secretary Robert Gibbs," White House, March 18, 2010.

20. John Aravosis, "VIDEO: Lt Dan Choi Marches to White House & Handcuffs Self to Fence," AMERICAblog, March 18, 2010, http://americablog.com/2010/03/video-lt-dan-choi-marches-to-white-house-handcuffs-self-to-fence.html; The Dish, "Face of the Day," *The Atlantic*, March 18, 2010, http://dish.andrewsullivan.com/2010/03/18/face-37/.

21. Kerry Eleveld, "Activists Stage Sit-in, Push Pelosi on ENDA," *The Advocate*, March 18, 2010, http://www.advocate.com/News/Daily_News/2010/03/18/Protesters_Urge_Pelosi_Move_on_ENDA/; see also, Kerry Eleveld and Andrew Harmon, "Choi Arrested at White House Gates," *The Advocate*, March 18, 2010, http://www.advocate.com/news/daily-news/2010/03/18/dan-choi-protests-front-wh.

22. "DOD News Briefing with Secretary Gates and Adm. Mullen from the Pentagon," US Department of Defense, March 25, 2010, http://www.defense.gov/Transcripts/Transcript.aspx?TranscriptID=4592.

23. On Obama reentering the health negotiations, Sheryl Gay Stolberg and David M. Herszenhorn, "In Health Talks, President Is Hands-Off No More," *New York Times*, January 16, 2010, http://query.nytimes.com/gst/fullpage.html?res=9E0DE4DE153EF935A25752C0A9669D8B63; on passage of health reform, Shailagh Murray and Lori Montgomery, "House Passes Health-Care Reform Bill Without Republican Votes," *Washington Post*, March 22, 2010.

24. Tucker Reals, "Obama's Approval Rating Hits New Low," *CBS News*, April 2, 2010, http://www.cbsnews.com/news/obamas-approval-rating-hits-new-low/.

25. On the DNC, "DNC Reports March Haul," CNN, April 20, 2010, http://politicalticker.blogs.cnn.com/2010/04/20/dnc-reports-march-haul/; on Obama, Julie Mason, "Obama Jumps In to Help Dems Bring in Big Money," *The Examiner*, April 16, 2010; Christine Simmons, "Obama Helps Democrats Raise $1M at DC Fundraiser," Associated Press, April 30, 2010.

26. Seema Mehta and Tom Hamburger, "Obama in L.A. for Boxer," *Los Angeles Times*, April 20, 2010.

27. On the White House pooler, author interview with Robin McGehee, August 19, 2013.

28. On the protest, author interview with Dan Fotou, March 9, 2012, and author interview with Zoe Nicholson, March 5, 2014.

29. On positioning, author interview with Dan Fotou, March 9, 2012, and author interview with Zoe Nicholson, March 5, 2014.

30. "Remarks by the President at Fundraising Event for Senator Boxer and the DNC," White House, April 19, 2010.

31. On cupping his ear, "LGBT Activists with GetEQUAL Heckle Obama at Boxer Fundraiser," YouTube, uploaded April 19, 2010, https://www.youtube.com/watch?v=hY3qX-O_aKE.

32. On locking eyes, author interview with Dan Fotou, March 9, 2012.

33. "Remarks by the President at Fundraising Event for Senator Boxer and the DNC," White House, April 19, 2010.

34. On crowd chants, White House pool report received by the author on April 19, 2010; on "Shut the fuck up," author interview with Dan Fotou, March 9, 2012.

35. "LGBT Activists with GetEQUAL Heckle Obama at Boxer Fundraiser," YouTube, uploaded April 19, 2010, https://www.youtube.com/watch?v=hY3qX-O_aKE.

36. "Remarks by the President at Fundraising Event for Senator Boxer and the DNC," White House, April 19, 2010.

37. On stepping away from the mic, "LGBT Activists with GetEQUAL Heckle Obama at Boxer Fundraiser," YouTube, uploaded April 19, 2010, https://www.youtube.com/watch?v=hY3qX-O_aKE.

38. White House pool report received by the author on April 19, 2010.

39. Marc Ambinder, "Outing the Debate: An Insider Account of the Struggle to End 'Don't Ask, Don't Tell,'" National Journal, December 9, 2010, http://www.nationaljournal.com/magazine/the-battle-to-end-don-t-ask-don-t-tell--20101209.

40. On the e-mail, author interview with Robin McGehee, August 19, 2013, and author interview with Paul Yandura, May 21, 2013.

41. On the protest, John Aravosis, "6 Military Vets Handcuff Selves to White House Gates to Protest Obama Inaction on DADT," AMERICAblog, April 20, 2010, http://americablog.com/2010/04/6-military-vets-handcuff-selves-to-white-house-gates-to-protest-obama-inaction-on-dadt.html.

42. On Aravosis, "White House Closes Lafayette Park Due to DADT Protesters, Kicks Out Media," YouTube, uploaded April 20, 2010, http://home.realclearpolitics.com/video/2010/04/20/police_chase_reporters_covering_gay_protesters_at_white_house_fence.html.

43. On Smith's post and Schlosser's statement, Ben Smith, "Most Transparent White House Ever . . . " Politico, April 20, 2010, http://www.politico.com/blogs/bensmith/0410/Most_transparent_White_House_ever.html.

44. Kerry Eleveld, "Gibbs: DADT on Hold Until 2011?" The Advocate, April 21, 2010, http://www.advocate.com/news/daily-news/2010/04/21/gibbs-says-dadt-may-be-hold-until-2011; see also, "Briefing by White House Press Secretary Robert Gibbs," White House, April 21, 2010.

45. Ibid.

46. Igor Volsky, "Gibbs Says White House Will Wait for Pentagon to Complete DADT Review Before Pushing for Repeal," ThinkProgress, April 21, 2010, http://thinkprogress.org/justice/2010/04/21/176755/gibbs-study/; Pam Spaulding, "Robert Gibbs Finally Admits the Obama Administration Has No Intention of Pushing DADT Repeal in 2010," Pam's House Blend, http://pamshouseblend.firedoglake.com/2010/04/21/robert-gibbs-finally-admits-the-obama-admin-has-no-intention-of-pushing-dadt-repeal-in-2010/.

47. On outing himself, Alexander Nicholson, *Fighting to Serve* (Chicago: Chicago Review Press, 2012), 114.

48. Kerry Eleveld, "White House Sends Mixed Messages on DADT Repeal," *The Advocate*, 4.21.2010, http://www.advocate.com/news/daily-news/2010/04/21/white-house-sends-mixed-messages-dadt.

49. Ibid.

50. Kerry Eleveld, "Sources Rebut WH 'Shut Down' Story on DADT," *The Advocate*, April 22, 2010, http://www.advocate.com/news/daily-news/2010/04/22/sources-refute-wh-shut-down-dadt.

51. On Sarvis, Press Release, Servicemembers Legal Defense Network, September 12, 2007, http://www.sldn.org/news/archives/aubrey-sarvis-named-executive-director-of-servicemembers-legal-defense-netw/.

52. On Stachelberg, "Staff Biography: Winnie Stachelberg," Center for American Progress, http://www.americanprogress.org/about/staff/stachelberg-winnie/bio/; on Herwitt, "Staff Biography: Allison Herwitt," Human Rights Campaign, Human Rights Campaign, http://www.hrc.org/staff/profile/allison-herwitt.

53. In fact, Secretary Gates would later write: Robert M. Gates, *Duty: Memoirs of a Secretary at War* (New York: Knopf, 2014), 438.

54. Anne Flaherty, "Military Tells Congress to Keep Gay Ban for Now," Associated Press, April 30, 2010; see also, "Pentagon: Don't Lift Gay Ban Yet," Agence France Presse, May 1, 2010.

55. On reactions, Andrew Harmon and Kerry Eleveld, "Politicians, DADT Repeal Advocates React to Secy. Gates's Letter," *The Advocate*, April 30, 2010, http://www.advocate.com/News/Daily_News/2010/04/30/Gates_tells_Congress_Members_to_Keep_DADT_for_Now/.

56. On April being tense, Gates, *Duty*, 438–439.

57. On not having the votes to pass ENDA, background author interview with Democratic House aide, March 18, 2014 and background author interview with LGBT advocate, March 3, 2014.

58. Correspondence released by Senator Carl Levin's office: Senator Carl Levin, US Senate Committee on Armed Services, to Secretary Robert Gates, May 3, 2010, and Secretary Robert Gates, Secretary of Defense, to Senator Carl Levin, US Senate Committee on Armed Services, May 6, 2010, http://web.archive.org/web/20121214055202/http://www.levin.senate.gov/imo/media/doc/supporting/2010/letters.DADT.050710.pdf.

59. Frank Oliveri, "Levin Wants to Include Repeal of 'Don't Ask' in Authorization Bill," *Congressional Quarterly*, May 11, 2010, http://www.sldn.org/news/archives/congressional-quarterly-levin-wants-to-include-repeal-of-dont-ask-in-author/.

60. On Levin telling advocates about Gates's explanation, author interview with Alexander Nicholson, February 27, 2014.

61. On Hoyer/civil rights, background author interview with Democratic House aide, April 17, 2014; on Lieberman/civil rights, author interview with Clarine Nardi Riddle, chief of staff to Senator Lieberman, April 7, 2014.

62. On securing the votes, author interview with Todd Stein, legislative director to Senator Lieberman, April 7, 2014; on Murphy having the votes, Kerry Eleveld, "Skelton Quashes DADT Debate," *The Advocate*, May 19, 2010, http://www.advocate.com/News/Daily_News/2010/05/19/Skelton_Quashes _DADT_Debate/.

63. On Nicholson/delayed implementation, Kerry Eleveld, "Gay Military Group Pushes New Repeal Plan, *The Advocate*, February 10, 2010, http://www .advocate.com/news/daily-news/2010/02/10/gay-group-pushes-new-repeal -plan; on Stachelberg's twist, author interview with Winnie Stachelberg, July 1, 2014; see also, Alexander Nicholson, *Fighting to Serve* (Chicago: Chicago Press Review, 2012), 168–169.

64. The Department of Defense's Military Equal Opportunity (MEO) Program, *Department of Defense Directive 1020.02*, February 5, 2009, http://www .dtic.mil/whs/directives/corres/pdf/102002p.pdf.

65. On Hoyer/Gates conversations, author interview with Mariah Sixkiller, senior policy adviser to Representative Steny Hoyer, May 13, 2015, background author interview with Democratic House aide, April 17, 2014; on sending new language to the Department of Defense, ibid.; on Schiliro calling Hoyer's staff, background author interview with Democratic House aide, April 17, 2014.

66. Kerry Eleveld, "Discharges Might End, But Discrimination Might Not," Equality Matters, February 3, 2011, http://equalitymatters.org/blog /201102030001.

67. On groups summoned, Alexander Nicholson, *Fighting To Serve* (Chicago: Chicago Review Press, 2012), 171–173; on concurrent meetings, background author interview with Democratic House aide, April 17, 2014; see also, Kerry Eleveld, "A Deal on DADT?" *The Advocate*, May 24, 2010, http:// www.advocate.com/news/daily-news/2010/05/24/deal-dadt.

68. Letter from Peter Orszag, director of the Office of Management and Budget to Representative Patrick Murphy, May 24, 2010, http://www.scribd .com/doc/31896931/0524-Rep-Murphy; see also, Kerry Eleveld, "White House Green-Lights Repeal," *The Advocate*, May 24, 2010, http://www.advocate.com /news/daily-news/2010/05/24/white-house-green-lights-repeal.

69. Kerry Eleveld, "View from Washington: The DADT Deal," *The Advocate*, May 25, 2010, http://www.advocate.com/news/daily-news/2010/05/25 /view-washington-dadt-deal.

70. On Lieberman's office requesting, author interview with Todd Stein, legislative director to Senator Lieberman, April 7, 2014.

71. On Lieberman having the votes, ibid.

72. On Nelson, Igor Volsky, "After Robert Gates Endorses Compromise, Ben Nelson Says He Will Support DADT Repeal," ThinkProgress, May 26, 2010, http://thinkprogress.org/justice/2010/05/26/176803/nelson-dadt-gates/; on the Senate vote, Kerry Eleveld, "Congress Moves to End DADT," May 27, 2010, http://www.advocate.com/news/daily-news/2010/05/27/senate-committee-passes-dadt-amendment.on; the House vote, US House of Representatives, "Final Vote Results for Roll Call 317," May 27, 2010, http://clerk.house.gov/evs/2010/roll317.xml.

73. On Reid adding DREAM, Andrea Nill Sanchez, "Reid Announces He Will Include DREAM Act in Defense Authorization Bill," ThinkProgress, September 14, 2010, http://thinkprogress.org/security/2010/09/14/176270/reid-dream-act/; on the filibuster, US Senate, "US Senate Roll Call Votes 111th Congress—2nd Session," September 21, 2010, http://www.senate.gov/legislative/LIS/roll_call_lists/roll_call_vote_cfm.cfm?congress=111&session=2&vote=00238; see also, Matthew Jaffe and Devin Dwyer, "Senate Republicans Block Defense Bill," ABC News, September 21, 2010, http://abcnews.go.com/Politics/senate-vote-repeal-ban-gays-military/story?id=11685658.

74. On the order, John Schwartz, "Judge Orders U.S. Military to Stop 'Don't Ask, Don't Tell,'" New York Times, October 12, 2010, http://www.nytimes.com/2010/10/13/us/13military.html?pagewanted=all; on "pure panic," background author interview with a former Department of Defense official, March 19, 2014.

75. "Hearings Before the Committee on Armed Services, U.S. Senate, 111th Congress, Second Session: Statement of Hon. Jeh C. Johnson, General Counsel, Department of Defense," December 2 and 3, 2010.

76. On Solmonese, author review of notes from a meeting participant, dated October 26, 2010; see also, Nicholson, Fighting to Serve, 213.

77. On Frank, ibid. and background author interview with meeting participant, March 17, 2014.

78. On the exchange, ibid.

79. On Obama's response, background author interview with meeting participant, July 3, 2014.

80. On Obama/Gates agreeing on the study, Kerry Eleveld, "Obama: 'Prepared to Implement,'" The Advocate, December 22, 2010, http://www.advocate.com/news/news-features/2010/12/22/exclusive-interview-president-barack-obama-dadt; on the risk to military effectiveness, US Department of Defense, "Report of the Comprehensive Review of the Issues Associated with a Repeal of 'Don't Ask, Don't Tell,'" November 30, 2010, http://www.defense.gov/home/features/2010/0610_dadt/DADTReport_FINAL_20101130(secure-hires).pdf, 3; on the data, ibid., 68.

81. On urging the Senate, US Department of Defense, "DOD News Briefing with Secretary Gates and Adm. Mullen from the Pentagon," News Tran-

script, November 30, 2010, http://www.defense.gov/Transcripts/Transcript .aspx?TranscriptID=4728.

NOTES TO CHAPTER 6

1. Kerry Eleveld, "Obama on Marriage: 'Attitudes Evolve, Including Mine,'" *The Advocate*, October 27, 2010, http://www.advocate.com/news/daily-news /2010/10/27/obama-marriage-times-are-changing.

2. Ibid.

3. On Obama aides, author interview with Joe Sudbay, August 30, 2013.

4. On pickup, Josh Gerstein, "Obama Says He's Evolving on Gay Marriage," *Politico*, October 27, 2010, http://www.politico.com/blogs/joshgerstein/1010 /Obama_says_hes_evolving_on_gay_marriage.html.

5. Author review of Joe Sudbay's notes on the encounter, dated December 8, 2010.

6. On Obama unloading, author interview with Joe Sudbay, August 30, 2013.

7. On prioritizing START and tax cuts, White House, "Statement by the President after Meeting with Bipartisan Leadership," November 30, 2010; on Gibbs, Kerry Eleveld, "Gibbs: DADT Still a Priority," *The Advocate*, November 17, 2010, http://www.advocate.com/news/daily-news/2010/11/17/gibbs-says -dadt-still-priority; see also, "Press Gaggle by Press Secretary Robert Gibbs," White House, November 17, 2010; Kerry Eleveld, "Plan B for DADT?" *The Advocate*, December 1, 2010, http://www.advocate.com/news/daily-news /2010/12/01/plan-b-dadt; "Press Briefing by Press Secretary Robert Gibbs," White House, December 1, 2010.

8. On the White House/Senate negotiators, Sheryl Gay Stolberg and David M. Herszenhorn, "In Health Talks, President Is Hands-Off No More," *New York Times*, January 16, 2010.

9. On not shooting down DADT, Kerry Eleveld, "Gibbs: DADT Still a Priority," *The Advocate*, November 17, 2010, http://www.advocate.com/news/daily -news/2010/11/17/gibbs-says-dadt-still-priority; see also, "Press Gaggle by Press Secretary Robert Gibbs," White House, November 17, 2010; Kerry Eleveld, "Plan B for DADT?" *The Advocate*, December 1, 2010, http://www.advocate .com/news/daily-news/2010/12/01/plan-b-dadt.

10. On no mention, Kerry Eleveld, "View from Washington: Dead Duck," *The Advocate*, December 6, 2010, http://www.advocate.com/news/2010/12/06 /view-washington-dadt-dead-duck; see also, C-SPAN, "Senate Session, December 4, 2010," (Time: 2:40:00), http://www.c-span.org/video/?296907-1/senate-session.

11. Ibid.

12. Kerry Eleveld, "View from Washington: Dead Duck," *The Advocate*, December 6, 2010, http://www.advocate.com/news/2010/12/06/view -washington-dadt-dead-duck.

13. Kerry Eleveld, "Reid, Collins Negotiate on DADT," *The Advocate*, December 8, 2010, http://www.advocate.com/news/daily-news/2010/12/08/reid-collins-negotiate-dadt.

14. On the vote, US Senate, "Roll Call Votes 111th Congress—2nd Session," December 9, 2010, https://www.senate.gov/legislative/LIS/roll_call_lists/roll_call_vote_cfm.cfm?congress=111&session=2&vote=00270.

15. On the press conference, "DADT Press Conference," YouTube, uploaded December 10, 2010, https://www.youtube.com/watch?v=PA6lcGsJkG0; see also, Kerry Eleveld, "Senate DADT Vote Fails," *The Advocate*, December 9, 2010, http://www.advocate.com/news/daily-news/2010/12/09/senate-dadt-vote-fails; on GOP tax pledge, Alan Silverleib, "Senate GOP Pledges to Block All Bills Until Tax Dispute Resolved," CNN, December 1, 2010, http://www.cnn.com/2010/POLITICS/12/01/gop.senate.demands/.

16. On Lieberman saying for weeks, Kerry Eleveld, "Lieberman on DADT: We Have 60," *The Advocate*, November 18, 2010, http://www.advocate.com/news/daily-news/2010/11/18/lieberman-dadt-we-have-60-votes; on Lieberman's strategy, author interview with Todd Stein, legislative director to Senator Lieberman, April 7, 2014.

17. "DADT Press Conference," YouTube, uploaded December 10, 2010, https://www.youtube.com/watch?v=PA6lcGsJkG0.

18. On being hastily arranged, author interview with Todd Stein, legislative director to Senator Lieberman, April 7, 2014; on contacting Collins, ibid.; on only discussing Plan B internally, ibid.

19. On meeting with Powell, "Remarks by the President and General Colin Powell After Meeting," White House, December 1, 2010.

20. On Gibbs, Kerry Eleveld, "Gibbs: START's Up Next," *The Advocate*, December 13, 2010, http://www.advocate.com/news/daily-news/2010/12/13/gibbs-start-next; see also, "Press Briefing by Press Secretary Robert Gibbs," White House, December 13, 2010.

21. Ibid.

22. On taxes, Kim Dixon and Richard Cowan, "Senate Passes $858 Billion Tax-Cut Plan," Reuters, December 15, 2010; on Brown, Murkowski, and Snowe, Jennifer Steinhauer, "House Easily Passes 'Don't Ask, Don't Tell' Repeal," December 15, 2010, http://thecaucus.blogs.nytimes.com/2010/12/15/house-easily-passes-dont-ask-dont-tell-repeal/.

23. On fewer procedural hurdles and House passage, ibid.

24. "Press Briefing by Press Secretary Robert Gibbs, Secretary of State Clinton, Secretary of Defense Gates and General Cartwright," White House, December 16, 2010.

25. On Reid's comment, Kerry Eleveld, "Will Reid Schedule a Vote or Not?" *The Advocate*, December 16, 2010, http://www.advocate.com/news/daily-news/2010/12/16/will-reid-schedule-vote-or-not.

26. On $8 billion in earmarks, John Fritze, "GOP Senators Slam $1.1 Trillion Spending Bill," *USA Today*, December 15, 2010.

27. On McConnell's one-eighty and Reid pulling the bill, David Rogers, "Democrats Concede Budget Fight to Republicans," *Politico*, December 16, 2010, http://www.politico.com/news/stories/1210/46520.html; see also, Robert Costa and Andrew Stiles, "National Review: How the Omnibus Fell," NPR, December 17, 2010, http://www.npr.org/2010/12/17/132132081/national-review-how-the-omnibus-fell.

28. Kerry Eleveld, "Gibbs Bullish on DADT," *The Advocate*, December 17, 2010, http://www.advocate.com/news/daily-news/2010/12/17/gibbs-bullish-dadt.

29. On Lieberman's staff, author interview with Todd Stein, legislative director to Senator Lieberman, April 7, 2014.

30. "Graham Shrugs Off Gaga," YouTube, uploaded September 21, 2010, https://www.youtube.com/watch?t=38&v=6Rnh10RpphY.

31. On documented cases, Nathaniel Frank, *Unfriendly Fire: How the Gay Ban Undermines the Military and Weakens America* (New York: Thomas Dunne Books, 2009), 178–183.

32. "McCain Defends DADT," YouTube, uploaded September 21, 2010, https://www.youtube.com/watch?v=By-ohi3vO2w.

33. On thirteen thousand, Brian Witte, "Admirals, Generals: Repeal 'Don't Ask, Don't Tell,'" Associated Press, November 17, 2008.

34. YouTube, "McCain Defends DADT," uploaded September 21, 2010, https://www.youtube.com/watch?v=By-ohi3vO2w; see also, Andy Towle, "Watch: McCain Lies, Gets Testy with Journalists over 'DADT' Facts," Towleroad, September 21, 2010, http://www.towleroad.com/2010/09/watch-mccain-lies-gets-testy-with-journalists-over-dadt-facts.html.

35. On Almy, "Hearing Before the Committee on Armed Services, US Senate, 111th Congress, Second Session," March 18, 2010, http://www.gpo.gov/fdsys/pkg/CHRG-111shrg57495/html/CHRG-111shrg57495.htm.

36. Joe Sudbay, "When Kerry Eleveld Wouldn't Let John McCain Lie About DADT," AMERICAblog, September 21, 2010, http://americablog.com/2010/09/when-kerry-eleveld-wouldnt-let-john-mccain-lie-about-dadt.html.

37. Ron Wyden, "Senate Clears Path to End 'Don't Ask, Don't Tell,'" December 18, 2010, http://www.wyden.senate.gov/news/press-releases/senate-clears-path-to-end-dont-ask-dont-tell.

38. On Lieberman walking, author interview with Clarine Nardi Riddle, chief of staff to Senator Lieberman, April 7, 2014.

39. C-SPAN, "Senate Debate on Don't Ask, Don't Tell and the DREAM Act," December 18, 2010, http://www.c-span.org/video/?297168-4/senate-debate-dont-ask-dont-tell-dream-act.

40. US Senate, "Roll Call Votes 111th Congress - 2nd Session, H.R. 2965," December 18, 2010, http://www.senate.gov/legislative/LIS/roll_call_lists/roll_call_vote_cfm.cfm?congress=111&session=2&vote=00279.

41. On the vote, ibid.; Servicemembers Legal Defense Network, "Dixon Steps Down," April 23, 2007, http://www.sldn.org/blog/archives/dixon-steps -down/.

NOTES TO CHAPTER 7

1. On Lieutenant Hester, "Freeheld: About the Film," Freeheld.com, accessed July 8, 2014, http://www.freeheld.com/film.html.

2. Randy Shilts, *The Mayor of Castro Street: The Life and Times of Harvey Milk* (New York, St. Martin's Press, 1982), 365.

3. On *Newsweek*, "*Newsweek* Poll: Support for Gay Marriage Grows," *Newsweek*, December 4, 2008, http://www.newsweek.com/newsweek-poll -support-gay-marriage-grows-83187; on the Public Religion Research Institute Poll, "Survey—A Shifting Landscape: A Decade of Change in American Attitudes About Same-Sex Marriage and LGBT Issues," Public Religion Research Institute, accessed July 8, 2014, http://publicreligion.org/research /2014/02/2014-lgbt-survey/.

4. On Bush/Cheney, Robin Toner, "Cheney Stakes Out Stance on Gay Marriages," *New York Times*, August 25, 2004, http://www.nytimes.com/2004/08/25 /politics/campaign/25cheney.html.

5. "Strong Support for Gay Marriage Now Matches Strong Opposition," Pew Research Center, accessed June 6, 2015, http://www.pewresearch .org/daily-number/strong-support-for-gay-marriage-now-matches-strong -opposition/.

6. The Center for Information and Research on Civic Learning and Engagement, "New Census Data Confirm Increase in Youth Voter Turnout in 2008 Election," accessed April 14, 2015, http://www.civicyouth.org/new -census-data-confirm-increase-in-youth-voter-turnout-in-2008-election/.

7. On hospital visitation, "Presidential Memorandum—Hospital Visitation," White House, accessed June 13, 2014, http://www.whitehouse.gov/the-press -office/presidential-memorandum-hospital-visitation; on the Langbehn article, Tara Parker-Pope, "Kept from a Dying Partner's Bedside," *New York Times*, May 18, 2009, http://www.nytimes.com/2009/05/19/health/19well.html?_r=0.

8. Tara Parker-Pope, "No Visiting Rights for Hospital Trauma Patients," *New York Times*, September, 30, 2009, http://well.blogs.nytimes.com/2009/09/30 /no-visiting-rights-for-hospital-patients/.

9. On Rahm handing off the article, background author interview with a former White House official, June 1, 2014; on the poll, "*Newsweek* Poll: Support for Gay Marriage Grows," *Newsweek*, December 4, 2008, http://www .newsweek.com/newsweek-poll-support-gay-marriage-grows-83187.

10. On the second case, "AG Coakley's Fight for Marriage Equality," Attorney General of Massachusetts, accessed April 14, 2015, http://www.mass.gov/ago

/news-and-updates/initiatives/doma/; see also, "Massachusetts Attorney General Martha Coakley Files Constitutional Challenge to Federal Defense of Marriage Act," Attorney General of Massachusetts, accessed June 16, 2014, http://www.mass.gov/ago/news-and-updates/press-releases/2009/ag-coakley -files-constitutional-challenge-to.html#materials.

11. *Gill v. Office of Personnel Management*, 699 F. Supp. 2d 374, (D. Mass. 2010).

12. On being "too narrow," *Romer v. Evans*, 517 U.S. 620 (1996); on DOMA, "PUBLIC LAW 104–199—SEPT. 21, 1996," US Government Printing Office, accessed June 16, 2014, http://www.gpo.gov/fdsys/pkg/PLAW-104publ199 /pdf/PLAW-104publ199.pdf.

13. On being the first federal case, "Prop 8 Trial Set to Begin Monday in San Francisco," *Bay City News*, January 10, 2010, http://abclocal.go.com/story ?section=news/state&id=7211121.

14. On the 136-page ruling, "U.S. District Court Decision: *Perry v. Schwarzenegger*," *New York Times*, http://documents.nytimes.com/us-districtcourt-decision-perry -v-schwarzenegger.

15. Ibid.

16. Ibid.

17. Ibid.

18. On Lamb, Court Transcript, *Perry v. Schwarzenegger*, Trial-Day 05, January 15, 2010, http://www.afer.org/wp-content/uploads/2010/01/2010–01–15 -Perry-Trial-Day-05-Lamb-Zia-mini.pdf; see also, Bob Egelko, "Gays Make Fine Parents, Psychologist Testifies," *San Francisco Chronicle*, January 16, 2010, http://www.sfgate.com/nation/article/Gays-make-fine-parents-psychologist -testifies-3275685.php.

19. On Walker, ibid.

20. "U.S. District Court Decision: *Perry v. Schwarzenegger*," *New York Times*, http://documents.nytimes.com/us-district-court-decision-perry-v -schwarzenegger.

21. On the leak, Andrew Harmon, "Proposition 8 Overturned," *The Advocate*, August 4, 2010, http://www.advocate.com/news/daily-news/2010/08/04 /breaking-prop-8-overturned; see also, Eli Sanders, "Prop 8 (Reportedly) Ruled Unconstitutional," *The Stranger*, August 4, 2010, http://slog.thestranger.com /slog/archives/2010/08/04/prop-8-reportedly-ruled-unconstitutional.

22. On the statement, Kerry Eleveld, "White House Statement on Prop 8," *The Advocate*, August 4, 2010, http://www.advocate.com/news/daily-news /2010/08/04/white-house-statement-prop-8.

23. On Guthrie, "Transcript: David Axelrod on MSNBC's 'The Daily Rundown,'" *NBC News*, August 5, 2010, http://www.nbcnews.com/id/38578941 /ns/nbc_press/t/transcript-david-axelrod-msnbcs-daily-rundown/#.U6nLuii Chpz.

24. Ibid.

25. On Obama's remarks, "Transcript: Jake Tapper Interviews Barack Obama," *ABC News*, June 16, 2008, http://abcnews.go.com/WN/Politics/story ?id=5178123&page=1&singlePage=true.

26. On the White House lawyers' conclusions, background author interview with a former White House official, June 1, 2014; on the first brief, ibid.

27. On concluding a reasonable argument could not be made, ibid; on believing heightened scrutiny was the proper test, ibid.

28. On the 'deep recognition,' ibid.

29. On the binder, ibid; on the letter being statutory protocol, 28 U.S.C., Sec. 530D, "Report on Enforcement of Laws," US Government Printing Office, accessed June 18, 2014, http://www.gpo.gov/fdsys/pkg/USCODE-2011-title28 /html/USCODE-2011-title28-partII-chap31-sec530D.htm; on nearly every president, "Duty to Defend: Letter from Andrew Fois to Orrin G. Hatch," Journal of Law, accessed June 17, 2014, http://journaloflaw.us/1%20Pub.%20 L.%20Misc./1–1/JoL1–1,%20PLM1–1,%20%20Fois%20to%20Hatch%20 1996.pdf.

30. On two federal appellate judges, Carol J. Williams, "Rulings on Gay Couples' Spousal Benefits Question the Defense of Marriage Act," *Los Angeles Times*, February 6, 2009, http://articles.latimes.com/2009/feb/06/local/me -marriage-act6.

31. On never considering not enforcing, background author interview with a former White House official, June 1, 2014.

32. On the White House lawyers/heightened scrutiny, background author interview with a former White House official, June 1, 2014.

33. On the August 10, 2010, meeting, background author interview with LGBT legal advocate, May 28, 2014, background author interview with LGBT legal advocate, June 2, 2014, background author interview with LGBT legal advocate, June 3, 2014, and author correspondence with LGBT legal advocate, October 9, 2014.

34. On there only being one possible outcome, ibid.

35. On not being able to indefinitely duck, ibid.

36. On White House lawyers deciding by Fall 2009, background author interview with a former White House official, June 1, 2014.

37. On Kneedler, "2014 Finalist—Career Achievement Medal," Service to America Medals, accessed June 19, 2014, http://servicetoamericamedals.org /SAM/finalists/cam/kneedler.shtml; on the Solicitor General's Office purpose, "About the Office (of the Solicitor General)," US Department of Justice, accessed June 19, 2014, http://www.justice.gov/osg/about-osg.html; on the Solicitor General's Office structure, Organizational Chart, US Department of Justice, accessed June 19, 2014, http://www.justice.gov/jmd/mps/manual/orgcharts/osg.gif.

38. On Katyal replacing Kagan, "Indian American Legal Eagle Will Be Acting Solicitor General," *The Economic Times*, May 19, 2010, http://articles

.economictimes.indiatimes.com/2010-05-19/news/28399528_1_solicitor
-general-elena-kagan-neal-kumar-katyal-top-legal-counsel; on the back and
forth with Katyal/Kneedler, background author interview with a former
White House official, June 1, 2014; on Kneedler being strongest proponent,
background author interview with former White House official, June 1, 2014,
and background author interview with an LGBT legal advocate, May 28, 2014;
on Katyal concurring: background author interview with a former White
House official, June 1, 2014; see also Sari Horwitz, "Justice Department Debated Handling of Law Denying Benefits to Gay Couples," *Washington Post*,
June 27, 2013, http://www.washingtonpost.com/world/national-security/justice
-department-had-debated-handling-of-law-denying-benefits-to-gay-couples
/2013/06/27/06e56304-df4d-11e2-b94a-452948b95ca8_story.html.

39. On the memos, background author interview with a former White
House official, June 1, 2014.

40. On the White House lawyers memo, background author interview with
a former White House official, June 1, 2014.

41. On Univision/Ebony, Amanda Terkel, "Obama to Be First President to
Appear on Univision's Sunday Public Affairs Show, Al Punto," ThinkProgress,
September 18, 2009, http://thinkprogress.org/politics/2009/09/18/60944
/obama-al-punto/; press release from EBONY magazine, "Ebony® Magazine's
January 2009 Barack Obama Collector's Issue Breaks Sales Records," *Ebony*, February 12, 2009, http://www.gwu.edu/~action/2008/media08/ebony021209
.html; see also, Rachel L. Swarns, "Obama Brings Flush Times for Black News
Media," *New York Times*, March 27, 2009, http://www.nytimes.com/2009/03/28
/business/media/28press.html.

42. On the candidate questionnaire, "Obama Once Backed Full Gay Marriage," *Windy City Times*, accessed July 2, 2014, http://www.windycitymedia
group.com/gay/lesbian/news/ARTICLE.php?AID=20229.

43. On the 2013 study, "New Patterns of Poverty in the Lesbian, Gay, and Bisexual Community," June 2013, The Williams Institute, http://williamsinstitute
.law.ucla.edu/wp-content/uploads/LGB-Poverty-Update-Jun-2013.pdf.

44. On the 2013 study, "A Broken Bargain for Transgender Workers," September 2013, Movement Advancement Project, http://www.lgbtmap.org/file
/a-broken-bargain-for-transgender-workers.pdf.

45. Kerry Eleveld, "Obama: 'Prepared to Implement,'" *The Advocate*, December 22, 2010, http://www.advocate.com/news/news-features/2010/12/22
/exclusive-interview-president-barack-obama-dadt.

46. Ibid.

47. Ibid.

48. Ibid.

49. On "It's a lot of pressure," author review of audio from the interview,
December 21, 2010.

NOTES TO CHAPTER 8

1. On pushing the administration right from the outset of 2011, Kerry Eleveld, "Next Up for Obama: Marriage Equality for Gay Americans," *Washington Post*, January 21, 2011, http://www.washingtonpost.com/wp-dyn/content/article/2011/01/20/AR2011012005148.html.

2. On alienating black voters, Josh Kraushaar, "Why Obama Isn't Backing Gay Marriage," *The Atlantic*, March 23, 2012, http://www.theatlantic.com/politics/archive/2012/03/why-obama-isnt-backing-gay-marriage/255002/.

3. On 68 percent support for open service, "CBS News Poll—The Republican Nomination Race: Romney, Cain Move to the Top," *CBS News*, accessed July 23, 2014, http://www.cbsnews.com/htdocs/pdf/TheRepublicanRace.pdf; on the Kaiser poll, "Kaiser Health Tracking Poll—September 2011," Kaiser Family Foundation, accessed July 23, 2014, http://kff.org/health-reform/poll-finding/kaiser-health-tracking-poll-september-2011/.

4. On no member of Congress being targeted, author interview with Aubrey Sarvis, September 15, 2014.

5. On the rift at the Justice Department, Jo Becker, *Forcing the Spring* (New York: Penguin Press, 2014), 256–257; on the Civil Division/heightened scrutiny, ibid., 256; on the Solicitor General's office, ibid.

6. On the Department of Justice calling Kaplan, author interview with Roberta Kaplan, August 24, 2013.

7. Ibid.

8. Ibid.

9. On being mindblowing, author interview with James Esseks, director of the ACLU Lesbian Gay Bisexual Transgender & AIDS Project, May 30, 2014; on Esseks/Kaplan and the New York marriage case, Anemoma Hartocollis, "New York Judges Reject Any Right to Gay Marriage," *New York Times*, July 7, 2006, http://www.nytimes.com/2006/07/07/nyregion/07marriage.html?pagewanted=all.

10. On Kaplan's reaction, Kerry Eleveld, "It's All About Edie," *The Advocate*, March 21, 2013, http://www.advocate.com/politics/marriage-equality/2013/03/21/supreme-court-case-lawyer-says-its-all-about-edie.

11. "Letter from the Attorney General to Congress on Litigation Involving the Defense of Marriage Act," US Department of Justice, February 23, 2011, http://www.justice.gov/opa/pr/letter-attorney-general-congress-litigation-involving-defense-marriage-act.

12. On Gallup, "For First Time, Majority of Americans Favor Legal Gay Marriage," Gallup, accessed July 9, 2014, http://www.gallup.com/poll/147662/first-time-majority-americans-favor-legal-gay-marriage.aspx; on Pew, "Behind Gay Marriage Momentum, Regional Gaps Persist," Pew Research Center for People and the Press, accessed July 9, 2014, http://www.people-press.org/2012/11/09/behind-gay-marriage-momentum-regional-gaps-persist/.

13. On Silver, Nate Silver, "Gay Marriage Opponents Now in Minority," *New York Times*, April 20, 2011, http://fivethirtyeight.blogs.nytimes.com/2011/04/20 /gay-marriage-opponents-now-in-minority/?_php=true&_type=blogs&_r=0.

14. Kerry Eleveld, "Obama and Religion: Where Will He Stand on Same-Sex Marriage in 2012?" Equality Matters, March 10, 2011, http://equalitymatters .org/blog/201103100012.

15. Kerry Eleveld, "What Will Obama Tell the Gays Under the Shadow of Lady Liberty?" Equality Matters, June 21, 2011, http://equalitymatters.org/blog /201106210015.

16. "Remarks by the President at a DNC Event," White House, June 23, 2011, http://www.whitehouse.gov/the-press-office/2011/06/23/remarks-president -dnc-event.

17. Author interview with Joy Tomchin, May 2, 2014; "Obama Gets Heckled About Gay Marriage at LGBT Reception June 23, 2011," YouTube, uploaded June 24, 2011, https://www.youtube.com/watch?v=94Z7X80p4cw; Kerry Eleveld, "Can Obama Bridge the Enthusiasm Gap?" Equality Matters, June 24, 2011, http://equalitymatters.org/blog/201106240016.

18. Author interview with Joy Tomchin, May 2, 2014.

19. "Remarks by the President at a DNC Event," White House, June 23, 2011, http://www.whitehouse.gov/the-press-office/2011/06/23/remarks-president -dnc-event.

20. "President Obama's Remarks at the 2011 LGBT Dinner in New York," YouTube, uploaded June 23, 2011, https://www.youtube.com/watch?v =tf5mmSQXHeA&app=desktop.

21. On progressive commentators, Greg Sargent, "The Morning Plum: Obama Hints He'll Come Out for Gay Marriage in Second Term," *Washington Post*, June 24, 2011, http://www.washingtonpost.com/blogs/plum-line/post/the -morning-plum/2011/03/03/AGJVQsiH_blog.html.

22. Kerry Eleveld, "Can Obama Bridge the Enthusiasm Gap?" Equality Matters, June 24, 2011, http://equalitymatters.org/blog/201106240016.

23. On not trusting Cuomo, Jen Chung, "Ed Koch Held Decades-Long Grudge Against Cuomos over 'Vote for Cuomo, Not the Homo' Posters," Gothamist, February 1, 2013, http://gothamist.com/2013/02/01/ed_koch _forgave_mario_and_andrew_fo.php.

24. On the March 9 meeting, Michael Barbaro, "Cuomo, in Push to Legalize Gay Marriage, Will Hold a Strategy Session with Advocates," *New York Times*, March 9, 2011, http://query.nytimes.com/gst/fullpage.html?res=980CE5DE1 F39F93AA35750C0A9679D8B63; on soaring in the polls, "Cuomo Ratings at All-Time High & 72 Percent Support His Budget," Siena College Research Institute, accessed July 22, 2014, http://www2.siena.edu/uploadedfiles/home /Parents_and_Community/Community_Page/SRI/SNY_Poll/SNYFeb2011Poll ReleaseFinalC.pdf.

25. On Spitzer's push, Danny Hakim, "Spitzer Vows to Push for Gay Marriage," *New York Times*, October 7, 2006, http://www.nytimes.com/2006/10/07/nyregion/07gays.html; on Paterson's failed attempt, Jeremy Peters, "New York State Senate Votes Down Gay Marriage Bill," *New York Times*, December 2, 2009, http://www.nytimes.com/2009/12/03/nyregion/03marriage.html?_r=0; on Paterson's quote: Kerry Eleveld, "Could Spitzer's Woes Have a Silver Lining?" *The Advocate*, March 10, 2008, http://web.archive.org/web/20080925090053/http://www.advocate.com/exclusive_detail_ektid52612.asp.

26. On the June 2009 poll, "New York State Voters Support Same-Sex Marriage, Quinnipiac University Poll Finds," Quinnipiac University, accessed July 25, 2014, http://www.quinnipiac.edu/news-and-events/quinnipiac-university-poll/ohio/release-detail?ReleaseID=1340.

27. On Tim Gill starting the PAC, Kerry Eleveld, "New York Fights Back," *The Advocate*, March 17, 2010, http://www.advocate.com/news/daily-news/2010/03/17/new-york-fights-back?page=0,0; on the PAC intake, "Campaign Financial Disclosure—List of All Contributors to Fight Back New York," New York State Board of Elections, accessed July 25, 2014, http://www.elections.ny.gov:8080/plsql_browser/CONTRIBUTORA_COUNTY?ID_in=A75577&date_From=10/10/2009&date_to=06/01/2011&AMOUNT_From=1.00&AMOUNT_to=900,000.00&ZIP1=&ZIP2=&ORDERBY_IN=A&CATEGORY_IN=ALL.

28. On the unseating of three lawmakers, Jacob Gershman, "Gay Marriage Voted In," *Wall Street Journal*, June 25, 2011, http://online.wsj.com/news/articles/SB10001424052702303339904576406201312879150; on flooding the district, Kerry Eleveld, "New York Fights Back," The Advocate, March 17, 2010, http://www.advocate.com/news/daily-news/2010/03/17/new-york-fights-back?page=0,0; on Monserrate losing, "Statement of Canvass—13th Senate District," New York State Board of Elections, accessed July 28, 2014, http://www.elections.ny.gov/NYSBOE/Elections/2010/Special/13thSDResults.pdf; on Stachowski/Padavan, "NYS Senate Election Returns for November 2, 2010," New York State Board of Elections, accessed July 28, 2014, http://www.elections.ny.gov/NYSBOE/elections/2010/general/2010SenateRecertified09122012.pdf.

29. On raising $1.5 million, author interview with Ken Mehlman, August 8, 2014.

30. Kerry Eleveld, "View from Washington: Duel," *The Advocate*, September 24, 2010, http://www.advocate.com/news/2010/09/24/view-washington-duel?page=full.

31. On the contributions of Singer/others, background author interview with an adviser to Paul Singer, July 29, 2014; Nicholas Confessore and Michael Barbaro, "Donors to G.O.P. Are Backing Gay Marriage Push," *New York Times*, May 13, 2011, http://www.nytimes.com/2011/05/14/nyregion/donors-to-gop-are-backing-gay-marriage-push.html?pagewanted=all.

32. On Mehlman disclosing, Marc Ambinder, "Bush Campaign Chief and Former RNC Chair Ken Mehlman: I'm Gay," *The Atlantic*, August 25, 2010, http://www.theatlantic.com/politics/archive/2010/08/bush-campaign-chief-and-former-rnc-chair-ken-mehlman-im-gay/62065/; on Mehlman's regrets, Kerry Eleveld, "The Ken Mehlman Interview," *The Advocate*, August 26, 2010, http://www.advocate.com/news/daily-news/2010/08/26/ken-mehlman-interview.

33. On raising $750,000, Jennifer Bendery, "Rufus Gifford: The Man Behind Obama's Historic Fundraising Machine," Huffington Post, November 10, 2011, http://www.huffingtonpost.com/2011/11/10/rufus-gifford-obama-fundraising_n_1086188.html.

34. On the final vote tally, "Bill A8354–2011—Enacts the Marriage Equality Act Relating to Ability of Individuals to Marry," New York State Senate, accessed July 28, 2014, http://open.nysenate.gov/legislation/bill/A8354–2011; on Skelos, "Statement from Senate Majority Leader Dean Skelos on Same-Sex Marriage Legislation," New York State Senate, accessed July 29, 2014, http://www.nysenate.gov/press-release/statement-senate-majority-leader-dean-skelos-same-sex-marriage-legislation; on the GOP caucus debate, Nicholas Confessore and Michael Barbaro, "New York Allows Same-Sex Marriage, Becoming Largest State to Pass Law," *New York Times*, June 24, 2011, http://www.nytimes.com/2011/06/25/nyregion/gay-marriage-approved-by-new-york-senate.html?pagewanted=all.

35. Author interview with Steven M. Cohen, secretary to Governor Andrew Cuomo, January 25, 2012.

36. On the moment Cohen wouldn't forget, ibid.

NOTES TO CHAPTER 9

1. Nate Silver, "Cuomo's Presidential Moment Forms Contrast with Obama," *New York Times*, June 25, 2011, http://fivethirtyeight.blogs.nytimes.com/2011/06/25/cuomos-presidential-moment-forms-contrast-with-obama/.

2. Maureen Dowd, "Why Is He Bi? (Sigh)," *New York Times*, June 25, 2011, http://www.nytimes.com/2011/06/26/opinion/sunday/26dowd.html.

3. Dana Milbank, "On Same-Sex Marriage, Obama Still Has Cold Feet," *Washington Post*, June 28, 2011, http://www.washingtonpost.com/opinions/on-same-sex-marriage-obama-still-has-cold-feet/2011/06/28/AGmAlmpH_story.html; on "leading from behind," Ryan Lizza, "The Consequentialist," *New Yorker*, May 2, 2011, http://www.newyorker.com/magazine/2011/05/02/the-consequentialist.

4. Andrew Sullivan, "A President, Not a Governor," Daily Beast, June 29, 2011, http://dish.andrewsullivan.com/2011/06/29/a-president-not-a-governor/.

5. Ibid.

6. Kerry Eleveld, "Why Obama Must Endorse Gay Marriage," Daily Beast, July 6, 2011, http://www.thedailybeast.com/articles/2011/07/06/obama-argues-federalist-approach-but-states-rights-wrong-for-marriage-equality.html.

7. Ibid.

8. On Plouffe/Cutter saying Obama would evolve, background author interview with a Democratic consultant, June 13, 2014; background author interview with a Democratic operative, August 14, 2014; on advising Obama to come out, ibid.

9. Background author interview with a Democratic consultant, June 13, 2014.

10. On Mehlman talking to a dozen Republicans, author interview with Ken Mehlman, August 8, 2014.

11. On more upsides than downsides, ibid.

12. On Obama's speech, "Transcript of Obama speech," *Politico*, March 18, 2008, http://www.politico.com/news/stories/0308/9100.html.

13. On switching positions soon, author interview with Ken Mehlman, August 8, 2014.

14. "Press Conference by the President," White House, June 29, 2011, https://www.whitehouse.gov/the-press-office/2011/06/29/press-conference -president.

15. Ibid.

16. Ibid.

17. Ibid.

18. Ibid.

19. Mark Halperin and John Heilemann, *Double Down* (New York: Penguin Press, 2013), 160.

20. On wanting to be asked about being a state legislator, background author interview with a Democratic operative, August 14, 2014.

21. On internal polling, background author interview with a Democratic operative, August 14, 2014; on Obama winning youth voters, "Young Voters Supported Obama Less, But May Have Mattered More," Pew Research Center for the People and the Press, accessed August 19, 2014, http://www.people-press.org /2012/11/26/young-voters-supported-obama-less-but-may-have-mattered-more/.

22. On what Mehlman drew from, author interview with Ken Mehlman, August 8, 2014; on the e-mail, ibid. and Jo Becker, *Forcing the Spring* (New York: Penguin Press, 2014), 291–292.

23. Becker, *Forcing the Spring*, 291–292.

24. On Wolfson/Jarrett conversations, Molly Ball, "The Marriage Plot: Inside This Year's Epic Campaign for Gay Equality," *The Atlantic*, December 11, 2012, http://www.theatlantic.com/politics/archive/2012/12/the-marriage-plot -inside-this-years-epic-campaign-for-gay-equality/265865/; on Plouffe/Axelrod and data, background author interview with Democratic operative, August 14, 2014, background author interview with Democratic consultant, June 13, 2014, and see also, Halperin and Heilemann, *Double Down*, 634–635; on Cutter, background author interview with Democratic consultant, June 13, 2014; on Messina being most nervous, background author interview with Democratic

operative, August 14, 2014, and see also, Halperin and Heilemann, *Double Down*, 634–635.

25. On Minnesota, Tim Nelson, "House Sends Same-Sex Marriage Ban to 2012 Ballot," *MPR News*, http://www.mprnews.org/story/2011/05/22 /house-approves-marriage-amendment; on Maine, Esmé E Deprez, "Maine Gay Rights Groups Submit Names for Marriage Referendum," *Bloomberg News*, January 16, 2012, http://www.bloomberg.com/news/articles/2012-01-26/maine -gay-rights-groups-submit-105-000-names-to-back-marriage-referendum; Elaine Thompson, "Washington State Lawmakers Pass Gay Marriage Bill," Associated Press, February 9, 2012; Aaron Davis, "Maryland Senate Passes Same-Sex Marriage Bill," *Washington Post*, February 23, 2012, http://www .washingtonpost.com/local/md-politics/maryland-senate-passes-same-sex -marriage-bill/2012/02/23/gIQAfbakWR_story.html.

26. On the amendment's coinciding with Republican primary, Marc Solomon, "Op-Ed: Trouble in the Tar Heel State," *The Advocate*, September 19, 2011, http://www.advocate.com/politics/commentary/2011/09/19/trouble-tar-heel -state; on the amendment polling, Public Policy Polling, "N.C. GOP Legislators' Popularity in the Toilet," January 12, 2012, http://www.publicpolicypolling .com/pdf/2011/PPP_Release_NC_011212.pdf; Public Policy Polling, "Marriage Amendment Leading by 24, Perdue Down," November 4, 2011, http://www .publicpolicypolling.com/main/2011/11/marriage-amendment-leading-by-24 -perdue-down-9.html.

27. On the "get out the vote" e-mails, Joe Sudbay, "OFA Tells Mainers to Get Out and Vote Without Mentioning Anti-Gay Ballot Measure," AMERICAblog, November 2, 2009, http://americablog.com/2009/11/ofa-tells-mainers-to-get -out-and-vote-without-mentioning-anti-gay-ballot-measure.html; on Jeremy Kennedy, who was heading up: Andrew Harmon, "Will The Democrats Pony Up?" February 2, 2012, *The Advocate*, http://www.advocate.com/news/2012/02/02 /will-democrats-pony.

28. On winning North Carolina in 2008, Micah Cohen, "In North Carolina, Obama's 2008 Victory Was Ahead of Schedule," *New York Times*, September 4, 2012, http://fivethirtyeight.blogs.nytimes.com/2012/09/04/in-north-carolina -obamas-2008-victory-was-ahead-of-schedule/.

29. On the marriage plank initiative, "Democrats: Say I Do," Freedom to Marry, accessed October 1, 2014, http://www.freedomtomarry.org/blog/entry /democrats-say-i-do.

30. Ibid.

31. On letting Democratic Party/White House officials know in advance, author interview with Evan Wolfson, August 22, 2014.

32. On Wolfson's thesis, Adam Polaski, "Evan Wolfson's 1983 Thesis on the Freedom to Marry Featured in Harvard Law Library," Freedom to Marry, April 2, 2013, http://www.freedomtomarry.org/blog/entry/evan-wolfsons-1983 -thesis-on-the-freedom-to-marry-featured-in-harvard-law-l.

33. On Freedom to Marry's two goals, author interview with Evan Wolfson, August 22, 2014; on Democrats' 2000 platform, "Democratic Party Platform of 2000," The American Presidency Project, August 14, 2000, http://www.presidency.ucsb.edu/ws/?pid=29612.

34. On Villaraigosa, "New Report: Moving Marriage Forward," Freedom to Marry, accessed September 24, 2014, http://www.freedomtomarry.org/blog/entry/new-report-moving-marriage-forward.

35. On Yellin, Chris Johnson, "Obama Campaign Ducks Question on Marriage in Dem Platform," Washington Blade, March 7, 2012, http://www.washingtonblade.com/2012/03/07/obama-campaign-chief-ducks-question-on-marriage-plank-in-dem-platform/.

36. Ibid.

37. "'This Week' Transcript: David Plouffe and Rep. Michele Bachmann," ABC News, March 25, 2012, http://abcnews.go.com/Politics/week-transcript-david-plouffe-rep-michele-bachmann/story?id=15987702.

38. Ibid.

39. On polling showing solid Democratic majorities, "Half of Americans Support Legal Gay Marriages," Gallup, accessed September 2, 2014, http://www.gallup.com/poll/154529/half-americans-support-legal-gay-marriage.aspx.

40. On being granular in thinking, background author interview with Democratic consultant, June 13, 2014; background author interview with Democratic operative, August 14, 2014.

41. On Bruni, Frank Bruni, "To Know Us Is to Let Us Love," New York Times, June 25, 2011, http://www.nytimes.com/2011/06/26/opinion/sunday/26bruni.html.

42. On sixteen states, "A State-by-State Examination of Nondiscrimination Laws and Policies," Center for American Progress, accessed September 2, 2014, http://cdn.americanprogress.org/wp-content/uploads/issues/2012/06/pdf/state_nondiscrimination.pdf.

43. On 90 percent, "Poll Shows Huge Public Support for Gay and Transgender Workplace Protections," Center for American Progress, accessed September 2, 2014, http://www.americanprogress.org/issues/lgbt/news/2011/06/02/9716/polls-show-huge-public-support-for-gay-and-transgender-workplace-protections/; on the Blueprint, copy of transition document obtained by author; see also, "A Blueprint for Positive Change," Human Rights Campaign, accessed April 19, 2015, http://www.hrc.org/resources/entry/a-blueprint-for-positive-change.

44. On adding transgender protections, "Obama Administration Policy Advancements on Behalf of LGBT Americans," Human Rights Campaign, accessed April 15, 2015, http://www.hrc.org/resources/entry/obama-administration-policy-legislative-and-other-advancements-on-behalf-of.

45. On Raghavan providing tickets, author interview with Heather Cronk, codirector of GetEQUAL, September 25, 2014; on Scarbrough/Sewell, Igor Volsky, "Gay Couple Makes Case for Nondiscrimination Order at White House Egg Roll," ThinkProgress, April 9, 2012, http://thinkprogress.org /lgbt/2012/04/09/460648/gay-couple-makes-case-for-nondiscrimination-order -at-white-house-egg-roll/.

46. On the HRC poll, Michael Cole-Schwarz, "Americans Overwhelmingly Support Banning Discrimination Among Federal Contractors," Human Rights Campaign, March 28, 2012, http://www.hrc.org/blog/entry/americans -overwhelmingly-support-banning-discrimination-among-federal-contr; see also, "Americans Overwhelming Support Executive Action to Ban Anti-LGBT Workplace Discrimination," Human Rights Campaign, accessed September 5, 2014, http://www.hrc.org/resources/entry/americans-overwhelmingly-support -executive-action-to-ban-anti-lgbt-workplac; on seventy-two members of Congress, "Letter from the Congress of the United States to President Barack Obama," dated April 3, 2012, accessed September 30, 2014, http://www .washingtonblade.com/content/files/2012/04/LGBT-Workplace-Non -Discrimination-EO-Letter-To-President-Obama.pdf; on Jackson's and Welker's stories, David Jackson, "Gay Couple Want to Question Obama at Easter Egg Roll," USA Today, April 6, 2012, http://content.usatoday.com/communities/theoval /post/2012/04/gay-couple-wants-to-question-obama-at-easter-egg-roll/1# .T4q21hxcnPG; Kristen Welker, "Gay Couple Presses White House on Executive Order," MSNBC, April 9, 2012, https://web.archive.org/web/20120801011704 /http://firstread.msnbc.msn.com/_news/2012/04/09/11105744-gay-couple -presses-white-house-on-executive-order?lite.

47. David Jackson, "Obama's New Slogan: 'We Can't Wait,'" USA Today, October 24, 2011, http://content.usatoday.com/communities/theoval/post /2011/10/obamas-new-slogan-we-cant-wait/1#.VTR09yhGHtA; see also, "We Can't Wait," White House, https://www.whitehouse.gov/economy/jobs/we -cant-wait.

48. Peter Wallsten, "Gay Rights Groups Vow More Pressure on Obama to Sign Nondiscrimination Order," Washington Post, April 12, 2012, http://www .washingtonpost.com/politics/2012/04/12/gIQAz5pTDT_story.html; see also, Laura Meckler, "Obama Won't Issue Ban on Gay Discrimination," Wall Street Journal, April 11, 2012, http://www.wsj.com/articles/SB1000142405270230 4444604577338383749279166; Jackie Calmes, "Obama Won't Order Ban on Gay Bias by Employers," New York Times, April 11, 2012, http://www.nytimes .com/2012/04/12/us/politics/obama-wont-order-ban-on-gay-bias-by-employers .html.

49. On the statements, Jackie Calmes, "Obama Won't Order Ban on Gay Bias by Employers," New York Times, April 11, 2012, http://www.nytimes.com/2012 /04/12/us/politics/obama-wont-order-ban-on-gay-bias-by-employers.html.

50. On the statement, Scott Wooledge, "$100,000 Tasked to Fight 'A Political Calculation That Cannot Stand,'" Daily Kos, http://www.dailykos.com /story/2012/04/12/1082832/--100-000-tasked-to-fight-A-political-calculation -that-cannot-stand.

51. "Press briefing by Press Secretary Jay Carney," White House, April 12, 2012, https://www.whitehouse.gov/the-press-office/2012/04/12/press-briefing -press-secretary-jay-carney-41212.

52. Ibid.

53. Ibid.

54. On A. Phillip Randolph, "Executive Order 8802: Prohibition of Discrimination in the Defense Industry (1941)," Ourdocuments.gov, accessed April 19, 2015, http://www.ourdocuments.gov/doc.php?flash=true&doc=72; on executive order 11246, "Executive Order 11246, as Amended," US Department of Labor, accessed April 19, 2015, http://www.dol.gov/ofccp/regs /statutes/eo11246.htm.

55. "Press Briefing by Press Secretary Jay Carney," White House, April 12, 2012.

56. On ten minutes, author review of the briefing footage.

57. "Sin of Omission," *New York Times*, April 12, 2012, http://www.nytimes .com/2012/04/13/opinion/sin-of-omission.html?_r=3.

58. Ibid.

59. On fifty-six stories, author review of press clippings from those days; on being picked up by the Tribune News Service, Kathleen Hennessey, "Obama Declines Action on Anti-Gay Discrimination from Contractors," April 12, 2012, http://www.latimes.com/news/politics/la-pn-obama-declines-action-on -antigay-discrimination-from-contractors-20120412,0,7737562.story; on other pickup, Jennifer Bendery, "White House Defends Obama's Not Ordering LGBT Worker Protection," Huffington Post, April 12, 2012, http://www.huffingtonpost .com/2012/04/12/obama-lgbt-workplace-protections-enda_n_1422041.html; Joe Sudbay, "Carney Gets Pummeled over LGBT Executive Order at WH Briefing," AMERICAblog, April 12, 2012, http://www.americablog.com/2012/04 /carney-gets-pummeled-over-lgbt.html; Anne Gearan, "Obama Won't Ban Discrimination on Gay Contractors," Associated Press, April 12, 2012.

60. On Johnson, Chris Johnson, "Carney: No Change in White House Position on ENDA Stopgap," *Washington Blade*, April 17, 2012, http://www .washingtonblade.com/2012/04/17/carney-no-change-in-white-house-position -on-enda-stopgap/; on La Raza, Igor Volsky, "Largest National Hispanic Civil Rights Group Calls on Obama to Issue Nondiscrimination Order," ThinkProgress, April 16, 2012, http://thinkprogress.org/lgbt/2012/04/16/465242 /laraza-eo/; on Merkley, Chris Johnson, "Merkley Criticizes White House for Inaction on ENDA Stopgap," *Washington Blade*, April 12, 2012, http://www .washingtonblade.com/2012/04/12/merkley-criticizes-white-house-for

-inaction-on-enda-stopgap/; on Polis, Jessica Brady, "White House Pressed on Gay Rights Issue," Roll Call, April 18, 2012, http://www.rollcall.com /issues/57_123/White-House-Pressed-on-Gay-Rights-Issue-213871-1.html.

61. On the Daily Show, "Gaywatch—Workplace Protections, North Carolina's Marriage Laws & Candy Divorce," The Daily Show with Jon Stewart, April 30, 2012, http://thedailyshow.cc.com/videos/8tw92l/gaywatch-workplace protections-north-carolina-s-marriage-laws-candy-divorce.

62. On the campaign kickoff, Jonathan Lemire, "President Obama Launches His Re-election Bid, Vowing 'It's Still About Hope. It's Still About Change,'" New York Daily News, May 5, 2012, http://www.nydailynews.com/news /election-2012/president-obama-launces-re-election-bid-vowing-hope -change-article-1.1073084; on the matter they overlooked, Halperin and Heilemann, Double Down, 811.

63. On the Biden interview, "Meet the Press Transcript," May 6, 2012, NBC News, http://www.nbcnews.com/id/47311900/ns/meet_the_press-transcripts /t/may-joe-biden-kelly-ayotte-diane-swonk-tom-brokaw-chuck-todd/#.VA4 wlCiChpw.

64. On the call to Volsky, author interview with Igor Volsky, August 21, 2014; on the headline, Igor Volsky, "Breaking: Joe Biden Endorses Same-Sex Marriage," ThinkProgress, May 6, 2012, http://thinkprogress.org/lgbt/2012 /05/06/478786/biden-marriage/.

65. On Volsky's thinking, ibid.

66. On caveats, "Joe Biden Appears to Endorse Gay Marriage," Buzzfeed Politics, May 6, 2012, http://www.buzzfeed.com/buzzfeedpolitics/joe-biden -appears-to-endorse-gay-marriage#.jmpNjLGoZq; Mark Halperin, "Biden Seems to Endorse Gay Marriage," Time, May 6, 2012, http://thepage.time.com /2012/05/06/biden-seems-to-endorse-gay-marriage/.

67. On the tweet, David Axelrod, Twitter, May 6, 2012, https:// twitter.com/davidaxelrod/status/199130006998364160; on the vice president's statement, Edward-Isaac Dovere, "President Obama Pressed on Gay Marriage," May 6, 2012, http://dyn.politico.com/printstory.cfm?uuid=95E22989 -34E0-44FA-83BE-3B6C651D2CB8.

68. Luke Johnson, "Arne Duncan Supports Gay Marriage," Huffington Post, May 7, 2012, http://www.huffingtonpost.com/2012/05/07/arne-duncan-gay -marriage_n_1495224.html.

69. On forty-four questions, "Press Briefing by Press Secretary Jay Carney," White House, May 7, 2012, http://www.whitehouse.gov/the-press-office /2012/05/07/press-briefing-press-secretary-jay-carney-5712.

70. Ibid.

71. On gay bundlers, Peter Wallsten and Dan Eggen, "Biden Comments on Same-Sex Marriage Expose Internal White House Divisions," Washington Post, May 7, 2012, http://www.washingtonpost.com/politics/biden-comments-on

-same-sex-marriage-expose-internal-white-house-divisions/2012/05/07
/gIQAd0A88T_story.html.

72. On Rosen/Elmendorf, Maggie Haberman, Jonathan Martin, and Glenn Thrush, "President Obama's Marriage Muddle," *Politico*, May 8, 2012, http://dyn.politico.com/printstory.cfm?uuid=3C6A4FAF-5690-4085-8964 -2FCCE7846407.

73. On the campaign statement, Luke Johnson, "Obama Opposes Amendment One, North Carolina Ballot Question Banning Gay Marriage," March 16, 2012, Huffington Post, http://www.huffingtonpost.com/2012/03/16/obama -amendment-one-north-carolina-gay-marriage_n_1354302.html; on the vote, "North Carolina Same-Sex Marriage, Amendment 1 (May 2012)," BallotPedia, accessed September 10, 2014, http://ballotpedia.org/North_Carolina _Same-Sex_Marriage,_Amendment_1_(May_2012).

74. Peter Wallsten, "Obama May Clarify Position on Same-Sex Marriage in Interview Today," May 9, 2012, *Washington Post*, http://www.washingtonpost .com/blogs/post-politics/post/obama-may-clarify-position-on-same-sex -marriage-in-interview-today/2012/05/09/gIQAGr61CU_blog.html.

75. "Transcript: Robin Roberts ABC News Interview with President Obama," *ABC News*, May 9, 2012, http://abcnews.go.com/Politics/transcript -robin-roberts-abc-news-interview-president-obama/story?id=16316043.

76. Author interview with Brian Bond, August 25, 2014.

77. Author interview with Gautam Raghavan, September 25, 2014.

78. Author written correspondence with a former White House official, October 16, 2014.

79. Author interview with Gautam Raghavan, September 25, 2014.

80. "Democratic Party Platform of 2012," The American Presidency Project, http://www.presidency.ucsb.edu/papers_pdf/101962.pdf.

81. On fundraising, Ari Shapiro, "Obama Saw Immediate Fundraising Spike After Same-Sex Marriage Announcement," NPR, June 27, 2012, http://www .npr.org/sections/itsallpolitics/2012/06/27/155854165/obama-saw-immediate -fundraising-spike-after-same-sex-marriage-announcement; on the Mehlman polling, "Right Side Battleground States Election Night Survey Results," Project Right Side, accessed September 30, 2014, http://www.projectrightside .com/contentimages/Right_Side_Election_Night_Survey_Findings_Memo.pdf; on 58 percent of independent voters, Ken Mehlman, "Making the Same-Sex Case," November 20, 2012, *Wall Street Journal*, http://online.wsj.com/news/articles /SB10001424127887323353204578128912891255410717.

82. "Inaugural Address by President Barack Obama," White House, January 21, 2013, https://www.whitehouse.gov/the-press-office/2013/01/21/inaugural -address-president-barack-obama.

83. Ibid.

NOTES TO CONCLUSION

1. On the DREAM Act vote, Elise Foley, "DREAM Act Vote Fails in Senate," December 18, 2010, http://www.huffingtonpost.com/2010/12/18/dream-act-vote-senate_n_798631.html; on direct actions of Dreamers and climate change activists, Kerry Eleveld, "What Gay Rights Activists Can Teach the Left About Winning," *The Atlantic*, September 26, 2011, http://www.theatlantic.com/politics/archive/2011/09/what-gay-rights-activists-can-teach-the-left-about-winning/245471/.

2. On deeply disappointing progressives, Sam Youngman, "White House Unloads on Professional Left," *The Hill*, August 10, 2010, http://thehill.com/homenews/administration/113431-white-house-unloads-on-professional-left; on children's health insurance and Lily Ledbetter passing, "Obama Signs Children's Health Initiative into Law," CNN, February 4, 2009, http://www.cnn.com/2009/POLITICS/02/04/schip.vote/index.html?eref=onion.

3. On the *Hollingsworth v. Perry* brief, Kerry Eleveld, "The Supreme Court's Middle Option: A Nine-State Solution," *The Advocate*, March 22, 2013, http://www.advocate.com/politics/marriage-equality/2013/03/22/supreme-courts-middle-option-nine-state-solution; on the 2015 "friend of the court" brief, Chris Geidner, "Obama Administration Urges Nationwide End to Same-Sex Marriage Bans," BuzzFeed News, http://www.buzzfeed.com/chrisgeidner/obama-administration-urges-nationwide-end-to-same-sex-marria#.peVy734Xa1.

4. On federal benefits, US Office of Personnel Management, "Memorandum for Heads of Executive Departments and Agencies," Chief Human Capital Officers Council, June 28, 2013, https://www.chcoc.gov/transmittals/Transmittal Details.aspx?TransmittalID=5700; on immigration services, "Statement by Secretary of Homeland Security Janet Napolitano on the Implementation of the Supreme Court Ruling on the Defense of Marriage Act," US Department of Homeland Security, July 1, 2013, http://www.dhs.gov/news/2013/07/01/statement-secretary-homeland-security-janet-napolitano-implementation-supreme-court; on Secretary Kerry, "Announcement on Visa Changes for Same-Sex Couples," US Department of State, August 2, 2013, http://www.state.gov/secretary/remarks/2013/08/212643.htm; on the military, "Extending Benefits to the Same-Sex Spouses of Military Members," US Department of Defense, August 13, 2013, http://www.defense.gov/home/features/2013/docs/Extending-Benefits-to-Same-Sex-Spouses-of-Military-Members.pdf; on taxes, "All Legal Same-Sex Marriages Will Be Recognized for Federal Tax Purposes," US Department of Treasury, August 29, 2013, http://www.treasury.gov/press-center/press-releases/Pages/jl2153.aspx; on Labor, "New Guidance Issued by US Labor Department on Same-Sex Marriages and Employee Benefit Plans," US Department of Labor, September 18, 2013,

http://www.dol.gov/opa/media/press/ebsa/EBSA20131720.htm; on education, "Education Department Announces That All Legal Same-Sex Marriages Will Be Recognized for Federal Financial Aid Purposes," US Department of Education, December 13, 2013, http://www.ed.gov/news/press-releases/education -department-announces-all-legal-same-sex-marriages-will-be-recognized-f.

5. On the travel ban, Julia Preston, "Obama Lifts a Ban on Entry into U.S. by HIV-Positive People," *New York Times*, October 30, 2009, http://www .nytimes.com/2009/10/31/us/politics/31travel.html; on federal contractor and gender identity protections, "Executive Order—Further Amendments to Executive Order 11478, Equal Employment Opportunity in the Federal Government, and Executive Order 11246, Equal Employment Opportunity," White House, July 21, 2014, https://www.whitehouse.gov /the-press-office/2014/07/21/executive-order-further-amendments-executive -order-11478-equal-employmen.

6. On passports, "New Policy on Gender Change in Passports Announced," US Department of State, June 9, 2010, http://www.state.gov/r/pa/prs /ps/2010/06/142922.htm; on Social Security, "Transgender People and the Social Security Administration," National Center for Transgender Equality, June 2013, http://transequality.org/sites/default/files/docs/kyr/SSAResource_June2013.pdf.

7. On advancements at Health and Human Services, "Obama Administration Policy Advancements on Behalf of LGBT Americans," Human Rights Campaign, accessed April 21, 2015, http://www.hrc.org/resources/entry/obama -administration-policy-legislative-and-other-advancements-on-behalf-of.

8. "Key Policy Letters from the Education Secretary and Deputy Secretary," US Department of Education, June 14, 2011, http://www2.ed.gov/policy /elsec/guid/secletter/110607.html.

9. Department of Veterans Affairs, "Providing Health Care for Transgender and Intersex Veterans," VHA Directive 2011-024, June 9, 2011, accessed June 15, 2015, http://www.paloalto.va.gov/docs/VA_Transgender_Directive.pdf.

10. "Discrimination Against Same-Sex Couples in Rental Housing," US Department of Housing and Urban Development, accessed May 18, 2015, http:// www.huduser.org/portal/pdredge/pdr_edge_research_071513.html.

11. "Statement by Attorney General Eric Holder on Federal Recognition of Same-Sex Marriages in Utah," US Department of Justice, January 10, 2014, http://www.justice.gov/opa/pr/statement-attorney-general-eric-holder-federal -recognition-same-sex-marriages-utah.

12. On 63 percent, Rhonda Evans, "A History of the Service of Ethnic Minorities in the U.S. Armed Forces," The Palm Center, June 1, 2003, http://www .palmcenter.org/publications/dadt/a_history_of_the_service_of_ethnic _minorites_in_the_u_s_armed_forces#_ftnref87.

13. On sixteen states, "Loving v. Virginia," Legal Information Institute, accessed May 18, 2015, https://www.law.cornell.edu/supremecourt/text/388/1;

on 70 percent, Evan Wolfson, "Letter: Do Not Deny a Minority the Right to Marry," *New York Times*, November 30, 2008, http://www.nytimes.com/2008/11/30/opinion/l30gay.html.

14. On Obama's quote, "Remarks by the President at LGBT Pride Month Reception," White House, June 29, 2009, https://www.whitehouse.gov/the_press_office/Remarks-by-the-President-at-LGBT-Pride-Month-Reception.

15. On Title VII, Kerry Eleveld, "The Title VII Awakening," *The Advocate*, July 15, 2014, http://www.advocate.com/print-issue/current-issue/2014/07/15/title-vii-awakening; see also, *Macy v. Holder*, No. 0120120821, 2012 WL 1435995 (E.E.O.C. Apr. 20, 2012).

INDEX

Award-winning journalist KERRY ELEVELD covered Obama for four years for *The Advocate*, first on the campaign trail and then at the White House, interviewing Obama three times including once in the Oval Office. Currently a columnist for *Daily Kos*, she lives in Berkeley, California.